ROOTS OF THE PAX AMERICANA

MANCHESTER
1824

Manchester University Press

Roots of the Pax Americana

Decolonization, development, democratization and trade

P. ERIC LOUW

Manchester University Press

Published by Manchester University Press
Altrincham Street, Manchester M1 7JA, UK
www.manchesteruniversitypress.co.uk

British Library Cataloguing-in-Publication Data is available

Library of Congress Cataloging-in-Publication Data is available

ISBN 978 0 7190 9668 6 paperback

First published by Manchester University Press in hardback 2010

This paperback edition first published 2015

Printed by Lightning Source

Contents

List of maps and tables

Maps

Tables

Acknowledgements

Thanks to Nico Louw for producing the maps and to Rose Louw for copy-editing this book. Thanks are also due to the staff of both Manchester University Press and the University of Queensland's library. Special thanks go to Marcos Riba of the University of Queensland's library, who was consistently helpful.

List of abbreviations

America	United States of America
APEC	Asia Pacific Economic Cooperation
EEC	European Economic Community
EU	European Union
GATT	General Agreement on Tariffs and Trade
IMF	International Monetary Fund
NATO	North Atlantic Treaty Organization
NGO	non government organization
OAU	Organisation of African Unity
OECD	Organization for Economic Cooperation and Development
OWI	Office of War Information (US)
UN	United Nations
WTO	World Trade Organization

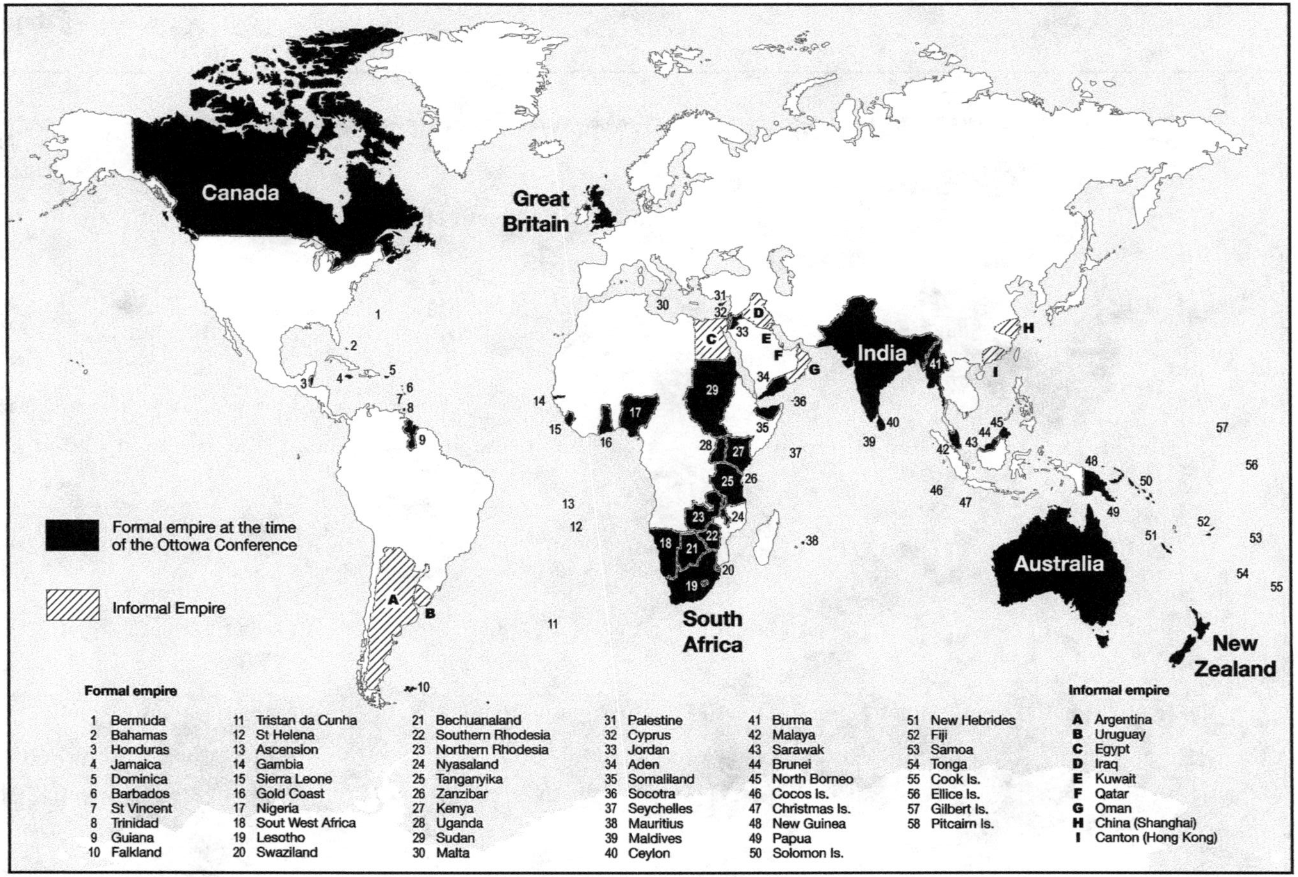

Great Britain

Canada

India

Australia

New Zealand

South Africa

Formal empire

1 Bermuda
2 Bahamas
3 Honduras
4 Jamaica
5 Dominica
6 Barbados
7 St Vincent
8 Trinidad
9 Guiana
10 Falkland

11 Tristan da Cunha
12 St Helena
13 Ascension
14 Gambia
15 Sierra Leone
16 Gold Coast
17 Nigeria
18 Sout West Africa
19 Lesotho
20 Swaziland

21 Bechuanaland
22 Southern Rhodesia
23 Northern Rhodesia
24 Nyasaland
25 Tanganyika
26 Zanzibar
27 Kenya
28 Uganda
29 Sudan
30 Malta

31 Palestine
32 Cyprus
33 Jordan
34 Aden
35 Somaliland
36 Socotra
37 Seychelles
38 Mauritius
39 Maldives
40 Ceylon

41 Burma
42 Malaya
43 Sarawak
44 Brunei
45 North Borneo
46 Cocos Is.
47 Christmas Is.
48 New Guinea
49 Papua
50 Solomon Is.

51 New Hebrides
52 Fiji
53 Samoa
54 Tonga
55 Cook Is.
56 Ellice Is.
57 Gilbert Is.
58 Pitcairn Is.

Informal empire

A Argentina
B Uruguay
C Egypt
D Iraq
E Kuwait
F Qatar
G Oman
H China (Shanghai)
I Canton (Hong Kong)

■ Formal empire at the time of the Ottowa Conference

▨ Informal Empire

Map 1 British empire, 1932

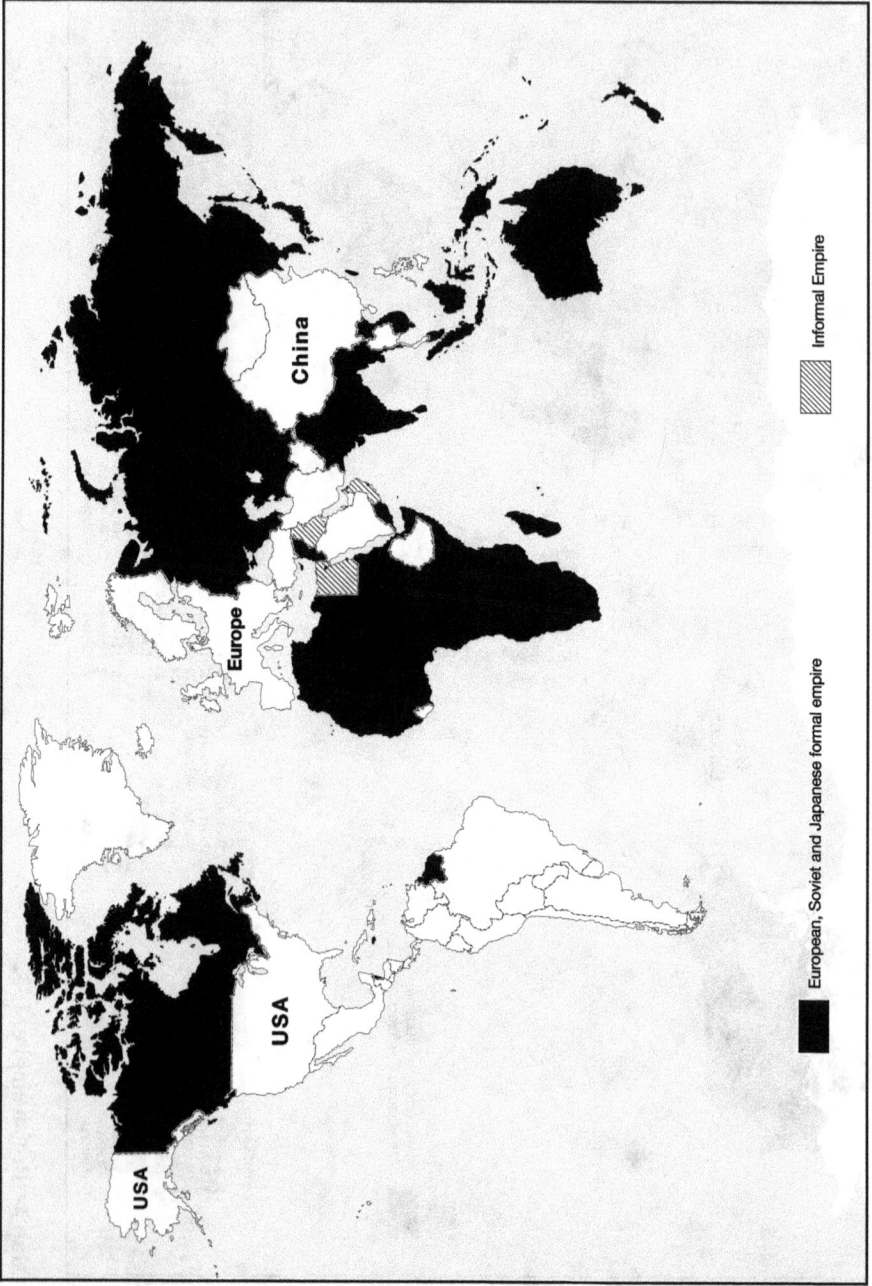

Map 2 The world, 1932

European, Soviet and Japanese formal empire

Informal Empire

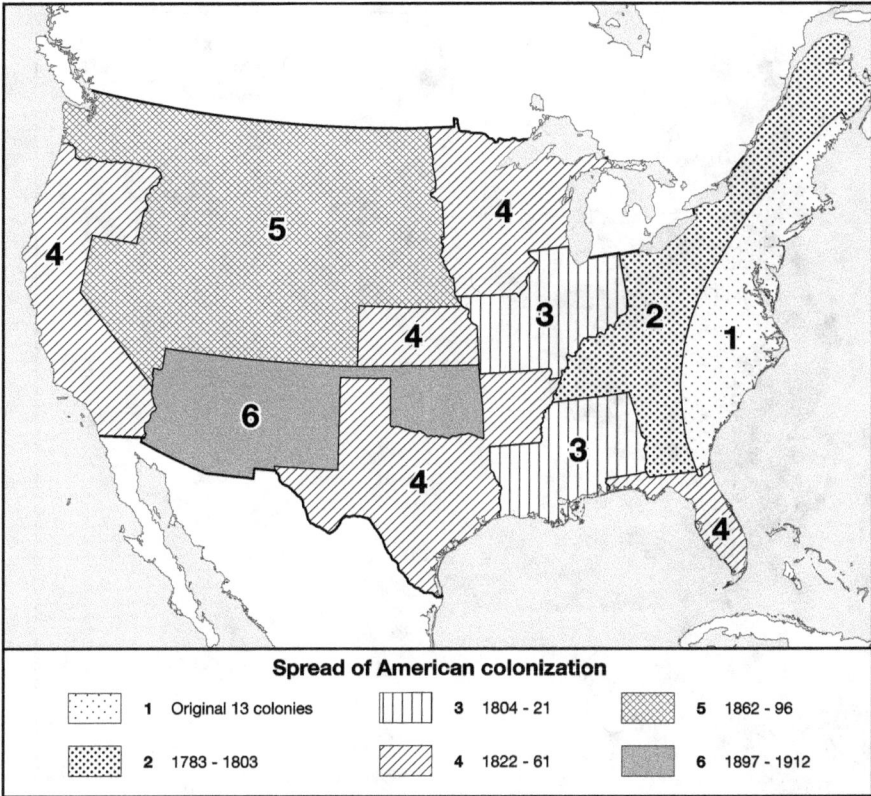

Spread of American colonization

1	Original 13 colonies	3	1804 - 21	5	1862 - 96
2	1783 - 1803	4	1822 - 61	6	1897 - 1912

Map 3 America's first empire

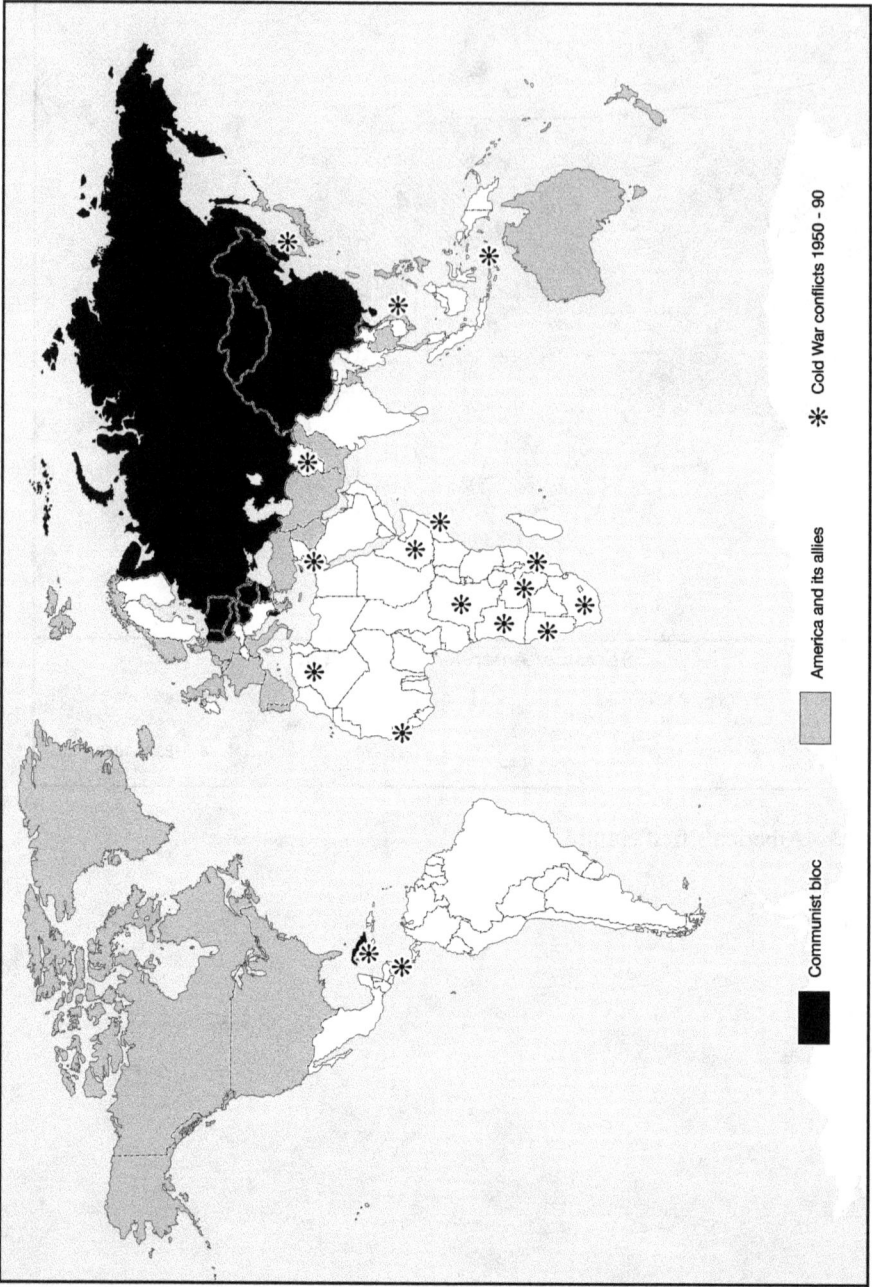

Map 4 Cold War world, 1957

Communist bloc

America and its allies

✳ Cold War conflicts 1950 – 90

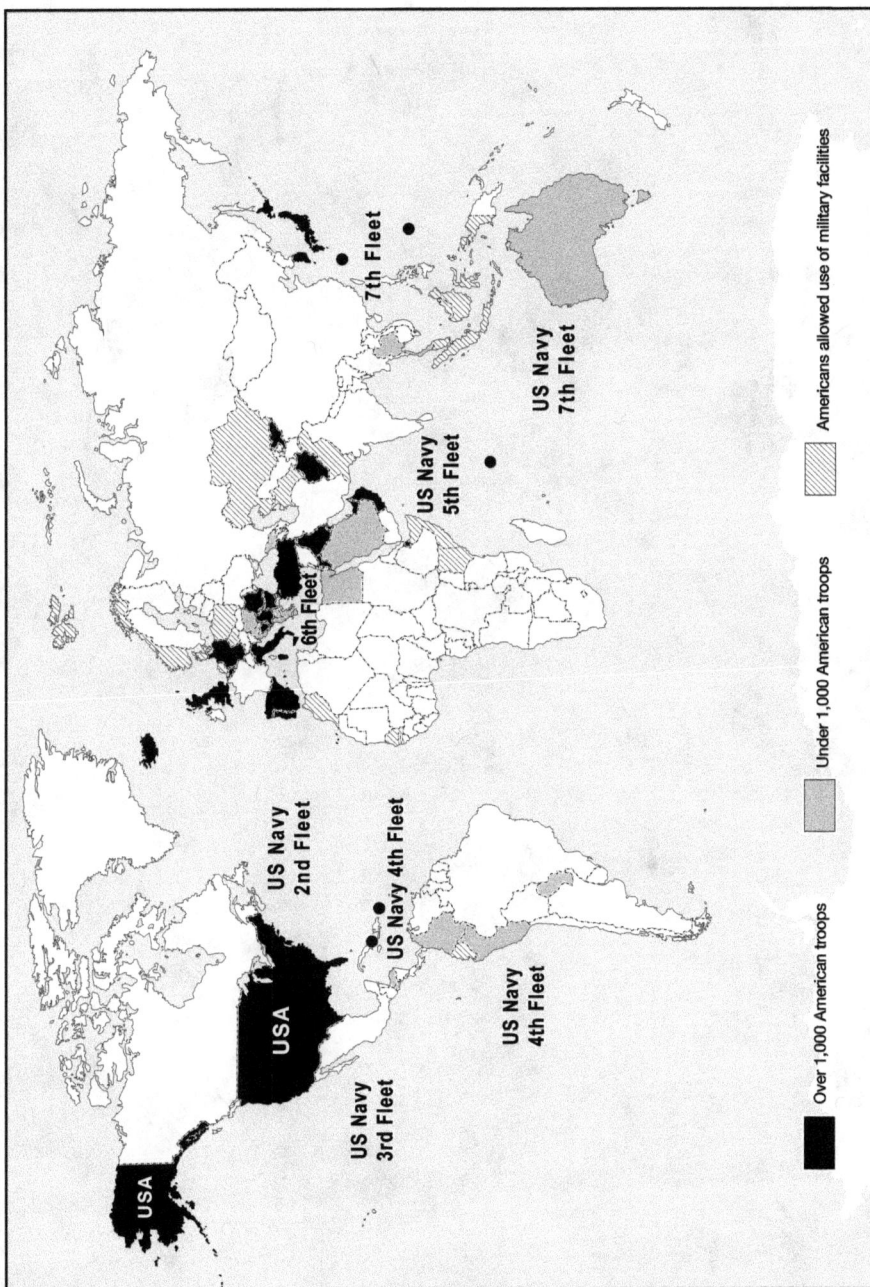

Map 5 Pax Americana military deployments, 2009

US Navy
2nd Fleet

USA

US Navy 4th Fleet

US Navy
3rd Fleet

US Navy
4th Fleet

USA

7th Fleet

US Navy
5th Fleet

6th Fleet

US Navy
7th Fleet

Over 1,000 American troops

Under 1,000 American troops

Americans allowed use of military facilities

1

What is the Pax Americana?

Modern American 'imperialism' is not like old British imperialism. It is much, much bigger. Britain once had an empire. America now has a superempire. (Porter, *Empire and Superempire*)

Informal empire [is] often based upon the intermediation of technically independent governments ... Each local society creates a collaborator class out of its own culture ... [with] the nature of the collaboration ... based on quite different forms of imitation, roleplaying, and ... interlocking ranges of transaction. (Winks 'On Decolonization and Informal Empire')

By the end of the twentieth century America was securely in control of an informal empire that reached across the globe, and there seems little doubt that the twenty-first century will be dominated by America. America's empire is noteworthy, firstly, because it is the largest empire in history, and, secondly, because of the way it is run as an 'informal'[1] or 'nonterritorial' empire.[2] Precisely because it is an informal empire many Americans believe they do not run an empire, and even believe themselves to be 'anti-imperialist'. The reality is, no one on the planet is untouched by the decisions made by America's rulers and that America's 'informal empire' is just as imperialist as was Britain's 'formal empire'. Because of its global reach and power the Pax Americana is clearly a phenomenon that warrants examination and debate.

There are many ways one could approach a study of America's empire. The *Roots of the Pax Americana* will examine this phenomenon by asking how and why Americans constructed the sort of (informal) empire they did. Understanding this empire's origins is important, because today's American empire functions as it does due to the way it was built in the past. Since the past gets encoded into the present, understanding the past can help us understand our contemporary world. Hence, this book aims to sketch out the origins of America's empire with a view to throwing light on the following sorts of questions. What is the Pax Americana? How and why did it come into being? How does America build, maintain and reproduce its empire? How and why did the Pax Americana replace the Pax Britannica? How have

Americans and non-Americans viewed this empire and its growth? Is the Pax Americana a valuable instrument of global governance or not? How does the Pax Americana rate when compared to the Pax Britannica?

So this is a book about empire-building of a particular sort – at heart it tells the story of the post-1945 informal empire that Americans built (and are still building). But in order to tell this story, some time must also be spent examining earlier forms of empire-building. Hence, the role played by the British empire in the emergence of the Pax Americana will be discussed, as will be America's pre-1945 imperial ventures. To these pre-1945 ventures we now turn.

Americans as empire-builders

America's post-1945 informal empire was by no means America's first venture in empire building. Americans have built three distinctly different empires over the past two centuries.

America's first empire involved the conquest and colonization of North America between 1783 and 1900, as shown in map 3. After Anglo settlers in the thirteen colonies had won their independence from Britain and established the United States of America, these settlers began moving America's frontier westward through an extraordinarily successful colonial exercise of conquest and colonization. The imperial project of expanding America until it reached the Pacific was explicitly called for by one of America's founding fathers, Thomas Jefferson. Jefferson's project of building an 'empire of liberty' was no less imperialist than building Britain's empire, or the Russian, French or Japanese empires. In fact, America's first empire, based upon waves of settlers moving westward, looked much like the other nineteenth-century Caucasian colonial projects in Canada, Australia, New Zealand, South Africa, Argentina and Siberia. Building this first American empire represented an enormous expansion of the Anglo (and European) world. From this American colonial expansion emerged the current coast-to-coast American Union, which provided Americans with a resource-rich territorial base from which to launch their second (formal) and third (informal) empires.

America ran a second 'formal' empire from 1898 until World War II. It began when America acquired new territory by winning the 1898 Spanish–American War. Significantly, when the Philippines, Guam, Samoa and Puerto Rico were acquired (in 1898/99) they were not incorporated into the American Union, but instead were organized as overseas imperial possessions. So, for example, American governance of the Philippines from 1898 to 1941 looked much like the sort of colonial rule deployed by Britain, France and the Netherlands in other parts of Southeast Asia.

America's third empire was launched after World War II, in 1945 as an informal empire. It is this third empire, or Pax Americana, that is the real concern of this book. Within this informal empire, independent states are enmeshed as clients into an American trading network. Consequently, no territory is annexed for incorporation into the American Union; neither are territories organized as (formal) overseas possessions. Instead, America works to build middle-class comprador-partners in independent states. These partner allies are relied upon to run their states in accordance with the needs of America's trading empire. Central to running such an informal empire is thus clientship and/or compradorship, with America using mostly 'soft power' to build comprador compliance. In addition, the Pax Americana has constructed a complex system of multilateral regulations that constitutes the global governance structure for this informal trading empire. The whole edifice rests upon America having more military power at its disposal than any other nation in history. The potential of American military violence is an omnipresent reality across the entire globe.

This third American empire was a consequence of the United States emerging as the chief victor of World War II – a war which expanded American economic and military infrastructures and which eliminated Germany, Japan and Britain as rivals. Germany and Japan were occupied; their cities destroyed by bombing; their territorial holdings dramatically stripped back; and their ruling elites decimated. Britain emerged from the war seriously weakened because, firstly, it was economically beholden to America; and, secondly, its empire was destabilized by growing calls for decolonization. In 1945 America was the only nation able to project its will globally. Washington was supremely powerful because it possessed large armies of occupation in Europe and east Asia (which have never been withdrawn); nuclear-warfare capabilities; and the world's largest industrial economy. The only alternative power centre to America was the Soviet Union, which occupied the East European power vacuum created by Germany's defeat. But in the face of America's nuclear capability, the Soviets were in reality a second-tier power.

America's third empire emerged as a consequence of World War II and the planning the American government engaged in during this war to conceptualize a post-war settlement. A 'new world order' was effectively designed by a US State Department team headed by Cordell Hull and Sumner Welles. These 1940s State Department planners were Wilsonians – drawing their inspiration from Woodrow Wilson's ideals. This planning process will be discussed in chapter 5. In 1945 America began imposing this new world order. The result was a globalized 'American Peace', emerging from the victory of liberal internationalists.[3] The resultant Wilsonian 'humanitarian imperialism' had four key features.

Firstly, it was grounded in an American belief that American-style democracy and liberalism should be universalized. Americans came to believe they had a duty (right?) to carry their vision of 'liberty' to the world. This will be discussed in chapter 3.

Secondly, empires were to be destroyed and replaced by independent states. This decolonization process was grounded in both Wilsonian idealism and American pragmatism. Pragmatically, it was difficult to build an American trading empire when facing competition from powerful states and/or empires. Replacing empires with small states facilitated building America's 'informal empire', because it was easier to incorporate weak states into an American trading empire on terms that suited Americans.

Thirdly, as many states as possible were to be meshed into America's trading network, or 'US corporations empire'.[4]

Fourth, American hegemony is precisely not based upon annexing territory. Instead, America's third (informal) empire has been grounded in economic, military and 'soft' power. America established (and dominates) a complex multilateral system, governed by a set of rules that 'regulates' international financial, trade and political relations. The resultant system (Pax Americana) manages a global 'peace' and economic relationships beneficial to American interests. Multilateral institutions became crucial for exerting American authority because they bind everyone else into an American-run world order.[5]

The result has been not only the construction of America's third empire, but also the construction of a new kind of international order, the Pax Americana.

An American-made new world order

Since 1945 Americans have reconfigured global political and trade relations as they built their third empire. A core feature of this reconfiguration was the massive twentieth-century power shift from British to American dominance of the world. This power shift was characterized by the deconstruction of Britain's 'formal' ('territorial') empire and its replacement by America's 'informal' ('nonterritorial') empire. This global power shift, which will be examined in chapters 2, 4 and 7, was a curious affair because it occurred without Britain and America going to war and, secondly, it involved a sort of 'familial' transfer of power, in which a parent nation (Britain) handed over global hegemony to its former off-spring (America). Significantly, this power transfer generated a new global hegemonic order that actually reproduced many continuities between Britain's global hegemony (globalization I) and America's (globalization II). Hence, on the one hand, the rise of a Pax Americana merely entrenched ongoing Anglo cultural domination of the world and maintained the export of Anglo socio-economic assumptions to the world. But, on the other hand, some features of the Pax Americana are uniquely American. These unique American dimensions – traceable back to America's colonial origins, the Civil War, and the growth of a particular brand of liberalism – will be explored in chapters 3 and 5.

Ultimately, the way American liberalism conceptualizes the world will be an important part of the story told in this book, because this particular brand of liberalism saw itself as engaged in a moral crusade against British, European and Japanese imperialism. By examining the assumptions and nature of this liberal crusade in chapters 5 and 6, much is revealed about why America adopted an informal empire model after 1945. Further, examining America's moral crusade deepens our understanding of the ideologies of 'anti-imperialism' and 'anticolonialism' which grew out of America's need to demonize formal empires and promote its own global hegemony grounded in the 'informal empire' techniques of free trade, multilateralism, soft power and politico-cultural colonization. The anticolonial demonization campaign will be explored in chapter 6, while attempts to diffuse Wilsonian liberalism and clone 'the American way' (i.e. politico-cultural colonization) will be explored in chapters 8, 9 and 10.

Differences between informal and formal empires

The building of America's third empire represented more than a global shift of power across the Atlantic. The emergence of this Pax Americana also signalled a new way of organizing global governance because the Americans exercise their global hegemony quite differently to how the British exercised theirs. At heart, the difference between pre- and post-1945 global governance is due to the fact that Britain ran a formal empire and America runs an informal empire. A summary of the differences between these two empires can be found in table 11.2 (chapter 11).

Perhaps the most obvious difference between the two empires is that Britain's formal empire was visible, while America's informal empire is opaque. Each independent state within the Pax Americana is allowed its own flag and own government. Hence although America's power may be omnipresent, there are fewer obvious symbols of this power than was the case when Britain dominated the globe.

A key to understanding American hegemony is the way decolonization was undertaken after 1945. Three features of this decolonization process are noteworthy.

Firstly, the Pax Americana retained the same administrative units created by the European imperialists (e.g. Iraq, Nigeria, Indonesia), and gave them independence as Woodrow Wilson's self-determination model was rolled out globally. Most of these administrative entities made no 'political' sense because they were not based on linguistic, ethnic or religious bonds. Generally, they were artificial constructs created when Europe's imperialists randomly drew boundaries on a map. The new states often threw together people with no desire to inhabit the same state and who often harboured historical animosities towards one other.

However, these administrative units were useful for the Pax Americana because they had been developed by European imperialists as economic entities. And since the Pax Americana was an informal (trading) empire, America was fundamentally interested in these states' economies (markets and resources), not in their political difficulties. What America wanted was for the 'economic entities' created by Europeans (e.g. Iraq or Indonesia) to keep functioning. But within the new world order they were to be tied to New York (rather than London, Amsterdam, Paris, etcetera). What the Pax Americana needed was effectively run sovereign states since such states formed the basis for functioning liberal capitalism.[6] Americans naively believed one could simply transform imperial administrative/economic entities into such functioning sovereign nation states.

Secondly, in each administrative entity created by European imperialism, a Westernized middle class had emerged. These Westernized middle classes usually lived in the cities, and were a minority of their country's population. To maintain their Western middle-class lifestyles, the economies built by the colonials needed to be maintained. America saw these Westernized middle classes as 'natural allies' (comprador-partners) of the Pax Americana and advocated power be transferred to them. Where European colonial possessions did not have 'native' middle-class populations large enough to run independent states, America encouraged the colonial powers to actively build such middle-class populations (as discussed in chapter 8). Successfully rolling out the American model meant transferring power to local Westernized elites, who stepped into the shoes of departing colonials[7] – effectively becoming administrators of new 'independent' states serving American economic interests. The model was based on the idea of a synergy between America (which needed comprador-partners in its far-flung informal empire) and Westernized minorities in each new state (who needed powerful overseas allies to help them maintain their affluent lifestyles and often precarious hold on power). Consequently, the Pax Americana came to be characterized by comprador-partnerships based on mutual need. America ruled 'indirectly' and 'informally' through comprador-allies. Thus, 'independence often brought not 'liberty', but rule by compradors who were often (but not always) corrupt, brutal and inept. But not all these Westernized populations turned into the 'natural allies' America had anticipated. Instead, some African, Asian and Latin American middle classes became radicalized and aligned themselves with the Soviet Union. None-the-less, America pursued its middle-class comprador-building model with vigour.

Thirdly, the ruling elites of these new states were allowed to have their flags and symbols of 'independence' as long as they conformed to the rules of the game – i.e. power effectively shifted from European empires to (non-state) multilateral financial organizations (e.g. the International Monetary Fund (IMF), the World Trade Organization (WTO), the World Bank); with American control of the global financial and monetary system consti-tuting the new locus of global governance.[8] Within the Pax Americana, the role of independent states is to 'administer' the 'linkages' of a global trading system (e.g. foreign affairs, finance and defence),[9] thereby facilitating a global market.[10] The rulers of these states operate as de facto functionaries of America's globalized trading system.

The Pax Britannica's colonial administrators fulfilled similar roles within Britain's globalized trading system. But whereas the 'rules' Britons administered were openly (and proudly) 'imperial', the Pax Americana disguises its 'rules' through a façade of 'independent' states. This is highly functional because it renders the Pax Americana opaque. Mustering resistance against an 'opaque' American hegemony is more difficult than challenging 'visible' formal empires.

Reconstructing the post-1945 world

The process of building America's informal (third) empire began in 1945. This involved replacing those structures associated with British global hegemony with American-designed global governance structures. It was a reconstruction project solidly grounded in Wilsonian-liberalism[11] – an ideology to be discussed in chapter 2. Western Europe's transition into American hegemony occurred from 1946 to 1958, during which time West European states adjusted their structures and national economies to the requisites of the new (Pax Americana) economic order.[12] To create their new 'liberalized' world order, America systematically exported the following to the world: (1) American business practices; (2) American labour–business relations; (3) financial and political 'rules' servicing the needs of the Pax Americana; and (4) American (liberal) discourses and values. Over time, 'market democracy' was spread across the developed world.[13] Once Western Europe (and Japan) had been reconfigured and incorporated into the Pax Americana, attention was turned to the Third World.[14] Consequently, by 1958 Britain no longer benefited economically from having an empire because America had reconfigured international financial rules (so wealth flowed to New York not London). At the same time pressures to 'develop' colonies began generating costs, making it economically sensible for Britain to acquiesce to decolonization pressures. This shift will be discussed in chapter 7.

Building America's new world order involved constructing a globalized 'open door' political economy, exclusive of the Soviet sphere, in which Western Europe and Japan, plus what became known as the Third World were all to be incorporated.[15] Creating this global hegemony involved bringing about four changes.

Firstly, power relations between the major states were transformed.[16] By permanently stationing American armies in Western Europe and Japan, Washington acquired enormous power in Europe and Asia. America used both 'persuasive powers', and 'coercive leverage', to get others to adopt liberal arrangements.[17] In Western Europe, America consciously used the Marshall Plan to shape the balance of forces within states.[18] Informal and formal actions were taken to marginalize Western Europe's left-wing and right-wing. Europeans advocating centrist, centre-right or centre-left positions, plus those favouring a European customs-union, were helped to emerge as the winners.[19] Across Western Europe (and Japan and Australasia) political forces aligning themselves to the Pax Americana were nurtured; with the promotion of European unity being perhaps the core 'liberal project' of the Pax Americana.[20] As the Pax Americana emerged, America effectively took on the role of a linchpin in an emerging (global) coalition of liberal forces.[21] The Pax Americana became able to function with no 'overarching authority' structure (as exists in formal empires) because ruling elites were developed and nurtured who shared a 'common, broad and deep commitment to liberal principles'.[22]

Secondly, the world's financial system was reordered. The West Europeans and Japan were pushed into accepting trade liberalization, exchange convertibility and a Hullian (liberal) open economy involving free access to raw materials, plus the free movement of goods, capital and technology.[23] American businesses gained access to resources and markets that they had previously been locked out of by the Japanese and European empires (as shown in map 2). Significantly, America also became coiner of the world's money,[24] and the international monetary and banking system effectively became extensions of American policy.[25] A system was created in which American money-and-other markets lead, and others follow.[26] Central to American hegemony has been the ability to set global financial (liberal) rules through the World Bank and IMF. This system – put into place by American power – has been economically, politically and ideologically biased in America's favour.[27] It has been suggested the American Fed ultimately controls this monetary system.[28] This global financial system grants America 'structural power', or the 'power to indirectly influence others'.[29] America also created the General Agreement on Tariffs and Trade (GATT) (later the WTO), to liberalize trade. Building multilateral mechanisms to govern and liberalize trade is central to the functioning of America's informal empire.

Thirdly, Americans used their power to reconfigure the world's state system. The Pax Americana came to be governed through two forms of state. In the developed world the 'neo-liberal state' was constructed by simply consolidating existing middle-class hegemonies where these existed.[30] Where they did not exist, America intervened to construct liberal middle-class hegemonies. The best examples of this were post-1945 Germany, Japan and Italy, which will be examined in chapter 9. Once consolidated, neo-liberal states were meshed into America's global trading network. Neo-liberal states created after 1945 were geared to stabilizing liberal capitalism by being economic actors and managing a corporatist system of business–labour cooperation. They promoted the interests of corporations, while simultaneously cushioning vulnerable social groups through a 'welfare state'.[31] Significantly, these states were enmeshed in (and could not secede from) the American-built system of globalized financial and trade regulation.[32] The core function of this globalized regulatory system was to tie independent states into America's trading network.[33]

In the Third World, 'neo-mercantilist' states were constructed. This form of government was designed to initiate capitalist development in the absence of an established middle-class hegemony.[34] These 'development' states were geared to integrating former European colonial possessions into America's global trading network.[35] This will be discussed further in chapter 8. Third World underdeveloped states were to be run by a Westernized urban petit bourgeoisie, who served as comprador-partners.[36] The comprador system became an important feature of the Pax Americana, and many compradors became dependent upon their links to partners in the developed world for their survival.[37] Hence, when America withheld support following the Soviet Union's collapse, many of these developmentalist regimes collapsed.

Fourthly, America's informal empire is premised upon rewriting the rules of international interaction and the way these rules are enforced. Because America runs an informal empire the nature of the rules governing international interactions is absolutely crucial. Under the Pax Britannica, Britain unilaterally enforced rules beneficial to themselves. But a central feature of the Pax Americana is that the rules are enforced multilaterally. Because the governance of America's informal trading empire is characterized by multilateralism, there has been a proliferation of multilateral arrangements (e.g. the UN, the North Atlantic Treaty Organization (NATO), World Bank, IMF, GATT, WTO, Organization for Economic Cooperation and Development (OECD), Asia Pacific Economic Cooperation (APEC), European Union (EU), G7, G20, etcetera). These multilateral organizations service the needs of America's 'corporations' empire by proceduralizing liberalism, running an 'imperial bureaucracy' and dispatching 'international peacekeepers' abroad whenever required.[38] An outcome of this multilateral system is 'structural power' accruing to America. As Strange says: 'the dynamic character of the "who-gets-what" of the international economy … is captured by looking not at that regime that emerges on the surface but underneath, at the bargains on which it is based'.[39] Strange notes the ground rules of the multilateral system were American built. So, not surprisingly, this multilateral system has proved immensely functional for the Pax Americana. It is a system that has generated unprecedented levels of global integration,[40] plus the globalization and naturalization of America's liberal 'rules of the game' and the proliferation of 'market democracy'. Interestingly, not all multilateral projects even look American. The EU, for example, is thought of as a 'European' project. Yet European unity – institutionalized by the EU and NATO – was a core post-1945 Pax Americana 'liberalization' project.[41] It was all about making Western Europe securely liberal and tying it into America's informal (trading) empire.

The importance of comprador partners in informal empires

After 1945, America set about constructing its new world order by incorporating into its globalized trading network the entire world outside the communist bloc (shown in map 4). During the Cold War Americans were unable to gain access to the resources and markets of the Second World (the communist bloc). The rest of the world, which was absorbed into the Pax Americana, consisted of two quite different 'systems' – a 'developed' First World and an 'underdeveloped' Third World. The First World was organized by a system of neo-liberal states allied to America, i.e. Western Europe, Japan, Canada and Australia.[42] The Third World was organized by a system of neo-mercantilist states in Asia, Africa, Latin America, the Caribbean and Pacific.[43] Both the First and Second Worlds were linked within the same globalized trading network, with its epicentre in New York. Since the collapse of the Soviet empire, America has worked hard to absorb as much of the Second World into its trading empire as possible.

The creation of independent neo-mercantilist states became the mechanism by which America managed its Third World 'corporations empire'. Effectively, client states were created and integrated into a global trading network and network of power relations – America became the epicentre of a world market reconstituted under American patronage after 1945.[44] Many of these states were born as a result of destroying Europe's empires. As these empires were deconstructed (mostly in the two decades following World War II), efforts were made to transfer power from colonial administrators to those deemed suitable to serve as allies and partners within the global trading network – i.e. a 'collaborator class'.[45] Effectively, the former colonies received 'independence upon imperial terms. At the very moment of birth the new nation was, in the eyes of many subgroups within it, fatally compromised, its form of government was not autochthonous, its independence being a gift'.[46] This process of independence-giving resulted in the birth of comprador-partners across the Third World.

Although comprador-partners became a significant feature of the Pax Americana, their roots lay in an earlier period. 'Compradors' originally emerged in nineteenth-century China from the practice of European traders recruiting locals to act as interpreters, purchasing agents and sources of intelligence. These compradors served as employed 'partners' or interme-diaries who facilitated Western penetration of China. From bases in Hong Kong and Shanghai, the British built a significant informal trading empire in China using such compradors.

In informal empires comprador-partners are essential. America's insistence on creating independent states meant it was essential to encourage the emergence of ruling groups who would collaborate – as compradors – with American interests. It was a system of managing peripheral economies that America had first developed in Latin America.[47] Effectively, compradorism is built upon a symbiotic relationship – America relies on comprador-partners to run Third World client states; while these comprador-partners rely on America to underpin their rule. America has preferred people who are culturally proximate and who have a vested interest in maintaining (or expanding) the old colonial-built economy. Whether the Americans deliberately sought 'junior' partners as suggested by Frank is a moot point.[48] But they certainly sought out comprador-partners for their multilateral networks. Fortunately for America, Europe's empires had created such people, in the form of Westernized middle-class Africans and Asians who wished to retain their Western lifestyles. Some of these middle classes had roots dating back to nineteenth-century educational infrastructures built by missionaries and colonial authorities in places like British India. Others were of more recent origins – e.g. in 1940s and 1950s British Africa, a Burkean strategy emerged to deliberately build a black middle class to serve as future comprador-partners. Whatever their origins, all the ex–imperial territories eventually possessed Westernized middle-class minorities. The decolonization agenda, promoted by the UN after 1945, offered these middle classes the opportunity to drive out colonial administrators, policemen and merchants and grab their jobs. Although some Afro-Asian middle classes became radicalized and resisted co-option into the Pax Americana, the bulk of these Westernized elites were quite happy to retain the socio-economic system built by colonials and serve as comprador partners of America's trading empire. Most were prepared to administer the client state and its economy on terms dictated by the multilateral system (created by America) as long as they – as comprador-partners – received a share of the profits. It was a perfect symbiotic relationship from which both sides benefited, as long as these compradors proved able to maintain the economic and political viability of their states. Those Afro-Asian middle classes who became radicalized and resisted the Pax Americana, were to discover there were major costs to being uncooperative with this informal empire.

Fanon suggests these Westernized compradors were an 'underdeveloped middle class ... in no way commensurate with the bourgeoisie of the mother country'.[49] He argued they did not possess the professional, entrepreneurial, managerial or agricultural skills of the departing colonials; and as an underdeveloped bourgeoisie, did not engage in 'production, invention, building or labour'.[50] Instead, their only vocation seemed to be to run a comprador 'racket'[51] based on demanding that the business of 'all the big foreign companies should pass through its hands'.[52] So these compradors discovered their 'historic mission' was being 'intermediaries'.[53] For Fanon these compradors constituted a parasitic group, incapable of carrying through the bourgeois project of building a developed capitalist society. As he said:

> The bourgeoisie of an underdeveloped country is a bourgeoisie in spirit only. It is not its economic strength, not the dynamism of its leaders, not the breadth of its ideas that ensures its peculiar quality as a bourgeoisie. Consequently it remains at the beginning and for a long time afterward a bourgeoisie of the civil service. It is the positions that it holds in the new national administration which give it strength and serenity. If the government gives it enough time and opportunity, this bourgeoisie will manage to put away enough money to stiffen its domination. But it will always reveal itself as incapable of giving birth to an authentic bourgeois society with all the economic and industrial consequences which this entails.[54]

Four decades after Fanon wrote this, the conditions in many Third World countries (most vividly seen in African and Pacific failed states), is testimony to his predictive capacities.

Effectively, Fanon deemed these compradors the creation of the Pax Americana. Fanon argued these parasitic 'junior partners' of America's informal empire might achieve considerable personal wealth (from being 'intermediaries'), but could never become equal partners, because they were defined by the way they acquired and retained their power. Their power is 'derivative' – derived, in effect, from three sources.

Firstly, America needs reliable middle-class partners if its trading empire is to function and (multilateral) global 'peace' is to be maintained. The system of (Wilsonian) liberal internationalism works best when America has reliable and competent allies in the peripheries to whom it can delegate responsibility.[55] The more responsibility that can be delegated the better, because this makes American hegemony both more efficient and more opaque. Hence, America actively seeks out people who it believes will be reliable compradors. It uses its financial and political leverage to 'intervene' wherever possible to try to encourage and groom the emergence of the 'right' leaders (while 'discouraging' the emergence of 'unhelpful' leaders). Woodrow Wilson bragged of his ability to use and control peripheral players in this way.[56] Because America does not directly control independent states, it is not always successful in creating compliant ruling elites. However, the rewards for collaboration are high; while the penalties for non-collaboration are high – as witnessed when leaders have not functioned as reliable compradors in Serbia, Iraq, Iran and North Korea.

Secondly, comprador-power was derived from gaining access to those levers of state power built by European-colonials. Once in control of these levers, they tended to be unprepared to let go. Usually the departing colonials handed power to an urban middle class because:

- Having acquired literacy, they were the obvious candidates to fill the shoes of departing colonial administrators.

- The Westernized middle classes lived in the colonial-built cities where the levers of power were located.

- As a minority who had been Westernized, they were culturally proximate to Americans and Europeans, and hence they were sought out as allies and partners.

- America's desire to integrate independent states into its global trading network necessarily implied encouraging 'economic growth' and modernization. This advantaged the Westernized middle class, and disadvantaged 'traditional' people (usually a majority of the population).

- America's desire to replicate its own liberal-democratic system advantaged the middle classes and disadvantaged 'traditional' people and workers (who had not been educated/Westernized to the same extent).

As decolonization pressures grew after 1945, independence movements led by the Westernized middle classes, proliferated. In general, those deploying populist nationalism (which often included unrealistic promises to unsophisticated electorates) were elected into power. Once in power they captured the state's bureaucracy, plus the military-and-police infrastructures created by Europe's empires. This gave these middle classes a base from which to ensure they remained in power. Many of these middle-class compradors ran into difficulties when they could not deliver on their populist promises; or when other social groups began mobilizing against them. This is when some abandoned all pretence to democratic governance and used military–police power to entrench themselves. The resultant military-dominated regimes often made reliable comprador-partners for the Pax Americana because they created stable environments for Western corporations and implemented modernization (Westernization) programmes – e.g. Indonesia. This was preferable to failed states where all semblance of governance broke down, and warlords took control.[57]

Thirdly, comprador-power was derived from members of the indigenous middle classes recognizing the value of having powerful Western backers. They learned the art of 'translating' between two worlds – the Western world and their own local (Third) world. A key to being successful was using 'appropriate' language, so as to 'please' Westerners. In this regard, it is worth noting how America (and its European allies) sought, wherever possible, to assist 'moderates' (usually those mobilizing 'nationalist' language) to come to power; while they discouraged 'radicals'. Ultimately those who became successful compradors mastered the following. They:

- avoided contradicting what those running the Pax Americana wanted to hear. For example, the Pax Americana was premised upon creating independent nation states. Yet few of the new states being created were 'nations'. Rather, they were administrative territories inhabited by a plethora of ethnic groups. But if Americans wanted 'nations' the Westernized middle classes were quite prepared to say they existed and to put themselves forward as the leaders of such nations. And so they conjured into existence new national identities (such an Indonesian, Zambian, Nigerian and Iraqi) which often had no meaning beyond the limits of one or two cities;

- agreed to play by the international rules of the game established by the multilateral system of economic and political global governance (encoded in the IMF and UN);

- maintained conditions in the states they controlled which facilitated American access to resources and markets;

- maintained conditions in which Western corporations could function profitably, and which protected Western property;

- facilitated Westernization through education, development programmes, and allowing America's culture industry unbridled access;

- maintained law-and-order so their territory could not be used by those the West defined as criminals or politically dangerous.

When compradorism works it is an ideal way of managing client states, because an informal empire, run by comprador-partners, can appear not to be to an empire, and so more difficult to challenge. After all

The final irony of an informal empire was that, precisely because it was informal, it was the most tenacious of all. For what else could follow in the wake of withdrawal … there being no new flag of independence to run up the pole, what else except internal struggle between shifting, bereft collaborators seeking new positions on the rungs of an endless ladder?[58]

But compradorism has its downsides. For one thing, it is easier to compel someone inside a formal empire than someone in an informal empire. Washington has to build its hegemony (rather than enforce it) – this means deploying a particular style of leadership and 'guidance' that achieves the deference and cooperation of other states.[59] Hence the workings of the State Department and the huge multilateral infrastructure of the UN, IMF, etcetera, have become immensely complex affairs. Simply put, managing comprador-partners requires more hours of diplomacy, tact and negotiation, than managing formal empires. It is thus a management process with more likelihood of error than in a formal empire. Examples are, the way 'mistaken communication' about Kuwait produced the Gulf War; or the way inept compradors produced the 1980s debt crisis. The Pax Americana has also produced many failed states, crony capitalisms and corrupt cleptocracies. In formal empires such problems could be fixed more easily from the centre. This is one reason the Pax Americana has proved a less successful form of global governance than the Pax Britannica.

Running an informal empire

The global system emerging after 1945 involved inventing ways to run an informal empire. Because the Pax Americana was to be an opaque 'anti-imperial' empire, new institutions, mechanisms-of-control and ideologies needed to be developed. Ultimately, the system built was characterized by five features.

Firstly, the Pax Americana was above all else a mechanism whereby Americans organized globalized resource extraction, wealth making and trade. The key mechanism for this was the corporation. But under the Pax Americana, corporations themselves mutated to become globalized entities.[60] As power was privatized (in accordance with liberal ideology), multinational corporations became important coordinating mechanisms within America's informal empire. Washington's political infrastructures were deliberately mere 'background facilitators' geared to assisting multinational corporations extend their reach. Washington tried to be as opaque as possible, while globally promoting trade liberalization and multilateralism. So whereas formal empires and national states fought over territory under a system of 'privatized power', corporations now fought for market share,[61] and their governments simply helped them achieve this. But this struggle over market share now occurs within an American-designed multilateral system of global financial governance. Naturally, American corporations benefited from the fact that the 'rules of the game' were American conceptualized. The outcome has been the privatization of power into the hands of multinational corporations and 'the market'.[62] Within this system, transnational networks/ alliances (negotiated by multinational corporations) become key mechanisms of global governance, because corporate-players now make decisions that globally influence the lives of millions – e.g. Wal*Mart's 'buying policies' played a major role in relocating industrial production from America to southern China (a global phenomenon with potentially significant long term geopolitical ramifications). Arguably, some corporate actors now exercise more global power and influence than political actors. But significantly, the global negotiations carried out by corporations are 'private' affairs. Hence, America's informal liberal empire has effectively developed mechanisms of global governance that are at best opaque, but are often completely hidden because they are 'private' business (even if their effects are not 'private').

Secondly, the Pax Americana has built a globalized economy which reaches even further than the one built by Britain. An important feature of this has been the internationalization of production – factories are located where profit can be maximized.[63] Often different components of a final product are made in different continents before being assembled elsewhere. This internationalization of production has stimulated new technologies, new management practices and new global communications. Managers can now control this globalized production from global cities like New York, Los Angeles, Chicago and London. As Strange notes, 'the location of productive capacity is far less important than the location of the people who make the key decisions on what is to be produced, where and how'.[64] Ultimately, what matters is that much of the production takes place under the direction of executives of American corporations.[65] America has built a corporate empire that effectively commands the resources and productive capacity of much of the world. Americans remain in charge no matter where the factories, mines and farms are located.

Thirdly, the Pax Americana created a global market through actively promoting trade liberalization. That products are sold globally has enormous cultural implications because selling a product also involves the selling of behaviours associated with the use of that product. Hence, global corporations have promoted the homogenization of consumer behaviour on a global scale.[66] This has contributed to the phenomena called Americani- zation and cultural hybridization (semi-Americanization) as discussed in chapter 10. The Pax Americana has promoted the emergence of a globalized culture associated with individualism, consumerism and materialism. Consequently, social values are becoming increasingly homogenized and/or hybridized across the globe, as American-driven modernization undermines traditional cultures everywhere. These processes of cultural change have been greatly encouraged by the growth of a globalized culture industry; by waves of migration (driven by business seeking to lower labour costs); and by modernization and liberalization of the Third World and ex-Soviet empire.

Fourthly, the smooth functioning of the Pax Americana depends upon America finding comprador-partners in every independent state across the globe. The best compradors are those sharing similar values and motivations to middle-class Americans. Consequently, the Pax Americana has come to resemble a huge global alliance of middle-class people who share similar educational profiles and lifestyles. This is why the Pax Americana can be termed 'an empire by invitation'[67] – an empire built upon cloning middle-classness; and then relying on these middle classes (scattered around the globe) to seek out partnership deals with America. All of these middle-class partners are then networked into a functioning international 'team'. Consequently, America's trading empire relies upon building and maintaining globalized networks which bind together a global coalition of liberal elites. Although New York is the metropolitan epicentre of this network, the network has become a truly globalized phenomenon within which some power is delegated to sub-metropoles like London, Frankfurt and Tokyo. Running such a network requires an effective communication system facilitating instantaneous global communication. The Internet now provides this. This has given rise to a highly reflexive economy where power has congealed in those global cities with significant concentrations of cultural capital. Effectively, within the corporations empire 'knowledge' is power.[68] But it is a particular sort of knowledge that is required. It should come as no surprise that today's global economy advantages those with the sort of knowledge, technical skills and information-processing habits acquired in Anglo-run (or Anglo-derived) education systems. The Pax Americana is very much associated with the use of English as a lingua franca;[69] with Anglo habits of mind (e.g. pragmatism and empiricism); and a system of rules and regulations largely produced by Anglo-Americans.

Fifth, the Pax Americana has mainly rested upon a 'soft type of coordination'[70] rather than direct American interventionism. Much of this soft coordination was encoded into the rules of multilateralism – Bretton Woods-system, IMF, GATT, UN, NATO, OECD, APEC and WTO. America has usually occupied a dominant position within these organizations such that it could steer and consensus-build through multilateral negotiations.[71] Effectively America has learned to 'supervise the relationships' between politically independent societies and build its hegemony by getting 'elites in the secondary states' to believe they are benefiting by acquiescing to American leadership.[72] Multilateralism, when it works, is immensely valuable to the Pax Americana because it provides a mechanism to coordinate a world of independent states, yet does so in a way that 'hides' American power, especially when America gets its allies to act as surrogates and proxies (in proposing and promoting American agendas). Multilateralism also provides the Pax Americana with an imperial bureaucracy to manage global 'peacekeeping'; a system of international law; and a mechanism to deal with transnational socio-economic issues like global health, food supplies, refugees, labour, and development. The Pax Americana has even been able to turn some 'problem' territories into multilaterally run protectorates, e.g. Bosnia. For the Pax Americana, multilateral organizations have served three purposes:[73]

- A strategic purpose was served whenever multilateral organizations assisted America in achieving foreign policy goals. However, Washington's support for multilateral organizations like the UN and World Court has waxed and waned, depending upon the extent to which American interests were being serviced or frustrated at a particular point in time.

- An adaptive purpose was served whenever multilateral organizations helped facilitate coordination between states. This is required to 'coordinate' politically independent states within America's global trading system. The system of multilateral financial organizations has generally worked well, allowing America to coordinate economic and technical arrangements needed for effective global trade.

- A symbolic purpose was served whenever multilateral organizations allowed all players to declare themselves in favour of some symbolic 'good' (a declaration) while leaving states free to pursue their own interests and do exactly as they wish anyway. Much of the UN system was reduced to symbolism once it failed to deliver the strategic outcomes desired by America.

Because the multilateral system was designed to facilitate 'soft coordination', America was never able to compel compliance with its will. Consequently, the American designers built in failsafe mechanisms for those occasions when American diplomacy, financial leverage or ideological osmosis failed. America's UN Security Council veto serves this purpose. Within the Bretton Woods system, America simply allocated itself a dominant voting-position.

Because finance is the glue in the Pax Americana-system, the Bretton Woods system (of international rules, institutions and procedures for financial and commercial interaction) was central to building an American informal empire. Bretton Woods promoted the globalization of American-style liberal capitalism and open trade based upon a system of convertible currencies and the use of the US dollar as the world's reserve currency. Significantly, Wilsonians established their open trading system through the use of multilateralism because their policy of open liberal trading (promoted by an alliance of Wall Street and the State Department) was meeting some resistance at home. Creating a system of multilateral organizations became a way of by-passing home opposition.[74] Wilsonian liberals realized if multilateralism could be institutionalized, liberal global governance could be 'professionalized' into the hands of technical experts and an imperial bureaucracy, thereby minimizing the impact of American opposition groups. Building an international multilateral system (operating alongside and parallel to America's internal government) had the benefit of transforming decision-making into something 'experts' did in multilateral negotiation forums which made it possible to sidestep America's internal democracy if need be. A similar process drove the creation of the WTO – when trade lawyers promoted the WTO as a means to overcome 'commitment problems' to free trade on the part of sections of American society.[75] The result is a form of 'concealed' multilateral global governance driven by a 'sort of international freemasonry that has grown up over two or three decades between English-speaking economic officials'.[76] Attitudes helpful to facilitating the global expansion of liberal capitalism have become so naturalized within this multilateral system of negotiators, experts and imperial bureaucrats, that the Pax Americana can now almost run on autopilot. Hence even when the formalized Bretton Woods system unravelled in 1971, it did not matter. The Smithsonian Agreement simply replaced Bretton Woods with a new multilaterally managed international monetary system. And ultimately a new multilateral Bretton Woods system emerged.[77] Further, in the process of dealing with the 1980s debt crisis, the 'international freemasonry' simply learned how to replace legal obligation by a new kind of consensus formation based on 'ideology' and 'correct' behaviour.[78] The result was the 'Washington Consensus' which advocated applying the same 'correct' (liberal) behaviour to both the First and Third Worlds.[79] Naturally, American hegemony has always been more secure at the centre of the system and less secure at the Pax Americana's peripheries.[80] However, even at the peripheries, the World Bank and IMF have been able to secure a remarkable degree of conformity towards the 'correct' behaviours of the Washington Consensus through a system of rewards and penalties.

But because the Pax Americana prefers 'soft coordination', the resultant informal empire is a 'messy' affair – its various components (independent states, NGOs and multilateral organizations) differ enormously from one another, and each is tied to the centre in different ways. It is an informal empire in which power is dispersed amongst a range of actors,[81] and which is held together by a complex hierarchy of power relationships and influence. Thus, for example, Britain has considerable influence within the corridors of the multilateral system; while Botswana has almost none; and some NGOs are independent actors while others are surrogates. Client states and comprador-partners derive sufficient benefits from being tied into the global trading network to give them a vested interest in its maintenance. Ultimately, it is a global system of power centred upon America – America's structural power effectively giving it the capacity to restrict the 'options' available to all other players.[82] It is an 'American Peace' precisely because American structural power is omnipresent. The brilliance of this informal empire is that American hegemony is strengthened by being opaque.

Achieving hegemony in an informal empire: structural power

Roosevelt's planners had decided America did not need territorial expansion to achieve global hegemony. Hegemony 'could be achieved by a combination of military alliances and a world economy opened up to trade, investment and information'.[83] For Strange, American power is grounded in its ability to change the options of other governments, foreign banks and trading corporations.[84] So how is this achieved? The answer is, after 1945 America successfully implemented a new system of global governance – an American-designed multilateral power system which effectively placed 'structural power' in American hands. The essence of this system is that whoever possesses or controls all sources of the power structure is able to shape the choices of others without directly putting pressure on any of them.[85] Strange contends the Pax Americana has constructed four interlocking sources of structural power:[86]

- A security structure grants America the ability to threaten or defend; or to deny or increase other people's security from violence. Since 1945 America has dominated the world militarily, although during the Cold War, the Soviets offered some counter-balancing force to American military power. America's pre-eminent capacity to project violence globally has always been a core feature of the Pax Americana; its military power making America primus inter pares in organizations like the UN and NATO. America has the power to defend and enforce its global economic system and its role as global hegemon.[87]

- A finance structure grants America the ability to offer, withhold or demand credit. America has the ability to control the supply of credit because Washington is the only government capable of creating dollar assets. America also possesses a huge and innovative capital market. Further, America has been primus inter pares in key organizations like the World Bank, IMF, WTO, OECD, APEC and G7.

- A production structure determines the locus, mode and content of wealth creation. The locus of power is revealed by who decides what to produce, how to produce it where to produce it, and for what reward. Strange argues if such key decisions are made by Americans and/or by corporations headquartered in America, then the world's production structure is dominated by America. America's 'corporation empire' ensures that the key locus of decision-making remains American.[88] So no matter where the factories are located, Americans remain in control. The same is true of the services sector and oil production – key decision-making is largely located in America for two reasons.[89] Firstly, America developed the world's first mass market for manufactured consumer goods and mass cultural products. As a result, Americans invented the modes of production and business practices that underpin today's global economy. The system was quite literally 'made in America', and Americans have consequently always been embedded (and remain) at the heart of this system. Secondly, the laws and policies required to operate corporations were originally developed by Americans. These laws and policies are being globalized as America's 'corporation empire' proliferates. The result has been the globalization of an 'American-made' productive system that necessarily encodes American values into its routines and practices. This necessarily advantages managers who are American (or who have been Americanized).

- A knowledge structure is about the production, acquisition, communication and storage of knowledge. How knowledge is structured impacts on who will have the most influence on the circulation of ideas in society (and whose ideas will be marginalized or repressed). This structure impacts on the ability to influence ideas and beliefs, and therefore impacts on which kind of knowledge is socially prized and sought after; plus who gets access to what knowledge. America dominates the world's knowledge structure – it leads the world technologically; has an enormous (and wealthy) university-and-research sector; has built and 'dominates' the internet and global telecommunications; plus the world's major data-banks are now located in America. America now also dominates the world's mass culture industry through Hollywood and globalized television. The global diffusion of American ideas, beliefs, technology, knowledge and entertainment complements the production structure by helping to spread materialism, consumerism, individualism and attitudes/work-practices helpful for expanding a capitalist trading network. This is called 'soft power' (discussed in chapter 10).

America has exercised this structural power since 1945. At various times it has been suggested American hegemony is in decline. Even when the school of American decline became very influential, Strange disagreed.[90] For example, she argued in the 1980s there had been no decline in American hegemonic power, 'only a change in the basis of American power, as when a person shifts weight from one foot to another. Simply, the American corporation empire spills out over its frontiers, and is consolidating an entirely new kind of non-territorial empire. It is this non-territorial empire (of corporate investment, financial institutions, the media, dollar markets, military bases and oil pipelines) that is truly the flourishing economic base of US power, not the goods and services produced in the United States'.[91] Once the Soviet Union collapsed and economic problems emerged in Asia, the school of American decline fell silent. At the start of the twenty-first century, America was supremely powerful; with its informal empire and structural power having never been more entrenched. And far from diminishing the Pax Americana, the 2008 financial crisis merely served to confirm how the entire world is meshed into an American-run economic system.

Securing America's informal empire with military power

America's informal empire is premised upon ensuring American businesses have access to all the resources and markets of the world. The European empires achieved this by annexing territories outright and sending occupation armies to ensure direct control of key resources and markets. Because the Pax Americana constructs its hegemony differently, the American military has learned to deploy force differently to the way the European empires did.

A core feature of the Pax Americana is that American military power underpins American political and economic hegemony. America has overwhelming military superiority because its military spending accounts for almost 50 per cent of the world total.[92] This means no state, or even coalition of states, can muster enough strength to challenge or restrain America.[93] And because all other states understand the enormous destructive capacity Washington possesses, America does not even have to use this capacity. Ultimately, only states with nuclear weapons can in any way 'challenge' America.[94] But there are not many such states, and the multilateral system banning nuclear proliferation is designed to keep it that way. All other political players must pay attention to American aspirations because Washington can project military violence to any part of the globe, and challenging American policy runs the risk of significant penalties. The basis of American power is five-fold.

Firstly, America's network of military bases straddles the globe, as shown in map 5. These army, navy and air force bases, together with America's fleet of aircraft-carriers, give America a strike capacity in every region of the world. America's military bases are positioned differently to those of the earlier British empire because British bases were designed to protect a maritime trading network, whereas American bases are geared to protecting a maritime and aviation trading network. The Pax Americana shifted global trading routes, and created new global trading hubs, new production centres, new global communication networks, and a new (globally dispersed) elite of liberal collaborator partners. Because these routes, hubs, communication networks and elites constitute the lifeblood of American economic power, they need to be protected by strategically positioned bases. America's navy dominates all the world's oceans; its airforce technologically outperforms all others; and America is the preeminent power in outer space.

Secondly, America has built up a network of multilateral and bilateral military alliances in Europe, Asia and Australasia. The most important is NATO, which America uses to maintain its hegemony over Europe.[95] NATO, in fact, well illustrates how Washington uses multilateralism to secure the Pax Americana. Following World War II, America wished to reconfigure Western Europe in two ways. Firstly, Germany was to be locked into a politico-economic union with other European states, especially France (to constrain Germany from trying to unilaterally become a world power). Further, as part of the Wilsonian exercise to promote open trade, America wanted to establish a European customs union. This, however, created the potential danger of building a united Europe that could eventually grow to challenge American global hegemony. However, by creating NATO, any future united Europe was locked into a multilateral alliance with America – which positioned large American military bases in Europe; and limited the possibilities that either a united Europe, or Germany, could develop a military force commensurate with their economic power. The multilateralism of NATO also services American-interests by simultaneously enhancing American power, yet making it opaque.

Thirdly, America's corporation empire has generated unprecedented levels of wealth for Americans. America now has at its disposal huge resources to spend on its military machine and military research. When the Soviet Union tried to keep up with American defence spending, they spent themselves into bankruptcy. Effectively America has built up a military machine that out-guns all others combined. America's military is not only ahead of all others in size and technological terms; it is backed by a research infrastructure that ensures it stays ahead.

Fourthly, America's military can project fire-power to every region of the world. This gives America an impressive ability to enforce its particular vision for 'peace' globally. Yet, interestingly, despite this enormous fire-power, the Pax Americana has proved to be a less effective world police officer than the Pax Britannica, as witnessed by the re-emergence of piracy in many places (which the British had repressed).

Fifth, the Pax Americana has constructed a defensive system grounded in the notions of multilateral security (administered through NATO) and multilateral peacekeeping (administered though the UN). A great innovation of this multilateralism is that it inherently spreads the costs of enforcing global stability (the American Peace) beyond America. The multilateralism of the UN system is also useful to the Pax Americana in so far as it is an inherently conservative system – making it very difficult to change the boundaries agreed to by the Allies after World War II.[96] These global arrangements and administrative entities conveniently service America's liberal trading empire, but the UN Charter virtually compels action against anyone wanting to challenge these arrangements. So America has cleverly designed a multilateral system for blocking changes it does not favour (including changes to the administrative boundaries of its empire). Further, any actions taken by this multilateral system are defined as being in the interests of 'peace'; while 'peace' is defined as a 'universal good' (like motherhood). This means defending the 'American Peace' (i.e. defending America's informal trading empire) becomes a 'universal good'. But because the system is multilateral, the centrality of American power and interests within this stabilizing-system is obfuscated.

Having established what the Pax Americana is, we will now turn to examine how this empire was created.

Notes

1 Winks, R.W., 'On Decolonization and Informal Empire', *The American Historical Review*, 81, 3 (1976), 540–556.

2 Strange, S., 'The Future of the American Empire', *Journal of International Affairs*, 42, 1, (1988), 6.

3 Cox, R., *Production, Power and World Order* (New York: Columbia University Press, 1987), 214.

4 Strange, S., 'The Future', 10.

5 Daalder, I. & Lindsay, J., *America Unbound* (Washington: Brookings Institute, 2003), 197.

6 Mandelbaum, M., *The Ideas that Conquered the World* (Oxford: Public Affairs, 2002), 77.

7 Fanon, F., *The Wretched of the Earth* (New York: Grove Press, 1968), 152.

8 Underhill, G.R.D., 'Global Money and the Decline of State Power', in Lawton, T. *et al.*, *Strange Power* (Aldershot: Ashgate, 2000).

9 Cox, *Production*, 228.

10 Underhill, 'Global', 131.

11 Mandelbaum, *Ideas*.

12 Cox, *Production*, 215.

13 Story, J., 'Setting the Parameter: A Strange World System', in Lawton *et al.*, *Strange Power*, 34.

14 During the Cold War the term 'Third World' was widely applied to underdeveloped states to differentiate them from developed capitalist states ('First World') and communist states ('Second World'). Although the Cold War is over and some have suggested these terms be abandoned, 'Third World' continues to have widespread currency and descriptive power; hence its use in this book.

15 Cox, *Production*, 211.

16 *Ibid.*, 212.
17 Strange, S., 'The Persistent Myth of Lost Hegemony', *International Organization*, 41, 4 (1987), 561.
18 Cox, *Production*, 215.
19 *Ibid.*, 215–216.
20 *Ibid.*, 373; Mandelbaum, *Ideas*.
21 This book uses the European understanding of 'liberal' (not the American version where liberal means 'left-leaning').
22 *Ibid.*, 375; Mandelbaum, *Ideas*.
23 Cox, *Production*, 215–216.
24 *Ibid.*, 221.
25 *Ibid.*, 217.
26 Strange, S., 'Cave! Hic Dragones. A Critique of Regime Analysis', *International Organization*, 36, 2 (1982), 483.
27 Gilpin, R., 'The Retreat of the State', in Lawton *et al.*, *Strange Power*, 197.
28 *Ibid.*, 208.
29 Helleiner, E., 'Still an Extraordinary Power, But for How Much Longer? The United States in World Finance', in Lawton *et al.*, *Strange Power*, 231–232.
30 Cox, *Production*, 218.
31 *Ibid.*, 220.
32 *Ibid.*, 224.
33 *Ibid.*, 228.
34 *Ibid.*, 218.
35 *Ibid.*, 231.
36 *Ibid.*, 325–236.
37 *Ibid.*, 237–238.
38 Strange, 'Future', 10.
39 Strange, 'Cave', 496.
40 Story, 'Setting', 19.
41 Mandelbaum, *Ideas*, 373.
42 Cox, *Production*, 219–230.
43 *Ibid.*, 231–244.
44 Story, 'Setting', 24.
45 Winks, R.W., 'On Decolonization and Informal Empire', *The American Historical Review*, 81, 3 (1976), 550.
46 *Ibid.*, 541.
47 Frank, A., *Capitalism and Underdevelopment in Latin America* (New York: Monthly Review Press, 1969).
48 *Ibid.*, 429.
49 Fanon, F., *The Wretched of the Earth* (New York: Grove Press, 1968: 149).
50 *Ibid.*, 150.
51 *Ibid.*, 159.
52 *Ibid.*, 152.
53 *Ibid.*, 152.
54 *Ibid.*, 178–179.

55 Strange, 'Future', 11.

56 Bell, S., *Righteous Conquest. Woodrow Wilson and the Evolution of the New Diplomacy* (Port Washington: Kennikat Press, 1972), 102.

57 In such cases corporations employed mercenaries to provide security for their operations (e.g. executive outcomes were used in Sierra Leone). Alternatively Western governments began direct interventions to restore law-and-order in the absence of competent comprador-allies (e.g. Solomon Islands, Papua New Guinea and Haiti).

58 Winks, 'Decolonization', 556.

59 Keohane, R., *After Hegemony* (Princeton: Princeton University Press, 2005), 46.

60 Cox, *Production*, 263.

61 Strange, 'Persistent', 564.

62 Story, 'Setting', 26.

63 Cox, *Production*, 244.

64 Strange, 'Future', 5.

65 *Ibid.*, 5.

66 Cox, *Production*, 245.

67 *Ibid.*, 61.

68 *Ibid.*, 244.

69 Strange, S., 'Finance, Information and Power', *Review of International Studies*, 16 (1990), 274.

70 Cox, *Production*, 258.

71 *Ibid.*, 258.

72 Keohane, *After*, 45.

73 Strange, 'Cave', 484.

74 Goldstein, J., 'The United States and World Trade. Hegemony by Proxy?', in Lawton *et al.*, *Strange Power*, 253, 255–256.

75 *Ibid.*, 267.

76 Cox, *Production*, 257.

77 Doole, M., Folkerts-Landau, D. & Garber, P., 'An Essay on the Revival of the Bretton Woods System' (National Bureau of Economic Research, September 2003).

78 Cox, *Production*, 259.

79 Williamson, J., 'What Washington Means by Policy Reform', in Williamson, J. 'Latin American Adjustment: How Much has Happened?' (Washington, DC: Institute for International Economics, 1990).

80 Cox, *Production*, 268.

81 Gilpin, R., 'The Retreat of the State', in Lawton *et al.*, *Strange Power*, 198.

82 Strange, 'Finance', 266.

83 Strange, 'Cave', 482.

84 Strange, 'Finance', 266.

85 Story, 'Setting', 32.

86 Strange, 'Persistent', 565–570; 'Future', 13.

87 Keohane, *After*, 39.

88 Lawton, T.C. & Michaels, K.P., 'The Evolving Global Production Structure:

Implications for International Political Economy', in Lawton *et al.*, *Strange Power*, 57.

89 Strange, 'Persistent', 568.

90 *Ibid.*

91 Story, 'Setting', 30.

92 The Stockholm International Peace Research Institute calculated America accounted for 47 per cent of the world's total military spending in 2003.

93 Layne C., 'America as a European Hegemon', in Skidmore, D., *Paradoxes of Power* (Boulder: Paradigm Publishers, 2007), 47.

94 Most states with nuclear weapons have such limited arsenals they can offer no meaningful resistance to American forces.

95 Layne, 'America', 41–43.

96 America's decision to support Kosovo independence has much potential to undermine this long-standing freezing of international boundaries.

2

The twentieth-century power shift

By ... 1947 the United Kingdom lay naked before the world, stripped of its status, its aspirations, and much of its pride. Like Greece and Rome before it, Great Britain was forced to step aside before younger, more virile nation-states. (Hathaway, *Ambiguous Partnership*)

Roosevelt was a moral-imperialist on a super-Wilsonian scale, determined not only to make as much of the world over into the American image as was possible, but also prepared to contemplate the large-scale, and presumably enforced, movements of population of an immensity which makes Hitler's and Stalin's efforts seem quite small scale. (Donald Watt, *Succeeding John Bull*)

At the start of the twentieth century Europeans (especially the British) dominated the globe. By the end of the twentieth century America reigned supreme. In the early twentieth century the discourses of imperialism and colonialism legitimated European power. At the close of the twentieth century the discourses of democratization, self-determination, free trade, multilateral peacekeeping, universal rights and globalization legitimated American power (while the discourses of imperialism and colonialism had been de-legitimated). This represents one of the great political and cultural power shifts in human history. Understanding this huge transformation in the global balance of power requires grappling not only with America's motivations and actions, but also with the motivations and actions of Britons, whose power America overcame.

The shift from Pax Britannica to Pax Americana involved ending British hegemony over vast swathes of the globe and filling the power vacuum (created by Britain's retreat) with new American hegemonic arrangements. A key feature of this hegemonic shift was the change from a system of global 'peace' based upon Britain's (mostly) formal empire to a system of global 'peace' based upon America's informal empire. That the Pax Americana deployed an informal empire model is due to the fact that America established its global hegemony whilst Wilsonian-liberals were hegemonic in Washington (between 1933 and 1953). So understanding the Pax Americana requires examining how Wilsonian liberals conceptualize the world.

Wilsonian liberalism

Liberals have been remarkably successful in diffusing liberal ideology and imposing liberal hegemony upon the world in a hegemonic struggle that began in 1789. The liberalization of the world has, so far, taken place in two stages.[1] During phase one –the 'long nineteenth century' (1789–1914) – liberals systematically pushed back the powers of Europe's aristocracy, while simultaneously building modern liberal-capitalist states in Europe, North America and Australasia.[2] Then the 'short twentieth century' (1914–91) saw liberals decimate traditional institutions and values, plus defeat two key anti-liberal ideologies (communism and fascism).[3]

Liberalism has mutated into a number of different versions. For the purposes of understanding the Pax Americana, Wilsonian liberalism is the most important version. This form of liberalism emerged while Woodrow Wilson was America's President (1913–21). Wilsonianism is liberalism applied to international relations.[4] Wilson, like all liberals, favoured 'small' government. Consequently, he argued for democracy, free trade and control on armaments. All three involve restraints on government power.[5] From this emerged liberal internationalism,[6] a vision of international relations which seeks to establish 'impersonal universal rules to govern politics, economic and security'.[7] Wilson effectively sought to establish a global liberal hegemony by 'universalizing' ('globalizing') liberal procedures for running states, economies and the international system. Within the Wilsonian model America 'conquers' the world by diffusing its values and practices; and by 'naturalizing' and 'institutionalizing' ('proceduralizing') liberal governance across the globe. The aim is to make liberalism appear as the most sensible, natural and preferably 'only' way to do things. If this 'American way' could be proceduralized everywhere, then a liberalized global system would effectively 'run itself' (and liberalism, as ideology, would be rendered invisible). Had Wilson succeeded, this would have created conditions for liberal capitalism and an American-run global trading system to flourish globally. But Wilson failed; and it was only under a new generation of Wilsonians, led by Franklin Roosevelt, that Wilsonianism was finally implemented.

Wilson's liberal internationalism was, at heart, grounded in a concern to expand American trade throughout the world. This trade agenda saw Wilson attempt to assert American hegemony and turn American capitalism outwards.[8] Wilson's concern grew from his recognition that the closing of America's land settlement frontier in the late nineteenth century created the danger of economic stagnation, unless new markets could be found for northeastern America's factories. Wilson explicitly rejected the idea of building a formal America empire to create new markets. Instead, Wilsonian liberal internationalists proposed to build a new sort of (informal) 'liberal empire' that explicitly differed from the (formal) empires constructed by the Europeans.[9] There were six components to Wilson's vision.

Firstly, it was grounded in the logic of Jeffersonian 'empire of liberty' which was premised upon the notion that American 'democracy', 'freedom', and state formation were simply superior. The Jeffersonian model advocated spreading the American model across the American continent within an 'Enlightenment vision of a benign imperial order'.[10] This 'moral imperialism' produced America's first empire (shown in map 3) – an empire based on conquest, colonization and cloning. The Wilsonian model was grounded in Jeffersonian logic,[11] but extended this logic to the rest of the world – i.e. the American model (of building 'liberal states') was now to be replicated across the world.[12] But these new states were not to be incorporated into the American Union; instead they were to become sovereign democratic states with whom America could trade.

Both the Wilsonian and Jeffersonian models assume 'the American way' is inherently superior, and so deserves to be universalized. Hence a Pax Americana grounded in Wilsonianism is not just an economic project; it is also a missionary project, proselytizing on behalf of 'liberal democracy', 'American values' and a vision of 'progress' grounded in Western Enlightenment thinking.

Secondly, trade lay at the heart of Wilson's concerns. 'Again and again Wilson stressed the closing of the old continental frontier and the necessity of a new one in world trade.'[13] Wilson conceptualized a world of 'open trade' and the building of an American informal empire based upon an American-run global trading system. He called this the 'righteous conquest of foreign markets'.[14] Although Wilson was not personally successful in creating such an informal (trading) empire (in part because European imperial powers like Britain blocked American aspirations after World War I), his vision ultimately become the basis upon which the post-1945 Pax Americana was constructed.

Third, American middle-class values and democracy were to be cloned such that comprador-partners would be created in each of the sovereign democratic states. The creation of such compradors would facilitate the building of an informal (trading) empire (i.e. a Pax Americana). Since this empire would be governed by comprador-partners it would also be cheap to run.

Fourth, promoting global free trade, market capitalism and individual rights underpinned the Wilsonian model. The aim was to globally clone American liberalism – i.e. a mix of 'consumer sovereignty' (capitalism) and 'popular sovereignty' (democracy).

Fifth, Wilson adopted an anti-imperial position by advocating self-determination and trusteeship (primarily geared to dissolving the Austrian, German and Ottoman empires).

Sixth, Wilsonianism proposed a liberalized international system of multilateral institutions and procedures to keep world order, promote 'open trade', enforce arms control and maintain peace.

Significantly, Wilson was quite prepared to shoot people into self-determination.[15] Since Wilson believed America was the most progressive state in the world, using force to spread 'liberty', 'democracy' and (American) 'civilization' was apparently justified.[16] Wilson's idealism, plus his belief in free markets, democracy, multilateralism, and universalizing the 'American way' have been a feature of Wilsonian liberals ever since.[17] This has been described as a new form of 'absolutism' in which American norms are taken to be 'self-evidently' correct.[18] This vision produced a 'moral imperialism' that can appear arrogant to non-Americans because universalizing American values, democracy and capitalism necessarily implies destroying the value systems and social structures that other cultures have built.[19]

Wilson never personally realized his vision because he was defeated both inside the American political system, as well as externally, by Europe's imperial powers. Rooseveltian Wilsonians succeeded where Wilson had failed; with Roosevelt's team both reinvigorating Wilsonian liberalism within America, and proving very adept at playing the international political game.

Significantly, at the end of World War I Britain was deeply in debt to America,[20] plus America's economy clearly outranked the British economy.[21] Yet, under Wilson, America did not succeed in translating American economic power into political power. Politically and diplomatically the British simply outperformed the Americans for the first three decades of the twentieth century.[22] Consequently, Britain remained the world's leading power.[23] It was under Roosevelt and his Secretary of State Cordell Hull that Americans learned to turn economic power into political power and to make Wilsonianism a force to be reckoned with on the global stage.[24] After 1940 Roosevelt began acting like a moral imperialist on a super-Wilsonian scale.[25] What Roosevelt Hull and Sumner Welles[26] did was to adopt Wilson's vision of 'open trade' and multilateralism and add to these a call for the ending of Europe's empires through decolonization.

Roosevelt's administration saw World War II as an opportunity to eliminate all empires – German, Japanese, British, French, Dutch, etcetera. They opposed empires for two reasons.

Firstly, they saw empires as an obstacle to the creation of an American informal trading empire. Such an empire could not be built until global free trade was established. Americans believed empires locked them out and denied them access to resources and markets. The Rooseveltians were especially unhappy about the British empire because of the 1932 Ottawa system of imperial tariffs. America's press had long created the impression

Britain's empire was bursting with wealth.[27] This generated much populist resentment about Americans being denied access to this wealth. Essentially, the Pax Americana could not be built until Britain's empire was removed. So, during the 1940s, Roosevelt's administration launched a media attack upon British imperialism, as discussed in chapter 4.

Secondly, there was a moral dimension to Roosevelt's anti-imperialism. Roosevelt (as Wilsonian) believed every nation state had the right to self-determination, and overlordship of one nation over another was not acceptable.[28] He made it clear he disliked British imperialism[29] and even blamed poverty in many parts of the world on colonial exploitation.[30] Roosevelt, Hull and Welles saw Britain's empire as morally unacceptable because it was deemed to be the opposite of American 'liberty' and 'democracy'. For Welles, destroying Europe's empires was a great moral crusade[31] geared to ending what he believed was an authoritarian and tyrannical system.[32] American hostility to imperialism partly sprang from America's war of independence against Britain. But in addition, migrants from Ireland, plus the Hapsburg and Russian empires carried with them powerful anti-imperialist sentiments to America. This fed into an American populist mood of anti-imperialism grounded in idealism, naivety and reductionist thinking about how Britain's empire functioned. Effectively, there existed a clash of political cultures; with Americans believing their own 'moral universe' and political system (grounded in political egalitarianism) was superior to the way (they believed) Europeans ran their empires. And when liberal internationalists believe someone is violating their 'moral universe' they believe they have a 'right' to intervene – this has been the basis of much American (moralistic) interventionism, seen recently in Kosovo.

Because empires violated their 'moral universe' the Roosevelt-Wilsonians decided to 'make over' both their enemies (Germany and Japan) and allies (Britain) in America's image.[33] The key statement of this intent was the 1941 Atlantic Charter.

World War II presented Roosevelt's administration with an opportunity to transform American economic strength into global political power. Roosevelt's team proved to be skilled political players – they effectively succeeded in using the power shifts caused by others, and successfully intervened to generate power shifts of their own. They aimed to build a new world order (grounded in Wilsonianism) and they succeeded. In this regard, it is worth noting Roosevelt was a man of his times who shared much in common with his key rivals Stalin and Hitler. All three men sought to change the world (and build new world orders). All three were social engineers who believed it was legitimate to use the state to radically reconfigure the world and people's lives. Roosevelt and his team were liberal social engineers who 'engineered' huge social changes (in the interests of liberal-capitalism) – the Rooseveltians transformed America (through the New Deal); reconstructed Germany and Japan into liberal societies (discussed in chapter 9); destroyed Britain's empire (to be discussed in chapter 7) which was replaced with Third World 'developmental states' (to be discussed in chapter 8); and laid the foundations for the Pax Americana (to be discussed in chapter 5).

Shifts in the balance of power

To understand why Roosevelt's team was successful, whereas Wilson had failed, we need to unpack the balance of power between the key political players (Britain, America, Germany, Japan and the Soviet Union), and how this shifted between the 1920s and 1940s. In 1920 Britain and America were the two leading powers. Americans were frustrated Britain dominated the world (even though America was the world's leading economy). There was also great American frustration that London's financial system (and the sterling bloc) retained so much global influence. Consequently, America made a number of (unsuccessful) moves in the 1920s to challenge British political and economic power[34] – they struggled over control of oil, undersea cables, air routes, China, and naval build-ups.[35] Americans were heartened by challenges to Britain's empire in Ireland, India, Iraq, Afghanistan, Persia and Palestine between 1919 and 1922. However, Britain's diplomats outperformed their American challengers, and British colonial administers stabilized the empire's trouble spots. By the mid-1920s Britain's empire was in clear revival mode and Britain's global supremacy was secure.[36]

Between World Wars I and II America was the world's growing economic giant. However, America remained a regional rather than a global power[37] – with Washington's power confined to the America's. Only British power was truly global, and Britain remained unambiguously 'the world's policeman'. Changes were triggered by the rise of German and Japanese power, plus moves by Axis powers (Germany, Japan and Italy) to build empires. For Britain this posed a problem, because not since 1779 had London faced three aggressive challengers all at the same time.[38] Britain did not deal with these challenges particularly well. In fact, British policy-makers and diplomats performed remarkably badly from 1930 onwards[39] – which contributed to Britain's loss of power (and the eventual loss of empire). Britain responded to the Axis bloc in two ways. Firstly, Britain decided to build up French power to create a shield against Germany. London believed a British–French alliance could contain German power. Secondly, because Italy was the Axis bloc's weakest link, Britain geared itself up to knock out the Italian empire first (which simultaneously facilitated expanding Britain's Middle East empire).[40]

Germany's defeat of France in 1940 radically transformed the balance of power. Britain (until then the 'world's policeman') was severely weakened by the defeat of its key European ally. Simultaneously, Germany was transformed into a great power, and America transformed from a regional power into a global player – because without American assistance, Britain could not defend itself against Germany. France's defeat presented Britain with two choices.

Option one – continue the war with Germany. But this required negotiating a deal with America for the supply of armaments. The problem was, Britain would presumably need to concede much to America. Firstly, Britain's empire would be threatened by the Roosevelt team's anti-imperialism; hostility to imperial tariffs; and American advocacy of self-determination. Secondly, the Americans had long sought to make New York (rather than London) the world's financial centre, and make the dollar (rather than sterling) the world's reserve currency. Thirdly, such negotiations could be expected to transfer considerable power from London to Washington, and turn Britain into an American ally *on America's terms*. Such negotiations carried the risk of allowing the birth of a Pax Americana at Britain's expense.

Option two – negotiate peace with Germany and join the German-led new European order. It was known Hitler had long wanted an alliance with Britain to facilitate war on the Soviet Union (geared to turning Soviet territory into Germany's empire). Further, since Hitler's book, *Mein Kampf*, advocated a continuation of Britain's empire, it was possible that negotiations with Germany might deliver a better deal than negotiating with America. The problem was, negotiations with Germany could be expected to transfer considerable power from London to Berlin, and turn Britain into a German ally *on Germany's terms*.

For Britain both options were disagreeable.[41] Britain's ruling elite was divided with some (particularly elites in the empire's dominions) inclined towards dealing with Germany.[42] Chamberlain appeased Hitler to avoid a deal with America precisely because he understood the dangers that this held for Britain's empire.[43] But Britain's Prime Minister Churchill was an Americophile, and his belief in an Anglo-American 'special relationship' guaranteed his support for option one.

When faced with choosing between aligning Britain with Germany or America, Churchill opted to align with America. In so doing he sealed the fate of Britain's empire. Roosevelt and his team handled the negotiations with Britain brilliantly. These negotiations ensured Britain was meshed into an alliance with America that guaranteed global power would shift across the Atlantic and make it possible, at last, for Washington to build

Wilson's informal trading empire, the Pax Americana. Conversely, British policy-making and negotiations under Churchill led inextricably to a loss of British power and the eventual end of Britain's empire.[44]

Ultimately, World War II contributed to the transfer of power across the Atlantic in a number of ways:

- Britain's economy was greatly weakened by the war because resources were allocated to the military instead of maintaining a viable economy. Rebuilding a peacetime economy would take time, and America was not interested in rolling over its loans to facilitate this.[45]

- British military forces did not perform especially well in Malaya, North Africa and Italy (which weakened Churchill's bargaining power relative to Roosevelt and Stalin).[46]

- The war undermined British legitimacy in parts of the empire – e.g. war was declared in India and South Africa without popular support. This undermined British claims about constitutional reform of the empire. The war also set back British moves to reform India into a dominion within the empire. Further, the fall of Singapore provided anti-imperialists (including America) with much ammunition to use against the Pax Britannica. Simultaneously, the war brought American forces into the empire, where they promoted an anti-imperial line.

- The war dramatically expanded America's economy and military capability. Plus America suffered no war damage to its economic infrastructure (unlike the Soviets, Britain, Germany, Japan and France). By 1945 American economic power was overwhelming, relative to all other countries.

- During the war America did much to build up Soviet power. This, coupled with the destruction of German power, left all of Europe vulnerable to the Soviets in 1945. This effectively made Western Europe dependent upon American power, leading to the phenomenon of an 'empire by invitation'.[47] Europe's vulnerability led to the formation of NATO which has kept American military forces (and hence American power) in Europe ever since.[48]

- Britain ended the war deeply indebted to America. From 1946 it was clear to London that Washington was going to use the leverage conferred by these debts to 'push' British policy-makers. The British Foreign Office became so concerned, it create an Interdepartmental Committee on American opinion and the British empire as a sort of 'general staff for the protection of the empire'.[49] Ultimately, Washington used its leverage; and when given the opportunity to push Britain's empire off the cliff the Americans did so.

And so Britain found itself at the end of World War II technically victorious, but actually strangely disempowered, relative to an assertive America. Consequently, 1945, 1946 and 1947 were peculiar years for

Britain's ruling elite. On the one hand, Britain's empire was at its absolute peak in 1945 with Britain having occupied during and after the war Libya, Eritrea, Ethiopia, Italian Somalia, Syria, Lebanon, southern Iran, Madagascar and Sumatra. With these acquisitions Britain administered virtually the entire coastline of the Indian Ocean. Yet despite this appearance of power, the British government found its room for manoeuvre severely curtailed by a powerful and assertive America to whom London was in debt. In 1930 Britain may have been the key global hegemon, but in 1945, it was all too clear to London the mantle had passed to America. And with this shift came American pressure to grant independence to India, and to partition Palestine into Jewish and Arab sectors, so that an Israeli state could be created.[50] This led inextricably to Britain's withdrawal from India and Palestine which set in motion the unravelling of Britain's empire.

The death of this empire was a curious affair, spanning twenty-seven years, and involved the transfer of global political power from London to Washington; and the transfer of global economic power from London to New York. The process began in 1940 and ended in 1967, and involved ten key events:

- France's 1940 defeat compelled Britain to start negotiating for American assistance.

- The 1941 Atlantic Charter signalled America's intention to end European (and British) imperialism.

- In 1946–47 America refused to allow Britain to roll over its war debts or delay sterling's dollar convertibility (triggering a British financial crisis and decision to withdraw from Palestine, India and Greece).

- The 1947 Truman Doctrine saw America assume responsibility for containing the Soviets and maintaining the European balance of power. The Truman Doctrine openly asserted American global power; with American global hegemony visibly replacing Britain's.

- In 1947 Britain dismantled its Indian empire, granting independence to India, Pakistan, Burma and Ceylon. This dramatically weakened imperial defence and British prestige. The injury this inflicted on Britain's empire proved to be terminal.

- In 1948 Britain withdrew from Palestine, further weakening British prestige.

- In 1956 America forced Britain and France to withdraw from Suez which signalled Britain was no longer a first-ranked power and America now exercised hegemony over Britain.

- The 1957 Eisenhower Doctrine signalled America intended to replace

Britain's informal empire in the Middle East with an America informal empire.

- The 1967 sterling bloc collapse signalled the victory of America's dollar as the world's reserve currency.

- London's 1967 announcement Britain was withdrawing its forces east of Suez confirmed Britain, stripped of its empire, was no longer a first-rate power.

Pax Britannica to Pax Americana

There are obvious differences between the Pax Britannica, as a (mostly) formal empire, and the Pax Americana, as an informal empire. Whereas the British were proud of, and revelled in their imperialist achievements, Americans like to deny their imperial behaviours.

Yet there are also strong continuities between the two empires. Both shared a number of features: Anglo culture; commitment to liberal-capitalism; and a desire to build a global trading network. Ultimately, the British and Americans, as the two great powerhouses of liberal capitalism, have effectively been the drivers of two centuries of globalization – with the British empire being the organizing force of globalization's first wave (in the nineteenth century) and the Pax Americana being the organizing force of the second wave (in the twentieth century). Together the British (globalization I) and Americans (globalization II) built trading networks spanning the globe; and globally spread capitalism, liberalism, the English language and Anglo-culture. Both shared the same commitment to the processes of modernization, liberalization and globalization. Consequently, the Pax Britannica and Pax American can clearly be seen as part of a single continuum – involving two interlinked projects which have been responsible for a series of massive political, economic, social, linguistic and cultural transformations of the globe. And it is a process of transformation that is not as yet complete.

Despite continuities between the two phases of globalization, dismantling Britain's empire and replacing it with a Pax Americana affected the lives of billions. Given the implications of this enormous power shift, it is curious that the transfer generated so little acrimony and dislocation. This has been attributed to the 'special relationship' that Britain and America are said to share because of their historical and cultural links. As a result, the 1940s–1950s transatlantic power shift involved a peculiar kind of transition somewhat akin to a family struggle in which one cousin forces another cousin to hand over the family inheritance. The transition was certainly characterized by rivalry between London and Washington, but this was moderated by the special relationship. This relationship, discussed by Hitchens,[51] has exercised the minds of many Americans, including Alfred Thayer Mahan, Josiah Strong, Andrew Carnegie, John Hay and Woodrow Wilson. It has also exercised the minds of many Britons like Rudyard Kipling, Cecil Rhodes, Joseph Chamberlain, Winston Churchill and Harold Macmillan. Over time various proposals have actually been made to strengthen this special relationship. For example, Mahan advocated a tight American alliance with the British empire; Chamberlain wanted British–American solidarity; Andrew Carnegie wanted America and Britain's empire to fuse or federate; Kipling was concerned with how to harness American strength to the British empire; Cecil Rhodes created the Rhodes Scholarship to build a joint British–American elite to govern the world; Josiah Strong and John Dos Passos saw Britain and America as engaged in the same project to Anglo-Saxonize the world; while Woodrow Wilson saw America and Britain as part of the same civilizing force in the world. And when it became clear in the 1940s there was to be a transfer of power over the Atlantic, one of America's leading intellectuals, James Burnham, actually called for a planned transition, saying the Pax Americana should formally become the 'receiver' for Britain's empire.[52] Because Burnham's 'receivership' proposal was never taken up, the actual transition became messy; with both sides grumbling through this transition – Britons complained about American 'imperialism' and Americans moaned about British 'colonialism'.[53] But despite grumblings, the transfer of power to the Pax Americana was largely completed by 1967. And within another two decades, the special relationship was repaired by Ronald Reagan and Margaret Thatcher and the two countries became allies and best of friends.

Cold War complications

When Rooseveltians began advocating the end of European imperialism and started pushing for self-determination in the 1940s, they assumed a Pax Americana could be unproblematically rolled out after World War II; and all the newly independent states would simply be absorbed into America's trading empire. This turned out to be naive. They did not reckon on the Soviet Union emerging as a post-war superpower.

Three events were to shift Washington's anti-imperialism stance, namely, the Soviets becoming a nuclear power (1949); China becoming communist (1949) and the Korean War. This created the realization in Washington that decolonization might lead to the new states joining the communist bloc instead of America's trading empire. Due to this threat, Washington re-evaluated its policy of dismantling Europe's empires. The State Department's European desk in particular argued Europe's empires were needed as bulwarks against the Soviets. This generated enormous relief in London, where for much of the 1950s, the British believed they would now be able to retain what was left of their empire. But this was not to be, because by 1950 the Pandora's box of anti-imperialist activism was open. Closing it was not going to be as easy as opening it. Britain (and America) now faced the following problems:

- Britain's empire had been terminally weakened by the loss of India, e.g. when Iran nationalized the Abadan oil refinery valued at £120million (or the equivalent cost of retooling and modernizing Britain's entire coal industry) London found without its Indian Army they were unable to protect their Iranian assets.[54]

- American anti-imperial rhetoric, combined with Indian independence, inspired decolonization activists across the Third World. Throughout the 1950s Afro-Asian activists organized themselves and demanded independence.

- The Soviets became active in promoting communist liberation movements in European colonies and showed they were willing to support and arm these decolonization activists if independence was refused.

America's response was to promote the idea of building 'moderate' middle-class elites in Asian and African colonies through 'development' and modernization, a phenomenon examined in chapter 8. The aim was to create middle-class comprador-partners.[55] Washington succeeded in getting Britons to adopt this 'development' idea in their empire. Both Washington and London assumed this would create 'moderate' nationalists who would be willing to join America's informal trading empire after independence was granted). But this did not always work, because 'development' sometimes created 'radical' middle classes (demanding immediate independence) who were inclined to align themselves with the Soviets rather than the Pax Americana.[56] Effectively 'decolonization' took on a life of its own. To halt the radicalization of independence movements, Britain, France and Belgium opted in the early 1960s to speed up decolonization and grant immediate independence to the most 'moderate' (pro-Western) politicians they could find in each colony.

Consequently Rooseveltian planners were only partially successful in rolling out their new world order. For example, although America was supremely powerful in 1945, much of the territory of the defeated German and Japanese empires was not acquired by the Pax Americana – because the Soviet empire acquired much of the former German empire; while much of the former Japanese empire was 'lost' to communist China. However, the Rooseveltians were successful in establishing a Pax Americana, and incorporated into this informal empire (called 'the Free World') Japan, the Pacific islands, Western Europe, Latin America, and a high percentage of the states created by decolonizing the British, French, Dutch and Belgian empires.

During most of the Cold War America adopted a policy of containment – i.e. working to prevent any part of 'the Free World' moving into 'the communist bloc'. This translated into America and the Soviets fighting a number of proxy wars in what had been the former colonial territories of the old European empires, e.g. Vietnam and Angola. However, Washington's defensive stance changed when Ronald Reagan became President. The Reagan Doctrine (1985) switched from containment to 'rollback' – i.e. seeking to 'take back' territories 'lost' to the Soviet bloc such as Angola, Nicaragua and Afghanistan. Reagan's assertive stance was also evident in the Strategic Defence Initiative (1983) geared to building a missile defence shield. Reagan's policy shifts made it dramatically more expensive for the Soviets to try and keep up with American defence spending. Ultimately America, with its much larger resource-base, pushed defence spending beyond what the Soviets could afford. This played a role in bringing about the Soviet Union's 1991 collapse.

Soviet collapse

When the Soviet Union collapsed, it finally became possible to establish the Pax Americana the Rooseveltians had conceptualized, because after this collapse America stood supremely powerful. No other country (or even alliance of countries) could challenge American power after 1991. Effectively, America became a global hyperpower.[57] So post-1991, (Wilsonian) liberal internationalism became globally 'hegemonic'. However, it did not become 'universal'– because it was globally 'imposed' by American power rather than universally 'believed'.[58]

One of the most dramatic effects of the Soviet collapse was that, for the first time, America could seek to expand its informal trading empire into what had been the Second World (the communist bloc). The resultant expansion of the Pax Americana was dramatic, when what had been the Soviet's East European empire joined both the EU and NATO. The Peoples Republic of China also adjusted itself to America's hyperpower status and tied its economy into America's trading empire. This produced a massive relocation of industry from America, Western Europe and Australia into southern China (where labour was much cheaper). This radically reconfigured the global division of labour. The 'liberalization' of the Second World and its integration into the Pax Americana remains a work in progress. But with the re-emergence of

Russian power, this integration process seems likely to become increasingly troubled and characterized by Moscow-Washington conflict.

Further, during the 1990s, all Third World states found themselves having to adjust to the political and economic requirements of an expanded and more powerful Pax Americana. Clearly states previously aligned with the Soviets had to make greater adjustments than those previously aligned to America. However, even Western-aligned states now found themselves having to make adjustments to new (more stringent) demands coming from Washington. Whereas during the Cold War Third World states could negotiate terms with Washington (and Moscow), from 1991 there was no counterweight to Washington's power and so they had to simply accept Washington's terms (the 'Washington Consensus'). Consequently, the 1990s generated considerable turmoil across the Third World as the processes of 'democratization' and economic 'liberalization' were imposed. Any states not fully acquiescing to the Pax Americana – e.g. North Korea, Iraq, Iran, Burma and Cuba – experienced the discomfort of refusing to adequately adjust to Washington's liberal 'consensus'.

America's post-1991 hyperpower status also generated highly interventionist presidencies. Bill Clinton adopted a classical Wilsonian 'moral empire' position and became a 'hyperinterventionist' when he sought to impose American 'morality' upon the world through wars in Haiti, Bosnia and Kosovo.[59] The Clinton Doctrine of humanitarian interventionism was also solidly Wilsonian in so far as it was grounded in multilateralism. The presidency of George W. Bush was equally interventionist. Interestingly, initially the Bush-team was opposed to interventionist foreign policies grounded in Wilsonian idealism.[60] But after 9/11 Bush slid into interventionism, replicating many features of Wilson and Clinton's 'moral empire' logic geared to spreading American 'democracy and freedom' to the world.[61] However, the Bush Doctrine of imperial interventionism deviated from Wilsonianism in so far as it eschewed multilateralism and also hybridized the 'idealist' and 'realist' strands of American foreign policy. One interesting by-product of Bush's 'democratizing' idealism was that it strengthened the British–American special relationship around a Bush–Blair Doctrine geared to globalizing Anglo-American liberal democracy via an 'aggressively utopian foreign policy'.[62]

The collapse of the Soviet Union not only freed up American power, it also made this power more obvious. The resultant hyperinterventionism of Clinton and Bush plus their heavy-handed promotion of American 'democratic capitalism' made America's global power clear to all. But it was the war in Iraq that really focused attention on America's relationship to imperialism because it looked as if this war signalled not only a shift away from Wilsonian multilateralism; but also a Bush-team policy redesign that looked set to produce a whole new kind of Pax Americana. However, an Obama presidency seems likely to restore the 'traditional' form of American imperialism as invented by the Rooseveltians – namely, an informal trading empire grounded in multilateralism and Wilsonian idealism.

Notes

1 Mandelbaum, M., *The Ideas that Conquered the World* (Oxford: Public Affairs, 2002), 63.

2 Key features of phase one were the French and American Revolutions and the Industrial Revolution.

3 The first targets of Europe's middle-class liberals were the traditional institutions and values of Europe's aristocracy. Thereafter, middle-class liberals turned to other continents where their 'modernization' agendas decimated the traditional societies of the America's, Africa and Asia. ('Modernizing' the Third World remains a work in progress.)

4 Mandelbaum, *Ideas*, 29.

5 *Ibid.*, 30.

6 Liberal internationalism has been most visible in the foreign policies of Wilson, Roosevelt, Truman, Kennedy, Clinton and Bush Snr and Jnr.

7 Mandelbaum, *Ideas*, 31.

8 Gardner, L.C., LaFeber, W. & McCormick, T., *Creation of the American Empire* (Chicago: Rand McNally, 1973), 298–299.

9 Bell, S., *Righteous Conquest. Woodrow Wilson and the Evolution of the New Diplomacy* (Port Washington: Kennikat Press, 1972), 41.

10 Onuf, P.S., *Jefferson's Empire. The Language of American Nationhood* (University of Virginia Press, 2000), 53.

11 Lipscomb, A. & Bergh, A., *The Writings of Thomas Jefferson, Vol. 12* (Washington DC: Thomas Jefferson Memorial Association of the United States, 1903).

12 Mandelbaum, *Ideas*, 77.

13 Bell, *Righteous*, 36.

14 Gardner, *Creation*, 299.

15 Bell, *Righteous*, 127.

16 *Ibid.*, 127.

17 Mandelbaum, *Ideas*, 33.

18 Hartz, L., *The Liberal Tradition in America* (New York: Harcourt & Brace, 1955), 58.

19 Watt, D., *Succeeding John Bull* (Cambridge University Press, 1984), 252.

20 McKercher, B., *Transition of Power. Britain's Loss of Global Pre-eminence to the United States, 1930–1945* (Cambridge: Cambridge University Press, 1999), 3.

21 Zakaria, F., *From Wealth to Power.* (Princeton: Princeton University Press, 1998), 131.

22 McKercher, *Transition*, 11, 27, 29.

23 *Ibid.*, 30–31.

24 *Ibid.*, 309–310.

25 Watt, *Succeeding*, 79.
26 Under Secretary of State.
27 Cain, P. & Hopkins, A., *British Imperialism 1688–2000* (Harlow: Longman, 2002), 485.
28 Greer, T., *What Roosevelt Thought* (East Lansing: Michigan State University Press, 1958), 156.
29 Louis, W., *Imperialism at Bay, 1941–1945* (Oxford: Clarendon Press, 1977), 147.
30 Greer, *Roosevelt*, 168.
31 Thorne, C., *Allies of a Kind* (Oxford: Oxford University Press, 1978), 217.
32 Watt, *Succeeding*, 226–227.
33 *Ibid.*, 96.
34 McKercher, *Transition*, 11.
35 Watt, *Succeeding*, 51, 60.
36 Gallagher, J., *The Decline, Revival and Fall of the British Empire* (Cambridge: Cambridge University Press, 1982).
37 McKercher, *Transition*, 32.
38 Gallagher, *Decline*, 128.
39 McKercher, *Transition*, 339.
40 Gallagher, *Decline*, 136.
41 Cain, *British*, 479.
42 *Ibid.*, 480.
43 *Ibid.*, 486.
44 Clarke, P., *The Last Thousand Days of the British Empire* (London: Allen Lane, 2007), 507, suggests Churchill's own actions hastened the downfall of the Pax Britannica.
45 *Ibid.*, 771.
46 McKercher, *Transition*, 320, 325.
47 Lundestad, G., 'Empire by Invitation? The United States and Western Europe, 1945–1952', *Journal of Peace Research*, 23 (September 1986).
48 Layne, C., 'America as a European Hegemon', in Skidmore, D. (ed.), *Paradoxes of Power* (Boulder: Paradigm Publishers, 2007), 41.
49 Watt, *Succeeding*, 107.
50 Clarke, *Thousand*, Part 4.
51 Hitchens, C., *Blood, Class and Nostalgia* (New York: Farrar, Straus & Giroux, 1990).
52 Hitchens, *Blood*, 245.
53 *Ibid.*, 265.
54 Louis, W., 'The Dissolution of the British Empire', in Brown, J. & Louis W., *The Oxford History of the British Empire, Vol. IV* (Oxford University Press, 1999), 339.
55 Mandelbaum, *Ideas*, 375.
56 Gallagher, *Decline*, 148.
57 Mandelbaum, M., 'The Inadequacy of American Power', in Skidmore, *Paradoxes*, 33.
58 Mandelbaum, *Ideas*, 38.

59 Krauthammer, C., 'Democratic Realism', in Skidmore, *Paradoxes*, 108.
60 Gordon, P., 'The End of the Bush Revolution', in Skidmore, *Paradoxes*, 267.
61 *Ibid.*, 268.
62 Krauthammer, 'Democratic', 113–114.

3

Manifest destiny
and the rise of American power

America was no ordinary nation, corrupted by time and tradition. Instead it was radically new, a nation that would bless all the nations of the world with the glories of the long anticipated millennial age. (Hughes, *Myths America Lives By*)

If we have to use force, it is because we are America. We are the indispensable nation. (Madeleine Albright, February 1998)

The contemporary actions of those driving the Pax Americana are the product of a particular worldview, and the roots of this worldview lie in America's colonial past. At its core America is a product of northwest European history and culture. More specifically, America is the off-shoot of a culture that has been particularly successful at expanding its territorial base – namely, Anglo-Saxon culture. As with other cultures that have become globally significant – Spanish, Arab, Russian and Chinese – this Anglo culture has aggressively colonized new territories at every opportunity, by annihilating, displacing or assimilating the smaller peoples who got in its way.

Roots of the American worldview

Of the numerous European colonial settlements established along the east coast of North America, one became the seedbed for America's vision of itself and its role in the world. This seedbed settlement was the 1620 Plymouth, Massachusetts, colony established by English Puritans. The Massachusetts colony was not even the first Anglo settlement in North America; in fact it was precisely established at Cape Cod Bay because this area lay outside the jurisdiction of England's Virginia colony. However, Massachusetts Puritans did something unique – they provided Americans, as a nation of immigrants, with a founding myth – the story of fleeing the oppression of an old corrupted world, and of moving to a new promised land to build a better future. This story ultimately transcended its Puritan roots, became secularized, and inculcated itself into the heart of America's self-image of how to build a better world.

The 1620 Massachusetts settlers, who arrived aboard the *Mayflower*, believed that, like the Israelites, they were God's chosen people. In their vision the world was perfectible and they believed themselves driven by destiny and duty to build a new and better world. The Massachusetts settlers had a truth – William Tyndale's protestant vision, modified by the Calvinism they imbibed during their exile in Holland. These Tyndale roots are highly significant in the story of the Pax Americana because they provided the builders of America's informal empire with a set of justifications for what they are doing.

Tyndale popularized the idea that England, like biblical Israel, had been chosen by God for a special mission in the world.[1] So not only did Englishmen have a 'truth', they had a God-given obligation to proselytize this truth in the world. This English mission mutated into an American mission when transplanted to New England by the Massachusetts settlers who had precisely fled England because they believed:

- England had become corrupt and ungodly. England's monarch was seen to have abandoned the covenant with God;

- by moving to the American wilderness they could build a new God-fearing society. Significantly, this was seen to provide them with a base from which to return to England and rescue the Old World from its corrupt ways;

- they were seeking freedom – the freedom to practise their 'truth'. Notions of 'freedom' and 'liberty' became a recurring theme in the American imagination. Significantly, the Puritans were interested in establishing freedom for their ideas to flourish. They were not particularly interested in establishing freedom for other people's ideas;

- as Congregationalists, that individual church congregations should rule themselves, rather than be ruled by established church hierarchies. Consequently, they carried with them two ideas that became recurrent themes in American thinking – namely, traditional hierarchical institutions of the old world are suspect; and American 'grassroots democracy' is superior to Old World hierarchies.

Significantly, the notion of being a 'chosen people' automatically encoded a God-ordained dichotomy – the world was divided into believers and heathens.[2] Within this dichotomy, it became possible for Puritan settlers to view Native Americans as 'agents of Satan'.[3] This worldview conveniently justified the sweeping away of (heathen) Native American societies to make it possible for God's chosen people to colonize the new lands. The scene was set for Anglo-colonization of North America over the next two hundred and fifty years.

It may seem remarkable that the worldview of a small group of Puritan settlers in New England could become so influential, but it is no exaggeration to say the *Mayflower* founding myth mutated into the core discourse underpinning the Anglo-American colonization of North America and the subsequent American proselytizing mission geared to carrying 'truth', 'freedom' and 'liberty' back to the Old World.

The Massachusetts Puritans represented the seminal moment in creating the American dream – a dream that is ritually reaffirmed every Thanksgiving Day. From these 1620 settlers America inherited the following notions that became central to how Americans now see their role in the world:[4]

- The idea of being a 'chosen nation' constantly resurfaces in America's vision of itself. Americans deem themselves 'special' because, as migrants, they remade themselves anew in the New World. This slipped into teleological thinking in which American becomes the most 'advanced' society because it is built on the best of the Old World, but in ways excluding the 'errors' of the Old World.

- America is seen as 'exceptional' because God chose Americans to carry out his mission of making the world a better place. Even today's secularized version of American exceptionalism is grounded in the original Puritan logic.

- America's mission is embedded in a 'national covenant', derived from Tyndale's 1534 New Testament translation. Although Americans avoid drawing attention to their Anglo roots, the reality is, one still hears echoes of Tyndale's view that God chose Anglos to play a special role in the world.

- American 'exceptionalism' also encodes the notion Americans, like the Puritan exiles, have abandoned the Old World's corrupt ways in order to build a non-corrupt New World.

- Like these Puritans, Americans believe they need to return to the Old World to fix it. Hence American foreign interventionism becomes a moral duty, carried out for the good of the world.

- The belief in a perfectible world mutated into a secularized belief Americans (individually and collectively) can make a difference. This mutated into America's upbeat 'can-do' culture with its preference for being 'positive'.

- Americans invented a form of Protestant populism derived from congregational self-rule and individual interpretations of the Bible. This became the secularized ideology of egalitarianism (tied to opposition of social hierarchies and elites).

Ultimately, from the 1620 settlers, Americans inherited a sense of destiny, and belief in themselves as 'good people' with a duty to make the world a better place. As America accumulated ever more power, this American vision became ever more salient for the rest of the world.

But Puritan settlers only provided the founding mythology. The emergence of an American worldview required a series of mutations to the original vision. The first mutation emerged from the American Revolution.

The American Revolution and American exceptionalism

The American Revolution and war of independence transformed the world by creating the United States and destroying the first British empire. The American Revolution also shifted America's worldview and sense of destiny by transforming and secularizing the founding Puritan myth. From this emerged an American self-image that still largely informs American actions to this day. As Hughes notes:

> The revolutionary and early national periods (between 1776 and 1825) stand at the centre of American self-understanding for several reasons. First the myths that emerged in those years seemed so self-evident, especially to Americans of European descent, that it was difficult to contest them at all. The American experiment simply reflected the way things were meant to be ... Second, the myths that emerged in this period had about them a certain timeless quality. According to these myths, America virtually transcended the particularities of time and place. These myths implicitly denied, for example, that the nation had particular historical roots.[5]

The founding myths were de-contextualized and de-historicized for practical political reasons. By 1776 North America's European settlements contained many different religions – Puritans, Anglicans, Presbyterians, Lutherans, Dutch Reformed and Catholics. Each wanted its version of Christianity recognized as the established religion. America's founding fathers recognized the dangers inherent in this, and so instead of identifying America with a Church-based God, they 'grounded the American experiment in a vision of 'Nature and Nature's God'; it was easy to imagine that the United States simply reflected the way God himself intended things'.[6] This produced a new kind of faith – one grounded in Enlightenment 'Natural order', wherein the new 'deity' became a set of (apparently universal) natural laws. This new faith neatly complements a society promoting individualism and materialism.

The founding fathers claimed to have discovered a set of moral standards God had built into nature.[7] By codifying these 'natural' standards they could build a secular state that, although effectively grounded in Christianity, did not need to formally proclaim its Christian roots. Because America was founded upon moral standards transcending individual religions, it claimed to represent a 'universal' moral order. This Enlightenment 'natural order' was able to absorb the Massachusetts Puritan vision. Hence Americans remained a 'chosen people' with 'destiny' on their side, but they were now transformed into a chosen nation grounded in a (secularized) Enlightenment faith. The Revolution actually strengthened Americans' faith in their exceptionalism – because 'America was no ordinary nation, corrupted by time and tradition. Instead it was radically new, a nation that would bless all the nations of the world with the glories of the long anticipated millennial age'.[8] In this millennialism could still be heard echoes of the Puritans' vision of creating a new and uncorrupted world.

America's Revolution produced a secularized political order, wherein church and state were formally separated. Despite this, American society remained grounded in its Christian roots. It also remained firmly embedded within its Anglo cultural roots. However, this Christian and Anglo heritage was made curiously 'invisible' within the new nation's founding mythology, precisely because Jefferson re-articulated Christian and Anglo particularistic 'truths' into 'universal truths' – an Enlightenment moral order that, according to the founding fathers, was apparently self-evident to all. Hence, the Declaration of Independence was explicitly framed as articulating a 'universal' truth –'We hold these Truths to be self-evident, that all Men are created equal, and they are endowed by the Creator with certain inalienable Rights, that amongst these are Life, Liberty, and the Pursuit of Happiness.' This founding myth reframed American identity as somehow autonomous of power-relations, of history and of tradition[9] – American identity was apparently no longer derived from its British, Western European or Christian heritage, but from some decontextualized 'truth' about the natural order of things. That Americans, as a chosen nation, had 'discovered' this de-historicized Enlightenment 'truth' served to confirm they were 'special' and 'ahead' of the rest of the world. Christian Americans could still choose to see the hand of God in this 'revelation' of 'truth'. But whether or not Americans chose to see God as the source of this revelation, they could all feel secure in the knowledge America was unique in being a polity grounded in 'the way things were meant to be'. This was simply self-evident;[10] a truth needing no formal proof.[11]

That Americans believed they had discovered a set of natural truths independent of history or tradition served to create a set of 'inalienable rights' in terms of which they planned to govern their new state. These rights were not universal. They were born of a particular context – the European Enlightenment and British history; and they encoded the values of Western Christendom and Anglo-culture. But once Americans believed they had de-contextualized and de-historicized their values, the scene was set for believing these American values applied to all humanity. This produced a pan-human universalism in which American 'inalienable rights' were actually deemed 'universal human rights'. And if America was a chosen nation, then Americans were licensed to export these 'rights' (freedom, democracy and self-government) to the world. Gray sees this as just another variant of Enlightenment 'utopian' thinking that seeks to impose itself on the world and in the process replaces the diversity of human cultures with a single universal civilization.[12]

This belief in 'chosen-ness', exceptionalism and pan-human universalism gave Americans an extraordinary self-assuredness that served them well as they colonized North America during the nineteenth century, and then set about establishing a Pax Americana during the twentieth century.

Further, fighting for their independence from Britain made Americans 'anti-imperialists'. Americans came to believe no nation should rule over another and all nations had a natural right to self-government, liberty and democracy. During the twentieth century this became something of an American mission – Americans came to see themselves as the champion of the rights of all nations to be free of imperial control and to assert their rights to freedom and self-government.[13] However, this American anti-imperialism was always somewhat ambiguous. For example, the right to self-determination did not apply to Native Americans whose lands were colonized by American settlers, and when America acquired the Louisiana Purchase, Louisianans did not have any right to opt for self-determination.[14] None-the-less, this American belief in anti-imperialism and self-determination did produce a particular genre of American imperialism – namely a post-1945 informal empire relying on comprador-partners. It is a form of imperialism that has not been an unqualified success (as discussed in chapter 11).

Manifest destiny 1: colonizing America

When the thirteen states became an independent nation, America's three million settlers lived mostly east of the Appalachians. For the next century America was a colonizing nation, as the frontier was pushed westward towards the Pacific. By 1820 the western frontier had crossed the Mississippi. After the Civil War, transcontinental railways were built and the Plains conquered and settled. At the end of the nineteenth century the land settlement frontier closed – America had been conquered, colonized and reordered in accordance with Jefferson's 'Empire of Liberty' model.

During the nineteenth century, Britain, Russia and America were amongst a number of states participating in imperialist-expansion. America's nineteenth-century imperialism subjugated Native Americans, French colons and Spanish–Americans. Their societies were swept away to be replaced with American colonists. America's colonial juggernaut simply pushed these conquered peoples into territory the settlers did not want ('Indian reservations') or assimilated them into America's homogenizing culture. But since Americans did not like to think of themselves as imperialists, they needed to construct a vision of what they were doing that differentiated American conquest from those of the other imperial nations. At the heart of this vision lay the notion of American exceptionalism, and America as a chosen nation. Effectively, Americans drew upon Jefferson's universalized moral standards to justify America's colonization and their destruction of existing societies/polities that got in their way. Americans justified their colonial expansion in five ways.

Firstly, American expansion meant growing the 'realm of liberty'.[15] Americans saw themselves as driven by a manifest destiny to spread Jefferson's self-evident truths as far and wide as possible. Like the Massachusetts Puritans, they were engaged in a 'moral' mission to expand Jefferson's 'empire for freedom'.[16] Indeed it was Jefferson who proposed the colonization of North America.[17] From within an American worldview, it was self-evident America was unique in being a polity grounded in 'the way things were meant to be'. Since American democracy was assumed to be superior, any expansion of America's hegemony necessarily expanded the part of the world where 'freedom' reigned. When Americans expanded their suzerainty, they were simply carrying out God's will to expand the 'universal' moral order discovered and codified by their founding fathers. Hence, Americans could believe Providence drove the expansion and that they were not motivated by selfish self-interest like the other imperialists. Instead, American expansionism and Americanization could be seen as being in the interests of all humanity.[18] These views continue to underpin the Pax Americana.

Secondly, Americans arrived as European colonists.[19] They navigated their way using maps showing a European conception of the land – these maps showed the outline of the continent, the rivers and the mountains. These became the focus of the Americans' attention – where to draw the 'natural' boundaries of the new nation. Before long it seemed logical to assume all of North America should be incorporated in the United States.[20] To Americans, this did not appear to be 'imperialist' because their maps showed no human geography. In Europe, Herder had argued the frontiers between linguistic groups imposed 'natural limitations' on imperialist expansion.[21] But in North America there appeared to be no such 'natural limitation' – the continent was theirs for the taking. This geographical conceptualization neatly complemented the American penchant for de-historicized thinking – before the settlers arrived the continent was seen to have had no history. From the maps drawn it appeared to be a contextless tabula rasa, awaiting American colonists to spread the realm of freedom and democracy from the Atlantic to the Pacific. It was easy to imagine America had a manifest destiny to occupy the whole continent, because except for the seashore, there appeared to be no other natural restraints. This geographical conceptualization was later to blur into a notion of a Western hemisphere destiny – i.e. America was seen to have 'special interests' across all of the Americas. This was encoded into the Monroe Doctrine.

Third, from the earliest days of the revolution national security became an American concern. Hamilton articulated this concern when arguing America had a natural right to boundaries affording the state security.[22] American expansionism has constantly been justified by this.

Fourth, from the beginning America was enmeshed in trade. From the revolution onwards, Americans demanded the right to free navigation to facilitate trade. This was given an interesting twist by the 1788 Convention of Kentucky, which argued free navigation of the Mississippi was an American right because this was required by Americans to develop their property.[23] In this way, the right to free navigation was tied to two other founding American discourses. Firstly, the 'inalienable rights' Americans had to expect their state to help them accumulate wealth and property (in order to pursue their 'inalienable right' to happiness). Secondly, the Puritan notion that Americans were God's agents for developing the soil. Without access to free navigation (to facilitate trade) God's invocation to develop the land could not be met. This free navigation notion ultimately led to America's first major exercise in expansionism – the incorporation of Louisiana so the Mississippi and New Orleans could become a conduit for opening up America's interior to colonization and economic development. But the free navigation/trade argument did not end there – it became central in driving America's expansion in the Caribbean, Panama and across the Pacific. And the nexus of free navigation, trade and God's invocation to develop the land remains alive and well in the discourses of one of America's more recent creations – the WTO.

Fifth, Americans believed their colonialism simply fulfilled the Bible's invocation to 'Fill the earth and subdue it'. American settlers believed this was exactly what Native Americans had not done.[24] Hence whites had a superior claim to the land because they were using it as God intended[25] – they were turning wilderness into civilization. This belief acquired a sort of commonsensical tangibility because as the frontier moved westward, the settlers could actually see the civilization they were building. Similar theological justifications for white colonization were used in Australia, South Africa and Canada. Benjamin Franklin went as far as suggesting the extermination of Native Americans was useful, and intended by Providence, because it made room for the 'cultivators of the earth',[26] i.e. America's manifest destiny to civilize the world justified a genocidal war of conquest against Native Americans.

So how have Americans reconciled their long-standing opposition to imperialism (and imperialist subjugation of other people) with their conquest and colonization of enormous swathes of territory? After all,

American expansionism was often more vicious than that practised by the other imperial powers – i.e. American colonization was accompanied by the annihilation or enforced assimilation ('Americanization') of those already inhabiting North America; while British and Russian imperialists subjugated, but generally did not exterminate those being conquered. The answer lies in the way Americans mobilized a different set of standards by which to judge their own actions; plus developed strategies making it possible to avoid 'looking' like imperialists (who subjugated others). Hence, during the building of their first empire, Americans simply ensured there were no indigenous people left in their conquered territories to be subjugated. This was achieved by either annihilating or assimilating conquered people. And when building their third empire, Americans used the comprador model to avoid the obvious subjugation of other peoples. However, America's third empire has proved to be as destructive of other people's cultures and ways of life as their first empire.

Manifest destiny 2: civilizing the world through liberal economics

Two events transformed America's sense of mission – the Civil War and the closing of America's land settlement frontier. These shifted America's sense of destiny away from a narrow focus on the American continent, and towards a concern with the wider world.

The American Civil War

It is impossible to overstate how much the Northern States victory in the Civil War was to impact on the world, because this victory represented the triumph of a particular economic model of development – a model that ultimately became enmeshed with America's worldview and sense of global destiny.

The American Civil War was a struggle over the nature of the economic regulatory system within which US economic development would occur. In particular, it was about whether America would have a uniform labour market. By the mid-1800s a manufacturing economy had emerged in New England and mid-Atlantic states. Northeast American manufacturing capitalists wanted to expand their commercial and industrial economy which would be greatly facilitated by:

- A larger supply of cheap labour. Ending slavery would transform slaves into 'free labour'. This would increase labour supplies and lower labour costs.

- An expanding market for their products. This would be facilitated by free settlement of America's new western territories and by transforming the Southern states' economies.

- Breaking Britain's economic hegemony over the Southern states. Before the Civil War the Southern states were geared to producing raw materials for British factories, placing a huge percentage of American resources outside the reach of northeastern capitalists. Destroying Southern plantation economies would simultaneously damage Britain and open up the Southern states to America's northeastern capitalists.

- Preventing the Southern states from expanding their economic system westwards (which would limit the territory and resources available for northeastern capitalists to exploit).

- Creating regulatory and ideological uniformity across the whole USA. If all America adhered to laissez-faire capitalism, and a uniform (northern-led) system of tariffs-and-trade regulation, northeastern capitalists would dramatically increase their opportunities for profit-making and expansion – because all America would become a single labour-pool and single market. (Not the case while Southern plantation economies survived).

The above vision of a new America was encapsulated by the Republican Party's advocacy of three principles: the promotion of middle-class enterprise; 'free labour'; and the 'opportunity' for white settlers to colonize Western territories free of competition from black slave labour.[27] After the Civil War these three principles became encoded into how Americans understood their destiny.

The Southern elites resisted Northern attempts to undermine their economic system, which produced the Civil War (1861–65). When the North won it set the scene for America's transformation. Over the next thirty years America shifted from an agricultural nation into a leading industrial nation. Industrial cities grew, as did infrastructures to support such cities, e.g. railways and mines. Washington geared itself to meeting the needs of manufacturing capitalists, who emerged as America's new power elite. Tariffs protected the new industries, while government regulations facilitated industrial development and allowed a freewheeling financial system to arise. Despite enormous population shifts from rural America to the slums of the new cities, there were still insufficient workers for the expanding industrial economy. Consequently, America took to importing workers from Europe. From this grew America's 'melting pot' society wherein people from a diversity of cultures were assimilated into America's homogenizing Anglo-culture. Such Americanization also involved assimilating migrants into America's belief-system of self-evident truths and its sense of manifest destiny and exceptionalness. Building a public school system was a core feature of this assimilation process.

The Civil War also altered America's notion of 'chosen-ness'. The rise of a manufacturing-capitalist elite brought with it a new dominant ideology. There was 'a radical transformation of the myth of the chosen nation. The older myth spoke of a covenant for the entire nation. The newer myth spoke of a covenant for the individual'.[28] This new ideology promoted the following:

- Jefferson's self-evident truth about the right to pursue 'happiness' was now interpreted as the accumulation of wealth. Materialism became central to the American dream and Jefferson's doctrine mutated into a materialist secularism.

- Radical individualism was foregrounded.[29] Whereas the Puritan and revolutionary creeds promoted a collective identity, the new capitalist creed promoted the idea America was an instrument to facilitate each individual maximizing their own self-interest.

- Competition now became the key mechanism binding American individuals together. American-ness became defined as individuals competing for wealth; a worldview encoding Darwin's 'survival of the fittest' idea.[30] So the credo of post-Civil War America became unbridled 'free enterprise' capitalism.

- The 'ideology of egalitarianism' was already part of the American dream; but now 'egalitarianism' became enmeshed with the competition for wealth. This resulted in the idea that individuals who became wealthy were the most industrious; while poverty was the outcome of laziness. Since America was an egalitarian society where everyone was afforded an equal opportunity to become successful, the failure to become wealthy was due to the individual's own faults. So individuals learned to blame themselves.

- Economic growth and the incessant expansion of markets were now deemed socially 'good'. Because growth was required to maximize opportunities for individuals to accumulate wealth, expanding trade opportunities became a key focus for manufacturers and government.

This ideological shift was to have significant implications for the world because 'the gospel of wealth, interpreted through the lens of social Darwinism, served to justify American expansion around the globe at the expense of the smaller nations of the earth'.[31] This expansionist drive unfolded in two stages – firstly, America's westward colonial expansion to the Pacific; then building a globalized trading network. Once America's land settlement frontier closed, it was easy to transfer America's 'manifest destiny' onto a global stage and to see America as a natural civilizing agent (through exporting trade and economic growth to distant shores). From within this worldview, expanding American global trade was equivalent to fulfilling the Bible's invocation to 'Fill the earth and subdue it'. This American vision manifested itself in building the Panama Canal, when trade and strategic interests were deemed equivalent to the collective interests of all humanity.[32] It was an easy step from this, to the notion that America as 'world policeman' served global civilization.[33] By the end of the twentieth century, this vision of America's destiny had mutated into the idea of 'globalization'. By the start of the twenty-first century the global media routinely circulated the idea globalization was an irreversible process and global free trade was good for everyone. So a worldview originally promoted by the rising class of northeastern American capitalists in 1860s, was 'universalized' to become the creed of a new world order with its epicentre in New York. Effectively, the Pax Americana has successfully constructed a globally networked liberal alliance who believe global free trade and globalizing liberal economics will bring about world peace (as expressed in the McDonaldization thesis that 'no two countries with a McDonald's restaurant have declared war on each other'). This Pax Americana liberal alliance now drives globalization II.

The closing of America's land settlement frontier

But not only the Civil War impacted on how Americans came to see their destiny. The closing of America's land settlement frontier significantly impacted on how America's governing elite viewed their options. Until the 1890s, the colonization and economic development of America's western territories provided America's economy with a natural engine of growth. But once America ran out of land to settle, there was the danger of the economy stalling unless new markets could be found. A stalled economy carried with it the danger of growing unemployment and hence of political unrest. The obvious solution was to refocus the energies of America's manifest destiny onto foreign shores and seek new economic opportunities overseas. This shift triggered American–British rivalry because once Americans began looking for overseas trading opportunities, they encountered Britain's empire. The rivalry was most evident in Asia, where Britain had a huge, and still expanding trading network.

In his 1902 book, Woodrow Wilson demonstrated a keen understanding of the challenges facing America by drawing attention to the closing of the land settlement frontier and the socio-economic implications of this for America.[34] Wilson realized unless alternative markets were found, the closing of the frontier could undermine economic growth and thereby create 'unemployment and social distress at home'.[35] Wilson argued the frontier's closing necessitated the 'conquest of world markets'.[36] This obviously meant America would find itself in direct competition with empires already straddling the globe in 1900. For Americans, the empires of Britain, France, Netherlands, Belgium, Russia, Austria and Ottoman Turks, locked up resources and markets America wanted access to. Because these empires blocked American economic wellbeing, they became the focus of American opposition. For Wilsonians, such empires were unacceptable because they stood in contradistinction to America's free trade ('open door') model and to America's self-evident truths of how societies and governance were supposed to be organized. For Wilsonians, the expansion of an American trading network across the globe made good economic and moral sense, because it served to grow America's economy while simultaneously spreading American values.

Although Wilson's vision of an American trading empire became a seminal moment in the Pax Americana's story, he was not the first to conceptualize American overseas expansionism based on trade. The pioneer-thinker was William Henry Seward.

Seward's expansion plans

Seward was Secretary of State from 1861 to 1869 – the period when Northeast American manufacturing capitalists were establishing their hegemony over America. Seward, as a member of Abraham Lincoln's cabinet, succinctly encapsulated the desire of these industrialists. His proposals neatly summarized their desire to see their commercial and industrial economy grow and expand across North America, and then across the oceans.

Seward sketched out a coherent plan for the building of an American informal trading empire. He 'exhorted Americans to achieve their destiny of dominating the markets of Asia'.[37] This required deliberately extending American hegemony over the Pacific in order to secure access to Asian markets. For Seward, projecting American hegemony across the Pacific was paramount because he saw Asia as the 'new theatre of human activity'.[38] He argued, if America achieved commercial dominance in Asia, America would become the most powerful state. In fact, he predicted it would become the most powerful state that had ever existed.[39] Interestingly, Seward's fascination with China's market has remained a feature of American thinking ever since.

Significantly, the commercial empire Seward envisaged was not like Europe's formal empires. Instead, he envisaged securing American global power through the construction of an economic and trading hegemony. In terms of Seward's model, America would only need to annex small amounts of strategically located territory for the construction of naval bases, to guard trade routes tying America to its foreign markets. So America's power was to be used not to annex new territory, but rather to establish freedom of the seas,[40] control of the Pacific, and 'open-door' trading. For Seward, America's core foreign policy goals should be to 'command the empire of the seas, which alone is real empire',[41] and to secure American access to all markets (global free trade). In the 1890s Captain Mahan picked up Seward's model and popularized the idea of building a powerful American navy. Ultimately, within Seward's model, the key agents of American expansionism would be its merchants;[42] the task of American governments would be merely to facilitate the merchants' expansionist activities.

This was a visionary conceptualization, clearly ahead of its time. Seward's plan did not come to pass during his lifetime for three reasons:

- Americans had not yet fully colonized North America. This 'internal' colonial task would provide enough of an outlet for America's expansionist energies for the next three decades. Effectively, until the 1890s there was no need to look overseas for opportunities for markets and economic growth.

- America did not as yet have the capacity to globally project itself politically or economically. America first had to strengthen the powers of its executive branch of government;[43] improve and professionalize its foreign service; and develop a military force (especially navy) able to project power overseas.

- America did not as yet have the capacity to dislodge Britain's empire, which controlled the world's oceanic trading routes.

None-the-less, Seward's plan was truly prophetic. One cannot but be struck by the extent to which today's Pax Americana conforms in large measure to Seward's model.

Seward's model

There were six components to Seward's expansionist plan.

Firstly, he was proposing a new kind of empire – one in which America would construct global commercial hegemony. For Seward, the true basis of 'empire' was 'commercial domination' rather than territorial expansion,[44] and the only empire worth having was a commercial one.[45] Consequently, American global power was to be built upon the principle of constructing an open-door commercial empire[46] based upon Seward's assumption that 'political supremacy follows commercial ascendancy'.[47] Seward's idea was that:

> The United States should possess commercial hegemony of the world. By virtue of its superior political, moral, and commercial institutions, Seward believed America was destined to dominate the trade routes and markets of the globe, and especially of Asia. But mere increase in wealth was not the only goal for Seward. In actuality, the commercial empire was the means to other ends, for through commercial domination political and cultural changes could be introduced American ideals and values transmitted, and the Christian religion spread over the globe.[48]

American domination of the Chinese market was a core feature of his vision.

Secondly, Seward's vision involved engaging in a 'Westernizing' and 'liberalizing' mission, in the sense that Asian societies would need to be reconstructed if they were to be transformed into viable trading partners for America. Hence, *development* of the Asian 'other' was implicit in Seward's plan. American-led socio-economic change and the industrial and commercial development of Asia was encoded into Seward's imperial plan that proposed America's commercial empire being engaged in a great civilizing mission consisting of two elements – the 'regeneration' of an apparently 'exhausted' Asian civilization;[49] and bringing Asia, Europe and America together into a single great trading bloc (with America at its heart). America was to become the world's 'leader' by engaging in this 'civilizing task' of bringing about the 'co-mingling' of the 'exhausted' civilization of Asia with the 'ripening' civilization of western Europe. This vision is still evident in today's American foreign policy.

Thirdly, Seward recognized the centrality of communication in building empires. As a man of his time, Seward focused on the telegraph, railways and shipping routes. However, by the middle of the twentieth century, America had added global air travel and air routes to Seward's list. By the start of the twenty-first century, the internet was added to this list. Seward's objective was to construct (and control) a global system of communication that would tie the world to America. In particular, he envisaged New York as London's successor – New York was to be made the nerve centre of a global commercial empire so that the world's wealth flowed into America rather than Britain.[50] For this to happen, New York needed to become the nodal point of a global system of communications which would give Americans the capacity to communicate with (and thereby manage/control) its empire's resources. Seward, in particular, focused upon the value of building a global telegraph system which, by the mid-nineteenth century, could provide almost instantaneous communication.[51] He especially wanted to see a telegraph route running from New York to San Francisco and then across the Pacific to Asia. This, for Seward, was the way to lock Asia into America's economic sphere of influence. Within Seward's imperial vision California loomed large. Transcontinental railways would tie Californian ports to America's northeastern industrial base, thereby becoming launching-pads for trade with Asia – from California would radiate America's sea-routes.

Seward also recognized the importance of America becoming the heart of a global monetary system. He noted a standardized coinage system had existed under the Roman Empire and realized if America could achieve something similar this would place global markets under American hegemony.[52] Consequently, Seward's plan discussed the need to build an American-run telegraph and coinage system that would reach every corner of the globe.[53] This would, according to Seward, ensure New York became the globe's financial centre.[54]

Fourthly, Seward was impressed by Britain's industrial and maritime capacity and recognized Britain would be America's chief rival.[55] Seward knew Britain was a huge obstacle to his plan to grow American power[56] because Britain:

- controlled a successful empire straddling the globe;

- dominated the world's postal system;

- operated a vast global network of steam-ship routes that dominated global trade;

- operated a network of coaling stations, ports and naval bases at strategic points around the globe;

- had developed a network of merchants around the globe that served to make London the heart of a global trading centre;

- was at the centre of a global financial system – with sterling operating as international currency; with London's financial system serving as banker, broker and insurer to the world.

If Seward's plan was to come to fruition, then clearly America needed to dislodge the British and break their existing global commercial hegemony.

Fifth, although Seward rejected building a formal territorial empire, he recognized the need for America to control key strategic points around the globe to protect American trade routes and commercial interests. Amongst the places identified as strategically important for an informal trading empire were Panama, plus some Pacific and Caribbean islands (e.g. Hawaii). From Britain's empire, Seward learned that operating a global network of coaling stations and naval bases was central to running a trading empire.[57] Hence he suggested copying Britain. Seward's purchase of Alaska was tied to his strategic vision of establishing American hegemony over the Pacific, to facilitate Asian trade.

Sixth, in Seward's plan, America would not accumulate power through territorial expansion. Instead, America would 'be aggrandized by peace'.[58] Seward's empire-building plan involved stealth – dispatching merchants, not soldiers. Merchants would establish trade networks that effectively tied foreign populations to America. Seward realized global commercial growth required global law-and-order (i.e. peace). The Pax Britannica's peace was militarily imposed. But Seward advocated an 'American Peace' could be secured differently – i.e. America would work to develop a network of foreign partners who established their own local hegemonies (local 'peace'). America-as-partner would provide these local comprador-partners with the resources needed to build their local hegemonies/peace. In this way the Pax Americana could expand its area of influence without needing to engage in costly warfare. America's partners would enact appropriate legislation and maintain law-and-order to facilitate American profit-making and trade.

America would sometimes intervene militarily in foreign conflicts. However, it would not intervene to annex foreign territory; it would only intervene to ensure foreign countries had 'appropriate' and functioning governments – i.e. governments that facilitated American trade, and/or served the interests of America's business. The Pax Americana might not mean direct American control, but it would mean subservience to American hegemony and US economic interests. Seward's model was first applied in 1898 when America militarily intervened in Cuba to assist Cuban rebels against the Spanish government. After defeating Spain, America installed an 'independent' Cuban government. The result was a 'semi-protectorate', with Cuba nominally free but (as Theodore Roosevelt said) 'a part of our international political system'.[59] Even the American Cuban military base at Guantanamo Bay was not annexed outright. Technically, Guantanamo remained Cuban territory, but was occupied by America in perpetuity. Cuba became a model for how the Pax Americana would operate – as an informal empire within which American power was 'disguised' by establishing client states run by comprador-partners. And when Americans intervened in other countries, they liked to frame their actions as altruistically serving the interests of 'others'.

The 1898 American–Spanish War kick-started American experimentation with imperialism when Washington dealt with the spoils of this war in four ways. Firstly, America sometimes annexed strategically important areas whose populations were so small that absorption would not alter the nature of American culture and society, e.g. Puerto Rico and Guam. Secondly, areas with large populations not seen as culturally 'absorbable' were not annexed outright. This partly reflected fear about the danger to American culture of incorporating large foreign populations who could not be easily assimilated (Americanized).[60] Consequently, the Philippines became a protectorate. Filipinos were then 'developed' (i.e. comprador-partners created); and the Philippines eventually became independent *within* the Pax Americana. Thirdly, areas already containing potential comprador-partners (able and willing to run client states) were granted nominal independence. This was Cuba's fate. Fourthly, America has established strategic military bases without formally annexing the territory these bases occupy, e.g. Guantanamo Bay.

However, only during the Woodrow Wilson era was Seward's informal empire model put firmly back on Washington's agenda.

The Wilson Doctrine

At the start of the twentieth century three emerging powers had a capacity to stamp their influence on the world, namely America, Germany and Japan. The rise of these new powers (and the interactions between them) was to have a profound impact on the world. In this regard, Wilson's tenure as President was significant because it laid the foundations for:

- an emerging American vision for how America would exercise its power during the twentieth century;

- how America would deal with the rise of Germany and Japan as competitors;

- the development of an American approach for dealing with imperial powers.

The Wilson doctrine was a vision deeply embedded in American liberalism.[61] A cornerstone of Wilson's thinking was his belief American business needed to 'conquer' world markets. At his 1912 acceptance speech Wilson said US industries had 'expanded to the point they will burst their jackets if they cannot find a free outlet to the markets of the world'.[62] As Wilson noted in *History of the American People*, the closing of the land settlement frontier created the potential for economic stagnation and hence social unrest. To solve this problem, America needed access to world markets and resources to keep its economy growing. So it was in America's interests to establish global free trade and end the division of the world into imperial trading blocks. If American laissez-faire capitalism was to keep growing, the wider world needed to become America's new expanding frontier.[63] Other nations – notably Germany and Japan – were to mobilize similar logics during the twentieth century, when they also argued their need for resources and expansion. But Wilson advocated American expansionism not based upon building a formal empire (as proposed by Germany and Japan), but based upon building an informal empire supported by a new multilateral international order. As Wilson said in 1918: 'The aim of America is henceforth to be the development of constitutional liberty in the world and the United States will never seek one additional foot of territory by conquest.'[64] But if territorial conquest was ruled out, American expansionism needed to be achieved by other means. Wilson's model had four dimensions.

Firstly, Wilson advocated an ideology that can be termed 'One Worldism'. It remains a powerful ideology up to the present. One Worldism contains two elements – an 'economic' and a 'values' dimension. Within American expansionism the two are inextricably intertwined. The economic dimension is unambiguous – Wilson, like Seward, was focused on expanding US trade. American power was to be grounded in the fact that America sat at the heart of an American-led global trading network. Trade would become the glue binding the rest of the world to America. This required that America build a global system of communication, plus a worldwide network of managers beholden to US corporations. From this America would derive enormous 'informal power'. America would also need to export to the world its organizational practices and the values of consumerism and materialism. In this regard Wilson had outlined his vision thus in 1916:

> America had to finance the world to an important degree, and those 'who finance the world must understand it and rule it with their spirits and with their minds'. America had to sell the goods that would make the world 'more comfortable and more happy, and convert them to the principles of America'. Wilson's dream was of an American world empire of righteousness and trade, based on that world's recognizing the implicit goodness of the United States and the liberating and uplifting effects of American wishes and American cargoes.[65]

So the Pax Americana might not export colonial settlers to the world, but it would export its values. Hence, America's trading empire would be the vehicle for cultural colonialism and cultural homogenization (Americanization); or at the very least cultural hybridization (semi-Americanization). By expanding global trade (and creating a single global market), America would grow its global political and cultural power. The ideology that came to justify this American global power was One Worldism – an ideology with the capacity to disguise its American roots, and consequently win over non-American adherents. By the end of the twentieth century, the ideology of One Worldism was mutating into boosterist arguments promoting globalization.

To build his vision for America's twentieth-century mission, Wilson reached back to Jefferson's 'self-evident truths' and rearticulated these into a vision for global governance. From within Wilson's ethnocentric worldview, the 'American way' of doing things, plus freedom, democracy and self-government were simply assumed to be superior. In fact, these were explicitly 'universalized', such that American 'truths' were now deemed to be 'universal' values and 'rights' for all humanity – i.e. One Worldism encodes pan human universalism. This made it possible for Wilson to conceptualize the building of an American informal empire as grounded in a humanitarian mission to build a better world for all. He believed 'the rights of other men were served by the expansion of American influence'.[66] So Wilson became a leading exponent of building an American trading empire (which would 'develop' other peoples), while simultaneously being an opponent of European imperialism (which he saw as 'subjugating' others). From within Wilson's worldview, American expansionism was not like other people's imperialism, because it was geared to 'helping' other people by exporting American 'truths' and (economic) 'development'. In constructing this vision, Wilson simply drew upon the long-standing view of America as a chosen nation. America was now being 'chosen' to make the world a better place. If successful they would build 'one world', united by a 'superior' (American) set of values, wherein prosperity and 'peace' reigned. This version of American exceptionalism constructed a moral justification for building the Pax Americana. So Wilson's Pax Americana was to become a humanitarian imperialism,[67] which Americans believed was morally superior to the imperialisms of the Europeans. Wilson thereby claimed for America the right to 'moral leadership' of the world.[68]

Secondly, Wilson's model encoded the notion that through building a liberal trading empire, America was engaged in a 'civilizing mission'. Effectively, Wilson reconfigured America's manifest destiny. Americans could now believe they were 'chosen' to 'civilize' and 'develop' the world. Interestingly, Wilson's humanist vision had both a domestic and international dimension, which were intermeshed – for this civilizing mission to succeed, America needed the world and the world needed America. Wilson called his vision the 'New Freedom' and it involved building a global market from which America would derive the resources needed for prosperity, democracy and liberty (i.e. the 'Pursuit of Happiness'). But simultaneously, Wilson claimed America's informal empire would diffuse 'the good life' and America's 'self-evident truths' to others – by exporting products, freedom, democracy and self-government to the rest of the world. This reciprocity was a significant feature of Wilson's thinking – i.e. in the process of developing global influence, America would simultaneously revitalize its own political structures.[69]

> Wilson's new Freedom was a highly nationalistic, coordinated campaign to expand American trade throughout the world on the basis of domestic integration and cooperation, and with the leadership of a strong executive. It was predicated on the extension of an American liberal empire that would replace territorial expansion as the engine of domestic prosperity and tranquillity. The test of this program would be the reception it got abroad.[70]

So Wilson conceived of his humanitarian imperialism as both a mission to civilize and save the world (from the scourge of warfare and great power imperial rivalries), as well as to make domestic America a better place (by ending American isolationism; removing tariffs, protectionisms and special privileges; taming US corporations by giving them a global mission; plus creating American prosperity that would be more equitably distributed).

Wilson recast American exceptionalism and projected it outwards – from now on America 'would illuminate the globe with truth, justice, goodness and democratic self-government'.[71] Wilson gave Americans a mission – to help other nations copy America's independence from Britain by throwing off their chains and claiming self-government. Wilson's vision proved extremely helpful to America's power-brokers because it seemingly gave Americans a 'moral' reason to intervene in the affairs of others. Interventionism could be conceptualized as a 'moral' mission rather than grounded in American self-interest.

Thirdly, Wilson saw his policies as geared to the building of 'peace'. He proposed a binary opposition in which America stood for 'peace', while Europe's powers stood for imperial rivalry and competition over territory. Wilson's peace was to be secured by multilateralism in the form of the League of Nations. This also became a feature of the post-1945 Pax Americana – America's trading empire would impose its peace through multilateral organization for which America wrote the rules (e.g. UN, WTO).

Wilson was correct – for America to build its liberal trading empire, certain conditions were helpful, namely:

- peace, because wars disrupted the free flow of trade;

- maximizing the number of states cooperating in free trade arrangements. (Competing empires were generally not helpful in this regard);

- maximizing predictableness in foreign countries. Warfare and conflict were unhelpful because they generated unpredictable outcomes;

- maximizing stability and law-and-order in foreign countries;

- maximizing agreements (multilateral or bilateral) that put in place codes, rules and standards facilitating trade;

- maximizing the number of foreign states operating in accordance with America's preferred system (liberal laissez-faire capitalism);

- minimizing the capacity of foreign states to engage in actions creating unpredictability for businesses.

The question was – how was America to establish these conditions; to enforce its 'self-evident truths'; and impose a global peace serving its interests? Wilson provided his answer to these questions when addressing the 'League to Enforce Peace' in 1916:

> The United States either had to turn to some form of international cooperation 'in which America could lead', or arm itself as a great military power. A few days before, Wilson privately concluded that the United States must either make a 'decided move for peace' or else take steps to protect itself from Allied attacks on trade ... He drafted a proposal for a 'universal association of nations' to maintain security of the seas for all nations, and to prevent wars.[72]

So Wilson opted to build his Pax Americana on a system of US-led multilateralism. But before Wilson could attempt to implement his plan globally, he needed to convert enough American politicians to his vision. Had Wilson succeeded, his trading empire would be cheaper to run than Britain's empire because America would not directly administer or police new territories. Further, instead, of being a unilateral global policeman, America would co-opt others into a multilateralism, so many would share the task of policing a global peace serving American interests. Consequently, Wilson's Pax Americana would – like Metternich's nineteenth-century 'Congress System' – have operated as a (conservative) multilateral system for maintaining 'America's peace'.

But although Wilson claimed to be anti-imperialist and pro-peace, his trading empire was not going to be free of coercion. Where necessary, violence would be used to establish American hegemony. As Weinberg says:

> Curiously enough, it was not until the administration of the theoretically anti-imperialist Wilson that the American government carried police power to the point of imposing upon independent American states military governments which virtually jailed the alleged culprits. Haiti, the Dominican Republic and Mexico were all the scenes of military incursions which were not only without treaty sanction but were against the protest of native governments.[73]

Hence, the building of (an American) peace would often involve using force (sometimes called peacekeeping). But Wilsonians justified their (humanitarian) imperialism as something beneficial for those being coerced[74] – i.e. when the Pax Americana used violence it was justified (because Wilson's project was driven by a 'moral mission' to make the world a better and more peaceful place). When others used violence it was not justified. In this sense Wilson's Doctrine set the tone for the Pax Americana up to the present day – America's 'self-assumed role as spokesman for the world morality' made many Americans believe they had a right to force others to adopt America's 'self-evident truths'.

Fourthly, Wilson's model of a liberal empire implicitly encoded the notion that America needed to build and 'develop' comprador-partners. Wilson believed in 'the capacity of people to govern themselves once they were educated'.[75] He regarded Anglo-Saxon methods of organizing and governing society, plus the Anglo-American laissez-faire economic model as superior and believed America had an obligation to pass this superior knowledge onto others[76] – through education and development programs. Wilson saw this as a continuation of how Anglo-Saxon democracy had grown through a reformist process of gradually elevating and educating the masses.[77] For Wilson, the Anglo masses had already been civilized; now it was the turn of the rest of the world – i.e. Wilson's 'civilizing mission' now extended the 'elevating' process to the backward masses of Asia, Africa and Latin America; and it was America's manifest destiny to carry out this task (although Wilson sometimes spoke of Britain as a partner in this civilizing task). However, when applied to the rest of the world this 'elevating' and 'development' process became a form of Anglo-American cultural imperialism.

Given Wilson's model effectively spreads Anglo-American culture, it is not surprising to find the interrelated notions of free trade, globalization and 'One Worldism' have proven to be especially appealing to the now globally dispersed population of Anglos. What is perhaps surprising is that so many liberal Anglo-Americans are oblivious to how their (often well-meaning) interventions to export 'democracy', 'development' and 'civilization' can be viewed as arrogant, patronizing and self-righteous.

Although Wilson failed to implement his plan, his presidency was important for building a Pax Americana because:
While Wilson was president, economic (not political) power was transferred from Britain to America. By the end of World War I, New York took over from London the role of the world's leading banking centre; the US Treasury controlled the finances of much of Europe; and America owned nearly half the world's gold.[78] By 1918, America indisputably possessed the world's leading economy.[79]
Wilson founded an influential pool of Wilsonian thinking, and during the presidency of Franklin Roosevelt Wilsonianism re-emerged as a template for building a post-1945 Pax Americana.

One Worldism: an anti-imperial 'imperialism'

Between World Wars I and II Americans debated the pros and cons of whether America should use its power to intervene in world affairs or be isolationist. This debate resolved in favour of Wilsonian interventionism during the 1940s. It was this interventionism that effectively gave birth to the Pax Americana. This interventionist turn was in some ways serendipitous – the Wall Street Crash brought Roosevelt to power in 1933. During his three terms in office, Roosevelt did more than just reconfigure America's domestic economy; he simultaneously put Wilsonianism back on the foreign policy agenda at precisely the moment that circumstances conferred upon America the opportunity to build a global hegemony. In the 1940s Roosevelt's administration began planning a post-war American global hegemony. (Discussed in chapter 5). Furthermore, significant bipartisan agreement emerged (between Roosevelt and Willkie) that America's time had come; and that after the war America should assert its authority and reconfigure the globe. Ultimately, the ideas of these men were to broadly set the tone for how a post-war Pax Americana would look. These were:

- Roosevelt's Secretary of State, Cordell Hull, became a leading advocate of global free trade, tied to the notion of an American trading empire along the lines proposed by Seward and Wilson. Hull built a career trying to remove or lower tariff barriers and put in place agreements to enhance global trading. As a Wilsonian he believed economic competition between states and empires caused wars, and that a system of global free trade would therefore end the need for such warfare.[80] He saw empires (such as Britain's) as obstacles to the creation of American global trading because of the system of imperial tariffs. Hull also advocated multilateral mechanisms for maintaining the peace required for global trade. In this regard he helped prepare the blueprint for the UN. Hull played a central role in US planning for post-war American hegemony.

- Wendell Willkie, Republican presidential candidate in 1940, adopted the same Wilsonian position on foreign affairs as Roosevelt. Willkie popularized anti-imperialism in America. In fact, Willkie can be regarded as the man who did more to popularize anti-imperialism during the 1940s than any other person. The catalyst for his anti-imperial rhetoric was Willkie's 1942 world tour. During this tour he not only called for an end to European empires after the war, but said America should set timetables for granting self-determination to colonial peoples. On his return to America, Willkie made a national broadcast to the American people in which he outlined his opposition to Europe's empires; said the Atlantic Charter should apply to the whole world; and promoted the view that America should help colonial peoples achieve their freedom from such empires. Willkie then set about writing down his ideas. The result was his book *One World* which sold millions of copies,[81] appeared in condensed versions in newspapers and magazines and was even translated into foreign languages.[82] *One World* became a publishing phenomenon. Its impact in popularizing the ideology of One Worldism was immense. Willkie's role in de-legitimating Europe's empires and popularizing the idea of decolonization cannot be underestimated.

- Franklin Roosevelt was the central player in building a Wilsonian vision for a post-war Pax Americana. His 'four freedoms' rearticulated Jefferson's self-evident truths. He advocated making the American dream universal (and secure) through building a multilateral UN system,[83] as well as by spreading prosperity. He believed spreading prosperity required free trade (to give America access to global markets) as well as the active 'development' of the peoples of Asia and Africa.[84] This necessarily required the ending of Europe's empires, especially Britain's empire.[85] In this regard Roosevelt advocated and popularized the notion that self-determination was a right that every nation had.[86] He saw it as an American post-war mission to spread the American ideas of liberty and majoritarian democracy to the rest of the world.[87]

Taken together, the ideas of these three men blended around a common ideology of One Worldism. It was an ideology justifying the building of a curious form of American global hegemony – one grounded in an anti-imperial 'imperialism'. This ideology of One Worldism drew together and hybridized a set of beliefs that resonated with many Americans by the 1940s – i.e. the Roosevelt–Willkie–Hull model of American hegemonic-assertiveness integrated the following beliefs into a common vision of a new world order.

Firstly, America was no ordinary state because Americans had 'discovered' liberty, and created a superior system of (liberal-democratic) government. Once America was conceptualized as the citadel of democracy, any expansion of American influence could be deemed a good thing, because such expansion carried with it the widening of the realm of freedom, democracy and America's superior values. And once American values were transformed by the logic of pan-human universalism into 'human rights', the expansion of America's hegemony could be seen to represent the growth of an 'empire of liberty'.[88] This made it possible for Americans to believe themselves to be anti-imperialist, while simultaneously constructing their Pax Americana. The ideology of building 'One World' on the basis of 'self-evident truths' would prove to be a great comfort to Americans because Americans clearly needed a policy that would promote global expansion and, at the same time, allow Americans to believe that they were not imperialists but, rather, the benefactors of all humankind.[89]

Secondly, American economic expansionism is deemed good for all humankind because 'many Americans find axiomatic the proposition that the creation of free markets around the globe and the expanded production of wealth and material possessions will eventually launch a golden age that will bless the world'.[90]

Thirdly, Americans have transferred the Jewish 'chosen people' notion to themselves. Americans have apparently been chosen by providence to spread the blessings of liberty to the rest of humankind.[91]

Fourth, it is seen as America's destiny to Americanize the world. In many ways, this is simply an extension of the Anglo-Saxon task of 'civilizing' the world. In earlier times, American leaders – such as Theodore Roosevelt, Franklin Roosevelt and Woodrow Wilson – had no qualms about explicitly drawing attention to this Anglo-Saxon dimension, but in today's politically correct environment, leaders avoid such references so as not to be accused of 'racism' or 'ethnocentricity'.

Fifth, believing in American exceptionalism transforms America into the very heart of global liberty. From this perspective, protecting America is good for the whole world and it becomes possible to justify all manner of actions deemed necessary to make America secure – including foreign interventions and pressure; expanding American hegemony and warfare.[92]

Sixth, built into Wilsonianism was a binary opposition within which American power represented 'peace' and 'freedom' while European power represented 'warfare' and 'non-freedom'. For Wilson, the problem with

European powers was that they constantly sought to aggrandize and enrich themselves through territorial conquest, empire-building and subjugating others. This produced warfare and misery. Wilsonians portray America's informal empire as the building of global 'liberty' (from subjugation), 'peace' (by ending of territorial conquest) and 'prosperity' (through free trade). This makes it possible for Americans to view their particular type of empire building (and interventionism) as moral and just.

However, for Roosevelt to implement Wilsonian 'One Worldism', alternative power centres had to be eliminated. In the 1940s this meant Germany, Japan and the other European empires. For the Pax Americana's planners Britain's empire was an especially challenging obstacle because it was run by an American ally.

Notes

1 Hughes, R.T., *Myths America Lives By* (Urbana: University of Illinois Press, 2004), 20.
2 This dichotomy between believers and heathens has justified many other conquests and colonial enterprises, examples being, the Arab-Islamic conquests, and Dutch settlement of South Africa. In fact the South African pejorative term for blacks, 'kaffir' refers to those who do not believe in God. The term 'kafir' (nonbeliever) was brought to Cape Town by Muslim Malay settlers.
3 Hughes, *Myths*, 32.
4 *Ibid.*, 19–27.
5 *Ibid.*, 45.
6 *Ibid.*, 56.
7 *Ibid.*, 66.
8 *Ibid.*, 101.
9 *Ibid.*, 56.
10 Benjamin Franklin was responsible for the words 'self-evident' in the Declaration of Independence.
11 Hughes, *Myths*, 63.
12 Gray, J., *False Dawn. The Delusions of Global Capitalism* (London: Granta, 2002), 2.
13 Weinberg, A.K., *Manifest Destiny. A Study of Nationalist Expansionism in American History* (Chicago: Quadrangle Books, 1963), 18.
14 *Ibid.*, 33–35.
15 *Ibid.*, 101.
16 Lipscomb, A. & Bergh, A., *The Writings of Thomas Jefferson, Vol. 12* (Washington: Thomas Jefferson Memorial Association of the United States, 1903), 277.
17 Onuf, P., *Jefferson's Empire. The Language of American Nationhood* (Charlottesville: University of Virginia Press, 2000).
18 *Ibid.*, 107.
19 The non-slave population.

20 Weinberg, *Manifest*, 31.
21 *Ibid.*, 14–15.
22 *Ibid.*, 21.
23 *Ibid.*, 25–26.
24 Hughes, *Myths*, 113.
25 Weinberg, *Manifest*, 73.
26 *Ibid.*, 77.
27 Foner, E., *Free Soil, Free Labor, Free Men* (New York: Oxford University Press, 1970).
28 Hughes, *Myths*, 130.
29 *Ibid.*, 130.
30 *Ibid.*, 130–132.
31 *Ibid.*, 133.
32 Weinberg, *Manifest*, 342–343.
33 *Ibid.*, 350.
34 Wilson, W., *History of the American People* (New York: Harper & Bros, 1902).
35 Bell, S., *Righteous Conquest. Woodrow Wilson and the Evolution of the New Diplomacy* (Port Washington: Kennikat Press, 1972), 35.
36 *Ibid.*, 35.
37 Paolino, E.N., *The Foundations of the American Empire* (Ithaca: Cornell University Press, 1973), 29.
38 *Ibid.*, 28.
39 *Ibid.*, 29.
40 *Ibid.*, 29.
41 *Ibid.*, 27.
42 *Ibid.*, 47.
43 Zakaria, F., *From Wealth to Power* (Princeton: Princeton University Press, 1998), 130.
44 Paolino, *Foundation*, 24.
45 *Ibid.*, 25.
46 *Ibid.*, 24.
47 *Ibid.*, 27.
48 *Ibid.*, 210.
49 *Ibid.*, 29–30.
50 *Ibid.*, 34.
51 *Ibid.*, 44.
52 *Ibid.*, 89.
53 *Ibid.*, 76.
54 *Ibid.*, 40.
55 *Ibid.*, 2.
56 *Ibid.*, 33–34.
57 *Ibid.*, 40.
58 *Ibid.*, 12.
59 Weinberg, *Manifest*, 425.
60 *Ibid.*, 355, 361–362.

61 Hugh-Jones, E.M., *Woodrow Wilson and American Liberalism* (London: English Universities Press, 1947).

62 *Ibid.*, 204.

63 Bell, *Righteous*, 29.

64 Hugh-Jones, *Woodrow*, 183.

65 Bell, *Righteous*, 177.

66 *Ibid.*, 129.

67 Weinberg, *Manifest*, 435.

68 Bell, *Righteous*, 41.

69 *Ibid.*, 24.

70 *Ibid.*, 41.

71 Hughes, *Myths*, 91.

72 Bell, *Righteous*, 176.

73 Weinberg, *Manifest*, 434.

74 *Ibid.*, 435.

75 Hugh-Jones, *Woodrow*, 183.

76 Bell, *Righteous*, 88.

77 *Ibid.*, 15.

78 Walworth, A., *America's Moment. America's Diplomacy at the End of World War I* (New York: W.W. Norton, 1977), 4.

79 McKercher, B.J.C., *Transition of Power* (Cambridge: Cambridge University Press, 1999), 2.

80 Hull, C., 'Economic Barriers to Peace', Address on the Occasion of the Presentation of the Woodrow Wilson medal to the Hon. Cordell Hull, New York, 5 April. (Woodrow Wilson Foundation, 1937).

81 Willkie, W.L., *One World* (New York: Simon & Schuster, 1943).

82 Madison, J.H., *Wendell, Willkie* (Bloomington: Indiana University Press, 1992), 19.

83 Greer, T.H., *What Roosevelt Thought* (East Lansing: Michigan State University Press, 1958), 25.

84 *Ibid.*, 167.

85 *Ibid.*, 165.

86 *Ibid.*, 164–165.

87 *Ibid.*, 37.

88 Weinberg, *Manifest*, 101.

89 Hughes, *Myths*, 135.

90 *Ibid.*, 149.

91 Weinberg, *Manifest*, 128.

92 *Ibid.*, 417.

4

The British empire
as obstacle to American power

America, that country of gigantic capitalist growth, wherever it turns ... encounters obstacles in the shape of the strongholds already held by England. (Stalin, speech to the Central Committee of the Communist Party of the Soviet Union, 30 July 1928)

British trade and British investments blocked and threatened American business. (Donald Watt, *Succeeding John Bull*)

During the nineteenth century Britain's empire was a force for globalization because, while London's gentlemanly capitalists guided British imperial policy, the empire served to expand global free trade and draw the world together into an intermeshed economic/trading system. But from the 1880s a new imperial vision grew in Britain – a vision of welding the empire into a political federation and single economic bloc, which necessarily involved abandoning 'free trade' in favour of imperial tariffs. This vision emerged while Joseph Chamberlain was Colonial Secretary between 1895 and 1903 because Chamberlain believed Britain's tropical empire could be developed and made valuable within a unified imperial economy.[1] Chamberlain's vision to reorganize the empire and build tariff barriers was popularized in Britain, and by 1915 Britain had abandoned free trade. By 1917 there was much talk about creating imperial self-sufficiency in food and launching the planned migration of Britons into the empire to speed up imperial development.[2] For Americans like Wilson this was alarming because, with America's settlement frontier now closed, America needed open-door global trade.

Fortunately for America, a British power struggle saw London's gentlemanly capitalists steer the empire back toward free trade during the 1920s.[3] However, this was only temporary because following the Wall Street Crash, Britain veered back towards imperial tariff barriers. In 1932 Britain introduced a system of imperial tariffs and began promoting internal empire trade through a system of 'imperial preferences'. From an American perspective Britain's empire came to resemble an enormous (and rich) chunk of the world from which American business was locked out. This empire was a huge global trading network run from London through which Britain dominated many markets – e.g. India, Southern and East Africa, Argentina, the Caribbean, Australasia and the Middle East. London acted as the global banker and carrier of the world's commerce and trade.[4] This trade network was protected by Britain's political power which, in turn, derived from Britain's control of such a huge empire. The empire functioned as a power bloc in the world[5] with British power depending on its possession of colonies.[6] Americans wanted access to these colonial markets and the enormous resources Americans believed Britain's empire possessed. But Britain had sufficient power to lock them out. Worse still for America, British power looked secure – i.e. the period when Britain's empire looked to be in trouble (1919–22) had passed and from the mid-1920s this empire entered a period of revival.[7]

In 1933 Franklin Roosevelt became US President and Cordell Hull became his Secretary of State. Not surprisingly, Roosevelt and Hull came to see the British Empire as a barrier to global free trade, and given Britain's empire controlled 40 per cent of world trade in 1939,[8] Britain's empire came to loom large in the consciousness of American policy-makers during the 1930s and 1940s, because it was seen as an impediment to building an American global trading network.

To understand why Britain's empire was seen as a problem in Washington it is helpful to examine the size and functioning of this empire.

How Britain ran its empire

By the twentieth century Britain was running two empires – the 'formal' empire, (traditionally marked pink on maps), was territory actually annexed by Britain. The 'informal' empire was territory Britain had not annexed, but where British economic interests were so dominant that Britain effectively 'controlled' these areas. Britain's informal empire operated in the Middle East, Argentina, Uruguay and central and southern China. At the start of the twentieth century, Britain's formal empire covered 25 per cent of the earth's surface[9] (shown in map 1) and contained 400 million people.[10]

This empire was a very complex political organization. It had no constitution proclaiming its existence or ordering its governance;[11] had no institutions uniting all its parts and was not in any meaningful sense a political extension of the British state.[12] The only things holding it together legally were the symbol of the crown,[13] and the Privy Council as final court of appeal for the entire empire. In every other sense it was an empire of extraordinary diversity, broadly governed in three different ways: by self-governing white colonies; by the India Office; and by the Colonial Office. The self-governing colonies made their own laws; while laws for the dependent empire (controlled either by the Colonial Office or India Office) were made by Britain's Parliament. Culturally there were two empires – the first consisted of 'white colonies bound to Britain by blood, taste and common history'.[14] Then there was another empire, equal in size, of mostly tropical territory 'whose allegiance to the crown had been imposed on them and whose people had nothing in common with the British except the fact of sovereignty'.[15]

All these territories – self-governing colonies, dependent empire and informal empire – were tied to London through trading networks established by London's gentlemanly capitalists, through London's financial, banking and insurance sectors, and/or as members of the sterling currency bloc.

Self-governing white dominions

By the twentieth century Britain's white colonies were all self-governing. Canada was the empire's first experiment in self-government. It worked so well the model was extended to Britain's other white colonies. In 1931 the six white dominions became virtually 'independent' (albeit still within the empire) when the Statute of Westminster removed the British Parliament's right to pass laws applicable to Canada, the Irish Free State, South Africa, Australia, New Zealand and Newfoundland. Although the small settler society of Southern Rhodesia was never granted dominion status, its Parliament was granted considerable powers over internal governance and became, for all practical purposes, a self-governing colony.

There were differences between these white colonies. Australia and New Zealand were solidly 'British'; Anglo-French tensions characterized Canada (where Anglos were dominant), while Anglo-Afrikaner tensions characterized South Africa (where Afrikaners were dominant). Canada, Australia, New Zealand and South Africa had all received significant flows of British migrants; although interestingly, the empire never granted free movement as a right of British citizenship[16] – i.e. the empire never professed itself a haven for Britain (or Europe's) tired poor masses, and the colonies never accepted all newcomers. Instead, London agents of each colony selected the migrants they wanted.[17] Once in the colonies, millions of settlers constructed new identities around the ideologies of 'empire', 'colonialism' and 'Britishness'. This 'Britishness' became a feature of the empire – an identity often (ironically) stronger in the colonies than it was in Britain itself. Although Britishness was particularly a feature of the dominions, it was also taken to the dependent empire by British bureaucrats, traders, soldiers and policemen posted into the empire by the India Office and Colonial Office. By 1939 some twenty million Britons lived in the colonies. Ultimately Britishness was found in every part of the empire, forming something akin to a scattered global community of colonials. This constituted a powerful cultural glue for holding the empire together (albeit that some dominion citizens held themselves aloof from Britishness – e.g. Irish republicans, South African–Afrikaners and French–Canadians).

Dependent empire

The dependent (non self-governing) empire consisted of various types of British possessions – colonies, protectorates, protected states, trust territories, condominiums and mandates.[18]

At the heart of this empire lay India. After Britain lost its thirteen American colonies a second empire was built. This second empire (centred upon India) was, from the start, grounded in trade. From their Indian base Britain gradually built an Indian Ocean empire. Many nineteenth-century imperial possessions were added as strategic scaffolding to bolster Britain's Indian empire.

The dependent empire was run by governors (appointed by Britain's government) and colonial bureaucrats – employed either by the India Office or Colonial Office. The Colonial Office ran Britain's possessions through a network of Crown Agents in the field. An imperial system of telegraphs and undersea cables kept London in touch with these men in the field. Both the India Office and Colonial Office acted as advisors to Britain's government on policies and legislation pertaining to these dependencies. Although these offices sought advice from interest groups within the dependencies, they were not beholden unto these colonial interest groups. Instead, the dependent empire was governed by an 'enlightened despotism' of colonial officials.[19]

A significant feature of British imperial governance was that Britain built a dedicated caste of well-paid professional colonial administrators. They were deliberately chosen by London rather than by those who became their seniors in the field so as to prevent jobbery.[20] The colonial officials were nearly all drawn from Britain's upper class; had attended the same schools (i.e. private school system); and attended either Cambridge or Oxford University. Those recruited by the India Office tended to be intellectual men selected by stiff academic examinations. If they passed the first round of examinations, they spent a year's probation at an English or Scottish university (studying Indian languages, the history of India and the Indian legal system).[21] This was followed by a second examination which, if passed, gained them a posting to Britain's Raj. Britain's colonial administrators were expected to be men who stood out because of their diligence and strong work ethic.[22] They were men sharing the same values and were deliberately educated to be a ruling class.

That Britain possessed such a ruling class should not be overlooked. It is a notable difference between the Pax Britannica and Pax Americana, and a key reason Britain governed their empire so much more effectively than the Americans have governed theirs. One reason Britain possessed such an imperial ruling class was that Britain's middle classes had not succeeded in displacing their upper classes,[23] and (until World War II) Britain's government continued to be dominated by upper-class personnel because 'they liked governing'.[24] As Porter notes:

> Capitalists are, as a general rule, not all that keen on ruling. It doesn't come naturally to them. They tend to be hostile to 'government' generally, which they see mainly as a restraint on enterprise, and on a personal level, don't find 'ruling' half as worthwhile or satisfying as making money. This is why a terrifically capitalist power like the USA today is not at all keen on governing newly conquered countries like Afghanistan and Iraq, and is not, it has to be said, very good at it. Capitalists prefer to leave countries 'free'; or, by a more cynical way of looking at it, to dominate or control them in less direct and obvious ways. The positive side of this, and one clear difference between the old British and new American empires, is the latter's willingness – indeed, almost desperation – to devolve the government of its conquests to democratically elected governments as soon as possible. One negative aspect is that if this cannot be done – if democracy (or a compliant democracy) – seems not to be an option – the Americans do not have much to offer in its stead. Britain did.[25]

The British produced a competent imperial ruling class precisely because its upper class enjoyed governing, indeed felt they were specifically born to it. They were also groomed for it in their schooling. This saved Britain's middle classes from the bother of governing.[26] Britain's imperial ruling class was marked out by a number of characteristics that produced a particular type of governance. Their schooling taught them to despise capitalist values and the making of money, and to regard the middle classes as philistines. This had the advantage of making them less prone to corruption.[27] They were educated to have a strong sense of honour and service, and were governed by an 'ideology of 'fair play'.[28] They were generally not zealous about liberalism, free trade or Christianity; were dismissive of middle-class Jacobin 'social engineers' (whether of liberal or socialist hew); and were respectful of the languages, traditions and customs of their subjects.[29] This is one reason Britain's empire generally left indigenous cultures far more intact than the Pax Americana (which proselytizes and universalizes American middle-class values). The very fact the British empire's governing class were an elite not sharing middle-class materialist values meant they stood out as incompatible with America's 'ideology of egalitarianism', consumerism and zeal for promoting liberal modernity. In fact, British upper-class values were virtually incomprehensible from within the 'moral universe' of American consumerist egalitarianism. Not surprisingly, Britain's aristocratic ruling class and its colonial officials were demonized by America's anticolonial campaign; and their values made unfashionable by an Anglo media that became increasingly Americanized after 1945. The many American troops stationed in Britain (and its empire) also did much to diffuse American values and weaken the legitimacy of Britain's upper class.

A noteworthy feature of Britain's imperial ruling class of administrators, magistrates and district commissioners is that they moved to the colonies and actually lived in the same districts with the subjects they governed. They spoke the native languages, learned (and respected) native legal customs and effectively got to interact with and understand the people they were governing. A British colonial official would often live out his whole life in the colony to which he had been posted and so came to closely identify with, and intimately understand, the colony where he lived. Because they developed strong affinities with the areas where they lived, these colonial officials developed a personal interest in building good governance in 'their' colony[30] and often came to defend the interests of 'their natives'.[31] This is quite different to the way Americans govern the Pax Americana from the safe distance of comfortable American suburbs, from which they occasionally make flying inspection tours to the margins of their empire.

However, although Britain's colonial officials moved to the colonies, they did not 'go native'. Instead, they held themselves aloof in segregated cantonments[32] in much the way the Norman-French rulers of England had kept themselves aloof from their Anglo-Saxon subjects. In cantonments all over the empire, Britishness flourished. An imperial caste system emerged wherein Britons were the highest caste. A style of governance developed that was simultaneously benevolent and fair, yet aloof and paternalistic. Colonial officials believed their rule was for the 'natives own good' because they saw these natives as 'child-like' and unable to properly govern themselves.[33] There was no pretence about consulting the masses, but they did work closely with indigenous traditional leaders. This partly derived from their natural respect for traditional authority structures, but also grew from a long-standing British tradition of forming alliances with local elites (e.g. chiefs). Much of Britain's success at governing its empire was based upon working with indigenous local elites and co-opting existing traditional power structures into their own imperial machinery of governance.

But the 1920s and 1930s saw Britain's ruling classes begin seriously debating imperial reform, trusteeship, building representative structures in the dependent empire, and enfranchising the empire's Asian and African subjects.[34] Then, from the 1950s the Colonial Office shifted away from working with traditional elites and began implementing liberal reforms – i.e. creating democratic councils to give voice to the new middle classes being built (to service America's comprador model). Once the process of liberalization and building the new middle classes was underway, the pressure to wind back traditional governance rapidly mounted because the new middle classes used the new representative bodies to argue for ending the power of traditional chiefs. Ironically this served to undermine the colonial administration's traditional allies (who had been an important mechanism of imperial governance) at the very moment the Colonial Office needed allies to serve as a counterweight to middle-class nationalist demands for independence.

Facilitating trade

Cain suggests London's gentlemanly capitalists were responsible for driving the expansion of Britain's (second) trading empire from 1850 to 1914.[35] Britain's second empire was a trading empire based upon a global chain of trading posts protected by strategically placed naval bases.[36] But this empire was not exclusively the product of Britain's middle-class traders and financiers. It was the product of a nineteenth-century alliance between Britain's middle and upper classes (as encoded into the House of Commons and House of Lords). The division of Britain's ruling group into a middle and upper class served the empire particularly well, because these two classes complemented each other in the imperial project. This happened because the upper classes were willing to be posted to the far ends of the earth to build the machinery of bureaucracy and law-and-order. This government machinery then served as the fulcrum within which Britain's trading enterprises could flourish. Britain's middle and upper classes made a great team (even thought they despised each other) because they did not compete for the same rewards. The British middle classes were especially good at developing viable economies out of whatever resources they could find in the new imperial possessions. They were also outstandingly good at tying all their scattered global enterprises together into global financial and trading networks – as witnessed by the number of major trading cities in today's world that were originally founded by these middle-class entrepreneurs during the British empire era. But the middle classes could not have built these enterprises and trading networks if it had not been for the upper-class rulers of Britain's empire who created good governance[37] and British legal infrastructures in the colonies, which then provided the security required for colonial business to flourish.

Britain was the world's nineteenth-century economic giant, with the whole world (outside Europe) forming a periphery for Britain's economy.[38] Since Britons were used to looking seaward, it is not surprising Britain's middle-class merchants looked abroad for trading opportunities. Once abroad, these merchants acted in one of three ways. Firstly, they ignored and by-passed places where no developed economies/societies existed, and hence no people could be found deemed worthwhile trading partners (e.g. Western Australia). Secondly, where merchants found societies/ economies deemed organized enough to offer trading opportunities (e.g. China, Argentina and Persia), they simply worked through local comprador-partners to build trade. Thirdly, where merchants found places offering the potential for trade, but where they believed the locals had not organized society well enough to provide security (e.g. India and the Transvaal), they would intervene to establish order. It was the latter that led to the building of Britain's empire. Essentially, weak states and people deemed unable to govern themselves well enough to be viable trading partners were deemed fair game for annexation to the empire.[39] It was all about establishing satisfactory conditions for commerce and trade.[40] Britons argued they were doing the locals a favour because imperialism brought with it British law-and-order and economic development. In this sense imperialism was not only driven by European assertiveness, but also by the incapacity of some communities to provide the stability required by the first wave of globalizing capitalism.[41]

This led to Britons annexing two kinds of places. Firstly, places seen as having economic potential, but which first needed the establishment of good governance and law-and-order before this economic potential could be realized (e.g. tropical Africa). Secondly, places deemed strategic – i.e. needed to protect valuable colonies and/or Britain's seaborne trade routes (e.g. Aden and Cape Colony). But Britons never confined their trade or capital investments to only their empire. Building this empire was but one part of a much wider nineteenth-century process of British-driven trade, globalization and modernization.

By the twentieth century, Britain's economy had been substantively enmeshed with its imperial trading network and the empire was very important to Britain's economic welfare. For example, just before World War II the empire accounted for 39.5 per cent of Britain's imports and 49 per cent of its exports.[42] These percentages increased in the 1950s by which time Britain was dependent on Australia for 66 per cent of its wool, 50 per cent of its butter and 29 per cent of its meat; dependent on South Africa and Canada for 50 per cent of its non-ferrous metals; on India for 81 per cent of its tea; on Canada for 54 per cent of its grains; on the West Indies for sugar; on Malaya for rubber; and on tropical Africa for vegetables and metals.[43] So not surprisingly, when Britain lost its empire, and the Pax Americana realigned global trade networks from London to New York, Britain's economy experienced great pain. This was seen visibly in the death of ports like Liverpool, Southampton and Glasgow;[44] along with the collapse of British shipbuilding, which was no longer required once Britain had no further need for a large merchant marine fleet to carry empire trade.

Developing the empire

Because Britain's empire was driven by a desire to expand trade, it served as a huge engine for globalization and modernist-development. After all, annexing territory and leaving it fallow was of little use to London's gentlemanly capitalists, while economically developing imperial possessions made them useful for London's financiers and merchants. Imperial development made London not only the centre of a gigantic global trading network, but also the centre-point of a wave of modernization that spread across the world during globalization I.

Consequently, the notion British imperialism produced 'underdevelopment'[45] and 'backwardness' is simply myth.[46] Rather than producing underdevelopment,[47] Britain's empire built the infrastructures required for Western development, modernization and global trade[48] – railways, roads, ports, communication infrastructures (e.g. postal services, telegraphs/undersea cables, imperial wireless stations), commercial farms and plantations, irrigation systems, mines, new cities, schools, technical colleges and universities, and research facilities (in agriculture, mining and tropical medicine). The empire was also mapped and surveyed, health-care (and life expectancy) improved, and bureaucratic-and-legal infrastructures built (to facilitate the sort of good governance and stability required by economic investors). It was this British-led first wave of (modernizing) globalization that laid down the basic infrastructure for the current (second) wave of American-led globalization.[49]

The British significantly re-ordered the economies and the demographics of their imperial possessions. Usually, colonies were economically re-ordered and modernized such that each region specialized in the particular product they had a relative advantage in producing, e.g. rubber in Malaysia; copper in Northern Rhodesia; tobacco in Southern Rhodesia; gold in South Africa; wool in Australia; rice in Burma; tea in Ceylon and parts of India; rice and jute in other parts of India; sugar in the West Indies and Fiji.

This economic re-ordering process required building colonial labour forces who became specialists in producing a local crop or mineral. By learning to work within new economic structures these labour forces were modernized and Westernized. In some areas, indigenous labour was trained to staff the British-built economy, e.g. the Burmese Irrawaddy irrigation scheme for rice production. However, in some colonies the local indigenous population resisted modernization (i.e. would not join the labour force) or struggled to adapt to modernization.[50] When encountering this problem, the British often by-passed the indigenous people and imported labour from elsewhere, e.g. when Zulus refused to work on Natal sugar plantations, the British imported Indians. In Australia the British by-passed aboriginals and built Australia's working class out of convicts and the Irish. Malays were by-passed in

favour of importing Chinese and Indians into Malaysia. In Fiji, Fijians were
by-passed in favour of Indians. When there was insufficient indigenous labour
for Johannesburg's gold mines, labour was imported from China, Nyasaland,
Mozambique and Basutoland. In East Africa Indians were imported.
Underpinning all of this was Britain's attempt to build economically viable
colonies that paid their own way. Naturally, all colonial enterprises (mines,
commercial farms, plantations) also required British staff in the form of
imported managers, accountants, engineers, geologists, etcetera.

So Britain's empire generated large population movements which brought
people together in new configurations. This created three varieties of new
society. Firstly, new societies were born by drawing colonial boundaries
that threw people together who had not previous lived as citizens of the
same state, e.g. Nigeria, Sudan and Kenya. Sometimes the people thrown
together had a history of conflict. Secondly, new multiracial societies were
created when Britain built new economies by importing labourers from
elsewhere, e.g. Malaysia and Singapore (now inhabited by Malays, Chinese
and Indians); Fiji (Fijians and Indians); and South Africa (blacks, whites
and Indians). These mixed-race economies often produced fraught societies,
characterized by racial conflict. Thirdly, the empire built Anglo-settler
societies, e.g. USA, Australia, New Zealand and Canada.

By the start of World War II, large swathes of the empire had been
economically developed and intermeshed within the global economy. The
modernization process had not reached everywhere, so the empire consisted
of a mix of modern people (working in modernized economies), pre-modern
people (in subsistence traditional economies), and people making the
transition from pre-modern to modern. So although the empire contained
large areas awaiting modernization/development, it contained a number of
modern economies and bustling cities like Bombay, Calcutta, Singapore,
Toronto, Montreal, Sydney, Melbourne, Johannesburg and Hong Kong.
These were tied to London, and each other, through imperial seaborne trade
routes and imperial telegraph/cable networks. These colonial economies
were highly productive and proved invaluable to Britain during World War
II. They were eyed with envy by America's Wilsonian free traders.

London as hub

Britain's empire was never run as a centralized polity. Rather, one of its
strengths was the flexibility derived from being governed in a multiplicity of
different ways. None-the-less, London was the empire's hub both politically
and economically.

The empire successfully placed London at the heart of a global trading
system. London was effectively the centre of global trade and commerce
– a role it first assumed in the early eighteenth century when England

(London) supplanted Holland (Amsterdam) as the dominant global trading power.[51] From London Britons coordinated an enormous merchant fleet and a communications infrastructure that tied the farthest reaches of the empire to London. Whereas as Americans now use the internet to coordinate the Pax Americana, the British were pioneers in developing a global system of telegraphs, undersea cables and wireless, plus an empire-wide postal service. London became a global communications hub. Within this hub-city were concentrated an extraordinary array of specialists for moving and investing capital; trading and moving goods; insuring the movement of goods; drawing up legal contracts; promoting new technologies; and coordinating major economic projects (from irrigation in the Punjab, to mining in Canada, or railway construction in Kenya). London also accumulated much knowhow about governing diverse regions; gathering and processing intelligence; mobilizing and projecting power; and setting monetary policy. The latter was an important source of British power because the sterling currency bloc was a major asset in dominating world trade and ensuring wealth poured into Britain's coffers from across the globe.

The end of the Pax Britannica terminated London's role as the world's key coordinating hub. This role moved across the Atlantic to New York and Washington. Although London has retained considerable influence as a sub-metropole of the Pax Americana, London is now a secondary hub; not the key driver of globalization.

The world's policeman

Global trade suffers when large swathes of the globe are infected by disorder, insecurity, warlordism, conflict and piracy. Given the Pax Britannica was grounded in trade, it is not surprising the British took upon themselves the role of being the world's policeman during the nineteenth century. British military power was positioned to dominate the world's trade routes. British naval bases were strategically scattered around the globe to give Britain the ability to command the world's oceans. Until 1897 Britain had absolute naval dominance.[52] British naval bases, sea charts, coaling stations and its enormous merchant marine fleet created the basis for imperial trade. In fact, the power derived from Britain's navy (coupled with the navies of its dominions and India) came to underpin not just Britain's seaborne empire but also the wider European dominance of the world, since safe seas made it possible for all Europeans to operate trading links with the world. (Even America's Monroe Doctrine relied upon British naval power to keep other Europeans away from the Americas). By preventing piracy and keeping the world's trading routes safe, Britain made globalization I possible.

Ports like Aden, Gibraltar, Cape Town, Singapore and Hong Kong were not just important British naval bases, but also became significant hubs for trade in their regions. And Britain's total command of the Indian Ocean meant Britain virtually monopolized Indian Ocean trade.[53]

However, although Britain was commonly thought of as a naval power, the empire also possessed a significant land fighting capacity. Although Britain and each of the dominions possessed their own army, the most important part of Britain's land forces was the Indian Army which, at its peak, comprised two and a half million men. Although under British command, this Indian Army was financed by Indian taxpayers. The Indian government also financed the one third of the British army permanently garrisoned in India, hereby lightening the costs of imperial defence for British taxpayers.[54] Britain used these Indian forces across the world. And because Britain controlled a huge naval force and merchant marine fleet it had the logistical capacity to move its armies around with ease when trouble erupted in different parts of the world. In addition, the three hundred and fifty thousand men in the armies of the Indian states were also available to Britain.[55] Overall the empire was collectively able to mobilize a significant military force as seen in the way the dominions, colonies and India mobilized five million soldiers to fight for Britain during World War II.[56]

Britain's capacity to mobilize large sea and land forces, and to project this power globally, made Britain a major global player as late as the 1940s. This power was derived from the empire operating as a single bloc at the behest of London. Because India was the linchpin in this empire, Indian self-determination was a precondition for constructing a Pax Americana. When India became independent, taking the Indian Army out of the empire, Britain's global power was severely compromised, because 'with the loss of India ... the keystone of the arch of our Commonwealth defence was lost and our imperial defence crashed'.[57] The loss of their Indian Army prevented London from protecting British oil interests in Abadan when Iran nationalized these.[58] This, in turn, seriously undermined Britain's post-war finances. Once Attlee decided to give India its independence, the whole edifice of empire built on Britain's Indian Ocean power-base melted away. Thereafter, Britain had no reason to play the world's policeman, and little capacity to do so. Significantly, each shock to British prestige after 1945 was associated with Britain's perceived inability to play the role of world policeman: Greece (1947), Palestine (1948), Abadan (1951) and Suez (1956). Britain simply ceased to be seen as a major power.

Anglo-American rivalry

Although America had amassed enormous economic power by the start of the twentieth century, and had been part of the alliance that defeated the German, Austrian and Ottoman empires in 1918, Woodrow Wilson found

America still did not have enough power to reconfigure international politics after World War I. The key obstacle to American power remained Britain's empire and its global trading network.

By the early 1920s rivalry over trade in China and a naval arms race precipitated considerable Anglo-American tension. But, this rivalry was contained by the 1921–22 Washington Conference which made China a free-trade zone and halted the American–British–Japanese arms race.[59] However, Anglo-American rivalry was reignited in 1932–33, by the Ottawa system of imperial tariffs and the return to power in Washington of Wilsonians. For these Wilsonians, a British empire straddling the globe and controlling 40 per cent of world trade was too great an impediment to their dreams of establishing an American global trading network. To make matters worse, the 1930s two rising powers, Germany and Japan, both made it clear they were now intent on building their own empires. So by the 1930s the threat to the Wilsonian free-trade model (from Britain, Germany and Japan) was intense. Washington's initial response was to focus on trying to contain Japan's empire-building in China (where America was trying to establish its own trading networks).

The outbreak of war between Britain and Germany was a godsend for America because this war offered the prospects of one, or both, being severely weakened. This war opened the possibility that creative American foreign policy could remake the world by helping Britain defeat Germany (so removing one rival), while simultaneously hoping such war would weaken Britain. By 1940 the US State Department was confident America was indeed going to emerge at the key beneficiary of World War II and so planning began for a post-war American hegemony. A significant part of this process involved working out how America could end the British empire (and other European empires) so that American businessmen could gain access to the markets and resources of these empires. So it was that during World War II London began to realize they were engaged in a serious struggle with their American allies over British rule in India; global air routes (that Britain controlled because of its empire); and Britain's Middle Eastern oil interests. Ultimately the struggle was about whether London could save its empire from an increasingly aggressive Washington intent on replacing the Pax Britannica with a Pax Americana. As Virgil Jordan, President of the National Industrial Conference Board of the USA told the Investment Bankers' Association on 10 December 1940:

> Whatever the outcome of the war, America has embarked on a career of imperialism in world affairs and in every other aspect of her life … At best England will become a junior partner in a new Anglo-Saxon imperialism, in which the economic resources and the military and naval strength of the united States will be the centre of gravity … The sceptre passes to the United States.[60]

Notes

1 Boyce, D.G., *Decolonisation and the British Empire, 1775–1997* (London: Macmillan, 1999), 17.
2 Cain, P.J. & Hopkins, A.G., *British Imperialism 1688–2000* (Harlow: Longman, 2002), 445.
3 *Ibid.*, 452.
4 Cain, P.J. & Hopkins, A.G., 'Gentlemanly Capitalism and British Overseas Expansion', *The Economic History Review*, 40, 1 (1987), 11.
5 Boyce, *Decolonisation*, 53–54.
6 *Ibid.*, 44.
7 Gallagher, J., *The Decline, Revival and Fall of the British Empire* (Cambridge: Cambridge University Press, 1982), 94.
8 Gardner, L.C., LaFeber, W. & McCormick, T., *Creation of the American Empire* (Chicago: Rand McNally, 1973), 429.
9 Louis, W.R., 'Introduction', in Brown, J.M. & Louis W.R., *The Oxford History of the British Empire, Vol. IV* (Oxford: Oxford University Press, 1999), 3.
10 *Ibid.*, 48.
11 Morris, J., *Pax Britannica* (London: Faber & Faber, 1968), 177.
12 Boyce, *Decolonisation*, 19.
13 *Ibid.*, 19.
14 Morris, *Pax*, 177.
15 *Ibid.*, 177.
16 Morris, *Pax*, 69.
17 *Ibid.*, 70.
18 Goldsworthy, D., *Colonial Issues in British Politics 1945–1961* (Oxford: Clarendon Press, 1971), 9,
19 Louis, 'Introduction', 7.
20 Morris, *Pax*, 185.
21 *Ibid.*, 185–186.
22 *Ibid.*, 187.
23 The signal Britain's upper class had finally been displaced was Tony Blair's 2007 House of Lords reforms.
24 Porter, B., *Empire and Superempire. Britain, America and the World* (New Haven: Yale University Press, 2006), 50.
25 *Ibid.*, 49.
26 *Ibid.*, 50.
27 *Ibid.*, 50–51.
28 Morris, *Pax*, 516.
29 Porter, *Empire*, 51.
30 Fieldhouse, D.K., *The West and the Third World* (Oxford: Blackwell, 1999), 89.
31 *Ibid.*, 77.
32 Morris, *Pax*, 131
33 *Ibid.*, 136, 139.

34 Hyam, R., 'Bureaucracy and "Trusteeship" in the Colonial Empire', in Brown & Louis, *Oxford*, 268–270.

35 Cain & Hopkins, 'Gentlemanly', 10–11.

36 Davis, L.E. & Huttenback, R.A., *Mammon and the Pursuit of Empire* (Cambridge: Cambridge University Press, 1986), 8.

37 During both globalization I and II, 'good' governance means governments facilitating global trade, providing capitalists with environments that are legally secure, have functioning infrastructures, and where law-and-order is maintained.

38 Tomlinson, B.R., 'Imperialism and After: The Economy of the Empire on the Periphery', in Brown & Louis, *Oxford*, 357.

39 Smith, T., *The Pattern of Imperialism* (Cambridge: Cambridge University Press, 1981), 49,

40 Gallagher, *Decline*, 7.

41 Smith, *Pattern*, 85.

42 Porter, B., *The Lion's Share. A Short History of British Imperialism 1850–1970* (London: Longman, 1975), 320.

43 *Ibid.*, 320.

44 Black, J., *The British Seaborne Empire* (New Haven: Yale University Press, 2004), 340.

45 Rodney, W., *How Europe Underdeveloped Africa* (Harare: Zimbabwe Publishing House, 1982).

46 Smith, *Pattern*, 50.

47 This 'underdevelopment myth' served the interests of Third World nationalists who deployed a variety of cut-and-paste Marxism to build 'national liberation' alliances between nationalists and Marxists. See Smith, *Pattern*, 69, 82.

48 Building Western economies meant shifting resources away from pre-modern sectors and infrastructures. This should not be equated with 'causing underdevelopment'.

49 Many writers have produced critiques of globalization, modernization and Westernization. These are not addressed in this book because they are tangential to the themes being explored.

50 Fieldhouse, *West*, 143, 352–353.

51 It was the Dutch who actually invented the sort of global trading system and merchant-based imperialism which later came to underpin both the Pax Britannica and Pax Americana. The system of global capitalism and trade that we today call globalization thus has its origins in the seventeenth-century 'golden age' of the Dutch Republic when the Dutch set up a maritime trading empire that reached from the Americas to Asia – they founded colonies as far apart as New Amsterdam (today's New York), Cape Town and Batavia (today's Jakarta) and operated trading ports in Japan, China, India, Sri Lanka, Brazil and the Caribbean. Just as the British and Americans would do later, the Dutch built a navy that allowed them to dominate sea trade across the world – i.e. theirs was a trading empire based on seapower and technological innovation (an approach the British and Americans would come to replicate). The Dutch also pioneered joint stock companies, stock exchanges and the sort

of capital accumulation that ultimately grew into capitalism. Their innovations in financial institutions, trade practices, global communications and liberal governance made Amsterdam the centre of global trade and commerce as well as a nodal point for the diffusion of liberal values into Europe and the Americas. But the Dutch proved unable to maintain dominance of this global trading network and lost control of world commerce to the English during the early eighteenth century. During the late seventeenth century the Dutch had formed an alliance with England (against the French); and the English effectively used this alliance to outmanoeuvre the Dutch and thereby transfer control of global trade from Amsterdam to London. Ironically, history was to repeat itself in the 1940s when America used an alliance with the British to transfer control of the global trading system from London to New York.

52 Louis, 'Introduction', 2.
53 Morris, *Pax*, 105.
54 Louis, 'Introduction', 7.
55 Morris, *Pax*, 411.
56 Porter, *Lion's*, 303.
57 Gallagher, *Decline*, 145.
58 Black, *Seaborne*, 315.
59 Buckley, T.H., *The United States and the Washington Conference* (Knoxville: University of Tennessee Press, 1970).
60 Dutt, 'Crisis', 149.

5

Planning for a future Pax Americana

We are going to have worse trouble with Britain [after the war] than we do with Nazi Germany now. (Roosevelt to an aide)

The European colonial powers, for their part, were sufficiently aware of these trends in American thinking to be greatly concerned over the future. (Christopher Thorne, *Allies of a Kind*)

During the course of World War II America began drawing up plans for a post-war settlement. Planners in both the Defense Department and State Department formulated schemes for the building of a new world order that would be American led. This planning began before America even formally entered the war. Because it was undertaken during Franklin Roosevelt's presidency, the plans were grounded in Wilsonian liberal thinking.

Wilson had failed to implement his vision of liberal internationalism after World War I, and only when Roosevelt became President in 1933 was Wilsonianism put squarely back on America's political agenda. By the 1940s Wilson's visions of liberal internationalism and free trade were dominant in the White House, the State Department and the US Treasury. With such important Washington power bases under their control, Wilsonians were finally in a position to try to implement their vision for a new world order. However, there was not unanimity between all Washington's players, with Defense Department planners (especially in the Navy[1]) often arguing for a different vision of the Pax Americana.[2] However, Roosevelt's views permeated his administration, giving the planning process much coherence. Until his death, Roosevelt's personal views were clearly discernible within the vision emerging for a post-war American informal empire. But Roosevelt was also very skilled in using other people to promote models he supported. In this regard he used Secretary of State, Cordell Hull, to push the trade dimension of his (Wilsonian) vision; used Under Secretary of State, Sumner Welles, to push the 'moral' dimension; and used Wendell Willkie to stir up public opinion against imperialism and colonialism.[3]

Ultimately, it was the State Department's planners whose model set the tone for the future Pax Americana. Central to their work were the subcommittees of the Advisory Committee on Post War Foreign Policy which needed to consider three interrelated issues. Firstly, what would be the form (and mechanisms) of American global hegemony? Secondly, how would defeated nations be treated and what was to be done with territory stripped away from the Germany, Japan and Italy? Thirdly, how would America deal with those allies (e.g. Britain and Russia) who would create future obstacles to building a Pax Americana? Britain, in particular, constituted a problem, because their empire straddled the globe. The very nature of Britain's empire as a trans-global trading block (which controlled many of the resources of Asia) meant British hegemony would necessarily interfere with American plans to build an American trading empire. For an American empire to be built, Britain's empire had to go.

When it came to conceptualizing America's 'ideal' post-war world, the key work was done by three (secret) State Department committees and one research body. The first two committees were charged with planning the post-war decolonization exercise; while the third committee was charged with planning a multilateral policing organization for securing the Pax Americana's security (i.e. what became the United Nations system of 'collective security). These bodies were:

1 the Subcommittee on Political Problems of the Advisory Committee on Post War Foreign Policy;

2 the Committee on Dependent Areas;

3 the Subcommittee on International Organization of the Advisory Committee on Post War Foreign Policy;

4 the State Department's Division of Special Research.

A Division of Special Research was launched in February 1941. Its staff of full-time political scientists and economists were charged with studying ways for reordering the post-war world in ways deemed most desirable to America.

The Subcommittee on Political Problems of the Advisory Committee on Post War Foreign Policy was especially important because it lay at the heart of the State Department's exercise in conceptualizing how world politics could be reordered. If an American informal empire was to be built, this was the committee that would work out how to do it. The subcommittee met for the first time in 1942 and consisted of five main players:[4] under Secretary of State, Sumner Welles who personally chaired this subcommittee, seeing it as the key vehicle to influence the direction of the whole post-war planning exercise; Stanley Hornbeck, State Department Far East expert; James Shotwell, historian and expert in British–French colonial competition, and mandate issues; Isaiah Bowman, president of Johns Hopkins University, with a special interest in Africa; and Anne Hare McCormick, foreign affairs writer for the *New York Times*, who infused into the deliberations a strong sense of moral outrage against European colonialism. Other members were: Leo Pasvolsky and Harley Notter (both from the Division of Special Research); Benjamin Cohen and David Niles (both White House staffers); Norman Davis, Hamilton Armstrong, Myron Taylor, Adolf Berle, Dean Acheson and Herbert Feis. Both Welles and McCormick were very anti-European and against Japanese imperialism. On 8 August 1942, Welles set the tone for the subcommittee by stating its purpose as:

> Liberation of the peoples should be the main principle. Many of these peoples cannot undertake self-government at this time. This is where trusteeship comes in. The United Nations [i.e. the Allied powers] should endeavour to develop the ability of these peoples to govern themselves as soon as possible.[5]

There was general agreement on the subcommittee that America was to bring to an end the European and Japanese empires (especially in Asia) and promote self-determination in line with the Atlantic Charter's vision. Hornbeck raised some potentially tricky implementation problems, e.g.: what was to be done if colonial settlers resisted these American moves? what would happen if some peoples decided they did not want self-determination? or if some decided they did not want trusteeship? The committee decided a universal self-determination model was not practical; and independence would need to be worked towards on a case-by-case basis.[6] Ultimately Welles' subcommittee became the strategic driver of American policy-making concerning the ending of European colonialism; the removal of Britain's empire; and how to use trusteeship as a transitional vehicle towards independence.

The Committee on Dependent Areas was chaired by Benjamin Gerig.[7] This committee systematically catalogued and analysed all the major problems existing in the colonial world. In this way they provided the information needed to understand the potential difficulties of implementing decolonization, trusteeship and development.

The International Organization Subcommittee met for the first time in July 1942. Its membership included Sumner Welles, Isaiah Bowman, Leo Pasvolsky, Ben Cohen, James Shotwell, Green Hackworth and Hamilton Armstrong. It was chaired by Welles. Welles, as an avowed Wilsonian and internationalist, wanted this subcommittee to succeed where Woodrow Wilson had failed. The committee was charged with finding ways to create a new League of Nations. This involved examining why Wilson's League had failed; drafting a constitution for a new multilateral global organization; examining the establishment of a UN trusteeship system (to replace the League's system of mandates); and examining ways for giving this new multilateral organization military capacities, so it could police the Pax Americana. This subcommittee created a blueprint for the UN.

Vision for an American-led new world order

In 1942 there were four main visions for how to order (or reorder) the world as follows.

- Germany's 'new order' was based on nationalism and national empires. Achieving this 'new order' involved a radical re-ordering of Europe and Asia. Germany's plan retained the European empires of Britain, France, Belgium, Portugal and Italy but added to them a new German empire (to be built in Eastern Europe and Russia). It also made provision for an expanded Japanese empire in Asia. This would be a global system stabilized by the empires of Germany, Japan and Britain.

- The Soviets advocated the end of states and empires through proletarian revolutions. These radical revolutions would create 'communist utopias' and 'people's democracies'.

- The British advocated a return to the old status quo – a world dominated by European empires, especially Britain's empire. This would be a global system stabilized by a Pax Britannica in alliance with America.

- America advocated a new world order based upon free trade and an American informal (trading) empire. This would be a global system stabilized by a Pax Americana, within which 'free trade' and 'global peace' would be enforced by an American-led multilateral system. How to achieve this re-ordered world is what engaged the minds of Roosevelt's Wilsonian planners.

This Wilsonian-strategizing was led by Roosevelt, Hull and Welles. Their vision for a new world order revolved around seven themes

Firstly, the core theme in US foreign policy was to expand American markets.[8] This required removing all obstacles to global free trade, such as Europe's empires. Hull, in particular pushed Wilson 'open-door' trading policy so America could gain access to resources and markets locked up in other people's empires. Hull argued that economic interdependence was the only way to ensure peace.[9] In fact, he blamed imperial competition and 'economic nationalism' (which created 'closed trading blocs' instead of 'economic interdependence'), as the main cause of warfare. For Hull, the key culprits of economic nationalism were Britain (which owned an empire) and Germany and Japan (which, in the 1940s were trying to create empires). Building a Pax Americana therefore required reorganizing the world's economy,[10] and breaking German, Japanese and British resistance to being incorporated into an American-led liberal system of global free trade. Hull's career had long been associated with fighting against tariff barriers such as Britain's system of imperial preference.[11] And Britain had long resisted Hull's attempts to remove imperial preferences, arguing 'open-door' trading would simply produce American domination, because America's economy outranked all others. This meant America would be best able to take advantage of the 'free-access' opportunity.[12] Britain argued Hull's proposals would create a set of international rules that would necessarily build American global hegemony – i.e. the Wilsonians would simply create a new type of 'imperialism' in the form of an American informal (trading) empire. The brilliance of the Hull doctrine was that it created American hegemony without any need to build a formal American empire.[13]

America's free-trade goals meant there was to be no toleration of European empires impinging upon the expansion of America's economy (shown in map 2). In those areas where America wanted to expand its trading network, European empires needed to be dismantled. Dating back to Seward's plan, America had focused upon expanding its informal empire across the Pacific into Asia. In the 1940s, Asia remained the key focus of American expansionist ambitions.[14] Hence, America's key concerns became Britain's informal (trading) empire in China; as well as British, French and Dutch formal empires in Southeast Asia and South Asia. As the State Department's Herbert Feis said: 'Never again would the great American nation allow the British and the Dutch to dictate the prices at which it would buy its tin and its rubber.'[15] But when it came to American expansion into Asia, by far the greatest obstacle was Britain's empire – with Britain's Asian investments and trade networks far surpassing America's.[16] Further, America grew increasingly interested in Britain's control of oil through its Middle East informal empire. In 1946 American officials explicitly told London that Britain would be allowed to retain its African empire if Britain withdrew from Asia, to facilitate America's penetration there.[17] Roosevelt's team developed an especially curious dislike of French and Portuguese imperialism which riled Americans because of the low levels of economic development in these empires.[18] French and Portuguese failure to fully exploit the resources of their colonial territories apparently violated the American expectation (derived from *Mayflower* puritans) that resources should be productively developed and used. French and Portuguese failures in this regard meant they 'sinned' against the American Puritan ethic by locking up resources (behind imperial tariff barriers) that America needed for growth/trade. So, for Roosevelt, these empires had to go.

A second theme in their strategizing was the way Jefferson's self-evident truths and American exceptionalism were taken for granted. This translated into a belief that the entire world would benefit from universalizing America's vision of liberty. From this derived justification for an American crusade to export to the rest of the world America's model of liberalism, democracy, nation-building and socio-economic organization. Roosevelt, for example, believed the lessons of American independence were simply applicable to India.[19] Ethnocentrism made it possible for Roosevelt to assume other people shared the same worldviews as Americans, and that they all wanted the same things as Americans. A core Wilsonian assumption was that all other people wanted (or could be educated to want) American-style self-determination and democracy within nation states functioning like America. Roosevelt's team shared a belief (with deep roots) that Americans had a mission to share their liberty with the rest of the world. Within Roosevelt's team this sense of mission manifested itself in two (interconnected) projects: ending imperialism and colonialism; and building new independent nations from these disassembled empires. Central features of Roosevelt's worldview were that nation states constituted the basic social unit;[20] every nation state had the right to self-determination, and overlordship of one nation over another was not acceptable.[21] When this vision was proclaimed to the world, it put Europe's empires on notice. The message was clear – America planned to use its power to rewrite the rules governing international political and economic relations; and was not going to tolerate the continued existence of Europe's empires. Roosevelt planned to export American liberty to the world by turning the 'administrative entities' created by Europe's empires (e.g. Indonesia, Iraq, Nigeria, etcetera) into independent 'nations'. And America was going to set the pace of decolonization by insisting on timetables for independence.[22] Roosevelt's policy neatly illustrated how Wilsonian idealism meshed perfectly with American self-interest.[23]

A third theme was that America was not going to allow a return to the old world order – Europeans would not be permitted to reconstitute their imperial power, since these empires violated both America's desire for global free trade and America's vision of liberty. Roosevelt attacked European colonialism and even blamed poverty in many parts of the world on colonial exploitation;[24] he made it clear he disliked British imperialism, and his anti-colonialist views were going to be acted upon.[25] Roosevelt's team, and sections of America's media, began demonizing Britain's empire as a dangerous and selfish anachronism.[26] Within this demonization process, Britain's empire was portrayed as the exact opposite of 'American liberty' – i.e. the empire was 'undemocratic', 'exploitative' and 'subjugated' people, whereas America was going to build global liberty (through 'free trade', 'democracy' and 'development'). For Welles, destroying European empires was motivated by more than economics; it was a great moral crusade.[27] Effectively, Welles mobilized a version of American exceptionalism that justified constructing a Pax Americana as a necessary adjunct to the (moral) deconstruction of the Pax Britannica. Although Roosevelt's team produced no clear anticolonial policy,[28] their pronouncements raised expectations in Asia and Africa. The Atlantic Charter, anti-British empire rhetoric, and the State Department's 1943 'Declaration of National Independence' all served to embolden nationalist groups within Europe's empires. This stirred rebellion within the empires which naturally served to weaken them. America welcomed and encouraged this, because any weakening of Europe's empires translated into a growth in American power, thereby enhancing American access to resources and markets previously controlled by others. And the process became exponential – the weaker the empires became the more rebellions grew; and the more power America acquired, the more it could leverage further change. But this ironically created a problem for American strategists because they realized Britain could only be a first-class power if it possessed an empire to exploit.[29] Not only was Britain an American ally, it was an important ally (growing ever more important as Soviet power grew). Hence, on the one hand, America wanted a strong Britain, but on the other hand, not a Britain strong enough to curtail the building of America's informal trading empire. This dilemma manifested itself within the State Department, where the European desk argued against pushing decolonization too far (since this would damage American allies), while the Asia desk advocated decolonization. Ultimately, the Asia desk won because there were so many American vested interests opposed to empires, such as, powerful members of Roosevelt's team; important sections of the State Department; Anglophobe opinion; African-American opinion in the National Association for the Advancement of Colored People (NAACP); plus sections of the mass media.[30]

A fourth theme was that the German 'new order' was to be extinguished. Germany and Japan would not be allowed to build empires. Instead, the Pax Americana would strip territory away from these two states (and their allies), reconfigure their socio-political systems, and integrate them into America's informal empire. Interestingly, although Welles disliked all imperialism, he had a particularly visceral dislike of Japanese imperialism.[31] Hence, the Japanese empire was to be uncompromisingly annihilated.

A fifth theme was the problem of what to do with those parts of the European and Japanese empires unable to govern themselves as independent states. Other empires had to be demolished and replaced with independent states for America to build its informal empire. But when the State Department began researching the actual mechanics of decolonization they encountered two problems:

- Some colonies were inhabited by people deemed too primitive to run modern states and economies.

- In some colonies the inhabitants had no desire to be independent.

Welles' committee identified Africa and Pacific micro-states as posing particular problems. The State Department could not find African agitation for independence, nor did they believe Africans had any conception of self-government.[32] Committee members, Bowman, Welles and McCormick concluded sub-Saharan Africa was not ready for independence because they believed Africans were 'on the lowest rung of the evolutionary ladder', who unlike the people of Asia or the Middle East had produced no civilization.[33] So what should be done with states not ready for independence? The committee was adamant the European imperial system had to be dismantled; and the imperial status quo could not be maintained with regard to these 'backward areas'. If they could not be granted independence, nor remain subjects of European empires, then a third option must be found. So a system of 'trusteeship' was developed, and became a core feature of the Roosevelt team's vision of decolonization – it entailed the Allies creating an international mechanism to supervise the transition from imperial 'dependence' to 'independence'. Effectively this meant 'development' and 'education' geared to producing the comprador-partners America needed for its trading empire to function. Roosevelt saw education (i.e. Westernization) as vital for building his new world order; believing subject peoples should only be held in 'tutelage' until they could 'stand on their own feet'.[34] But Roosevelt was a gradualist, not a revolutionary, and shared a widespread 1940s belief that it would take many decades or even centuries to 'raise' some 'backward' people to a level where they could be granted self-determination. There was no expectation in the 1940s State Department that the decolonization process would unfold as quickly as it did. Instead, it was expected a lengthy period of trusteeship (and development) would be required to prepare many colonies for independence.

America wanted Europe's empires replaced by a multilateral trusteeship system to be operated by the UN.[35] Britain resisted this notion, arguing for trusteeship by a single nation. But America insisted upon international (multilateral) trusteeship, and rejected 'national' trusteeship, seeing it as equivalent to continuation of Britain's empire (since it would leave Britain free to determine the timetables for development and independence). The British meanwhile opposed multilateral trusteeship, seeing it as equivalent to giving the Americans a role in governing Britain's empire during the transitional stage.

A sixth theme was the creation of a Pax Americana grounded in a system of multilateral policing. America wanted its 'global hegemony' and 'peace' to be enforced by the UN's 'four policemen' (America, Soviet Union, Britain and China). Effectively America conceptualized the UN as a vehicle for multilaterally securing American interests by: (1) getting others to share the load of policing the stabilization of new world order; and (2) internationalizing the process of decolonization (global reform). Conceptualizing the UN as a vehicle to serve American interests was extraordinarily innovative. Firstly, it was cheaper than trying to unilaterally secure the global 'peace' required for American trade to flourish. Secondly, it meant the creation of a new sort of 'neo-imperial bureaucracy' (at the UN). This new global bureaucracy would effectively administer an 'American Peace', which although disguised, was 'American' – i.e. when operating according to plan the UN would serve to simultaneously 'police' the Pax Americana, 'mask' American power and legitimate America's new world order.[36]

A seventh theme was the creation of multilateral mechanisms for regulating global trade and finance. It was not enough to remove the European and Japanese empires (as obstacles to free trade), it was equally important to restructure the world's economy in accordance with the needs of an American informal (trading) empire. At the centre of Hull's vision was the institutionalization of international rules and mechanisms to facilitate an American-led liberal-capitalist world order.[37] This would serve as the foundation for America's global hegemony. Hull's State Department may only have been partially successful in building its planned 'UN/four policemen' model, but it was completely successful in building its planned system of global finance and trade. The 1944 Bretton Woods conference gave birth to multilateral organizations in the form of the IMF and IBRD (International Bank for Reconstruction and Development). This was unambiguously an American-dominated system. From this eventually grew the World Bank and WTO – another part of the 'neo-imperial bureaucracy' for administering the Pax Americana.

Wilsonian concerns

Roosevelt, Hull and Welles believed that although Wilson had been unsuccessful in creating a liberal peace,[38] American power in the 1940s now allowed them to succeed where Wilson had failed. From this grew three core concerns that informed their planning for a post-war world.

Firstly, at the core of Hull's agenda lay a Wilsonian concern for breaking 'economic nationalism' and replacing it with global free trade. Hull was obsessed with the idea that economic nationalism, empire-building and warfare were all interconnected. Wilsonians argued that if a global system could be built guaranteeing all nations access to all resources and markets, then there would be no reason for anyone to go to war. For Hull, America was fighting against Germany and Japan to destroy their economic nationalism. But what was to be done about America's allies practising economic nationalism? In particular, what was to be done about Britain's sterling bloc which, by 1938, accounted for one-third of world trade. For America to reconstruct the world's economy, the sterling bloc presumably also had to be broken, so American businesses could gain access to this bloc's markets/resources. This became a core theme within American foreign policy under Hull.[39]

Throughout the 1940s, Hull's team tried to devise ways to 'prize open the oyster shell of the British Empire' through persuasion and pressure.[40] Britain resisted. But during the 1940s two schools of British thought emerged – one held Britain should acquiesce to America's model of free trade and multilateral regulation. The second believed 'Britain could use its position as the world's largest market for food and raw materials to conclude bilateral agreements with as many nations as possible'.[41] By 1944 most British experts favoured complying with the American model, but the British government continued to procrastinate. For Hull's team there could be no compromise on this issue – the building of America's informal empire required a system of global free trade. The British had to be made to acquiesce. Eventually they did.

Secondly, Roosevelt's team wanted imperial competition to be ended. Roosevelt believed if colonial empires continued to exist they would become the causes of future wars.[42] To secure America's global hegemony, this potential threat to the 'American Peace' had to be ended. Consequently, a central preoccupation of the Washington planners was to find ways to end Europe's imperialism because these empires represented alternative power centres that could challenge American power. Under Roosevelt, anticolonialism was promoted as a moral crusade. Imperialism and colonialism had to be so thoroughly demonized that it became inconceivable for such systems to survive. Welles, in particular, developed a high media profile as an anti-imperialist spokesman. But a growing anticolonial crusade also attracted the support of Vice President Henry Wallace, and powerful American politicians like Wendell Willkie, Tom Connally and Robert LaFollette. Once the ideologies of anti-imperialism and anticolonialism entrenched themselves in newsrooms (especially in the Hearst and Luce press groups), these ideologies were quickly diffused to the wider American public. Hence, as the war progressed, American public opinion grew increasingly hostile to imperialism in general, and to Britain's empire in particular. The Wilsonians had good reason to be pleased with the success of their moral crusade, which portrayed colonialism as 'morally indefensible', because the resultant 'moral outrage' against 'colonialism' this generated, provided Washington with much leverage when negotiating with Britain over the shape of the post-war settlement.[43]

Thirdly, as World War II progressed, American policy-makers began confronting the reality of what it was going to mean to become the dominant power in the world. At some point American policy-makers became concerned there were potentially billions of foreign enemies if America got its policy settings wrong. Significantly, Roosevelt chose to think through the problem in racial terms. A State Department official reported Roosevelt's concerns thus:

The President said he was concerned about the brown people in the east. He said that there are over 1,100,000,000 brown people. In many eastern countries, they are ruled by a handful of whites and they resent it. Our goal must be to help them achieve independence – 1,100,000,000 potential enemies are dangerous. He then added, Churchill doesn't understand this.[44]

Similarly, America's envoy to New Delhi, William Phillips, suggested if America did not support Indian nationalists against Britain, Asians would lose their belief in 'the American gospel of freedom'.[45] Phillips believed Asians would become anti-white if Washington was seen to align itself with European imperialism.[46] Such fears were mobilized by Wilsonians to justify supporting Third World nationalist groups. These fears also drove the Americans to project a particular image of themselves to the world which revolved around the notion of Americans as 'selflessly' bringing 'liberty' to the world. America represented 'liberty' and 'democracy' (as opposed to the undemocratic rule of Europe's empires) and 'economic development' (as opposed to the economic exploitation of European imperialism). Americans also portrayed themselves as:

- anti-racist (ironic given their treatment of African–Americans);
- anti-subjugation (ironic given their treatment of Native Americans, as well as American aggression carried out under the Monroe Doctrine);
- anti-colonization (ironic given their colonization of continental North America);
- anti-elitism (ironic given American class distinctions).

It was a well-crafted image that allowed America's agenda of building an informal empire to be obscured behind the rhetoric of anticolonialism. This meant the focus of attention was cleverly shifted away from how America was building global hegemony, to how America was assisting 'small nations' fight for their liberty. It was a public relations message that played well until the Soviet Union grabbed these anticolonial and anti-imperial messages and learned to present itself as:

- more anticolonial than America (ironic, given Russia was still engaged in colonizing its Asian and Siberian empires during the Soviet era);
- more anti-imperialist than America (ironic given Russia expanded its empire into eastern Europe after World War II);
- more anti-subjugation than America (ironic given the existence of Soviet Gulag forced-labour camps).

But America and the Soviet Union promoted these messages so well that they became irresistible in the Third World. The rhetorics of anti-imperialism and anticolonialism took on a life of their own and so the pressures for 'independence' mounted. In the process Roosevelt's trusteeship model was all but forgotten, and Europe's empires found themselves unable to resist the growth of nationalist and communist rebellions. As a result, the speed at which the empires were dismantled far outpaced the sort of timetables Roosevelt's planners had envisaged back in the 1940s.

Unfolding of Roosevelt's Wilsonian vision

The Wilsonian planning process ran from 1940 to 1945. The planning process was initiated when the Advisory Committee on Post War Foreign Policy met for the first time in January 1940. It ended with the April 1945 San Francisco meeting to convene the United Nations. America's vision for a post-war world unfolded in five stages.

Stage 1: establishing free trade

Because America's core concern was with building its global trading empire, the planning process began with Hull's desire to create an open-door trading system. This meant (1) identifying obstacles to global free trade; (2) considering ways to remove these obstacles; and (3) identifying mechanisms that would be helpful to build an American-led free trade system. Ultimately, America would demand access to all the world's raw materials and markets, the removal of tariff obstacles to American business, and the creation of a global monetary and trading system that facilitated the free flow of trade and capital.[47] Effectively, the planners wanted to establish a form of 'new internationalism' based on a restructured (multilateral) system of global trade, with New York at its heart. Stage 1 was a research and planning stage in which the two key obstacles were identified.

The first obstacle consisted of trading blocks which denied Americans access to resources and markets. The key culprits here were the European and Japanese empires (shown in map 2); and there was fear that Germany would successfully construct a new trading block (encompassing all of Europe, which would then be spread to Latin America). These trading blocks were to be removed (through warfare, pressure or negotiation) and replaced with many smaller states that America could more easily 'influence'.

The second obstacle consisted of four alternative power centres capable of challenging America (Britain, the Soviets, Germany and Japan). Germany and Japan were to be dealt with militarily. The question was, could anything be done about British power?

Roosevelt's planners conceptualized their ideal post-war world in which:

1 German and Japanese power was smashed.

2 The former territories of the European and Japanese empires were placed under the control of a multilateral system (run jointly by the big four Allied powers) who would administer a multilateral trusteeship system geared to preparing colonies for independence.

3 · A UN system of multilateral peacekeeping would be established to stabilize the Pax Americana.

4 A multilateral system of global finance and trade regulation would be established to facilitate America's informal empire.

5 A global network of American military bases would be created to protect America's trading network.

Much energy went into discussing the concept of trusteeship, because international (multilateral) trusteeship solved a number of the problems the planners had identified.[48] Firstly, it offered a mechanism to reform (liberalize) Britain's empire out of existence, thereby retaining Britain as an ally (while removing them as a competitor). Secondly, trusteeship meant America acquired partial control over the empires, and so could ensure these empires were opened up to free trade. Third, it solved the problem of what to do with people not developed enough for independence – they could be 'developed' and 'educated' into becoming comprador-partners. Fourth, trusteeship offered America a mechanism to gain access to Pacific islands for military bases, without the need to annex these.

In July 1941 (three weeks before the Atlantic Conference and five months before America entered the war) Welles revealed to the world Washington's Wilsonian vision for the post-war world during a speech at the Norwegian Embassy. His speech (certainly approved by Roosevelt) was broadcast across America and Europe, in twenty-six languages. In it Welles argued for open-door trade; a restoration of independence and sovereignty for nations around the world; the creation of a new League of Nations to ensure collective security.[49] It was a speech that not only put Germany and Japan on notice, it also put Britain on notice of America's future intentions.

Stage 2: Atlantic Charter

Sumner Wells was the main driver behind the Atlantic Charter.[50] As Roosevelt's son said, 'It was his baby.'[51] Significantly, Under-Secretary of State Welles (not his boss, Hull) accompanied Roosevelt to meet Churchill. The Atlantic Charter emerged as a joint American–British declaration from the Churchill–Roosevelt 1941 Newfoundland meeting. Welles saw the Charter as an opportunity to promote Wilson's vision and globalize the Monroe Doctrine.[52] Roosevelt saw it as a means to 'free people all over the world from backward colonial policy' and to promote free trade.[53] Although merely a press release, rather than a formal treaty, the Atlantic Charter was to have far-reaching consequences for the post-war world. Both Welles and Roosevelt knew perfectly well Britain was in a precarious position and desperately needed American assistance in its war with Germany. Welles and Roosevelt took advantage of this,[54] getting Britain to commit to clauses dealing with self-determination and open-door trade.

Although Churchill made sure the Atlantic Charter never referred to Britain's empire, the document effectively undermined this empire (as Welles had intended) for putting self-determination and decolonization onto the world's agenda. In the decades that followed, this Charter became a document to rally anti-colonial forces, and played a decisive role in creating a political climate that encouraged the destruction of European imperialism (thus promoting conditions conducive to creating a Pax Americana). A sign of things to come was that Clement Attlee, leader of Britain's Labour Party, announced the Atlantic Charter should be applied to Asians and Africans as well as Europeans.[55] Britain's Colonial Office immediately recognized the dangers posed to the empire by this Charter and recommended the War Cabinet not endorse it.[56] Having lost this battle, a shaken Colonial Office began trying to formulate arguments and reforms to save the empire.

Stage 3: Singapore falls

In 1942 Japan overran Britain's Far East empire. The February 1942 fall of Singapore was a catastrophe for Britain's empire because it emboldened the Americans, pressing for decolonization; triggered self-reflection about imperialism within Britain (which undermined the self-confidence of Britain's ruling classes); and destroyed the 'mystique' of invincible British power in Asia. The head of the State Department's Far East division said it lowered the prestige of the white race in Asia.[57]

In America, Walter Lippmann argued Singapore's fall meant America should now identify with 'the cause of freedom of Asian peoples';[58] while in Britain, Margery Perham pointed to weaknesses of the structures of British colonial societies.[59] Perham argued Singapore demonstrated the empire was not sustainable in its current form. She proposed reforms that built 'partnerships' between British colonials and Asian and African elites within the empire.[60] This notion of partnership was to become a cornerstone of British Colonial Office attempts to reform the empire so as to save it from American decolonization pressures. London proposed 'partnership' as an alternative to American 'trusteeship' (because partnership represented a rejection of multilateral/UN supervision). The most thorough attempt to implement this partnership notion occurred in the 1950s Federation of Rhodesia and Nyasaland.[61] But decolonization pressures unleased by the Atlantic Charter became far too powerful, and the partnership model collapsed in the face of criticism that it was just a new form of British (racist) subjugation.

Singapore's fall certainly emboldened Welles. Recognizing that Britain was vulnerable, Welles opted to go on the attack. He had always seen the Atlantic Charter as a weapon to weaken Britain's hold on its empire. Now, in the wake of Singapore, Welles deliberately reactivated the Charter, and in May 1942, launched an attack on Britain's empire during an Arlington Memorial Day address.[62] Welles reiterated the Charter's principles were applicable to the whole world. He described World War II as a 'people's war' and called for the complete liberation of all the peoples of the colonial world. Welles said America was fighting the war to end racial discrimination and imperialism and after the war America should lead a process of global reform in collaboration with the Soviets and China. He said America needed to assume the role of global power and to build a new world order in which there would be 'freedom from want'. Because Welles was Roosevelt's right-hand man, London realized this was a speech to be taken seriously. In his nationally syndicated column, Walter Lippmann, noted this was not a utopian speech, but, rather, signalled serious policy.

Welles' Arlington speech was big news. The *New York Times* carried the story on page one under the headline 'Age of Imperialism Ended'. Anne McCormick (who served on one of Welles' planning committees) said in her *New York Times* column the Arlington speech represented a 'New Deal for the world' – effectively a globalization of Roosevelt's New Deal. And clearly Welles wanted his message to impact inside Britain's empire because the US Office of War Information distributed his speech as a press release to hundreds of newspapers across India and had it broadcast on All India Radio. This emboldened India's nationalists who pursued with vigour their 'Quit India campaign'. Inside the State Department Welles now had the post-war planning committees focus their discussions on how to decolonize India and other colonial territories. He told the planners political consciousness favouring independence was springing up across the colonial world and America should seek to lead these movements.[63] He told Roosevelt India was on the brink of rebellion.

By mid-1942 it was clear both Welles and Roosevelt had decided to internationalize the empires through a multilateral trusteeship system that would prepare colonies for independence.[64] In July 1942 *Fortune* magazine carried a populist map of a future American 'defence belt' sweeping across the Pacific to Asian 'states of the future'. In accordance with Welles' 'end of empire' vision, the Japanese and European empires were gone. It could just as well have been Roosevelt's map of a future Pax Americana.[65]

Hull, however, thought Welles' had gone too far and tried to repair bridges with the British by suggesting independence should only be given to those who were ready for it. The tension between Hull and Welles became intense as they vied for Roosevelt's ear.

Stage 4: mobilizing public opinion

In 1942 Welles decided to launch an aggressive public relations exercise to promote his Wilsonian vision of a new world order.[66] Welles and his State Department planners were concerned there was not enough public support for their Wilsonian vision of internationalism (i.e. a League of Nations) and anti-imperialism. Consequently, 1942–43 became a period of intense publicity during which Welles' profile as an internationalist and anti-imperialist grew. This exacerbated tensions between Welles and Hull. Welles argued his public pronouncements were authorized by Roosevelt as 'trial balloons' on post-war policy.[67] This fits the wider picture of Roosevelt's style of being a skilful mobilizer of public opinion through exploiting mass media – Roosevelt was a master at manipulating journalists to manufacture public opinion and then using this public opinion to justify his actions.[68] Hull was incensed at how Welles' used the post-war planning process to build his own power-base. But incensed or not, 1942 was a year when Welles grabbed the media spotlight. In fact, Welles can be seen to have contributed greatly to shaping future American public opinion by successfully promoting the Wilsonian ideologies of anti-imperialism, decolonization, internationalism and American moralistic interventionism into world affairs. Welles' messages resonated because they drew upon pre-existing American beliefs (discussed in chapter 3). Also, his messages meshed into America's wider propaganda exercise of demonizing alternative (non-American) visions of the future, e.g. German Nazism, Japanese imperialism and British imperialism.[69] These demonization campaigns promoted the vision of the world shown in table 5.1.

America's demonization campaigns were immensely successful and generated long-lasting residues in America's vision of itself and the world. Sixty years later echoes of American wartime propaganda can still be heard in contemporary American mass media portrayals of the world; and the simplified dichotomy of table 5.1 has become so 'commonsensical' that it has become virtually unchallengeable within mainstream Western media.

Welles did not have to concern himself with demonizing Germany and Japan because that was part of official wartime propaganda. However, he did have to engage in demonizing British imperialism, because as an American ally, Britain was not on the official propaganda hit list. Welles' 1942 Arlington speech launched the anti-British-imperialism campaign. But Roosevelt, as a consummate engineer of public opinion, cleverly arranged the next major anti-imperial message came not from a Democratic Party Wilsonian, but from Wendell Willkie, his Republican Party presidential

Good	Evil
America	Nazi Germany
	Japanese imperialism
	European imperialism
• Democracy	• Undemocratic/authoritarian/
• Anti-imperialism	totalitarian
• Anti-colonialism	• Subjugation
• Anti-racism	• Domination by foreigners
• Anti-elitism	• Racism
• One Worldism	• Elitism
• Free enterprise capitalism	• Nationalism
• International cooperation	• Economic exploitation
(multilateralism)	• Economic nationalism

Table 5.1 Struggle between good and evil

opponent. From August to October 1942 Willkie undertook a state-sponsored global familiarization tour. This was a public relations exercise to cement America's alliances with the Soviets and China; while simultaneously distancing America from British imperialism. Willkie's trip was extensively covered by America's media. It became an exercise in demonizing Britain's empire, with Willkie calling for an end to imperialism. He advocated the freedom of colonial peoples, as well as timetables for independence.[70] On his return home, Willkie made a coast-to-coast American broadcast in October during which he said people across the globe now understood:

> That men's welfare throughout the world is interdependent. They are resolved, as we must be, that there is no more place for imperialism within their own society than in the society of nations.[71]

Asked to comment on Willkie's broadcast, Roosevelt endorsed it, saying the Atlantic Charter applied 'to all humanity'. The message to Britain was clear. But things were to get worse for the British. On 12 October 1942, *Time* magazine editors published an 'Open Letter to the People of England' stating Americans believed the British empire should be liquidated:

> [O]ne thing we are sure we are not fighting for is to hold the British Empire together. We don't like to put the matter so bluntly, but we don't want you to have any illusions. If your strategists are planning a war to hold the British Empire together they will sooner or later find themselves strategizing all alone.[72]

This was symptomatic of a growing anti-imperial mood in American newsrooms, as media moguls like Henry Luce and William Randolph Hearst climbed on board the anti-imperial crusade and used their magazines and newspapers to promote Welles' anti-British-empire line. The *Chicago Tribune* became especially vitriolic; and American broadcasting networks like CBS sent correspondents to British India to identify problems with the colonial system. This hostility spilled over into a flurry of anti-imperialism books published during 1943. Most significantly, Willkie published his 'observations' of his world tour in 1943 as *One World*. This book was a publishing sensation, selling millions of copies. *One World* stamped anti-imperialism and decolonization firmly into America's consciousness and popularized themes that were to become hallmarks of the Pax Americana, namely: One Worldism, international cooperation, free trade, Third World development and America as a global missionary of liberty and economic growth. Willkie's book was followed by *Prefaces to Peace*, in which Welles, Willkie and Wallace discussed their post-war aims; and *The World of the Four Freedoms*, a collection of Welles' wartime speeches.

Following Willkie's tour, Churchill hit back in November 1942, saying:

> Let me … make this clear, in case there should be any mistake about it in any quarter. We mean to hold our own. I have not become the King's First Minister in order to preside over the liquidation of the British Empire.[73]

Analysts in Britain's Colonial Office concluded America was intent on liquidating Britain's empire to make way for its own informal empire. These analysts noted America was intent on building a new kind of dependency by breaking up larger political units and creating a large number of smaller (and hence weaker) states that were economically tied to America. A Colonial Office minute noted, 'The Americans are quite ready to make their dependencies "independent" while economically bound hand and foot to them.'[74] Britain's government responded to this perceived threat in two ways. Firstly, they sought to salvage at least something of their empire by offering Washington a form of shared sovereignty over parts of the empire.[75] Secondly, Britain built a public relations machinery geared to presenting the pro-empire case to Americans[76] and to British soldiers fighting alongside American troops.[77] But compared to the Americans the British were public relations amateurs, and British publicity was no match for the momentum that had been built up by Welles' decolonization campaign.

Hull broadly shared the same Wilsonian vision for a post-war world as Welles. However, Hull worried Welles was inflicting too much damage on American–British relations. He was also angered by Welles' failure to clear things with him first. Consequently, in July 1943 Hull disbanded Welles' planning committees, thereby ending Welles' domination of the post-war planning process. However, although Welles left the State Department, his ideas did not. By the time Welles resigned in mid-1943 his vision for the post-war world had been largely codified into the findings of the Political Problems Subcommittee and International Organization Subcommittee. Only two of Welles' pet ideas fell into abeyance once he left, namely, compulsory trusteeship, and the idea of a UN structured as a set of regional blocs.

When Welles left, the intensity of the anti-colonial publicity lessened. However, London realized this did not mean Washington had changed its mind about their empire. And if the British needed any confirmation America was distancing itself from them, the lead-up to the 1943 Teheran Conference, provided this, because Washington consulted with the Soviets and Chinese about how a post-war Asia would look, but not with the British. At Teheran the Soviets acquiesced to America's vision of a new-look Asia and Pacific. The Teheran Conference also produced the 1943 Cairo Declaration which affirmed the American view that the Atlantic Charter applied to all continents.

By the end of 1943 Britain had clearly lost the public opinion battle. Welles' public relations campaign had successfully de-legitimated Britain's Asian empire, while simultaneously popularizing a Wilsonian vision for the future. This (combined with the ongoing retreat of the German and Japanese empires) effectively legitimated the building of America's new world order. In January 1944 two British empire dominions (Australia and New Zealand) saw the writing on the wall; so they abandoned Britain, and joined the American camp by publicly supporting an internationally supervised process of decolonization.[78] For London this was an ominous sign, and during the rest of the war, British intelligence saw America as fighting not only Japan, but also simultaneously conducting a war against Britain's Asian empire.[79]

Stage 5: institutionalizing a multilateral peace system

The Wilsonian vision for a new world order placed a high value on creating global stability. After all, peace and stability were required for trade to flourish in America's informal empire. But dismantling Britain's empire meant dismantling the peace established by the Pax Britannica. If the British were not going to maintain global peace and keep the international shipping routes open, someone else would have to. The Americans intended that this role would fall to a Pax Americana. However, the Wilsonians' conceptualization of global peacekeeping differed from the British model. The Americans did not want to carry the entire financial burden of policing the world. So instead of being the sole global policeman, they wanted to build a multilateral system of collective security. Hence America advocated a 'four policeman' system, wherein the wartime Allies would collectively maintain global peace. Within this system, Wilsonians envisaged America acting as primus inter pares (first amongst equals).

Since 'global trade' required 'global security' the State Department regarded the creation of a new League of Nations as very important. But if this new League was to be helpful to the Pax Americana, it needed to be able to:

- keep global order. This required military and/or policing capabilities;

- maintain the integrity of the new world order by being able to violently punish any attempt/s to change post-war boundaries agreed to by the Allies;

- attack and subdue any state violating the system of international norms/ rules the Wilsonians were putting into place. (In effect this meant policing and stabilizing America's informal empire);

- look autonomous of American control (given that America said it opposed imperialism and the subjugation of weak nations by strong nations);

- be structured in such a way that despite multilateral participation, America could veto any action/s it saw as violating its interests.

Between July 1942 and July 1943 the State Department's International Organization Subcommittee tried to envisage what kind of organization could fulfil the above criteria. The result was a blueprint for what was to become the UN. The core elements of the State Department's blueprint were: an Executive Committee consisting of the four policemen; a General Council consisting of all UN members; a set of regional committees (which clustered members into regional blocs); and a General Security and Armaments Commission. Welles' draft plan also included a number of UN agencies to shape the global socio-economic order in ways that would assist America's global trading network. Amongst the agencies proposed were: an International Health Organization; International Committee on Nutrition; Commission on Drug Trafficking; Organization on International Cultural Relations; International Communication Organization; Refugees Board; International Monetary Commission; International Labour Organization; and an Economic Commission.[80] After Welles left the State Department, Hull changed one feature of the original plan, namely, regional committees were eliminated because of fears such regionalism could create Asian and European power blocs that America would be unable to control. Hull opted instead for a single UN General Assembly. Ultimately, the 1944 Dumbarton Oaks Conference produced a UN structure that hardly differed from the original Welles' draft. Six months later the San Francisco Conference used this Dumbarton Oaks model as a template to create the UN.[81] From this has evolved the following complex UN system:

- A Security Council in which America, Soviet Union, Britain, China and France have veto rights; so ensuring the UN cannot transgress American interests.

- The General Assembly became a vehicle for driving the Wilsonian decolonization agenda; thereby clearing the way for America's informal (trading) empire.

- An Economic and Social Council oversees 14 specialist agencies and 11 funds/programmes. These agencies/programmes undertake work facilitating socio-economic development that is helpful for servicing America's global trading network. For example, these agencies/programmes promote:

  - the sort of education and skills-diffusion complementary to Western economic growth and Westernization;

  - the control and management of global health;

  - global food supplies and agricultural development;

  - global labour supplies.

- A Trusteeship Committee to supervise the trust territories (including former mandates). This committee ceased functioning in 1994 when the last trust territory became independent.

- An International Court of Justice which operates as a World Court, and a fulcrum for administering the sort of international laws and regulations required by a Wilsonian multilateral system of global trade and security.

- A World Bank Group overseeing:

  - a global monetary, financial and investment system (required for the functioning of a global trading system);

  - global trade routes (maritime, aviation, postal and communication networks);

  - global industrialization;

  - development programmes to improve economic and social infrastructures in the developing world (such that these regions can join the Wilsonian global trading network);

  - global intellectual property rights.

- An imperial bureaucracy that effectively services America's informal (trading) empire.

When the UN came into being in 1945, the Wilsonians within the State Department had every reason to be delighted, because a key linchpin of their new world order had been put into place.

Notes

1 Throughout the war, US Navy planners tended to hold views closer to Britain's Colonial Office than to other sections of the American government.

2 Louis, W.R., *Imperialism at Bay, 1941–1945* (Oxford: Clarendon Press, 1977), 18.

3 Wendell Willkie was the Republican Presidential candidate who opposed Roosevelt. The way Willkie was used to drive Rooseveltian agendas was masterful.

4 Louis, *Imperialism*, 160.

5 *Ibid.*, 161.

6 *Ibid.*, 161–162.

7 *Ibid.*, 114.

8 Kimball, W.F., *Churchill & Roosevelt. The Complete Correspondence I* (Princeton: Princeton University Press, 1984), 43.

9 *Ibid.*, 44.

10 Kolko, G., *The Politics of War* (London: Weidenfeld & Nicolson, 1968), 266.

11 Kimball, *Churchill*, 45–46.

12 Lefeber, W., 'Roosevelt, Churchill and Indochina, 1942–45', *American Historical Review*, 80 (1975), 1294.

13 Kolko, *Politics*, 294.

14 Hess, G.R., *The United States' Emergence as a Southeast Asian Power, 1940–1950* (New York: Columbia University Press, 1987), 49.

15 Thorne, C., *Allies of a Kind* (Oxford: Oxford University Press, 1978), 209.

16 Hess, *United*, 17.

17 Hathaway, R.M., *Ambiguous Partnership. Britain and America 1944–1947* (New York: Columbia University Press, 1981), 255–256.

18 Louis, *Imperialism*, 27–28, 165.

19 *Ibid.*, 149.

20 Greer, T., *What Roosevelt Thought* (East Lansing: Michigan State University Press, 1958), 161.

21 *Ibid.*, 156.

22 Louis, *Imperialism*, 9.

23 Lefeber, W., 'Roosevelt, Churchill and Indochina', 1294.

24 Greer, *What*, 168.

25 Louis, *Imperialism*, 147.

26 Thorne, *Allies*, 209.

27 *Ibid.*, 217.

28 *Ibid.*, 456.

29 *Ibid.*, 339.

30 Hathaway, *Ambiguous*, 234–235.

31 Louis, *Imperialism*, 165.

32 *Ibid.*, 170.

33 *Ibid.*, 170.

34 *Ibid.*, 148.
35 *Ibid.*, 148.
36 The UN has not always operated according to America's original conceptualization.
37 Hathaway, *Ambiguous*, 17.
38 Smith, D.M., *The Great Departure* (New York: John Wiley, 1965), 96.
39 Kolko, *Politics*, 249.
40 Kimball, W.F., *The Juggler* (Princeton: Princeton University Press, 1991), 49.
41 Hathaway, *Ambiguous*, 28.
42 Louis, *Imperialism*, 3.
43 *Ibid.*, 36–37.
44 Hess, G.R., *America Encounters India* (Baltimore: Johns Hopkins University Press, 1971), 155.
45 Thorne, C., *Allies*, 359.
46 *Ibid.*, 360.
47 Kolko, *Politics*, chapter 11.
48 See Louis, *Imperialism*.
49 O'Sullivan, C.D., *Sumner Welles, Postwar Plannning, and the Quest for New World Order* (New York: Columbia University Press, 2008), 10.
50 *The Atlantic Charter* (London: Whitcombe & Tombs Ltd, 1941).
51 Roosevelt, E., *As He Saw It* (New York: Duell, Sloan & Pearce, 1946), 39.
52 O'Sullivan, *Sumner*, 18.
53 Louis, *Imperialism*, 121.
54 O'Sullivan, *Sumner*, 13.
55 Louis, *Imperialism*, 125.
56 *Ibid.*, 128.
57 Thorne, *Allies*, 207.
58 Louis, *Imperialism*, 134.
59 *Ibid.*, 135–136.
60 *Ibid.*, 137.
61 Wood, J.R.T., *The Welensky Papers* (Durban: Graham Publishing, 1983).
62 Welles, S., (1942) *Sumner Welles, Under Secretary of State Memorial Day Address at the Arlington National Amphitheatre*, May 30, Office of War Information (www.ibiblio.org/pha/policy/1942/420530a.html).
63 O'Sullivan, *Sumner*, 8.
64 Louis, *Imperialism*, 157.
65 *Ibid.*, 158.
66 O'Sullivan, *Sumner*, 18.
67 *Ibid.*, 19.
68 Winfield, B.H., *FDR and the News Media* (Urbana: University of Illinois Press, 1990).
69 Interestingly, America did not demonize the Soviet model during World War II.
70 Louis, *Imperialism*, 199.
71 *Ibid.*, 199.
72 *Ibid.*, 198.

73 *Ibid.*, 200.

74 *Ibid.*, 247.

75 *Ibid.*, 257.

76 *Ibid.*, 190.

77 *Ibid.*, 457.

78 *Ibid.*, 290.

79 Hathaway, *Ambiguous*, 47.

80 O'Sullivan, *Sumner*, 10–11.

81 Russell, R.B., *A History of the United Nations Charter* (Washington: The Brookings Institute, 1958).

6

Promoting decolonization: de-legitimating European imperial power

In Africa, in the middle east, throughout the Arab world, as well as in China, and the whole far east, freedom means the orderly but scheduled abolition of the colonial system. (Wendell Willkie, national radio address, 1942)

Although the word 'independence' occurred in the document no less than nineteen times, the Americans are in fact trying to establish a sort of informal empire. 'Independence' is a political catchword which has no meaning apart from economics. The Americans are quite ready to make their dependencies politically 'independent' while economically bound hand and foot to them and see no inconsistency in this. (British Colonial Office analysis of American decolonization policy, 1943)

Because the Pax Americana could not be built while Europe's empires straddled the globe, America's wartime planners considered ways to deconstruct these empires. And within three decades of the war ending all Western Europe's empires were successfully eliminated without America having to use warfare to achieve this; and the Cold War eliminated Russia's empire.

In 1945, Washington resigned itself to a Soviet sphere that would be beyond their economic reach. But they were not prepared to let Western European empires remain an obstacle to US economic expansion. British 'imperial preferences' especially concerned Americans because they impeded American access to the British empire's resources and markets. Churchill knew, from Roosevelt's wartime correspondence, that America wanted Britain's special economic relationships with its empire removed so America's 'open-door' empire could be established.[1] America's dilemma was that Britain was an ally. This imposed limits to how much pressure America could deploy against Britain. With this in mind, America turned to 'soft' cultural power to de-legitimate, demonize and destabilize Western European imperialism by making:

- imperialism/colonialism morally unacceptable to journalists and intellectuals;

- decolonization appear inevitable;
- imperialism appear to be a 'lost cause'.

America's Wilsonians propagated the notion 'decolonization' was equivalent to 'progress' and imperialism/colonialism was equivalent to an anachronistic morally bankrupt system.

So successful was Wilsonian propaganda that today these ideas are accepted as 'truth' within mainstream Western media and intellectual circles. But in the 1940s such ideas were far from universally accepted, and America had to engage in a major ideological struggle to de-legitimate imperialism/colonialism. After all, in the 1940s, imperialism/colonialism had been mainstream (even dominant) West European ideologies for over five hundred years. The idea that empires and colonial settlement were 'good' had been widely naturalized and deeply embedded in mainstream European thinking, Further, imperialism had delivered major economic benefits to Europe, plus many Britons had family living as colonists in the empire. Naturally, there had always been some Europeans – e.g. socialists, communists and libertarian liberals – opposing imperialism. But they were a minority. Mainstream thinking in Western Europe did not question the 'correctness' and 'benefits' of imperialism, because, after all, mainstream European media, school books, most politicians, plus colonial-settlers (on return visits to Europe), all promoted the view imperialism was beneficial. Consequently, empires were widely seen as:

- civilizing missions. Empires were deemed good because they developed backward regions and people, and spread Christianity;
- a source of wealth. Empires delivered resources and markets which created jobs in Europe;
- a source of national prestige;
- a source of pride derived from imperial projects that 'opened up the wilderness' and developed it;
- a place where the entrepreneurial and adventuresome could go to build better lives. Colonial settlements were viewed as part of natural migratory processes that humans had always engaged in;
- agents for progress because they built global trade and changed the world for the better.

Such views were an obstacle to building a Pax Americana, so Europeans had to be sold a different view of imperialism – one which questioned the value and morality of empires and colonialism. If this was to be achieved the place to start was with opinion leaders – journalists (as the nation's story tellers) needed to be persuaded to write anticolonial narratives; educators needed to be persuaded to stop extolling the virtues of empire; while intellectuals (as the makers of knowledge) needed to be convinced that imperialism was an unworthy cause.

Those constructing and popularizing 1950s–1960s anticolonial rhetoric had two sources from which they could draw, namely, Wilsonian liberalism (with its advocacy of humanism, self-determination and free trade) and communism (with its advocacy of a people's revolution and socialist utopia). Both liberal humanism and communism challenged imperialism with powerful Jacobin idealisms.[2] Both promised human liberation. The pro-imperialists simply failed to construct a compelling counter-narrative or counter-idealism and so they lost the ideological battle. Consequently, anticolonialism proliferated, mutated and grew into such a powerful and fashionable ideology that, by the 1960s, was unique in being supported by liberals, socialists and communists. Faced with such a powerful coalition fewer and fewer opinion leaders were prepared to be dissidents and question decolonization. The resultant spiral of silence helped accelerate the destruction of Europe's empires.[3] Ultimately the ideology of decolonization became an irresistible force for change. The emergence and growth of this ideology revealing much about how ideologies are the outcome of both deliberate design and happenstance.

America and imperialism

Although anticolonial rhetoric became strongly associated with Third World and Soviet agitation, this ideology actually had its roots in America. America has always had a schizophrenic relationship to colonialism – i.e. America is the product of one of the most successful colonial ventures of all time, but Americans came to see themselves as champions of anticolonialism and self-determination. America's anticolonialism can be traced back to its declaration of independence from Britain. This was transfigured into a 'generalized' anti-imperialism. Further, many migrants to America came from ethic minorities in the Russian and Austrian empires; or were Irishmen opposed to British rule. Their disgruntlement fed into a generalized anti-imperialism within the American population. Consequently, even when America adopted imperialist behaviours during the 1898 Spanish–American War, this was justified as American opposition to Spanish imperialism. Actually, this supposedly 'anti-imperial' war was to prove a seminal moment for Washington policy-makers, because America conquered four new territories. This forced America to confront its new situation – i.e. with America's settlement frontier closed, any further expansion meant adopting one of four policies:

- annexing territory and exterminating the inhabitants (the approach deployed by America's first empire). For America's growing capitalist class such a policy was economically unsound because it reduced the size of potential markets for the trading empire they wanted to build;

- annexing territory and assimilating the inhabitants. This would build economic markets, but if conquered territories contained large populations with cultures fundamentally different to America's, America faced the danger of being swamped by cultural 'others'. Mainstream-America has long regarded Latin Americans as the 'other'[4] and sought to defend and protect[5] American identity against this 'otherness'.[6] So twentieth-century Americans adopted an assimilation approach for territories with small populations (Hawaii and Guam), but not for territories with large populations (Philippines and Cuba);

- subjugating conquered people within a formal empire. (Wilsonians rejected this approach);

- establishing a system of comprador-partners. Compradorism allowed foreign populations to be economically incorporated into America's empire without being politically incorporated (The Wilsonians' preferred model.)

America entered the twentieth century torn between three options: (1) building a formal empire and competing with European empires over territory (using warfare); (2) building an informal empire (using compradors); or (3) isolationism. Ultimately compradorism won out. From 1900 to 1939 Washington focused on learning how to build and maintain comprador regimes in Latin America – a process sometimes involving 'regime change' through military interventionism (i.e. Panama 1903–18; Nicaragua 1912–33; Mexico 1914 and 1916; Haiti 1915–34; Dominican Republic 1916–24; Cuba 1921–23 and 1933). Under Franklin Roosevelt compradorism was consolidated as America's preferred method for global expansionism.

World War II provided Roosevelt with the opportunity to globalize America's hegemony. With this in mind, Roosevelt's team began the task of globally propagating the following interrelated (Wilsonian) ideas:

- Liberalism, open trade and capitalist expansion (globalization) needed to be sold to as many people (Americans and foreigners) as possible.

- Any barriers to 'open trading' (e.g. Europe's empires) were to be demonized and de-legitimated.

- The idea of changing other people (i.e. 'development' and 'modernization') was advanced as a good idea (i.e. 'progressive'). Modernization/development meant teaching people how to run modern states/economies, and thereby become valuable partners within America's trading network.

- Cultural modernization ('Americanization') was seen as an adjunct to globalizing liberal capitalism. American values (individualism, materialism, consumerism, democracy) were to be promoted at every opportunity.

- Traditional societies (seen as 'backward') needed to be de-legitimated. America's 'development package' (of decolonization–modernization– Americanization) was equated with liberating Third World people from 'backwardness'. Roosevelt blamed 'backwardness' on imperialism/ colonialism.[7]

- The spreading of American democracy and liberty was 'good' for the world. (From this grew America's 'moral imperialism').

- America was scripted into the role of an anticolonial agent (which involved fudging America's historical record of colonial settlement).

From the 1940s Wilsonians (globally) propagated an ideology of decoloni-zation, which encoded all of the above elements. Like all ideologies it took on a life of its own as it spread around the world. This ideology evolved through seven phases, as discussed below.

Antecedents of the decolonization idea

Although decolonization was a post-1945 phenomenon, its antecedents can be traced to the start of the twentieth century.

The idea of decolonization emerged out of the ideology of anti-imperialism. A key source of this ideology was the British radical liberal, John Hobson, whose book *Imperialism* became seminal in activating liberal criticism of empire-building. Hobson's ideas resonated with Britain's anti-empire lobby, but because they were a small minority group, his ideas initially caused no major political repercussions for Britain's empire. However, Hobson's ideas also migrated across the Atlantic where they influenced American liberals. This was to become an important source of the decolonization idea because Wilsonian-liberals became such influential twentieth century opponents of Europe's empires.

Wilson's advocacy of self-determination is a core antecedent of decolo-nization.[8] Wilson developed the self-determination model to facilitate the post-World War I dismantling of:

- the Austro-Hungarian and Ottoman empires;

- Russian imperial control over Poland and the Baltic states; and

- Germany's empire in Africa and the Pacific.

Wilson proposed new independent states be created in Eastern Europe from former Austro-Hungarian, Russian and German territory. His self-determi-nation model was driven by two factors. Firstly, central European and Polish migrants to America successfully lobbied for such states.[9] Secondly, creating such states[10] prevented Germany and the Soviets from stepping into the power vacuum created by the collapse of Austrian power.[11]

But significantly, Wilson's self-determination model was only applied to Europeans. German and Ottoman empire territories were not given independence. Because they were not deemed able to govern themselves, they became 'mandates' – i.e. other states took over governing these territories on behalf of the League of Nations. These mandates became de facto (if not de jure) colonies of Britain, France, Belgium, Australia, South Africa and Japan. For this reason, 'self-determination' is not equivalent to 'decolonization'. But the roots of decolonization can be traced back to Wilson's self-determination model. The Fourteen Points Wilson brought to the 1918 Peace Talks were in many ways akin to the Atlantic Charter – they had no legal standing; but they significantly undermined imperialism. In fact, these Fourteen Points effectively ended the imperialist age since they made any future outright annexation of colonies unacceptable.[12] Consequently, for London, Wilson's Fourteen Points spelt long-term trouble since 'the very notion of self-determination was incompatible with the empire's survival'.[13] But whereas, in 1918 Britain was still powerful enough to ward off the full impact of this Wilsonian threat, thirty years later they would not be. Hence, when in the 1940s, Roosevelt's Wilsonian team extended Woodrow Wilson's self-determination concept so that it also applied to non-European people, the British were too weak to resist.[14]

Both the self-determination and decolonization notions are rooted in a Wilsonian anti-nationalism. Wilson's view of independent states is one tied to his Christian view that 'mankind had to become one brotherhood'.[15] This implied a world not made up of powerful autonomous nation states competing with each other; but rather a world of many small states locked together in peaceful cooperation. The basis of this cooperation was to be a globalized economy, structured by an American-led trading empire and secured by an American-led multilateral mechanism for securing global 'peace'. For Wilsonians, America's mission was to lead the world into a better (post-nationalist and liberal) future. This is because, for Wilsonians, America represented the pinnacle of evolutionary progress, and consequently had the redemptive (missionary?) task of universalizing its (superior) socio-economic system.[16] Wilson effectively tied together a belief:

- in the Christian 'Brotherhood of Man';

- in modernist 'progress';

- that America represented an 'ideal' all other states should emulate;

- that the world could be improved through liberal reform.[17]

Applying this Wilsonian vision to international relations was likely to produce a 'moral imperialism'.[18] It did.

However, in 1918, Wilson was unable to fully implement his vision.

Hence, although the Versailles/Sevres Treaties encoded elements of Wilson's worldview, they also preserved many features of the old European competitive-imperialist model. Consequently, despite America's power, Versailles/Sevres did not establish a Pax Americana. Instead, Versailles/Sevres entrenched (and expanded) Europe's empires (especially Britain's).

Effectively the years between World Wars I and II were an interregnum because America was now a major power, but was not (yet) able to dislodge the Pax Britannica. It was during this interregnum that opposition groups within Britain's empire (especially Indian, Irish and Afrikaner nationalists) discovered the shifting global balance of power offered them opportunities to challenge British rule. The resultant 1920s–1930s Indian agitation for political change became a media spectacle in America[19]– a spectacle that played a major role in transforming Wilson's 'self-determination' notion into the new notion of 'decolonization'. In the process America acquired a new stick with which to beat Britain and undermine the Pax Britannica.

Decolonization acquires a media face

The struggle against British rule in India played a major role in developing the ideology of decolonization. It is no accident the term decolonization was first used during Gandhi's 1932 agitation against British rule.[20] Indian resistance to Britain was nothing new, but unlike earlier resistance the twentieth-century struggle proved successful. This was partly because new communication technologies made it possible for newspapers and newsreel films to (timeously) convey stories and images of events across the world.

Gandhi, an activist with a flair for media performance, learned to exploit these media opportunities to mobilize liberal sympathy in America and Britain. The Indian Congress used Gandhi's 1920s–1930s 'passive resistance' campaigns to generate international publicity against British rule. Gandhi's performances were magnificent – scripted around the brilliant visual gimmick of a little man wrapped in a white dhoti, holding a bamboo stave who looked like a victim rather than a skilled political operator. Gandhi was a photojournalist's delight, so images of him were splashed across the pages of the world's press. Gandhi's carefully crafted image evoked sympathy in its target audience – i.e. liberal journalists and the Western liberal intelligentsia. His performances were so good he even managed to create sympathy in non-liberal newspapers.[21] Gandhi became a media darling in Hearst's newspapers. Gandhi understood that key decisions about British India were made overseas. It was London and Washington decision-makers who mattered. Hence Indian nationalists set out to persuade British leaders the liabilities of empire outweighed the benefits; and set out to recruit American leaders as allies against British imperialism. For this, Gandhi staged events geared to embarrassing India's British rulers, and to provoke them into arresting him – thereby making Britons look like heavy-handed villains. Gandhi's non-cooperation campaigns generated 'moral' pressure by leaving an impression of poor non-aggressive Indians victimized by an unjust, aggressive and bullying imperial machine. Gandhi was brilliant at evoking liberal sympathy. His performances during the 1930s Salt Marches; visits to the British Viceroy's New Delhi house, and to London were skilfully executed media events. His presence during these media events personified (and simplified) the struggle for journalists – providing Indian nationalists with a celebrity face for photojournalists to use; a carefully crafted face that was a public relations disaster for British imperialism. Western journalists so fixated on Gandhi's performance, they paid insufficient attention to the complex issues, power brokers, organizers and opinion leaders of India's independence struggle. Gandhi's performances made him not only a hero-victim and celebrity-politician, but an icon of anticolonialism. Essentially, Gandhi's successful use of the media helped make colonialism unfashionable with liberals. As Gandhi became a recognizable politician in America[22] he made India into a significant issue in America,[23] and US public opinion swung against Britain's empire.[24] As US power grew, this became deeply significant.

Gandhi's performances meshed well with the sort of simplistic 'good guy–bad guy' portrayals beloved by America's mass media. His performances created easy-to-understand images, which was a real political boon in America's highly visualized culture. The images were also profoundly memorable, and left emotional residues of sympathy for Indians-as-victims. Gandhi staged magnificent political theatre which provided Americans with victims to rescue. From this media-generated populism was to grow the notion of decolonization as 'rescuing victims' from villains – which meshed well with Hollywood's portrayal of the US cavalry riding to the rescue. Effectively, the US media's populist reading of Gandhi's struggle was to help set the stage for America's post World War II moral imperialism, in which American liberals wrote themselves into the script as the 'good guys', and European imperialists as the 'bad guys'.

American media portrayals of Indian nationalists, Gandhi and British colonials served to create a set of stereotypes and mythologies which profoundly influenced the emergent ideology of decolonization – an ideology that ultimately serviced the sort of 'independence' associated with compradorism. Effectively, when American journalists wrote about India (and later on, about the rest of the Third World) they constructed a narrative based on a naive American populism.[25] This narrative revolved around four sets of players – nationalist leaders; traditional leaders, the people, and colonials:

- Nationalist leaders advocating independence were generally eulogized by American journalists as heroes fighting against imperial tyranny. American journalists gravitated towards those people most culturally proximate to themselves, i.e. Third World Westernized middle classes who advocated modernization, development and nation-building, i.e. ideals which complemented an American-led global trading network. Western journalists sought out such people as sources, which laid them open to manipulation by Third World Westernized elites.[26] Ironically, it was precisely these Westernized middle classes who had most separated themselves from the mainstream (traditional) culture in their countries, and who were less socially integrated with 'the people' they claimed to represent than were the traditional leaders.[27] But since Westernized middle classes advocated policies that made 'sense' to American journalists, they were reported favourably. The Indian Congress and Gandhi fell into this category.

- Traditional leaders – who were generally closer to 'the people' than Westernized leaders – tended to be culturally incomprehensible to American journalists. Traditional leaders represented a world not be easily integrated into an American-led trading-network. They were generally despised by American journalists for 'collaborating' with colonial authorities and for being part of what Americans viewed as an undemocratic, elite-run antiquated and exploitative system.[28]

- 'The People' was a category constructed by nationalist leaders and journalists sympathetic to their cause. 'It implies a belief in the existence of a recognizable political entity, "the people" ... in colonially governed territories, with the consequential moral imperative that the exercise of sovereign power in these territories should rest on ... the "consent" of ... a majority of this political entity ["the people"]'.[29] Americans wanted to believe each colony had a recognizable 'people' within its borders (i.e. India had 'Indians'; Nigeria had 'Nigerians' and South Africa had 'South Africans').[30] This was a naive belief, bearing little relationship to the socio-political and ethic complexity of these territories.[31] But the concept of 'the people' helped American journalists report on political realities too complex to be comprehended by their audiences who wanted easy-to-understand populist explanations.[32] This poor journalism served compradorism, because it allowed journalists sympathetic to anticolonial nationalists to advocate power should be handed over to this Westernized minority.

- Colonial authorities were deemed automatically problematic by America's press. American journalists portrayed them as 'alien overlords' with no right to be in the colonially governed territories.[33] They were also an obstacle to creating an American-led trading network. Because they were not 'natives' of these territories American journalists simply assumed colonial administrators 'could never enjoy the confidence, or act in the best interests of the people they governed'.[34] So journalists automatically distrusted anything these colonials said. Consequently, in 'one of the ironies of history ...

those who knew the local societies best, that is ... those whose job it was to administer, maintain order and administer justice between the various separate elements which American opinion lumped so readily together as the Indian people'[35] were silenced. Their experience and knowledge was not taken into account when journalists reported on or when the theories of decolonization were being constructed. Had their views been solicited some of the errors of decolonization – that led to coups, corruption and failed states – might have been avoided.

American media reporting of the 1920s–1930s Indian nationalist struggle was seminal in giving birth to the American notion of decolonization. It was also a period when Indian nationalists learned to use the media to generate sympathy for their cause; and when Washington learned to use Third World newspapers to encourage nationalist insurrections against colonialism and promote the view America was an ally against colonialism.[36] Not surprisingly, Britain came to see this as a problem.[37] In response, the British government began censoring the Indian press and launched its own public relations campaign in America.[38] But Britain had nothing to match Gandhi's media flair. Decolonization had acquired a powerfully emotive media face – the face of a helpless 'victim' confronting imperialist 'villains'.

Planning decolonization

Gandhi's impact on American opinion was exactly what Roosevelt needed to reactivate Wilson's self-determination model. But Roosevelt's team went further and also applied self-determination to non-Europeans. Hence, 'self-determination' mutated into 'decolonization'. This produced phase three of the evolution of decolonization, when Roosevelt's team began planning a programme of decolonization.

Many have sought to understand Roosevelt's decolonization. Five explanations have emerged:[39]

- Roosevelt's decolonization was simply a stalking horse for building America's informal empire.

- He sought to destroy Europe's empires because was sincerely opposed to colonialism.

- He was a misguided populist whose ignorance and rhetoric prevented Europeans from implementing a rational decolonization.

- He was a politician playing to the crowd with sanctimonious self-righteous demagoguery.

- He compromised on decolonization because he needed West European allies against the Soviets.

Each has some explanatory power, and they are not mutually exclusive. What is clear is that under Roosevelt decolonization took root; the State Department initiated serious planning to build a post-World War II world which deconstructed Europe's empires. From the 1940s, 'decolonization' was not merely an idea, it became an American-government plan, with Roosevelt's first targets being British India and Dutch East Indies (Indonesia).[40]

Popularizing decolonization

Once Roosevelt's team had a plan, the next stage was to sell that plan. So phase four of decolonization's evolution was its popularization at home and abroad.

Roosevelt was highly adept at using the media to steer public opinion and generate bandwagon effects.[41] He understood only too well how to build public opinion into a force to exert political pressure. And he knew Britain would not be immune to growing American anticolonialism because ideas flowed back and forth across the Atlantic. So widening American support for decolonization would help in two ways. Firstly, it would provide Roosevelt with an excuse to pressure London (by claiming he was simply responding to his electorate).[42] Secondly, Britain's press and universities would clearly pick up such ideas and so grow British anticolonialism. This would increase the political costs of maintaining an empire. Consequently, Roosevelt's team set about promoting decolonization.

Roosevelt personally played a role in putting decolonization on the agenda through deploying his well-honed news management skills.[43] Roosevelt was a media master – he employed skilled spin-doctors, ran an effective public relations machine,[44] and developed the art of being personable with journalists, making him a media darling. Roosevelt had a proven ability to keep journalists on-side and maintain full control of the news agenda through press conferences, which he manipulated by planting questions.[45] He was also an excellent actor, ably using the new medium of radio to generate mass approval.[46] Roosevelt used his position as president to make important speeches attacking colonialism;[47] his media savvy keeping decolonization on the agenda. He was convinced 'pitiless publicity' would force Europe's imperial powers towards decolonization.[48] However, Roosevelt also understood the need not to go too far in personally antagonizing Britain. Consequently, he creatively deployed other people to mouth harsh anti-imperial messages and pressure Britain, e.g. Wendell Willkie, Henry Wallace, Welles, and (Roosevelt's Chinese ally) Chiang Kai-shek. Roosevelt also deployed public diplomacy against the British (such as the Atlantic Charter, which placed decolonization on the international agenda); and repeatedly sent US officials around the globe[49] to spread the gospel of independence.[50]

In 1942–43 Roosevelt launched an aggressive anticolonial public relations exercise, using Welles, as surrogate. Welles made a series of harsh anti-imperialist pronouncements, authorized by Roosevelt as 'trial balloons' on post-war policy.[51] As a result, Welles acquired the profile of a leading anti-imperialist spokesman. It was a PR campaign that put London on notice that after the war America was intent on ending European imperialism.

But it was Roosevelt's use of Wendell Willkie as anti-imperial spokesman that revealed his real brilliance for deploying surrogates to sway public opinion. Willkie had been Roosevelt's opponent in the 1940 campaign for President. What better than to deploy one's Republican opponent as surrogate spokesman. Consequently, Roosevelt sent Willkie on a 1942 world tour, as his personal representative, in a converted bomber. Willkie was used to focus attention on decolonization in general and India in particular.[52] As part of Willkie's entourage, Roosevelt sent two senior propagandists of the Office of War Information (OWI), namely the foreign propaganda supervisor and the director of domestic news.[53] This revealed Roosevelt had a domestic and international propaganda agenda. Because OWI's director of domestic news was especially competent, Willkie was big news in America every day throughout his global trip.[54] When he returned home Willkie made a nationwide radio address on 26 October 1942. This address deployed the carefully planned-and-scripted radio performances Roosevelt's PR team were so good at.[55] In this speech Willkie pushed a strong anti-imperial line, saying:

> We are also punching holes in our reservoir of good will every day by our failure to clearly define our war aims. Besides giving our Allies in Asia and Eastern Europe something to fight with, we have to give them assurances of what we are fighting for … Many of them have read the Atlantic Charter. Rightly or wrongly they are not satisfied. They ask: what about a Pacific Charter? What about a World Charter? … Many of them also asked the question which has become a symbol all through Asia: what about India? Now I did not go to India and I do not propose to discuss that tangled question tonight. But it has one aspect in the East which I should report to you. From Cairo on, it confronted me at every point. The wisest man in China said to me: 'When the aspirations of India for freedom were put aside to some future unguaranteed date, it was not Great Britain that suffered in public esteem in the Far East. It was the United States' … he was telling me, and through me, you, that by our silence on India we have already drawn heavily on our reservoir of good will in the east. People of the East who would like to count on us are doubtful. They cannot ascertain from our government's wishy-washy attitude towards the problem of India what we are likely to feel at the end of the war about all the other hundreds of millions of eastern peoples. They

cannot tell from our vague and vacillating talks whether we really do stand for freedom, or what we mean by freedom.[56]

Media coverage of Willkie's world tour, plus Willkie's radio broadcast transformed Roosevelt-and-Welles' decolonization agenda into an American domestic issue.[57] Then a 1943 book about this world tour was published. Willkie's *One World* became a publishing sensation, selling a million copies in eight weeks. This book played an enormous role popularizing anti-imperialism and decolonization in America. Roosevelt had every reason to be satisfied with this Willkie propaganda operation.

Willkie's *One World* represents a significant moment in the story of decolonization. This book encapsulated and popularized the Wilsonian vision for a new world order, and tied this vision to a justification for dismantling Europe's Empires. *One World* provided a clear populist exposition of America's post-war agenda. This book argued:

- America should 'lead' the world to 'freedom' by helping those fighting Western European empires for their independence;

- people in the world loved Americans because America represented freedom, and because America was not tainted by imperialism;

- for the creation of many small states that would be politically independent (but not economically independent or militarily powerful);

- for free trade;

- for Third World development and modernization as a means to build new markets for American-trade, and build middle classes across the Third World;

- Imperialists and colonials were responsible for Third World backwardness;

- America should end its alliance with Britain after the war (because of British imperialism);

- Americans should stop repressing non-white people within its own boundaries.

Willkie's book had an enormous impact. It provided an accessible text that summarized the Wilsonian vision of 'open trade', international brotherhood and the Americanization of world values. It complemented Vice-President Henry Wallace's populist call to make the twentieth century 'the century of the common man'.[58] Willkie's book captured the imagination of American journalists. It also created a handy vehicle to promote Wilsonian internationalism on university campuses across the Anglo world.

Roosevelt's team had every reason to be satisfied with their decolonization PR campaign. It was an immensely successful popularization exercise that helped build an active constituency of liberal internationalists in America,

Canada, Britain and Australia. It also weakened Europe's empires by inspiring and energizing pro-independence nationalists in the colonies.

Decolonization and the intelligentsia

Roosevelt also realized the importance of spreading his decolonization ideas amongst university intellectuals and journalists. If he could make decolonization and anti-imperialism mainstream discourses in key newsrooms and university campuses in the Anglo-world, the causes of Wilsonian-internationalism and building a new world order would be greatly advanced. Of course, there already existed a body of socialist and Marxist intellectuals who opposed imperialism and colonialism. But in America and Britain, such intellectuals had been an ineffective minority before 1939.[59] Further, as Leftists they would be unlikely to support American plans for a trading empire. Roosevelt realized he needed to widen the pool of anti-imperial intellectuals, plus align anti-imperialism with America's post-war decolonization agenda, i.e.:

- nurture and recruit as any many opinion leaders as possible into supporting liberal anticolonialism (i.e. replacing European empires with American free trade);

- co-opt as many left-wing opinion leaders as possible into supporting Wilsonian-internationalism;

- silence pro-colonial opinion leaders (by making imperialism/colonialism 'politically incorrect').

By the end of World War II this had largely been achieved within America, with Roosevelt saying to a friend, 'The intellectuals are nearly all with us.'[60] However, real success required also impacting on the trans-Atlantic intelligentsia. In this regard Fabians proved most helpful to the Wilsonian cause, because it was they who succeeded in transforming 'anti-imperialism' from a left-wing, into a more mainstream-liberal position. This had to do with morphing the Marxist 'anti-imperial' discourse into a liberal 'decolonization' discourse. The resultant new discourse was ambiguous enough to be simultaneously acceptable to Marxist, neo-marxist and liberal intellectuals. Effectively, Roosevelt Wilsonians created a 'common ideology' (of 'decolonization') acceptable to a remarkably broad spectrum of intellectuals.[61] The wartime American–Soviet alliance helped facilitate this.

But creating the decolonization discourse was not enough. This discourse needed, if possible, to be made hegemonic on university campuses. In part, this was achieved by creating the binary opposition of 'progressive' versus 'antiquated' thinking; and making it embarrassing for intellectuals to hold views deemed backward or antiquated. Effectively, if intellectuals wanted to be seen as progressive and at the cutting edge of new thinking, they needed to be seen to espouse the following views:

- imperialism = antiquated, morally irreprehensible system of subjugation;
- imperialism = exploitation = unacceptable;
- imperialism = racism = unacceptable;
- imperialism = exploitation = unacceptable;
- decolonization = freedom/democracy = good;
- decolonization = ends imperialist exploitation = good;
- Third World development = modernization = good.

Any intellectual not espousing these views was deemed 'backward'; and even worse, could be accused of supporting racist subjugation. Following World War II this could mean being associated with Nazism. Effectively linking imperialism/colonialism to 'racism' made it very difficult to mount an argument against decolonization.[62] Not surprisingly, once the 'progressive-antiquated' binary opposition was naturalized, intellectuals disagreeing with decolonization were likely to be 'embarrassed' into silence, and intellectual debate was terminated. Consequently, by the late 1950s European imperialism/colonialism had been thoroughly de-legitimated. British intellectuals became increasingly able to pressure their Colonial Office to refocus its energies on 'development'[63] and officials in Britain's Colonial Office adjusted their language to be able claim the empire was about progressive modernization (as Americans understood it).

The notions 'development', 'democracy' and 'internationalism', which became intellectually fashionable, were useful because they:

- could be espoused by both liberals and Marxists;
- enabled liberal-Wilsonians to co-opt many Western leftists into supporting their agendas; and
- deflected attention away from America's economic self-interest in promoting decolonization, free trade and modernization.

Effectively Roosevelt's anti-imperial campaign built a diverse pool of decolonization intellectuals across the globe – including libertarians, socialists, Marxists and Third World nationalists – who all rallied behind a common call to end Europe's empires.[64] This post-war intellectual phenomenon demonstrates how power and wealth can influence and 'guide' knowledge production. The post-war discourses of 'decolonization' and 'anti-colonialism' effectively derived from 'American ... idealism backed up by power'.[65] In this regard, Watt notes how 'the illusions of the mighty can assume a pseudo-reality by virtue of the strength of those who hold them',[66] and discusses how the 'naive populism' promoted by America led to 'decolonization' becoming intellectually fashionable.[67] This produced a self-referential decolonization discourse that only selectively examined the issues, e.g. many intellectuals uncritically accepted the word of independence activists, but automatically dismissed anything colonial officials said, based on the naive assumption that colonials and colonial officials had 'dishonourable motives', while independence activists had 'honourable motives'.

But naive, or not, the 'decolonization idea' was to have enormous practical consequences beyond the campuses (and newsrooms) where it became so fashionable.

The result was, 'American ignorance and insouciance as to the political and social reality in Asia and Africa, reshaped these continents after World War II.'[68] A clear example of the impact of the 'decolonization idea' was how Congo's independence derived from the agitation of pro-decolonization Belgian intellectuals.[69] The Congo example illustrates the role played by intellectuals in the decolonization process; how Wilsonian ideals were successfully exported to Europe; how Europe's intelligentsia came to promote American agendas; how ivory tower intellectualism could have catastrophic consequences (in this case for central Africans); and how even unsuccessful decolonization exercises could service American needs (because Congo/Zaire became an American client state).

Institutionalizing decolonization

But Wilsonian liberals did not rely merely on intellectuals and journalists to promote decolonization. To make sure decolonization became a reality, they succeeded, during the sixth phase of decolonization's evolution, in having the concept institutionally embedded in the UN. This was a brilliant move because, although America remained the chief beneficiary of deconstructing Europe's empires, America no longer had to take the lead in promoting decolonization. Effectively, decolonization was made an international political issue, with the UN providing a platform for vocal advocates of change. This sprang from Roosevelt outmanoeuvring Churchill at the Yalta Conference and getting him to agree international accountability existed over Europe's empires.[70] Churchill agreed as long as the colonial powers held sole trusteeship over colonial territories. He (wrongly) believed this preserved imperial sovereignty. In fact it opened the door to colonial issues becoming matters for UN debate. The UN platform produced new voices demanding decolonization. Pressure for decolonization became virtually irresistible as the following voices merged into an unrelenting demand for rapid deconstruction of Europe's empires:

- an Afro-Asian bloc at the UN, that grew larger with each new state given independence. This bloc was constructed around an assertive race-based 'identity politics'. The advocacy of 'decolonization' was enmeshed with this 'identity';

- the Soviet bloc in the UN. The Soviets were motivated by a Leninist belief in anti-imperialism; a vested interest in reducing West European power; plus a desire to build alliances in Asia and Africa. Once the Soviets joined America in advocating decolonization it necessarily became a very powerful global discourse;

- independence movements in the colonies (both nationalists and communists);

- Western intellectuals advocating decolonization/anti-imperialism were a lobby group who knew how to mobilize pressure and publicity against imperial governments. These intellectuals often developed links with independence movements which assisted decolonization activists;

- journalists sympathetic to independence movements produced good coverage for anti-colonial voices and negative publicity for those opposing decolonization. This encouraged independence movements and their Western sympathizers;

- liberals advocating immediate independence for 'moderates' to undercut support for 'radicals' (communists).

Within this cacophony of voices, the UN became an important platform for generating pressure upon the empires.[71] This produced a spiral of imperial decline – UN pressure inspired anticolonial rebellion, which triggered colonial reform and defensiveness; which generated more rebellion; which often triggered colonial police/military actions, which attracted negative media coverage; thereby generating further UN condemnation. For the colonial powers this spiral of international attention–unrest–attention became a nightmare absorbing ever-more government resources.

For America institutionalizing decolonization within the UN proved to be a two-edged sword. It certainly generated pressure on the European colonial powers, and sped up the collapse of Europe's empires. However, Washington lost control of the decolonization exercise. The decolonization process took on a life of its own, and eventually delivered some outcomes not pleasing to Washington, e.g. the Soviets learned to use decolonization to their own advantage; some Third World independence movements began aligning themselves with Moscow or Beijing; and some Third World leaders began criticizing America's informal empire as 'neo-colonialism'.[72] So despite the American–British 1940s conflict over colonialism; during the 1950s–1960s America and Britain found their policies once again converging around a shared goal of creating comprador-partners – i.e. developing strategies to create independent states ruled by 'moderates', and preventing 'radicals' from coming to power in the Third World.[73]

Decolonization triumphs

Decolonization's first wave took place in Asia because Asia was America's primary concern – the place where, ever since Seward, Americans had dreamed of building a trading empire. Decolonization started when America gave the Philippines independence in 1946, arguing this provided Europeans with a model to follow. Filipino independence conformed to the comprador model – the country was ruled by Filipinos, allied to and dependent upon America; America continued to control Filipino resources; and US hegemony over the Philippines remained intact.[74] Independence for other Asian states followed quickly: India (1947), Pakistan (1947); Ceylon (1948); Burma (1948), Korea (1948), Indonesia (1949), Vietnam (1949), Cambodia (1949) and Laos (1949).

In Asia this left Britain holding Malaya (and fighting a communist insurgency)[75] plus Hong Kong; Americans holding Pacific islands (as trust territories); Portugal holding Timor, Goa and Macao; and Russian–Soviets holding central Asia. It also left European empires holding Caribbean and Pacific islands as well as most of Africa.

In the late 1940s, Africa's British, French and Belgian rulers argued (because of Africa's 'backwardness') decades of education, development and tutelage were needed to prepare their African subjects for independence. So in the late 1940s/early 1950s it was assumed Europeans would retain their African empires, but in a modified form – i.e. African colonies would be restructured and developed under European control. However, these African territories soon came to be seen as a liability because:

- After World War II America rewrote the terms of global trade and finance. Consequently, much of the wealth that used to flow to Europe from the empires, flowed instead to America.

- The Pax Americana insisted upon Third World development (to build trading partners and compradors). For Europe this meant spending money on development projects just as the empire was delivering fewer economic benefits. Essentially after America rewrote the rules of the game in 1945, formal empires no longer made economic sense.

- Anticolonial rebellions emerged in a number of African colonies (inspired by the Atlantic Charter and Asian independence). Policing these rebellions became expensive (and unpopular).

- As the ideology of decolonization became hegemonic in Western universities, newsrooms and international organizations it became increasingly difficult to defend imperialism/colonialism. This generated a growing sense of hopelessness and defeatism within Europe's governing elites, and the will to rule over empires began to wane.

African decolonization, when it came, was a messy and ad hoc affair as Britain, France and Belgium tried to come to terms with a rapidly changing global-and-African context that militated against them holding onto their empires.[76] African decolonization was triggered by Ghana's independence in 1957, followed in 1958 by Guinea. Then in 1960 seventeen African states became independent, which terminated the Belgian and French African empires, with the exception of French Algeria. Algeria, Kenya and Rhodesia were, in fact, to become the African territories most difficult to decolonize because they contained sizeable white settler populations who rejected America's decolonization model and majoritarian democracy. Zanzibar also presented a decolonization problem because it was ruled by an Arab minority who similarly rejected majoritarian democracy. In each of these territories independence consequently only transpired following conflict: Algeria (1962), Kenya (1963), Zanzibar (1963) and Zimbabwe (1980). Portugal was the only colonial power to resist the very principle of decolonization.[77] The Portuguese (who allied themselves with South Africans and Rhodesians) ignored UN pressure, and fought guerrilla wars against (communist and nationalist) anti-colonial insurgents. But in 1975, Portuguese military forces, tired of fighting wars in Africa, overthrew their government in a coup and implemented decolonization. Europe's last empire was terminated.

Eventually, even the microstates of the Pacific, Caribbean and Indian Ocean were given independence. Then in 1991 the Russian–Soviet empire collapsed, and in 1997 the last significant European imperial possession, Hong Kong, was transferred from Britain to China. With this, decolonization was triumphant, and America seemingly acquired untrammelled trading access to the entire globe. At last the Wilsonian dream of globalization seemed possible – globalized 'open trading' and a Pax Americana with global reach could finally be realized.

Notes

1 Kimball, W.F., *Churchill & Roosevelt. The Complete Correspondence I* (Princeton: Princeton University Press, 1984), 356–357.
2 Morris, J., *Farewell the Trumpets* (London: Faber & Faber, 1978), 210.
3 Noelle-Neumann, E., 'The Theory of Public Opinion. The Concept of the Spiral of Silence', in Anderson, J.A. (ed.), *Communication Yearbook 14* (Newbury Park: Sage, 1991).
4 Asians were also traditionally the 'other'. Until 1965 American laws restricted Asian immigration.

5 Until 1952 US naturalization laws were race based – only whites and Africans could become American citizens.

6 Weinberg, A.K., *Manifest Destiny. A Study of Nationalist Expansionism in American History* (Chicago: Quadrangle Books, 1963), 355, 362.

7 Within the American teleological conceptualization of 'progress', European imperialism was also deemed an archaic nineteenth-century system associated with a 'backward' European 'feudal' elitism.

8 Walworth, A., *America's Moment. America's Diplomacy at the End of World War I* (New York: W.W. Norton, 1977), chapter 9.

9 Walworth, *America's*, 174.

10 To be protected by British and French power.

11 Walworth, *America's*, 184.

12 Morris, *Farewell*, 208.

13 *Ibid.*, 211.

14 Louis, W. & Robinson, R., 'The United States and the Liquidation of the British Empire in Tropical Africa 1941–1951', in Gifford, P. & Louis, Wm.R. (eds), *The Transfer of Power in Africa. Decolonization 1940–1960* (New Haven: Yale University Press, 1982), 31–32.

15 Spillman, K., 'Wilsonian Ideas and European Politics', in Den Hollander, A., *Contagious Conflict* (Leiden: E.J. Brill, 1973), 156.

16 *Ibid.*, 129.

17 *Ibid.*, 130.

18 Watt, D.C., 'American Anti-colonialist Policies and the End of the European Colonial Empires 1941–1962', in Den Hollander, *Contagious Conflict*, 125.

19 Collins, L. & Lapierre, D., *Freedom at Midnight* (London: Granada, 1982).

20 Gardiner, D., 'Decolonization in French, Belgian and Portuguese Africa', in Gifford, P. & Louis, W. (eds), *The Transfer of Power in Africa* (New Haven: Yale University Press, 1982), 515.

21 Hess, G., *America Encounters India* (Baltimore: Johns Hopkins Press, 1971), 15, 18.

22 *Ibid.*, 170.

23 Burns, J.M., *Roosevelt. The Soldier of Freedom* (New York: Harcourt Brace Jovanovich, 1970), 379.

24 Hess, *America*, 73, 83.

25 Watt, 'American', 123.

26 *Ibid.*, 123.

27 *Ibid.*, 102.

28 *Ibid.*, 103.

29 *Ibid.*, 123.

30 *Ibid.*, 118.

31 *Ibid.*, 123.

32 *Ibid.*, 117.

33 *Ibid.*, 100.

34 *Ibid.*, 100.

35 *Ibid.*, 101.

36 Clymer, K., 'Franklin Roosevelt, Louis Johnson, India and Anticolonialism: Another look', *Pacific Historical Review*, 57 (1988), 281–282.
37 Hess, *America*, 38.
38 *Ibid.*, 103.
39 Kimball, W., *The Juggler* (Princeton: Princeton University Press, 1991), 127.
40 *Ibid.*, 146.
41 Winfield, B., *FDR and the News Media* (Urbana: University of Illinois Press, 1990), 30.
42 Kimball, *Juggler*, 137.
43 Winfield, *FDR*, 29, 231.
44 *Ibid.*, 13, 236–238.
45 *Ibid.*, 30.
46 *Ibid.*, 17, 118.
47 Kimball, *Juggler*, 144–145.
48 *Ibid.*, 151.
49 Roosevelt also personally travelled around the colonial world, holding meetings with nationalist leaders to assure them of American support (Kimball, *Churchill*, 129).
50 Kimball, *Churchill*, 129.
51 O'Sullivan, C., *Sumner Welles, Postwar Plannning, and the Quest for New World Order* (New York: Columbia University Press, 2008), 19.
52 Kimball, *Churchill*, 135.
53 Johnson, D., *The Republican Party and Wendell Willkie* (Urbana: University of Illinois Press, 1960), 215.
54 *Ibid.*, 218.
55 Winfield, *FDR*, 104.
56 Hess, G.R., *The United States' Emergence as a Southeast Asian Power, 1940–1950* (New York: Columbia University Press, 1987), 61.
57 *Ibid.*, 61.
58 Burns, *Roosevelt*, 357.
59 Howe, S., *Anticolonialism in British Politics* (Oxford: Clarendon Press, 1993), 320.
60 Burns, *Roosevelt*, 515.
61 Kimball, *Juggler*, 103.
62 Howe, *Anticolonialism*, 325.
63 Louis & Robinson, 'United'.
64 Louis & Robinson, 'United', 38.
65 Den Hollander, A.N.J., 'On "Dissent" and "Influence" as Agents of Change', in Den Hollander, A.N.J., *Contagious Conflict* (Leiden: E.J. Brill, 1973), 6.
66 Watt, D., 'American Anti-colonialist Policies and the End of the European Colonial Empires 1941–1962', in Den Hollander, *Contagious*, 109.
67 *Ibid.*, 123.
68 Den Hollander, 'Dissent', 6.
69 Strengers, J., 'Precipitous Decolonization', in Gifford & Louis, *Transfer*, 323–325.
70 Kimball, *Churchill*, 153.

71 Kirk-Greene A., 'A Historiographical Perspective on the Transfer of Power in British Colonial Africa', in Gifford & Louis, *Transfer*, 579.

72 Nkrumah, K., *Neo-colonialism* (London: Heineman, 1968).

73 Gifford, P. & Louis, W., *The Transfer of Power in Africa* (New Haven: Yale University Press. 1982), 46, 49.

74 Hess, *United*, 249–250.

75 After defeating the communist guerrillas, Britain granted Malaysia independence to 'moderates' in 1963.

76 Gifford & Louis, *Transfer*; and Gifford & Louis, *Decolonization and African Independence* (New Haven: Yale University Press, 1982).

77 South Africa resisted the decolonization of Namibia.

7

Getting Britain to deconstruct its empire

Roosevelt ... had to gain British approval, or at least acquiescence, for decolonization. A military confrontation with Great Britain over the issue of empire was unthinkable. (Kimball, *The Juggler*)

The end of the mandate in Palestine was ... the most blatant signal of the dissolution of the British Empire. There could be no clearer example of the shift in power from the British Empire to a new dispensation where the United States could call the shots whenever it chose to do so. (Peter Clarke, *The Last Thousand Days of the British Empire*)

The two decades following World War II saw Britain's empire dismantled in three stages: beginning with Britain's Indian empire; followed by the Middle Eastern empire; and ending with the African empire. Curiously it was not dismantled due to a period of hegemonic breakdown. In fact, during the 1930s to 1950s the empire was more valuable to Britain than ever before. The deconstruction was largely driven from the centre, as London effectively reformed its own empire out of existence. The question is, why did British policy-makers do this? and were there signs before World War II, this empire's rulers were considering dismantling their empire?

Britain had been building its empire over centuries and by the middle of the twentieth century had constructed a very complex political entity. This empire's story was not one of uninterrupted expansion. Rather, British control had waxed and waned as Britons constantly struggled to secure, maintain and/or grow their globalized hegemony. Hence, there were periods of both expansion and contraction: periods when British hegemony over parts of the empire were challenged; and periods when Britain's hegemony over its domains was very secure. Not surprisingly, given the size of the empire, British hegemony was nearly always being challenged somewhere. During the twentieth century the most consistent opposition came (in bursts) from Irish, Indian, Arab and Afrikaner nationalists. However, British power was never seriously challenged by this opposition, because overall Britons were very skilled in co-opting local elites into alliances with themselves; in keeping opposition/rebellion localized (i.e. preventing empire-wide coalitions of opposition groups); and in always restoring control when opposition flared up (by mobilizing violence and legitimacy-building techniques). Effectively, Britain's success at maintaining long-standing global hegemony resulted from a well-honed hegemonic expertise.

The twentieth century, like previous eras, saw Britain having to work hard to secure hegemony across its far-flung domains. Two themes dominated twentieth-century imperial history. Firstly, the most troublesome areas were Ireland, India, South Africa and the Middle East. The key feature of Britain's response was the reform of imperial governance. These reforms decentralized power in order to co-opt 'moderate' Irishmen, Indians, Afrikaners and Arabs into political structures geared to stabilizing imperial rule. In part this signalled a shift back to 'informal' empire (as opposed to the 1880s–1890s 'formal' empire). In this regard, it is worth noting Britain's new Middle Eastern empire (built between World Wars I and II) was 'informal'. A second feature of the twentieth century was Britain's move away from a 'free trade' empire towards a 'closed' empire of tariffs. This was codified by the 1932 Ottawa Conference. British moves to turn the empire into a single economic bloc was a clear threat to US ('open-door') trading interests. Britain's closed-imperial trading system was perhaps unduly provocative and unwise, given it provoked American antagonism to the empire at the very time American power was growing (relative to Britain's).

Condition of Britain's twentieth-century empire

The first three decades of the twentieth century tested British hegemonic skills. The century opened with Britain fighting to secure control of South Africa through the 1899–1902 Boer War.[1] This war triggered four imperial difficulties Britain was to face during the twentieth century. Firstly, although the British eventually won this war, they were humiliated by many defeats and by the enormous imperial resources they had to mobilize to crush a small force of Afrikaner guerrillas. By exploding the image of British invincibility, the Boer War helped inspire players around the globe into believing they could realistically challenge British hegemony. Secondly, a force of Irish volunteers was formed to assist the Boers. This force became the Irish Republican Army (IRA), and the guerrilla warfare methods the volunteers learned in South Africa were to cause the British endless trouble in Ireland. Thirdly, the Boer War became a publicity disaster for London due to concentration camps built by the British.[2] This bad publicity mobilized anti-imperialist activists in London itself, and a significant consequence of this anti-imperial ferment was the publication in 1902 of a book by John Hobson[3] – a book that had enormous influence on twentieth century anti-imperial thinking, and which helped fuel the growth of anti-imperial activism over the next six decades. Lastly, the Boer War damaged British self-confidence, mortally wounded Anglo jingoism and began a process of undermining Anglo belief in their empire.[4] Effectively, the Boer War was for Britain what Vietnam became for America six decades later. It triggered turmoil in British politics – which brought to power a new government in London. This Campbell-Bannerman (Liberal) government, responding to the new British mood, began reforming India's colonial government. These reforms actually stimulated Indian resistance to British rule because they raised, then dashed expectations, while simultaneously creating the impression British confidence was declining. So, for Britain, the Boer War represented an inauspicious start to the twentieth century, not least because it directly stimulated nationalist resistance in Ireland and India.[5]

However, Britain did win the Boer War, and this war did not generate any crises fundamentally threatening to the empire. Actually Britain's responses to the empire's opponents during the early twentieth century was creative (and effective). It involved reformism geared to dividing its opponents. Once moderate and radical nationalists were successfully divided, the moderate nationalists were incorporated into reformed political systems as de facto British partners. In 1922, for example, the Irish Free State was created as a new dominion ruled by moderate nationalists. Likewise, from 1923 Indian Congress moderates were contesting elections in British India and Britain's Indian difficulties appeared manageable.[6] In South Africa moderate Afrikaner nationalists were co-opted into Anglo-Afrikaner governing coalitions. All these moves helped stabilize British imperial rule. Then in 1931 the Statute of Westminster was enacted to appease Afrikaner, French-Canadian and Irish nationalists.[7] This statute represented a significant reform of the British empire because it ended London's formal control over five white-ruled dominions. It also changed how Britons conceptualized their empire – a reconceptualization that became an important feature of how Britons later rationalized their post-1945 imperial retreat.

But between the two world wars these reforms were geared to strengthening, not scuttling, the empire. This mood of strengthening the empire is evident in the Imperial Conferences of 1923 and 1926, which sought to create a unified empire self-sufficient in food, raw materials and key industrial outputs[8] and to set up an imperial marketing board to encourage people across the empire to 'buy British'.[9] In 1932 the Ottawa Conference created a system of 'Imperial Preferences' (empire tariff system), so demonstrating political reforms did not mean the weakening of empire bonds. But not only economic bonds were strengthened between the wars. In addition, from the 1920s onwards, the British government systematically sent settlers into the empire to 'reinforce' the 'British element overseas, [and] strengthen the cultural and sentimental bonds of empire'.[10] During the 1920s alone one million Britons were settled across the empire.[11] Clearly, the British did not see their empire as being in decline.

Importantly, Britons built a whole new empire during the first half of the twentieth century – again demonstrating their empire was far from a spent force. This new empire was in the Middle East. It included Egypt, Sudan, Palestine, Jordan, Iraq, South Yemen, Oman, Qatar, Bahrain, Kuwait and southeast Iran.[12] Significantly much of Britain's Middle Eastern empire was 'informal' – hence, independent governments ruled in Egypt, Iraq, Jordan, Iran and the Gulf States. But, in reality, British writ held sway. Britain learned to rule the region through comprador-partners such as the conservative (anglophile) Hashemite ruling families. Anglo 'advisors' became ubiquitous in the region with the offices of the local British High Commissioner or British Residencies and Agencies becoming de facto centres of power. The heart of British Middle Eastern power was the High Commissioner's Office in Cairo. Although Egypt was supposedly an independent state, by the 1940s, Cairo was effectively the military capital of the British empire and a British Minister of State was in full-time residence there.[13] This informal empire gave Britain control of two assets – oil reserves and the Suez canal. The shift to informal empire demonstrates one of the key features of the British empire – namely, British flexibility in using different modes of governance to underpin their trading and strategic interests. Britain's informal Middle Eastern empire became a model for American hegemony over this region (and beyond) after World War II.[14]

In many ways 1940 represented something of a high-water mark for the British empire – with the entire empire economically galvanized to support Britain in its war with Germany and with millions of troops from across the empire fighting for Britain. In 1940 the empire did not appear in danger of being dismantled.

Critics of empire

Britain's empire had long had its critics. Some had even successfully challenged London and secured independence for the thirteen American colonies. But in the early twentieth century, the critics posed no serious threat to Britain's second empire.

Losing the American colonies triggered the building of a second British empire (centred on the Indian Ocean region) during the nineteenth century. The earliest voices raised against this second empire were those of British liberals in the 'Manchester School' led by John Bright and Richard Cobden. As nineteenth-century liberals, they argued colonial expansion involved too much government interference in the economy (e.g. taxation to pay for colonial wars) and advocated instead 'free trade' as a better way to build a globalized British trading network. In a sense the Manchester School founded a line of thinking that eventually produced Wilsonian liberalism which, in turn, came to underpin the Pax Americana.

However, Bright and Cobden's ideas did not resonate widely at the time they were advocated. Instead, during the last three decades of the nineteenth century, imperialist jingoism (of the Joseph Chamberlain variety) took hold in Britain. In the face of this Anglo-nationalist jingoism, voices critical of empire became muted, and the empire went into an expansionist mode. This only changed during the Boer War trauma – which stimulated intellectual critiques of imperialism and jingoism. But these critiques of empire never influenced more than a small minority of people in Britain and its empire and so posed no threat to imperial hegemony. However, these criticisms laid the foundations for what would later become more serious opposition. Hence, it is worth spending some time looking at these criticisms.

Seminal critiques of empire: Hobson, Morel, Lenin

The early twentieth century produced three important critiques of empire. Of these Hobson had the largest impact.

Hobson's *Imperialism* was important in the growth of anti-imperialism because his book influenced both Wilsonian-liberal and Marxist anti-imperialist thinking. One reason Hobson influenced both Soviet Marxists and American liberals was the hybridity of his thinking. He was clearly influenced by the Manchester School,[15] but Hobson took these ideas much further. Essentially, Hobson was a radical liberal humanist who focused his concern on economic reasons for Britain's imperial advances in South Africa. He concluded:

> The economic root of imperialism is the desire of strong organized industrial and financial interests to secure and develop at public expense and by the public force private markets for their surplus goods and their surplus capital.[16]

Hobson's conclusions were largely based on a critique of how Cecil Rhodes provoked the Boer War to serve his own financial interests.[17] However, significantly Hobson was not unambiguously opposed to all imperialism, because he argued 'lower races'[18] were not capable of developing their tropical lands, so consequently 'progressive people' from Europe needed to intervene to economically develop these regions.[19] However, Hobson argued this 'development' needed to be carried out for the 'good of the subject race' rather than for the good of capitalists like Rhodes.[20] Effectively, Hobson articulated a 'trusteeship' view of 'development'. It was an idea that became very influential during the twentieth century. Hobson's ideas on 'preparing' subject peoples for independence can, for example, be seen in the 'trusteeship' notion Wilsonian-liberals built into the League of Nations and UN,[21] as well as in Hull's call to replace European empires with a UN trusteeship model.[22]

But because of Hobson's economic focus, his book also had an important influence on Lenin's work on imperialism.[23] So although Lenin regarded Hobson as a 'bourgeois' theorist, he acknowledged his debt to Hobson's work. Thus did Hobson's liberal ideas mutate into a Marxist critique of imperialism. And once the Soviet Union became a global power intent on promoting Lenin's vision (after 1945), these anti-imperialist notions acquired the sort of force British policy-makers could no longer ignore. But equally significantly, Hobson's critique crossed the Atlantic and impacted on American liberal thinking. Hobson's critique became especially central to an American school of thinking on international issues[24] centred on Parker Moon's *Imperialism and World Politics*.[25] Hobson's ideas, in fact, became more influential in America than Britain.[26] Some have suggested British radical liberals, like Hobson, were partly responsible for Wilson's post-1918 failures precisely because Wilson focused so much attention on these British radical liberals: he mistook their minority views for the views of the wider British and European publics (publics not hostile to imperialism in the early twentieth century).[27] Certainly echoes of Hobson can be heard in the pronouncements of many Wilsonians (including Roosevelt, Hull and Welles). Effectively, Hobson helped generate a powerful twentieth-century negative vision of imperialism. This vision argued Britain was entering a state of capitalist decadence, because, having ceased to be the world's workshop Britain had become the world's banker, more and more dependent upon tribute from colonial and foreign borrowers.[28] Hobson's ideas served to affirm American prejudices against Britain's ruling elite and feed into the myth that Britain's empire was simply a 'vast system of outdoor relief for the upper classes'.[29] This Hobsonian/Cobdenite anti-elite idea meshed well with America's 'ideology of egalitarianism' and became an important factor in Roosevelt's moves to end the British empire.

Hobson's long-term role in undermining Britain's empire cannot be overstated because Hobson, as internationalist,[30] inspired both the key twentieth-century schools of internationalism – Marxist–Leninism and Wilsonian liberalism. And so, rather bizarrely, two different interpretations of the same book came to influence Soviet and American foreign policy. But ultimately, perhaps Hobson's impact on Wilsonian liberalism should be seen as most significant, given that Rooseveltian Wilsonians eventually played such a major role in bringing down European imperialism.

However, Hobson was not alone in criticizing European imperialism. Edmund Morel was another important critic who inspired Anglo radical-liberals. Whereas Hobson focused on economic reasons for imperialism, Morel was a British humanist concerned with exposing imperialism's impacts on people in the colonies. Morel's book *Red Rubber*,[31] published in 1906, mobilized considerable opposition to Belgian rule in the Congo. Morel's success in mobilizing British activists may be attributed to the fact the Congo was not Britain's colony. Ultimately, *Red Rubber* generated much emotive anti-imperial publicity in the Anglo world, and gave European imperialism a bad name in America. The moral indignation Morel stirred up could still be heard in the pronouncements made by Roosevelt and Welles decades later (and can sill be heard in America today).

Post-1945 critics of empire

By the mid-twentieth century, criticism of Britain's empire was no longer an insignificant minority view. When anti-imperialism was only espoused by a small group of leftists or radical liberals it did not matter. They posed no real challenge to imperialism because they had few followers and no resources.[32] But once these ideas spread into mainstream thinking, the situation changed. A post-war intellectual ferment, kick-started by Roosevelt's team, popularized the Wilsonian liberal notions of self-determination and trusteeship and spread 'anticolonialism' into the mainstream (e.g. Britain's Labour Party, the Anglo-media, and even sections of Britain's bureaucracy).

This created three challenges for the British empire's rulers. Firstly, anticolonialism grew increasingly popular within Western academic and journalistic circles. Secondly, in parts of the empire, nationalists and/or Marxists organized themselves to agitate for decolonization. Thirdly, after 1945 London found itself increasingly having to acquiesce to US policies. Hence, after 1945, British policy-makers wanting to retain the empire found themselves confronting the following groups advocating the opposite:

- an expanding British anticolonial lobby which included members of Britain's Labour Party caucus;[33]

- decolonization activists in the colonies (who often networked with British left-wingers);

- a US anticolonial constituency built by Roosevelt's team;

- members of Britain's bureaucracy influenced by anticolonialism, e.g. Andrew Cohen;[34] and

- the UN, which grew into an important anticolonial forum. An alliance of newly independent Afro-Asian states plus Soviet-bloc states used the UN to agitate for the decolonization of Europe's empires.

An important feature of the growth in anticolonialism was a trans-Atlantic traffic in ideas. Roosevelt's team, plus Willkie's 1940s tour had created an American anticolonial coalition. At the heart of this anticolonial coalition were Wilsonian liberals, but others in the coalition were America's tradition Anglophobes and the National Association for the Advancement of Colored People.[35] The (Wilsonian) Institute of Pacific Relations (IPR) ran a network of branches from New York, to disseminate anticolonial ideas amongst academics in America, Canada, Britain and Australia.[36] Britain's IPR branch was based at the Royal Institute of International Affairs at Chatham House. During the 1950s anticolonialism was diffused on university campuses across the Anglo world as radical liberal and Marxist intellectuals discovered a shared opposition to imperialism and colonialism. By the 1960s anticolonialism had become the dominant paradigm at Anglo universities. Prolific intellectuals like Basil Davidson and Thomas Hodgkin did much to popularize anticolonialism amongst undergraduates,[37] while Davidson's writings about Africa made black nationalism fashionable in the West and helped popularize African decolonization within the Labour Party.[38]

From the 1950s onwards, both the Wilsonian liberal and Marxist varieties of anti-imperialism grew into real threats to the British empire. When anti-imperialism became fashionable with academics and journalists, the stage was set for diffusing anti-imperialism/anticolonialism and decolonization into the wider public. Whereas during the 1940s a pro-empire view dominated in the British media, by the early 1960s anticolonialism was the mainstream discourse. In fact, it has been argued

> Anticolonialism was the most ubiquitous international ideology from the 1950s to the 1980s, uniting the whole Communist world, almost all articulate opinion in the developing world and most left-wing thought in the Western world.[39]

Because this ideology resonated with so many Anglo journalists, anti-imperialism/anticolonialism became a widespread news discourse during the last four decades of the twentieth century. It eventually became a virtually unchallengeable discourse in Anglo newsrooms, so the media routinely touted the idea colonialism was anachronistic and 'backward', while decolonization was 'progressive' and 'inevitable'. Consequently, 'the idea of empire' inspired fewer and fewer people and, in the face of the growing demonization of imperialism/colonialism, doubts about the rectitude of empire necessarily grew in Britain.[40] Eventually, even Britons favouring imperialism fell silent for fear of being labelled 'backward' or 'racist'. In places like Australia this triggered identity problems because Australian identity had long been constructed around a pride in being British colonials. For British politicians this anti-imperial mood increased the cost of advocating pro-empire policies.

But the challenge to Britain's empire came not only from ideas. Another challenge was nationalist and Marxist activists in Britain's empire. These activists had been emboldened by the Atlantic Charter; Roosevelt/Welles' anti-imperial rhetoric; and Britain's defeat in Singapore. They began demanding decolonization. Sometimes these nationalists and Marxist activists fought each other. But whenever nationalists and Marxists sank their differences and worked together, it produced the phenomenon of a 'national liberation struggle'. These decolonization activists received support and encouragement from leftist and anticolonial groups in Britain, America and Scandinavia. Further, an anticolonial pressure-group coalesced at the UN from ex-colonies already granted independence. UN support for anticolonial activists was to become a powerful anti-imperial force. Further, Cold War competition helped drive anticolonialism because the Soviets provided weapons and training to Third World Marxist-activists. This caused America to argue independence be speedily given to Third World 'moderates' (nationalists) so as to undercut the 'radicals' (Marxists). The US model of speedily granting independence to 'moderates' (prepared to function as US compradors) became an important factor in Britain's rapid deconstruction of its empire.

Shifts in the US–British balance of power

During the 1890s America overtook Britain to become the world's leading economic power. But despite America's economic strength, Britain entered the twentieth century as the world's leading political power. Even after Britain was weakened by World War I, America was still unable to dislodge Britain as the world's leading political actor (as seen in Wilson's inability to implement his vision). The key reason for Britain's continued political supremacy was its sprawling global empire. Britain, as the initiator of globalization I, still controlled an unparalleled global trading network of business interests linked to London by an enormous merchant fleet, plus railway and telegraph networks. So at the start of the twentieth century America may have possessed the world's largest economy, but British-staffed businesses were scattered across the globe, and Britain had colonial officials in situ around the globe to protect its economic and political interests. Further, Britain's navy controlled (and policed) the world's ocean trade routes; Britain had military bases across the globe; and Britain controlled the world's largest military force – the Indian Army. From this derived British political power.

Although Wilson wished to create a new international order, he was not driven to erase Britain's empire (in the way he wanted to erase the Austrian, Ottoman and German empires). Rather, Wilson wished to build an Anglo-global partnership/alliance within which Britain remained a first-class power (governing its empire as a 'trustee' for developing less advanced peoples).

Within Wilson's conceptualization, America would have taken the lead within a US–British partnership geared to building an Anglo-led system of globalized 'open trade'. Essentially Wilson, as Anglophile, believed in an American–British 'special relationship' (based upon a shared Anglo-Saxon heritage),[41] and he wanted to share global power with Britain. As it happened, British imperialists (in alliance with other European imperialists) thwarted Wilson's model of globalized 'open trade', causing America to withdraw into itself for two decades.

That British imperialists thwarted Wilson's 'open trade' internationalism after 1918 rankled and frustrated Wilsonians throughout the inter-war years. Consequently, the new Wilsonians (like Roosevelt and Hull) were never Anglophiles interested in retaining Britain as a first class power. Instead, they wanted to sweep away Britain's Empire to make America unambiguously both the world's economic and political leader. World War II gave these New Wilsonians the opportunity to tackle the problem of Britain's political power.

At the start of World War II Britain's hegemony over its empire looked secure despite on-going restiveness amongst Indians, Arabs and Afrikaners. But World War II changed this because four new pressures on their empire emerged. These would ultimately prove irresolvable.

Firstly, the war produced a new breed of anticolonial activists emboldened by Japan's occupation of Southeast Asia and America's strong advocacy of anticolonialism under Roosevelt. That America, as the rising global hegemon, was advocating decolonization naturally encouraged Third World revolt. Sedition was, in fact, often actively encouraged by American diplomats when they initiated meetings with nationalist leaders to express US support for independence.[42] Hence, although Japan was defeated and Europe's empires returned, anticolonial activists understood a shift had occurred, because Roosevelt's Atlantic Charter called for self-determination; and this Charter was now underpinned by American power, which had clearly supplanted British power. The war also undermined Britain's inter-war attempts to stabilize the empire through constitutional reform, because Indian and Afrikaner nationalists argued their countries' declarations of war (instead of remaining neutral) proved Britain's reforms had been a sham.

Secondly, Germany's defeat created a power vacuum which was filled by Soviet occupation of Eastern Europe. This transformed the Soviet Union into a global power. The Soviets became a major advocate of decolonization. (Although, their advocacy of decolonization never included Russia's own empire). The Soviets became a key anticolonial player because they actively encouraged armed rebellions against both Europe's empires, and what was termed 'neo-colonialism' – i.e. the Pax Americana's comprador-partners. The

1950s–1980s saw the Soviet Union and Warsaw-bloc provide finance, plus weapons-and-training to national liberation movements like the Viet Minh and Viet Cong (Vietnam), Pathet Lao (Laos), FLN (Algeria), FRELIMO (Mozambique), MPLA (Angola), PAIGC (Guinea-Bissau), ZAPU (Zimbabwe), PLO (Israel), ANC (South Africa), SWAPO (Namibia), and FRETELIN (East Timor). The Soviet AK–47 became the main weapon of rebel guerrilla forces everywhere. The Soviets also became an important anticolonial voice inside the UN.

Thirdly, international bodies like the UN, Organization of African Unity (OAU) and Commonwealth became mobilizing platforms for decoloni-zation. The UN especially became a problem for Britain once the Soviets and newly independent countries learned to use the UN to promote anticolonialism during the 1950s. And since every ex-colony granted independence joined these international bodies, the Afro-Asian anticolonial lobby kept expanding. The influence of this Afro-Asian bloc was greatly enhanced by American–Soviet Cold War competition, because Washington did not want to be outperformed by Moscow. This resulted in America adopting a 'shrill, moralizing and uncompromising tone' towards Europe's empires in order to distance itself from charges of supporting colonialists.[43] Consequently calls for decolonization grew ever louder and more insistent. And because anticolonialism became a dominant journalistic discourse from the late 1950s, the shrill anticolonialism emanating from the UN, Commonwealth and OAU was given prominence in mainstream Anglo media. By 1960, Britain simply found it increasingly difficult to resist these decolonization pressures.

Fourthly, during World War II it became clear to London Roosevelt's team were intent on deconstructing Britain's empire. This generated considerable consternation and even fear amongst British policy-makers and bureaucrats.[44] Britain's policy-makers split into two camps.[45] One camp, which congealed around the Foreign Office, argued Britain needed to adjust to the new realities of emerging American global hegemony. The Foreign Office concluded without American cooperation Britain would be unable to maintain its empire after the war.[46] Recognizing America's capacity to destroy the empire, meant making as many policy adjustments as were required to appease Washington in order to try and preserve as much of the empire as possible. The second camp, which congealed around the Colonial Office, argued Britain should not allow itself to look weak by 'acquiescing' to American pressure. Rather, Britain should simply stand firm in defence of its imperial rights (while 'reforming' the empire so as to secure British hegemony). But because Britain became deeply indebted to America during World War II, by 1945 Washington acquired the capacity to pressure Britain to reconfigure its empire according to Wilsonian principles of self-determination, open trade and trusteeship. Washington used its economic leverage to steer British policy in ways that hastened the empire's death.

Further, American armies poured into Britain and its empire during World War II. This also contributed to undermining the empire because these armies, and the media they brought with them, carried Roosevelt's anticolonial ideas. The US OWI was staffed by Rooseveltian New Deal social engineers interested in creating a 'world-wide social revolution'.[47] The Pacific Bureau of OWI, operating from California, was especially hostile to European imperialism and generated large amounts of wartime propaganda specifically geared to undermining Britain's empire.[48] OWI was also responsible for producing motivational and education packages for US troops sent abroad. These educational packages promoted anticolonialism and the Wilsonian trusteeship model. Interestingly, the British War Office (keen to keep the Americans on-side), did nothing to prevent the distribution of educational material promoting anticolonialism and trusteeship to British troops.[49] In addition, the huge numbers of US troops who poured into Britain and its empire brought with them America's ideology of egalitarianism and American prejudice against Britain's upper class.[50] This helped spread the idea the empire was an old fashioned exploitative and repressive anachronism, plus the notion this empire served only a decadent upper class of Britons. The impact of these ideas on undermining Britain's ruling class (plus its values of rank, service, loyalty, honour, etcetera), coupled with the promotion of US egalitarian consumerism, cannot be underestimated. Further, US troops stationed in the empire (including India) flouted imperial taboos which also destabilized Britain's imperial legitimacy.[51] By the end of World War II American notions of egalitarianism and anticolonialism had been widely diffused and this seriously undermined stability in Britain's empire.

British–American struggle over India

Pax Americana planners always had a particular interest in Asia, as seen in the considerable energy expended to keep China 'open' for US trade between the two world wars, and which culminated in a war with Japan.

Significantly, Britain's economic interests in India, China and Southeast Asia far outstripped America's during the 1930s.[52] If America was to grow its global power something had to be done to change this situation (as General Macarthur noted).[53] During World War II, London realized a core American objective was to shut down all empires in Asia – Japanese, French, Dutch and British – so America could expand its informal empire into Asia. In this regard, Washington even made it understood it would grant London a free hand to maintain Britain's African empire as long as London agreed to American post-war dominance in the Asia-Pacific.[54] Consequently, it was the Asian empires of Britain, France and the Netherlands that attracted America's attention;[55] and when Roosevelt spoke of decolonization his key targets were British India and Dutch Indonesia.[56]

Washington's support for Indian independence was of real concern to London, with British intelligence seeing America as 'conducting political warfare' against Britain's Asian hegemony throughout the war.[57] This triggered a British-American struggle over India's future. Both London and Washington realized the outcome of this struggle was central to the future of both the Pax Britannica and the Pax Americana because Indian independence would undermine British power and open the way for Pax Americana penetration of south Asia.

America's campaign for Indian self-determination was conducted in three ways. Direct communications with the British government made it clear Washington wished to see rapid reform of India's political system and movement towards Indian independence. Secondly, Wilsonian anticolonial discourse was actively diffused within British society. Thirdly, America encouraged anti-imperial rebellion and sedition within India, because when American diplomats established contact with nationalist activists in places like India,[58] these contacts left activists in no doubt of America's anticolonial views and persuaded them that after the war they would achieve independence under American guidance.[59] This necessarily energized anticolonial activism.

Given America's model of informal empire required comprador-partners, the US State Department worked to identify and assist 'moderate' (nationalist) anticolonial leaders in Europe's empire. By assisting 'moderate' leaders (and shunning 'radicals') American anticolonial activities not only played a role in destabilizing Britain's empire, but also effectively helped shape many post-colonial governments. In India, the Americans easily identified a group they believed would make splendid compradors, because, by the start of the twentieth century, British rule had already produced a Westernized Indian middle class. From this middle class emerged the Congress movement, which demanded Indian self-rule.

Although this Congress movement had long harassed the British Raj, Britain's hegemony over India remained intact in 1939. But after the fall of Singapore, American propagandists proved to be masters at promoting the idea of a weak and decadent British empire ready to fall over. Roosevelt had created a wartime information agency, the Office of Coordinator of Information (OCOI), and India was on OCOI's list of concerns.[60] In addition to OCOI propaganda encouraging Indian nationalism,[61] Roosevelt's unambiguous anticolonial stance and the Atlantic Charter inspired, empowered and energized anticolonial activists everywhere. It also mobilized British left-wing activists who allied themselves with nationalist struggles.[62] This obviously increased pressure on Britain in places like India.[63] In addition, anticolonial activists recognized America's growing power, plus Britain's growing dependence upon America. This realization generated the 1942 'Quit India' campaign, geared to mobilizing Washington pressure on London.[64] This campaign cleverly undermined Britain's hegemony by mobilizing new recruits into the ranks of the anticolonial movement; reduced the number of Indians prepared to openly ally themselves with British rule; and generated considerable bad publicity for the empire (in America).

Both the British government and Indian nationalists recognized that, in a world of growing US power, American attitudes became central to deciding international political agendas. Consequently, Indian decolonization became very much tied up with a battle for American public opinion, and both sides became involved in a 1940s public relations war targeting Americans.[65] Recognizing how important it was to secure American pressure on Britain, Indian Congress activists invested considerable energy into campaigns geared to influencing American journalists.[66] In this regard, Gandhi was especially effective because he was skilled in mobilizing liberal journalistic sympathy.[67] Gandhi generated significant American support for Indian independence, including amongst powerful Americans.[68] In response, Britain's Colonial Office established their own public relations department specifically targeting America.[69] And when Indian Congress public relations began working in Canada, the Colonial Office public relations department also turned its attention to Canada.[70] The Colonial Office grew deeply fearful about mounting American journalistic and public hostility to British rule in India, and their public relations department worked hard to try and explain to Americans why Britain's empire was an agent for good.[71] But ultimately, British propaganda was never going to persuade Washington's influential Wilsonian lobby; and was no match for the media-savvy Gandhi's ability to tap into American anti-imperial sensibilities. In the end, the synergy between Wilsonians and Indian nationalists made it impossible for London to overcome the perception (being diffused by Wilsonians) that the British Raj was an anachronism to be abolished. By 1945 the fate of British India was effectively sealed.

But India aside, during the last eighteen months of World War II American anticolonial rhetoric actually moderated (as Washington began recognizing the new threat posed by emergent Soviet power). As US anticolonial rhetoric was toned down, British policy-makers started to feel less threatened; and actually began planning for maintaining parts of the empire by 'reforming' it in accordance with Wilsonian 'trusteeship' notions.[72]

Although Washington made it clear they definitely wanted political change in Asia (India, Philippines, Indonesia and French Indochina), British policy-makers now believed much of Britain's empire (outside of India) was salvageable – i.e. they saw the 'white Dominions' were safely 'British'; the African empire appeared maintainable; and Britain's Middle Eastern informal empire looked secure. As American concern over Soviet power grew, so Britain's Colonial Office became increasingly convinced America would realize Britain's empire (reformed by the 'trusteeship' model) was a strategic asset to the West. This produced a new burst of energy and confidence in Britain's Colonial Office that lasted until the mid-1950s.

But the Colonial Office was wrong. Washington had not become a supporter of British imperialism, and due to the war, Britain lost its capacity to resist American anticolonial pressures. The reality is, World War II made Britain economically beholden to America because of lease–lend debts, and because Britain needed to borrow US funds to rebuild an economy ravaged by wartime capital depreciation.[73] The lease–lend agreements effectively ended Britain's self-sufficiency as a great power[74] and gave America influence over British policy-making.[75] Britain's lend–lease negotiator, Lord Keynes, made two mistakes. He miscalculated what the dollar–sterling exchange rate would be after the war,[76] and he assumed the negotiations were governed by English gentlemanly rules. After the war, he discovered America's way of doing business was different,[77] and 'much of what happened in 1945 was at variance with the warm words Keynes remembered hearing in Washington'.[78] After the war, what counted were written agreements granting America power over British policy. During the negotiations Keynes had committed Britain to financial arrangements that distorted Britain's post-war economy and made the reconstruction of its post-war economy impossible.[79] Washington had no interest in letting Britain rebuild itself into a serious rival to America, and so insisted the agreements be met. Britain's central problem became an agreement to make sterling convertible with the dollar by 1947. For Washington this was the key to establishing a Pax Americana, because it cemented the US dollar into the position of core global currency. By 1947 it became clear to London that if dollar convertibility was implemented, Britain could not afford to pay all its bills at the current exchange rate.[80] These bills included feeding civilians in a war-ravaged Germany,[81] and paying for wars in Greece and Palestine. To implement dollar convertibility Britain had to cut back on its overseas costs. This was the background to Attlee announcing Britain's withdrawal from Greece, India and Palestine. Further, as a result of signing lease–lend, Britain found itself forced to hand over global air transport routes[82] and military bases to America.[83] In so doing, Britain effectively conceded to the emergence of a Pax Americana. There is no doubt Washington used the leverage created by lease–lend to push Britain to adopt policies that ultimately destroyed its empire. Cordell Hull admitted America used its muscle to push for self-determination, open-door trading and trusteeship.[84] Washington pushed for Indian independence;[85] to open the British empire to American trade;[86] and to divide Palestine into Jewish and Arab states (which the British had resisted).[87]

Effectively, by 1945 the West European imperial powers (including Britain) were in no position to resist American economic pressure, and Washington showed a willingness to use its power to impose American political preferences on European states like Britain, the Netherlands, France, Germany and Italy.[88] This was most openly revealed when Washington used Marshall Aid to pressure the Netherlands to give independence to Indonesia.[89] Indonesian independence was a key moment, signalling to European governments (including London) that the old imperial game was up, and they had no choice but to acquiesce to America's trusteeship model. Acquiescence meant adopting the Pax Americana's Third World 'development' model – geared to 'developing' colonies into viable trading partners for the Pax Americana, and building Westernized middle classes in these colonies. The building of 'moderate' middle-class compradors capable of taking over government at independence was a central feature of the 'development' model imposed on Britain's empire.

The shift from Pax Britannica to Pax Americana could have been a smooth and organized affair if the proposals of one of America's leading intellectuals had been acted upon. James Burnham[90] proposed a planned transition, saying the Pax Americana should formally become the 'receiver' of Britain's empire.[91] Burnham's 'receivership' proposal was never taken up. Consequently, the transition from Pax Britannica to Pax Americana was a disorderly affair:

> A mixed history of improvisation, secret diplomacy, covert action, inter-Establishment jealousy and military disaster. There was under the affection of Anglo-American solidarity, a continuation of the old politics by other means. Elements of this mutual suspicion though seldom stressed, endure to this day. They arise from the original lack of synchronicity and from the British habit of only giving up where they had to. As a result the United States very often had to pick up where a sudden British scuttle had left off.[92]

Both sides grumbled through this transition. Yet within a few decades of the process being completed, the British and Americans were able to rebuild their 'special relationship'. In fact, Hitchens suggests it is this special relationship that meant the British felt less aggrieved than other Europeans about their loss of empire – after all Britain's possessions simply passed into the hands of their Anglo cousins across the Atlantic.[93]

British response 1: Britain stumbles, 1947–48

The years 1947–49 set in motion the destruction of Britain's empire. Britain effectively bankrupted itself during World War II by committing all its resources and then borrowing from America, its dominions and India. Consequently, London lost the power to resist American demands for imperial reform.

In 1945 American policy-makers were split between those supportive of European colonialism and those supporting anticolonial nationalists.[94] Ultimately, America backed the nationalists, partly due to the belief that if independence was not granted to nationalists, then ultimately communists would come to power.[95] The rise of Soviet power consequently served to modify, not end, America's anticolonial agenda, because it encouraged a belief in speeding up imperial reform and granting independence to 'moderates' (nationalists who would function as compradors) in order to undercut support for 'radicals' (communists). Significantly, British Prime Minister Attlee was persuaded that managed reform (leading to rapid independence) was preferable to revolution. Attlee, in turn, tried to persuade the Dutch.[96] Although, by the late 1950s British colonial policy (under Macmillan and McLeod) was completely geared to this imperial-reform agenda, in the late 1940s, British colonial policy was not so clear cut – because there was still struggle (and confusion) amongst British policy-makers.

In the late 1940s all British policy-makers agreed the empire should be preserved. The question was how, and in what form. Two broad positions emerged:

> The Tories held in general that the Americans should be kept out of the Colonial Empire because it was a British concern. The Labour view affirmed the desirability of co-operation with the United States in colonial development.[97]

The anti-reform group, which coalesced around Churchill, believed Britain had the capacity to keep its empire intact; and Britain should fight American pressure to scrap or modify the empire. A second group felt the old empire could not be saved (because of anticolonial pressures) or should not be saved (because they disapproved of the empire). However, this second group believed a modified empire could be salvaged by reforming it in accordance with America's 'trusteeship' model. For these reformers, the colonies would be 'developed' into self-governing dominions (like Canada, South Africa and Australia), which would become 'independent' but remained tied to the British crown – i.e. the empire would be transformed into the Commonwealth through a process of liberalization, democratization and development of the colonies. This reform group included Britain's Labour Party and some senior members of Britain's Colonial Office, such as Sir Andrew Cohen. Cohen not only supported America's development model, he believed American economic assistance should underwrite the development of Britain's empire.[98] Effectively Cohen was proposing something similar to James Burnham – that America be formally recognized as the 'receiver' of Britain's empire. Ultimately, both Attlee's reformers and the Americans agreed on a model of gradualist imperial reform. But neither the Americans nor British ever anticipated the speed with which the empire would then unravel.[99] Essentially, the reformers were naive not to anticipate how their reforms would take on a life of their own; and simply failed to grasp how attempts to build middle-class compradors would slip out of their control. The gradualist model proved untenable.

With hindsight, it is clear four decisions set in motion a chain of events that unravelled the British empire. All four were taken by Clement Attlee, who became Prime Minister in July 1945.

- In September 1945 Attlee called elections in India with a view to establishing a constitution-making body for a self-governing India. This accorded with American wishes and made it inevitable that the British Raj would be terminated. Effectively, Attlee was conceding to the (overt and covert) pressure America had been directing at Britain to withdraw from India.[100] Attlee's September announcement naturally dramatically energized and empowered India's anticolonial activists. The 1945 elections brought to power Congress activists (demanding an independent India) and Muslim League activists (demanding an independent Pakistan). By 1946 the British Raj was in turmoil because British colonials lost heart and began preparing their departure; Indian Army officers pragmatically shifted allegiance; anticolonial activists became more assertive; and a Hindu–Muslim struggle for power erupted.

- In January 1947 Attlee announced (in the face of British public hostility)[101] India would be given independence no later than June 1948.[102] India was finally given independence in August 1947 as part of the spate of decolonization fulfilling America's desires for the termination of empires in Asia, i.e. Philippines (1946), India (1947), Pakistan (1947), Burma (1948), Ceylon (1948), Indonesia (1949), Vietnam (1949), Cambodia (1949) and Laos (1949).

- In February 1947 Attlee announced Britain was withdrawing its army from Greece, (where Britain was fighting communist guerrillas) because Britain could no longer afford this war.

- In May 1948 Attlee pulled British forces out of Palestine (with support from the British public). The British had found themselves under enormous American pressure to establish a Jewish state by dividing Palestine into two states. The British (who opposed Washington's pro-Jewish policy) clearly found America's pressure un-nerving because it was indicative of how Washington was prepared to use Britain's debt as leverage. Ultimately London simply walked away from the Israel–Palestine problem without formally transferring power to any successor state as a way of effectively conceding to American pressure,[103] while not formally doing so.[104] This dishonourable withdrawal signalled to the world Britons were either unwilling or unable to enforce their preferred Palestine settlement. This sent another signal of British weakness to anticolonial activists. Effectively, Attlee discovered it was difficult to oppose Washington's preferred options, and with the Indian Army no longer under British control, Britain no longer had the power to impose its preferred options in Asia and the Middle East.[105]

Given the importance of Attlee's Labour government in ending the empire, it seems worthwhile asking why the Labour Party took these decisions. It is worth noting, as soon as the Atlantic Charter was published, Attlee personally agreed with Roosevelt this Charter should be applied to Britain's empire.[106] When the Labour Party came to power in 1945 it already had colonial policies supporting America's view that India become independent. The impact of both the Fabians and anticolonial-left on developing these Labour Party policies was significant.[107] In fact, Attlee's decision to quit India was clearly driven by pressure from both his own party's anticolonial lobby and US pressure.[108] Many in the Labour Party had imbibed the ideas of Hobson, Morel and Lenin and were very receptive to Roosevelt's 1940s anticolonialism. Amongst those strongly associated with Labour's anticolonial lobby was Secretary of State for the Colonies, Arthur Creech Jones. Not only had Creech Jones co-founded the Fabian Colonial Bureau,[109] but he had also pushed Fabian ideas within the Labour Party.[110] It was during the Attlee period that Creech Jones worked closely with Andrew Cohen to develop a Fabian model of British imperial reform and empire 'development'.[111] This Fabian model was, fortuitously for Washington, highly compatible with the Rooseveltian 'trusteeship' model and thereby complemented the shift to a Pax Americana.

Attlee's two 1947 announcements (on Indian independence and Greece) were powerful signals a Pax Americana was supplanting a Pax Britannica. When Britain withdrew from Greece, America immediately stepped in to take over Britain's role. This triggered the Truman Doctrine, by which America assumed responsibility for containing Soviet power, and maintaining the European balance of power.[112] The Truman Doctrine openly asserted US global power; with American global hegemony visibly replacing Britain's. Essentially, this doctrine was as close as America came to operationalizing the sort of formal transfer of power suggested by James Burnham.[113] The Truman doctrine signalled the formal birth of the Pax Americana.

However, from a British empire perspective, the announcement of Indian/ Pakistani independence was far more dramatic. The damage to the empire was huge because Britain's Indian Army had been the linchpin of imperial defence.[114] Losing this army undermined Britain's fighting capacity to such an extent Australia and Canada realigned their security alliances away from Britain and towards America,[115] which further weakened British global power. Withdrawal from India also made Britain look weak; emboldening anticolonial activists elsewhere. As if to confirm Britain's weakness, the empire's two other trouble-makers also became more politically assertive – in 1948, Afrikaner nationalists won control of South Africa and began displacing Anglo hegemony;[116] then in 1949, the Irish dominion severed ties with Britain to become the Republic of Ireland. So, during this 'stumble period', Britain rather symbolically lost control of the empire's three 'traditional' trouble-spots, India, Ireland and South Africa. But most significantly, it was during the Truman era that Britain was dislodged (by America) as an Asian power.[117] With its dislodgement from Asia,[118] Britain's days as a global superpower were over.

America's Cold War policy adjustment

If Britain's dislodgement from India, Pakistan, Burma and Ceylon signalled American triumph, Washington did not get to celebrate for long because four events heralded a new threat to American global ambitions. These were the Soviet blockade of Berlin (1948), the Soviets becoming a nuclear power (1949), China acquiring a communist government (1949) and the start of the Korean War (1950). Each illustrated not merely the arrival of the Soviets as a new global superpower, but also demonstrated Soviet willingness and ability to challenge American power. So at the very moment Britain was removed as an obstacle to building a Pax Americana, another obstacle arose. The emergence of a communist bloc stretching from central Europe to the South China Sea (and powerful enough to defend itself against US pressures), was a disaster for those wishing to roll out America's informal empire. The 'fall' of China was especially disruptive given America's long-standing desire to incorporate China into its trading empire.

By 1950 Hull's original new world order plan was no longer implementable. Hull had been naive not to consider how bringing down the Japanese, German and British empires would create power vacuums that would lead to the emergence of new powers (like the Soviets). But if building a fully globalized Liberal order was impossible, this did not mean the Pax Americana project had to be abandoned. It simply meant reconfiguring Hull's model such that the world would be divided into two – a communist bloc, falling outside the Pax Americana, and the rest of the world, which would be integrated into

America's global trading empire (shown in map 4). The Americans called the latter the Free World; and the American–Soviets stand-off came to be called the Cold War. This emerged from Harry Truman's policy of containment, which meant America would work to prevent the spread of the communist bloc. Significantly, Truman's containment policy remained grounded in Hull's liberal and internationalist assumptions.

> Containment was influenced by liberal assumptions. That is to say, it was animated not simply by a determination to balance Soviet power, but by the desire to foster the strength of an internationalist order characterized by free trade, national self-determination, and liberal democracy. This meant that outside the Soviet bloc, among non-Communist countries, US policymakers sought to encourage free trade and economic interdependence, democratic reform, and gradual decolonization. Occupied countries such as Germany and Japan were liberalized, politically and economically. Europe's colonial powers were pressed to coopt nationalist movements in the developing world by devolving formal control over imperial holdings.[119]

Containment was a pragmatic response to Soviet power. Truman's containment policy had significant implications for Hull's decolonization plan, because the original American idea of forcing the decolonization of all Europe's empires now became too risky, due to the danger some new states might opt to join the 'communist bloc' rather than the 'Free World'. In fact, a core feature of the Cold War was that direct American–Soviet conflict was avoided (because nuclear weapons made direct confrontation too dangerous) and replaced by struggles between American and Soviet Third World surrogates.[120] Consequently, it was precisely those areas lost by Europe's empires that now became the key Cold War battlegrounds. This necessitated a rethink in Washington about how to strategically progress its policy of liquidating Europe's empires.[121]

The Cold War caused Washington to modify both its Third World and decolonization policies. Hull's earlier blanket support for Third World self-determination was moderated. Faced with the threat the Soviets might breach Truman's containment lines by winning allies amongst new Third World ruling elites, Washington decided decolonization needed to be managed more rigorously to ensure an outcome favourable to American global interests. Effectively, Washington discovered the continuance of empires (ruled by America's British, French and Portuguese allies) might be preferable to creating independent Third World states ruled by communists. This did not mean America abandoned its long-term vision of a decolonized world wherein new states were to be tied into America's informal empire through a system of comprador-partners. But it did mean reaching this goal would now be more difficult and drawn out; might necessitate short-term Washington support for maintaining Europe's empires (as long as these empires were reforming/liberalizing themselves); and might even involve American support for wars against anticolonial activists (if they were communist aligned). So under Truman a new decolonization model emerged that placed greater emphasis on 'development'. Essentially, America wanted to ensure that, at independence, power was handed over to ruling elites who functioned as reliable Pax Americana compradors. This took some pressure off Europe's empires, because America was now prepared to listen to European arguments that some colonies were far from ready for independence. The British Colonial Office latched onto America's new 'realism', seeing it as a way to 'salvage' the empire by reforming colonies and building compradors tied to London.

Once America accepted Europe needed to prepare their colonies for independence, decolonization became enmeshed with 'development', a phenomenon discussed in chapter 8. Consequently, from the 1950s Europe's colonial authorities were pushed to deploy 'development' to build 'moderate' middle-class compradors in each colony. This led to the growth of a Third World 'development industry' grounded in Western paternalism. 'Development' was geared to teaching the emergent middle classes how to govern liberal democracies and run the sort of economies that would make their states useful trading partners for the 'Free World'. For the Americans, none of this detracted from their long-term goal of creating an informal empire that was to include the (decolonized) former European empires – i.e. the Pax Americana was still premised upon creating independent states knitted together into an American-led globalized 'open' trading network. During the 1950s Britain undertook to steer its remaining empire in this direction, but argued it would take many decades of 'development' to produce Third World Westernized elites capable of self-government. The colonial powers argued, while this development was happening, their empires needed to remain in place – with imperial authorities acting as 'trustees' for developing their Third World subjects towards self-determination. For the Americans, such a managed transition over many decades seemed preferable to immediately creating unstable new states that might become Soviet allies. So the Cold War created a new spirit of compromise between Britain and America over colonial policy – a far cry from the pre-1947 era of British–American conflict over self-determination.

But if American foreign policy had evolved, so too had the notion of anticolonialism. Anticolonialism may have emerged as an American liberal concept when Roosevelt's team placed self-determination onto the 1940s international agenda. However, during the 1950s, the concept of anticolonialism was captured by the socialist left, who saw decolonization tied to (Fabian-type) imperial reform as a new type of Western imperialism called neo-colonialism.[122] From the mid-1950s the Soviets became skilled at promoting themselves as the true torch-bearers of an anticolonial/anti-imperial revolution. So successful was Soviet propaganda, that by the 1960s many Third World anticolonial activists (and their Western sympathizers) saw the Soviet Union (rather than America) as a preferred postcolonial model. So successful were the Soviets in capturing the anticolonial agenda (and redefining 'anticolonialism' and 'anti-imperialism') that America's role in inspiring the original 1940s anticolonial ferment was largely erased from the memory of new generations of anticolonial activists. Eventually, America was portrayed in anticolonial literature as a bastion of counterrevolution[123] because of how America was seen to have supported right-wing forces over left-wing struggles in China, Malaysia, Indonesia, Vietnam, Cuba, Guatemala, El Salvador, Nicaragua, Chile and Angola.

British response 2: salvaging empire through reform, 1949–56

Truman's containment policy boosted optimism in Britain's Colonial Office because they believed Washington would recognize Britain's (still large) empire as a Western bulwark against communist expansion. Believing the empire had a new role to play in the Cold War dramatically reinvigorated the Colonial Office – who saw their new role as deepening British penetration into Africa and the Middle East,[124] plus 'developing' the empire to make it economically and politically valuable to the 'Free World'. Consequently, the Colonial Office was expanded during the first half of the 1950s to equip it for the new (interlocking) tasks of 'development' and building Westernized middle-class elites. The Colonial Office's staff tripled, its budget quintupled, and in five years six and a half thousand new colonial officers were sent out to the colonies to implement the new 'development' vision.[125] A Colonial Development Corporation was established, and a new kind of empire emerged, run by reformers, planners, developers and economists.[126] The ideas of the Labour Party's Arthur Creech Jones, plus two Colonial Office officials, Andrew Cohen and Sydney Caine, featured prominently in the reform being implemented. This reform – geared towards shifting from formal to informal empire – overlapped with Wilsonian/Rooseveltian notions of 'trusteeship'.

London appeared to believe the 'Free World' had been divided into spheres of influence – America was to be dominant in Asia (where it was building its new informal empire out of the remnants of the Japanese, British, Dutch and French empires), while Africa (in which America was less interested) was regarded as a shared British/French sphere. None-the-less, Britain understood they did not have a free hand to do as they wished in their African empire, because Washington expected Britain to reform its African possessions into an informal empire. This reform was focused on Westernizing Africans and building middle-class elites to whom power could be transferred (in due course) – in accordance with the comprador model where power is transferred in order to actually keep power.[127] Andrew Cohen saw Africa's greatest problem as the lack of a middle class;[128] which meant creating African comprador-partners was going to be difficult. But the Colonial Office adopted this exercise with gusto; deploying Cohen's model for constructing an African middle class[129] and encouraging middle-class nationalism as a bulwark against communism.[130]

Converting the Colonial Office to imperial reform (liberalization) and development geared to building middle-class compradors generated dramatic shifts across British-ruled Africa.[131] Britain had traditionally administered its empire by working with and through traditional ruling groups, e.g. African chiefs. The 1950s roll-out of the Liberal comprador model saw chiefs abandoned in favour of new elected councils.[132] This accorded with America's vision of 'democracy' which values middle-class power and devalues traditional governance. Andrew Cohen's liberalization model assumed colonial officials, educators and development experts would be able to build stable new middle classes, steer them towards a moderate nationalism, and induct them into running new liberal-democratic governance structures. This would provide the foundation upon which Britain's remaining colonial possessions could be granted independence within an informal empire. (Whether it would be an American or British informal empire was a moot point.)

But the whole reform model proved to be a huge miscalculation that failed to produce the expected outcomes. Firstly, the new policies destabilized traditional rural governance structures (and hence weakened governance generally). Secondly, these policies created underdeveloped African middle classes who proved to be incapable of either effective governance or economic productivity.[133] Worse still, far from becoming moderates, these new middle classes often became radical nationalists, who often allied themselves with the new Soviet-aligned genre of anticolonial theory. So ultimately, Britain's policy shift towards 'development' and compradorism (adopted to please Washington) produced the following unintended consequences:

- Britain's empire was terminated more rapidly than anticipated because the reforms produced radical middle classes demanding immediate independence.

- Reform produced little meaningful economic progress because it was unable to build a fully developed bourgeoisie capable of economic entrepreneurship.[134]

- The failed reform policies left a legacy of fragile and failed states across Africa and the Pacific.

What is more, imperial reform did not generate any American sympathy for salvaging Britain's empire. Both Truman and Eisenhower rebuffed Churchill's attempts to reconstruct a 'special' bilateral relationship between London and Washington.[135] And even more telling was Dwight Eisenhower's response to the Suez affair (1956).

The Suez affair became a crucial moment for terminating Britain's empire. It began when America cancelled a promise to build the Aswan dam as part of an Egyptian 'development' plan. Egypt's President Nasser responded by seizing the Suez canal. This eliminated the last remnants of British power in Egypt. In response British, French and Israeli forces attacked Egypt. Fearing this would drive Egypt (and other Arab states) into an alliance with the Soviets, the Eisenhower administration forced the British and French to withdraw. When British Prime Minister Anthony Eden launched the Suez attack he acted as if Britain was still a global power able to act imperially. When America forced his capitulation, it signalled Britain was no longer a first-ranked power, and that America now exercised hegemony over Britain. This crushed Eden and taught Britons they could no longer behave imperially.[136] The British never tried to act imperially again.

British response 3: capitulation, 1957–67

Suez brought a new British Prime Minister to power in 1957, Harold Macmillan. During Macmillan's term, Britain's government concluded nothing of the empire was salvageable. So Macmillan, and his Secretary of State for the Colonies, Iain McLeod, set in motion the decolonization of Britain's African colonies, thereby terminating the empire. Given the enormity of the Macmillan/McLeod decisions, it is worth examining what led them to conclude the empire was unsalvageable. Eight factors seem to have been involved in this final capitulation.

Firstly, Suez showed Macmillan the Cold War did not mean America would allow Britain to go back to its old imperial ways. And even more significant was the 1957 Eisenhower Doctrine – which (following Suez) pledged American aid to any Middle Eastern government threatened by communism.[137] The Eisenhower Doctrine was a signal America intended to replace Britain's informal Middle Eastern empire with an America informal empire. So the Eisenhower Doctrine spelt out to Britain a new world order was in place within which the Pax Americana had unambiguously replaced the Pax Britannica,[138] and that Britain was now expected to hand over its oil-rich Middle Eastern informal empire. This meant the remnants of Britain's empire were now visibly subject to America's global hegemonic will. The message was clear – even reforming Britain's colonies into an informal empire would not be enough to please the Americans. The British empire was simply unsalvageable in the face of an expansionist Pax Americana, and ultimately Macmillan cared more about Anglo-American relations than about imperial links.[139]

A second problem Macmillan faced was imperial reform had produced radical middle classes led by men like Kwame Nkrumah. Macmillan confronted the fact, the Colonial Office had lost control of imperial reform, and had botched the implementation of the informal empire/comprador model. A naively led and poorly managed reform process had unleashed radical middle-class forces in ways that simply confounded the reformers. To make matters worse, an increasingly aggressive Soviet Union was only too happy to provide weapons to radical nationalists, creating the danger of national liberation struggles producing guerrilla wars of the sort Britain had fought in Malaya. Macmillan's key concern became halting the radicalization process threatening to produce communist governments in Africa.[140] Consequently, Macmillan simply opted to walk away from the turmoil reform had created, and to grant independence to the most moderate politicians he could find in each colony.

Third, Macmillan concluded the empire was becoming an economic burden because of the costs of imperial reform, development and building Westernized middle classes. Reforming colonial policies so as to make them conform to America's vision was expensive.[141] To make matters worse, the new global economic order (derived from the Bretton Woods system) was beginning to hurt Britain's economy as America's dollar displaced sterling, and Americans elbowed their way into what had been British markets. So imperial reform became a growing burden to British taxpayers at precisely the moment Britain was getting poorer because the Pax Americana was displacing the Pax Britannica. Macmillan realized Britain simply did not have sufficient resources to carry out the 'development' programmes being demanded of her. It made sense to walk away from an empire that had become a burden, not an asset.

Fourth, for the most part, Britain's political and intellectual elites no longer believed in empire. Hull's 1940s anticolonial propaganda campaign had been a huge success, and by the late 1950s anticolonialism had been widely popularized amongst academics and journalists across the Anglo world. Macmillan confronted the reality 'colonialism' and 'imperialism' had been successfully demonized. In fact, by the late 1950s, the empire was no longer simply being labelled an 'outdated anachronism', but was now also being associated with a powerful new boo-word, 'racism'. This made it increasingly socially costly for anyone to try and defend (and hence salvage) the empire.

Fifth, anti-empire pressures mounted as a coalition of newly independent states and the Soviet bloc learned to use the UN as a platform to call for decolonization. Simultaneously, decolonization became increasingly fashionable amongst journalists and intellectuals. Intellectuals like Basil Davidson successfully promoted the idea radical African nationalists were heroes fighting against villainous colonial forces.[142] This helped mobilize an increasingly vocal anticolonial left in Britain.[143] They, together with the activists in the colonies, ran a relentless and vociferous campaign directed at the British government. An interesting feature of this campaign was how activists deployed charges of 'racism' to demobilize defenders of the empire,[144] and because sloppy journalism allowed them to equate 'colonialism' with 'racism', the anticolonial left gradually silenced more and more of those inclined to support colonialism. Given the growing success of anticolonial campaigning and the mounting pressure from the UN, it is perhaps not surprising Macmillan opted to simply walk away from empire.

Sixth, by the late 1950s there was a mood shift amongst City of London capitalists about the value of empire. These 'gentlemanly capitalists' had always been key players in driving British imperialism.[145] The Wilsonian/ Hullian agenda of 'open trade' was premised upon New York replacing London as the core metropolis of global capitalism, which was initially very concerning to the gentlemanly capitalists. However, once it was clear London would remain a key sub-metropole within the new US-led global trading network and London's gentlemanly capitalists would remain central players within global capitalism, the pro-empire lobby lost a powerful ally. Macmillan took note.

Seventh, by the late 1950s British public opinion was shifting against imperialism, and once politicians sensed declining popular support for empire, they saw no advantage in supporting the imperial cause. After World War II American consumerist values had spread rapidly through Western Europe due to Hollywood movies and television, plus the presence of US military forces now permanently based in Europe. The British government increasingly found it needed to pay serious attention to these new consumerist values and materialist demands. And so economic issues at home became more important than 'imperial glories' in far-distant lands. Britons were also influenced by the late 1950s anticolonial and anti-imperial rhetoric being circulated by journalists and academics. Hence, when Attlee announced Indian independence in 1947, he was acting against British public opinion.[146] But a decade later British public opinion had shifted, and by the time Macmillan embraced decolonization, he simply reflected a growing British indifference to the empire's survival.

Eighth, British policy-makers became increasingly demoralized at developments in those parts of their empire where British settler populations lived. Because of the multiracial nature of Rhodesia and Kenya, the Colonial Office had assumed a different style of decolonization would be required in east

and central Africa.[147] In Kenya this involved special parliamentary representation for white settlers.[148] In the Federation of Rhodesia & Nyasaland, the
empire's reformers hoped to build a new kind of comprador group based upon
multiracial 'partnership' – i.e. white settlers would remain as 'development'
agents and 'partners' in the building of an independent Central African
Federation. The idea of Rhodesia & Nyasaland black–white 'partnership'
under British leadership was promoted as an alternative to both apartheid
and black nationalism.[149] But these British plans did not please middle-class
black nationalists in Kenya, Nyasaland, Northern Rhodesia and Southern
Rhodesia, who agitated for one-man-one-vote and independence. The use of
force to pacify Kenya's Mau Mau (1952–60) and Nyasaland (1959) created
much bad publicity for Britain's empire.[150] And in the Colonial Secretary,
Iain McLeod, it generated fear that a bloodbath would ensue if rapid decolonization did not take place, Consequently, McLeod began transferring power
from white to black hands in Kenya and Central Africa.[151] This triggered
white resistance to London and the Colonial Office. However, Africa's white
settlers failed to influence British policy because they had no representation
in Britain's Parliament[152] (which the Irish had possessed) and they were
portrayed as rich landowners, which did not generate much popular sympathy
in Britain.[153] McLeod said he speeded up the process towards independence
because 'in my view any other policy would have led to terrible bloodshed in
Africa ... Were the countries fully ready for independence? Of course not
... Of course there were risks in moving quickly. But the risks of moving
slowly were far greater'.[154] This is where attempts at imperial reform had led:
the reforms failed; the British became demoralized, and fled. In the end, for
the British 'all that mattered was that indigenous elite, with some degree of
local support, should exist and be willing to take over'.[155] As Duncan Sandys,
British Minister of Commonwealth Relations told Rhodesia & Nyasaland's
Prime Minister, Roy Welensky, in 1962, 'You see, we British have lost the
will to govern.'[156]

By 1960 the confidence of Britain's ruling class had been shattered by the
rise of American power and US pressure for imperial reform; by Suez; by
two decades of sustained anticolonial propaganda; and by losing control of
the reform process. Mohandas Gandhi had hypothesized Britain's empire
would die when the British 'will to rule' ended. Macmillan's period as Prime
Minister signalled that time had arrived. Macmillan's 'wind of change'
speech delivered to South Africa's Parliament on 3 February 1960 is often
seen as especially symbolic of Britain's shift from imperial reform to rapid
decolonization. In this speech Macmillan told white South Africans trying
to resist the swelling tide of black nationalism was futile. White South
Africans and Rhodesians were appalled at Macmillan's advocacy of capitulation. Washington, however, was delighted with Macmillan's speech,[157]

because it signalled Britain at last accepted the inevitability of America's informal empire and the demise of Britain's empire. After his wind of change speech Macmillan was able to repair the damage done by decades of US-British conflict over the empire, and start the process of rebuilding the US-British special relationship.[158] The significance of making Britain's imperial capitulation speech in South Africa should not be underestimated – since Macmillan was obviously trying to distance Britain from apartheid, given the success of anticolonial propaganda that equated 'empire' and 'colonialism' with 'apartheid' and 'racism'.

For Macmillan, the reality was, by 1960, imperialism was so thoroughly demonized that defending empire was simply too costly. Countries like Britain, France and Belgium faced unrelenting barrages of criticism. Interestingly, the Soviet Union, USA, China and Portugal, (who in the 1960s all still occupied territories won during their imperial-expansionist phases), now mobilized political discourses claiming they were not empires. The Soviet's claimed Russia's empire had been reconfigured into a voluntary federation of states (e.g. Russia, Lithuania, Kazakhstan and Uzbekistan). China claimed its national minorities were organized as 'autonomous' regions (e.g. Tibet, Inner Mongolia and Sinkiang Uighur) which were voluntarily associated with China. America simply claimed its North American territory were US states 'internal' to the Union. Portugal claimed its 'overseas' territories (e.g. Angola and Mozambique) were part of a single political entity called 'Portugal'. Interestingly, the Soviet, Chinese and American claims were deemed legitimate, perhaps because the territories concerned formed a contiguous bloc; while Portugal's claims were deemed illegitimate because its territories were scattered across the globe. In another interesting twist, South Africans claimed their apartheid policy was a form of 'internal decolonization' in which black people were to be given independent homelands in accordance with the American model of self-determination.[159] South Africa's claims were deemed illegitimate because they endangered UN and OAU principles of freezing 1945 political boundaries.

It fell to Macmillan and McLeod to wind up Britain's empire. Between 1960 and 1966 every major remaining British colony was granted independence, leaving Britain with only scattered islands and possessions deemed non-viable states. By 1967 only two significant colonies remained technically British, namely Hong Kong and Southern Rhodesia; and white settlers in the latter had in any case declared Rhodesia unilaterally independent in 1965. When the end came, the empire was dismantled with remarkable speed.

The 1967 announcement by Prime Minister Harold Wilson that Britain was withdrawing its forces east of Suez confirmed Britain, stripped of its Indian Ocean empire, was now a second rate power reduced to functioning merely in the European sphere. The British passed through a painful period of economic and cultural metamorphosis, as Britain's economy suffered from the consequences of being stripped of its empire and as Britons adjusted to being second-tier players within the Pax Americana. It was only during the 1980s, under Prime Minister Thatcher, that Britons came to terms with their new position in the world. By the twenty-first century Britain had completely adjusted to its new global role in which London served as an important financial centre of the Pax Americana, and the British government operated much like a deputy sheriff, dispatching troops to fight in America's imperial wars and in Pax Americana 'peacekeeping' operations.

Given the role played by America in the demise of the British empire, it seems remarkable that the British-American 'special relationship' was once again fully functional after Thatcher. Interestingly, while Macmillan was terminating the empire he rationalized what he was doing by formulating a new conceptualization of this 'special relationship' within which Britons' future role would be to act as 'civilizing agents' within the Pax Americana. As Macmillan said:

> These Americans represent the new Roman Empire and we British, like the Greeks of old, must teach them how to make it go ... We are like the Greeks ... the power has passed from us to Rome's equivalent, the United States of America, and we can at most aspire to civilise and occasionally to influence them.[160]

It is debatable whether Macmillan's conceptualization ever came to pass. But the British never seemed to feel quite as aggrieved as other Europeans about having their empire striped away. This is possibly because the Americans granted the British an important military role within the Pax Americana;[161] because London acquired an important post-imperial financial role within the Pax Americana;[162] and because Britain's empire merely passed into the hands of their Anglo-Saxon cousins across the Atlantic.[163] At any rate the Americans and British have learned to work together and a new intermeshed American–British elite (that spans the Atlantic) has effectively shaped up,[164] despite the fact many Britons (along with many of their fellow Continental-Europeans) are still far from convinced Americans are up to the task of governing an empire.[165]

But whatever Americans and Britons think of each other, one thing is clear, the Pax Americana would have been impossible without the Pax Britannica,[166] because the British empire represented globalization I; and this first wave of globalization created the conditions for the second wave associated with the Pax Americana. In more ways than one, the Pax Americana has inherited the legacy and infrastructure built by Britain's empire-makers. No amount of American anticolonial rhetoric can obfuscate these roots.

Notes

1 Pakenham, T., *The Boer War* (Johannesburg: Jonathan Ball, 1979).

2 Pretorius, F., *Scorched Earth* (Cape Town: Human & Rousseau, 2001).

3 Hobson, J.A., *Imperialism. A Study* (London: George Allen & Unwin, 1968).

4 Morris, J., *Farewell the Trumpets* (London: Faber & Faber, 1978), 93–104.

5 *Ibid.*, 96–97.

6 Gallagher, J., *The Decline, Revival and Fall of the British Empire* (Cambridge: Cambridge University Press, 1982), 94.

7 The Statute of Westminster was proposed by South African and Canadian Prime Ministers James Barry Munnik Hertzog and William Lyon Mackenzie King.

8 Walker, E.A., *The British Empire. Its Structure and Spirit* (London: Bowes & Bowes, 1953), 198.

9 *Ibid.*, 199.

10 *Ibid.*, 197.

11 *Ibid.*, 198.

12 During World War II the British expanded their Middle East informal empire by occupying Libya, Syria, Lebanon, southern Iran, Eritrea and Somalia.

13 Morris, *Farewell*, 438.

14 Callahan, R.A., *Churchill. Retreat from Empire* (Wilmington: Scholarly Resources, 1984), 100.

15 Cain, P.J., 'J.A. Hobson, Cobdenism and the Radical Theory of Economic Imperialism 1898–1914', *Economic History Review*, 31 (1978), 565–584.

16 Hobson, *Imperialism*, 106.

17 *Ibid.*, 201–202.

18 *Ibid.*, 235.

19 *Ibid.*, 227.

20 *Ibid.*, 235.

21 Louis, W.R., *Imperialism at Bay, 1941–1945* (Oxford: Clarendon Press, 1977), chapter 5.

22 Hess, G.R., *America Encounters India* (Baltimore: Johns Hopkins University Press, 1971), 74.

23 Lenin, V.I., *Imperialism. The Highest Stage of Capitalism* (Moscow: Progress Publishers, 1975).

24 Winslow, E.M., 'Marxian, Liberal, and Sociological Theories of Imperialism', *The Journal of Political Economy* 39, 6 (1931), 737.

25 Moon, P.T., *Imperialism and World Politics* (New York: Macmillan, 1927).

26 Winslow, *Marxian*, 747.

27 Spillman, K.L., 'Wilsonian Ideas and European Politics', in Den Hollander, A.N.J., *Contagious Conflict* (Leiden: E.J. Brill, 1973), 156.

28 Gann, L.H. & Duignan, P., 'Reflections on Imperialism and the Scramble for Africa', in Gann, L.H. & Duigan, P., *Colonialism in Africa, 1870–1961* (Cambridge: Cambridge University Press, 1969), 104.

29 Etherington, N., 'Reconsidering Theories of Imperialism', *History and Theory* 21, 1 (1982), 17.

30 Porter, B., *Critics of Empire* (London: Macmillan, 1968), 235.

31 Morel, T., *Red Rubber* (Honolulu: University of the Pacific Press, 2005).

32 Gallagher, *Decline*, 117.

33 Howe, S., *Anticolonialism in British Politics* (Oxford: Clarendon Press, 1993), 320.

34 *Ibid.*, 82.

35 Hathaway, R.M., *Ambiguous Partnership. Britain and America 1944–1947* (New York: Columbia University Press, 1981), 234–235.

36 Thorne, C., *Allies of a Kind* (Oxford: Oxford University Press, 1978), 212.

37 Howe, *Anticolonialism*, 192–195.

38 *Ibid.*, 221.

39 *Ibid.*, ix.

40 Morris, *Farewell*, 210.

41 Hitchens, C., *Blood, Class and Nostalgia* (New York: Farrar, Straus & Giroux, 1990), 124.

42 Newsom, D.D., *The Imperial Mantle* (Bloomington: Indiana University Press, 2001), 52.

43 Hathaway, *Ambiguous*, 303.

44 Lee, J.M. & Petter, M., *The Colonial Office, War, and Development Policy* (London: Institute for Commonwealth Studies, 1982), 137–138, 142.

45 *Ibid.*, chapter 4.

46 Callahan, *Churchill*, 96.

47 Thorne, *Allies*, 142.

48 *Ibid.*, 242–243.

49 *Ibid.*, 243.

50 US Vice-President Wallace advocated a 'century of the common man'; Lee, *Colonial*, 121.

51 Morris, *Farewell*, 466.

52 Hess, *America*, 17.

53 *Ibid.*, 49.

54 Hathaway, *Ambiguous*, 256.

55 Thorne, *Allies*, 76.

56 Kimball, W.F., *The Juggler* (Princeton: Princeton University Press, 1991), 146.

57 Thorne, *Allies*, 83.

58 Newsom, *Imperial*, 52.

59 Hess, *America*, 366.

60 Clymer, K.J., 'Franklin Roosevelt, Louis Johnson, India and Anticolonialism. Another Look', *Pacific Historical Review* (1988), 57.

61 Many employees of OCOI/OWI were social activists strongly influenced by the ideas of Hobson, Moon and Morel.

62 Howe, *Anticolonialism*, 137.

63 *Ibid.*, 128.

64 Hess, *America*, 70.

65 *Ibid.*, 239.
66 Hess, *America*, 70, 29–30, 113, 122.
67 *Ibid.*, 15.
68 Clymer, 'Franklin', 262.
69 Lee, *Colonial*, 116–117; and Hess, *America*, 103, 128, 115–119.
70 Lee, *Colonial*, 137.
71 Thorne, *Allies*, 220–223, 457.
72 See Lee, *Colonial*.
73 Hathaway, *Ambiguous*, 231–232.
74 Callahan, *Churchill*, 99.
75 *Ibid.*, 96 & 147; and Howe, *Anticolonialism*, 140.
76 Clarke, P., *The Last Thousand Days of the British Empire* (London: Allen Lane, 2007), 471.
77 *Ibid.*, 264.
78 *Ibid.*, 263.
79 *Ibid.*, 373.
80 *Ibid.*, 489.
81 *Ibid.*, 418.
82 *Ibid.*, 235.
83 McKercher, B.J.C., *Transition of Power. Britain's Loss of Global Pre-eminence to the United States* (Cambridge: Cambridge University Press, 1999), 409.
84 Smith, T., *The Pattern of Imperialism* (Cambridge: Cambridge University Press, 1981), 160–161.
85 Thorne, *Allies*, 241.
86 *Ibid.*, 242.
87 Clarke, *Last*, 509.
88 Watt, *Succeeding*, 232, 245.
89 Louis, W.R. & Robinson, Wm.R., 'The United States and the liquidation of the British Empire in Tropical Africa, 1941–1951', in Gifford, P. & Louis, Wm.R. (eds), *The Transfer of Power in Africa. Decolonization 1940–1960* (New Haven: Yale University Press, 1982), 46–47.
90 James Burnham, who wrote *The Managerial Revolution*, exercised much influence over American intellectuals, politicians and journalists during the 1940s–1950s. The CIA often contracted him to write policy documents and he wrote the briefing notes for America's team at Yalta.
91 Hitchens, *Blood*, 245.
92 *Ibid.*, 252.
93 *Ibid.*, 261–262.
94 Hess, *America*, 182.
95 McMahon, R.J., *Colonialism and Cold War* (Ithaca: Cornell University Press, 1981), 277.
96 Louis & Robinson, 'The United States', 46.
97 Louis, W.R., *Imperialism at Bay, 1941–1945* (Oxford: Clarendon Press, 1977), 105.
98 *Ibid.*, 105.
99 *Ibid.*, 113.

100 Harris, K., *Attlee* (London: Weidenfeld & Nicolson, 1982), 355.

101 *Ibid.*, 385.

102 *Ibid.*, 355.

103 Britain knew America preferred its Palestine policy be implemented by the UN.

104 Clarke, *Last*, 509.

105 *Ibid.*, 397.

106 Louis, *Imperialism*, 125.

107 Howe, *Anticolonialism*, 135–136, 278.

108 Harris, *Attlee*, 366.

109 *Ibid.*, 135.

110 Howe, *Anticolonialism*, 93–102.

111 The Labour Party's radical left saw Fabian reformism as too conservative and set about changing Labour Party policy. By the mid-1950s they succeeded; so radical anticolonialism thereafter set the tone for much British Parliamentary discussion of colonial affairs.

112 Hathaway, *Ambiguous*, 301–302.

113 Hitchens, *Blood*, 257–258.

114 Gallagher, *Decline*, 145.

115 Watt, *Succeeding*, 117.

116 Louw, P.E., *The Rise, Fall and Legacy of Apartheid* (Westport: Praeger, 2004), chapter 2.

117 McKercher, *Transition*, 337.

118 America had also wanted Britain to transfer Hong Kong to China. This was shelved once communists took control of China.

119 Dueck, C., *Reluctant Crusaders* (Princeton: Princeton University Press, 2006), 89.

120 Gardner, L.C., LaFeber, W. & McCormick, T., *Creation of the American Empire: US Diplomatic History* (Chicago: Rand McNally, 1973), 476, 487.

121 Thorne, *Allies*, 600.

122 Nkrumah, K., *Neo-colonialism* (London: Heineman, 1968).

123 Smith, *Pattern*, 192.

124 Gallagher, *Decline*, 144.

125 Morris, *Farewell*, 503–504.

126 *Ibid.*, 503.

127 Louis & Robinson, 'The United States', 51.

128 Cohen, A., *British Policy in Changing Africa* (Evanston: Northwestern University Press, 1959), 99–100.

129 *Ibid.*, 32, 36, 60, 104, 106, 111.

130 *Ibid.*, 61, 114.

131 Winks, R.W., 'On Decolonization and Informal Empire', *The American Historical Review* 81, 3 (1976), 552.

132 Louis & Robinson, 'The United States', 24.

133 Fanon, F., *The Wretched of the Earth* (New York: Grove Press, 168), 149, 178–179.

134 *Ibid.*, 178–179.

135 Watt, *Succeeding*, 127.
136 Morris, *Farewell*, 526.
137 Gardner, *Creation*, 480.
138 Takeyh, R., *The Origins of the Eisenhower Doctrine* (London: Macmillan, 2000), 152.
139 Black, J., *The British Seaborne Empire* (New Haven: Yale University Press, 2004), 326.
140 Horowitz, D., 'Attitudes of British Conservatives towards Decolonization in Africa', *African Affairs*, 1, 274 (1970), 16.
141 Lee, *Colonial*, 249.
142 Howe, *Anticolonialism*, 220–221.
143 *Ibid.*, 231, 238.
144 *Ibid.*, 324–326, 329.
145 Cain, P. & Hopkins, A., 'Gentlemanly Capitalism and British Overseas Expansion', *The Economic History Review*, 40, 1 (1987).
146 Harris, *Attlee*, 385.
147 Horowitz, 'Attitudes', 9.
148 Pratt, C., 'Colonial Governments and the Transfer of Power in East Africa', in Gifford & Louis, *Transfer*, 261.
149 Wood, J.R.T., *The Welensky Papers. A History of the Federation of Rhodesia & Nyasaland* (Durban: Graham Publishing, 1983), 207.
150 Pratt, 'Colonial', 262.
151 Goldsworthy, D., *Colonial Issues in British Politics 1945–1961* (Oxford: Clarendon Press, 1971), 362.
152 Black, *Seaborne*, 324.
153 *Ibid.*, 325.
154 Goldsworthy, *Colonial*, 363.
155 *Ibid.*, 361.
156 Welensky, R., *4000 Days. The Life and Death of the Federation of Rhodesia & Nyasaland* (London: Collins, 1964), 319.
157 Watt, *Succeeding*, 135.
158 Hitchens, *Blood*, 282.
159 Louw, *Rise*, 62–65.
160 Hitchens, *Blood*, 24–25.
161 Smith, *Pattern*, 101.
162 McIntyre, W.D., *British Decolonization, 1946–1997* (London: Macmillan, 1998), 88.
163 Hitchens, *Blood*, 261–262.
164 *Ibid.*, 297–298, 306.
165 *Ibid.*, 295.
166 *Ibid.*, 286.

8

Cloning America 1: selling 'development'

I am firmly of the belief that if we are to arrive at a stable peace it must involve the development of backward countries. Backward peoples. (Franklin Roosevelt)

When President Clinton announced the 'we have it within our means ... to lift billions and billions of the people around the world into the global middle class' the barely disguised subtext was one that most Americans find reassuring: globalization meant that 'they' would become more like 'us'. (Andrew Bacevich, *American Empire*)

To function well, the Pax Americana as a comprador-based informal empire needs independent states, run by people 'sympathetic' to tying their countries into America's trading network. Generally, the best comprador-partners are middle-class people. Consequently, after World War II, much energy was invested into encouraging the growth of middle-class elites across the Third World, with the framework of what was called 'nation building'. From this grew a 1950s to 1960s development industry operating from North America and Western Europe. Initially, this industry was geared to preparing Europe's empires for independence by 'developing' urban middle classes with the necessary political, economic and administrative skills to lead each imperial possession to independence. Hence, 'development' effectively meant 'liberalization' – i.e. an attempt to promote liberal democracy and capitalism in these new Third World states. Because this was essentially an exercise in Westernization, the provision of Western education to Asians and Africans was a central feature of this development process.

This highlights some interesting similarities and differences between the American (informal) and British (formal) approaches to empire. Firstly, both were geared to building trading partners, and so both had a vested interest in 'development'. However, when the British encountered weak states and people whom they deemed unable to govern themselves well enough to be viable trading partners, they took control themselves by annexing these areas to the empire; then actively intervening to establish what they deemed satisfactory governance and infrastructures for commerce and trade to flourish.[1]

So Britons took direct responsibility for 'development' by going into the field to impose ('British') order, build infrastructures and establish businesses. America, on the other hand, prefers not to take such direct responsibility for establishing the governance and infrastructures needed for trade. Instead, Americans prefer local comprador-partners to do this for them. This means the Pax Americana faces difficulties the Pax Britannica did not – i.e. because the British appointed their own governors and officials they could ensure quality control over governance. In the Pax Americana, if compradors turn out to be corrupt, incompetent or simply demagogues (as has often been the case), Washington cannot fire them the way London could fire its governors. (Instead Washington has to mount expensive 'regime change' operations.) This is one of the reasons the Pax Americana has generated so many instances of poor governance, corruption and failed states.

Secondly, there are differences between the Pax Americana and Pax Britannica notions of 'development'. Lord Lugard (who had a major influence on British Colonial Office policy from the 1920s) argued the British empire had a 'dual mandate' to develop British trading interests and to simultaneously progress the 'native' peoples materially and morally.[2] Lugard's vision of development was, like America's, grounded in the promotion of global trade. He believed Britain's imperial interventions (driven by trade) were not only good for Britain, but were also good for natives of the colonial possessions, because Britain's efforts to build trade generated employment/ wealth and diffused skills in places like Africa. Lugard's key development argument was that Britain should train 'native' middle managers. These native middle managers (rather than white colonial officials) would become the 'face' of British governance with whom local people actually interacted on a daily basis. He saw this as part of a civilizing mission in which the wealth derived from trade was used to train locals in the art of good governance. Significantly, Lugard aimed to leave existing native authorities largely intact. Training would empower the traditional authorities by giving them the ability to govern effectively and thereby the ability to protect their local native producers (and their culture) against the intrusion of white planter economies. Within this Lugardian vision, Britain's empire was a 'trustee' for development and a long-term 'training academy in liberal democracy'.[3] It is important to note the Lugardian 'development' model differs from the Pax Americana 'development' model, because Pax Americana development is geared to producing Third World middle-class elites who are Westernized (i.e. 'clones' of middle-class America); whereas Lugard's model was geared to actually preserving existing local authorities and cultures, but then grafting onto these the techniques of good governance. So in the British model, the local middle managers would not resemble the British middle class, but would, rather, be 'translaters' between their own local culture and the culture of the British Colonial Office for whom they worked. In other words, British empire 'development' did not promote a middle-class social engineering model of radically transforming society (into new middle class-led 'nation states'). Rather, it was a gradualist development model promising to incrementally transform the empire into a multiracial Commonwealth based on Confederalism and cultural pluralism (an outcome quite different to the Pax Americana model of secularized independent nation states governed by Westernized compradors).

However, after World War II, the British Colonial Office, adjusted itself to the reality of American global power, and abandoned the Lugardian approach in favour of America's preference for developing (Westernized) middle-class elites prepared to run secular-liberal nation states and serve as comprador-partners of America's empire. This policy shift to 'modernization' was put into effect by the Colonial Development & Welfare Act 1945. Unfortunately for the British, this policy shift had the unintended consequence of producing radicalized middle classes who demanded immediate independence.[4] Refusing to grant independence threatened to produce (Soviet-funded) armed rebellion and communist governments. To halt this radicalization process, independence was eventually granted to many Third World states before the 'development' process had been completed – i.e. before they were deemed 'ready' for independence.[5] For the Pax Americana, this generated the problem of underdeveloped states ill-prepared to be valuable members of America's trading network. Consequently, Westerners concluded 'underdeveloped' states (who prefer to call themselves 'the developing world') needed to be taught, through 'development' programmes, the appropriate skills to govern themselves and run Western economies (so they could become reliable trading partners within the Pax Americana). This produced a new type of 'development industry' – one focused on already-independent states deemed poorly organized.

Effectively, the reconfiguration of the world under the Pax Americana has led to the emergence of five types of 'state'

- First-tier states are those inside the Union (e.g. California). Citizens of these fifty states get to vote not only for the United States of America government, but effectively also for the government of the Pax Americana.

- Second-tier states are liberal democracies with ties to America (e.g. Britain, Germany, Italy, Japan, Canada, Australia). These states are inside an American-led consultation network. Although citizens of second-tier states do not vote for the Pax Americana government, second-tier governments are consulted by Washington.

- Third-tier states are seen as both capable of organizing themselves and as valuable trading partners (e.g. China, Russia). However, because they do not organize themselves using America's preferred (liberal-democracy) model, they are viewed with some suspicion, excluded from Washington's consultation network, and some are seen as future political competitors.

- Fourth, are the states deemed 'rogues' (e.g. North Korea), which Washington sees to be in need of 'regime change' so they can be brought into the fold of the Pax Americana.

- Fifth-tier states are those deemed poorly organized – i.e. 'underdeveloped' states that still need to learn how to organize themselves economically and politically. They are deemed in need of 'development' in order to make them valuable to the Pax Americana's global trading network and/or to stop them serving as 'power vacuums' that can be used by criminal gangs, 'terrorists' or America's global competitors. During the 1950s the term 'Third World' began to be applied to these underdeveloped states.[6]

Fifth-tier states have presented Washington with a particular set of challenges. They are weak, fragile or even failed states characterized by poor governance, corruption, poor infrastructures and a lack of the cultural capital required to organize or develop themselves into the sort of 'nation states' preferred by Washington. Their weakness and poor governance makes them precisely the sort of places the British empire would have annexed in order to establish satisfactory conditions for commerce and trade. But what can Washington do to create satisfactory conditions for commerce and trade given that America (unlike Britain) does not run a formal empire; claims to be morally opposed to 'imperialism'; and does not possess the sort of ruling class capable and prepared to govern distant colonies. The Pax Americana's solution has been the growth of a 'development industry' (geared to 'teaching' good governance, and building cultural capital and functioning infrastructures). In effect, the 'development industry' was deployed as an alternative to formal imperialism (where imperialists directly intervened to establish 'satisfactory conditions'). The informal empire approach involves trying to 'improve conditions' through pedagogy, persuasion and consultation.

So what is the nature of the 'development' being undertaken? Answering this question requires unpacking some key assumptions of the Pax Americana's style of 'development'.

Assumptions underpinning Pax Americana 'development'

Americans came to see themselves as 'exceptional'. And once they came to believe that the American way of life, social order and political system was self-evidently superior, it was easy to reach the conclusion the whole world would benefit from adopting America's socio-political and economic system.

This belief in the superiority of 'the American way' underpins America's preferred model of 'development' and social change. At heart, this model can be traced back to Jefferson's conceptualization of spreading American 'liberty' westward across the continent to the Pacific.

Jefferson's 'empire of liberty'

Jefferson's 'empire of liberty' was premised upon the notion that American 'democracy', 'freedom' and state-formation were simply superior. Jefferson advocated spreading the American model across the American continent within an 'Enlightenment vision of a benign imperial order'.[7] Spreading this model across North America necessarily involved taking control of territory, then reconfiguring that territory politically, economically and socially until a new 'state' was deemed ready ('developed' enough) for incorporation into the Union. Each of these new states replicated America's model of state-building. Hence, rolling out the 50 states across the continent involved a cloning process. It was also an intensely imperialist process of incorporating other people's territory into America's own political formation. The result was America's first empire (shown in map 3) – an empire based on conquest, colonization and cloning. In this way Jefferson's republican union spread irresistibly westward through a proliferation (cloning) of 'free republican states'.[8] The irony is, this process of westward expansion and state formation ultimately produced an American political culture which, because it is now morally opposed to imperialism and colonialism, needs to obfuscate its own history.

The Jeffersonian model of cloning 'democratic states' did not die with the ending of America's first empire. Instead, a modified version of this Jeffersonian 'cloning' model now effectively underpins today's American vision of how (liberalized) 'development' should be rolled out across the 'underdeveloped' world – i.e. a key feature of America's (informal) third empire involves the idea of developing 'democratic states' across the world. Within America's third empire (operating since 1945), these new states are not created or developed by American settlers. Instead, they are run by their own indigenous people. However, since they are not deemed to be well run, the West operates a huge global development industry to teach people in fifth-tier states how to run democratic-capitalist societies. So a new form of 'control' called tutelage emerges. Another difference is that, once successfully developed, these new states are not destined to be incorporated into the American Union (as occurred in America's first empire). Instead, they are to be enmeshed, as client states, into the trade networks of America's (informal) third empire. So clientship replaces direct subjugation.

Universalizing 'democratic capitalism'

Jefferson's 'empire of freedom' idea was always grounded in an Enlightenment optimism and belief that Americans had found a 'recipe' to make the world a better place. It is an optimism that powerfully informed twentieth-century Wilsonian thinking about building a Pax Americana. But an important consequence of transferring Jefferson's 'empire of freedom' idea across to America's new informal empire is that Jeffersonian optimism tends to slide into a new kind of imperialism within which Americans increasingly look like they want to build a 'universal' global civilization. Effectively, Jefferson's democratic ideals are transformed into something akin to a religion of 'democracy' and 'universal human rights'. Within this religion, 'American democracy' and 'American values' slide into a pan-human universalism, which is intensely utopian. Hence, the Pax Americana, as globalization II, becomes ensnared in a new Jacobinism:

> It employs an idiom somewhat different from that of the earlier Jacobinism, and it incorporates various new ideological and other ingredients, but it is essentially continuous with the old urge to replace historically evolved societies with an order framed according to abstract, allegedly universal principles, notably that of equality. Like the old Jacobins, it does not oppose economic inequalities, but it scorns traditional religious, moral, and cultural preconceptions and social patterns ... The new Jacobins ... regard today's Western democracy as the result of great moral, social and political progress ... they see it as an approximation of what universal principles require ... [The new Jacobins] think globally. They put great stress on the international implications of their principles. The new Jacobinism is indistinguishable from democratism, the belief that democracy is the ultimate form of government and should be installed in all societies of the world. The new Jacobinism is the main ideological and political force behind present efforts to turn democracy into a worldwide moral crusade.[9]

The idea that Americans had found the 'recipe', which if applied to the whole world would make it a better place, is grounded in an 'American faith that it is a universal nation [which] implies that all humans are born American, and become anything else by accident – or error. According to this faith American values are, or will soon be, shared by all humankind'.[10]

At heart is the belief 'democratic capitalism' (in the form developed by Americans) is good for everybody.[11] Universalizing democratic capitalism certainly would be good for America, because a fundamental feature of America's organization is that 'American domestic vitality depends on continued expansion'.[12] This is because America's economy has to keep growing; which means continually searching for new markets. All three of America's empires have been grounded in this need to find new markets in order to keep the economy growing. The post-1945 informal empire is simply the most recent means to feed this market-driven economy. Clearly America's informal empire would work best if lots of little America-type 'democratic capitalist' states were cloned (or at least hybridized) across the globe. It would be better still if they were run by people who broadly shared American middle class values. Hence, not surprisingly, the Pax Americana's 'development industry' has not simply been intent on building infrastructures facilitating economic growth and trade; it has also been concerned with (Western) education and inculcating the sort of (Western secular materialist) values that drive American economic growth. This implies the simultaneous destruction of 'old' values and the traditional cultures in which they were embedded.

A Wilsonian informal empire

The problem faced by an informal empire like the Pax Americana is that when its trade-promotion agendas are impeded in fifth-tier states by poor infrastructures, poor governance and populations without the cultural capital required to run Western economies, it needs to employ *indirect* methods to try and rectify the situation. These indirect methods may not involve such drastic action as annexation (as used by formal empires) but they still involve intervention. And the preferred intervention of the Pax Americana has been to deploy specialists in Third World development – i.e. people working in the 'development industry' (often linked to the West's 'foreign aid industry'). The development industry has come to be inspired by a form of Jacobin thinking – i.e. a belief in middle-class-driven social engineering (of either a liberal or socialist variety). It is social engineering that intervenes into other people's lives to change them. Presumably those doing the intervention believe what they are doing is good – i.e. bringing about socio-economic change. In many ways this makes the development industry a form of contemporary 'missionary' activity in which (Western) 'believers' work to 'improve' non-Western societies.[13] But today's missionaries do not promote Christianity. Instead, the development agenda has been driven by a secular vision of social engineering that grew up in the context of building a Pax Americana after 1945. This agenda has been closely associated with a strong belief in 'education' as a key mechanism to roll out the skills (and attitudes) needed for 'progress'. Not surprisingly, we find the Wilsonian-liberal thinking of the Roosevelt/Hull-team (outlined in Table 8.1) has strongly influenced the broad trajectory of the development industry's vision of how to 'improve' the world.

The discursive framework of table 8.1, which has been widely propagated by Western intellectuals and journalists from the 1950s onwards, is highly compatible with the economic needs of America's informal trading empire, and with the 'moral universe' of middle-class America. When development

Positive	Negative
Democracy	Aristocratic elites and hierarchies/oligarchies/fascism/communism
Religious freedom within a secular state/society (Relativist pluralism)	Theocratized states/society
Cosmopolitanism	Ethnic-nationalism
Anti-imperialism Decolonization Self-determination within nation states Nation-building	Imperialism Colonialism Confederalism/Holism
Free trade/free movement of capital Capitalism Consumerism/materialism Property rights Liberalization	Anti-competitive behaviour/restrictions on trade/restrictions on enterprise and capital/tariffs/protectionism/imperial preference
Government creates conditions for capitalist-enterprise	Government decisions impeding capitalist-enterprise
Modernization and Development and Western education	Traditional society and Tribalism
Individualism	Collectivism
State formation around viable economic units (wherein different groups/nations/religions live together harmoniously)	Economic nationalism
Facilitating movement of labour: Migration Melting pot/assimilation Multiculturalism Cultural hybridization	Limiting movement of labour: Segregation Apartheid Racism Cultural autonomy
Peace (assured by multilateralism) Universalized 'human rights'	War (caused by imperialist and nationalist competition)
Progressive (teleology geared towards America as the 'universal state')	Reactionary

Table 8.1 Liberal thinking underpinning the post-1945 Western 'development industry'

programmes encoding these (Liberal) values are successfully rolled out, it produces populations sufficiently 'modernized' (i.e. 'Westernized' or culturally 'hybridized') to run self-governing client states and/or run Western economies that are valuable to America's informal trading empire.

American versus British 'development'

Both the Pax Britannica and Pax Americana engaged in development. And if we look at the development work done in the two empires there are some striking similarities. Most obviously, both the British and Americans built global trading empires which served to integrate the world's economy and create an international division of labour.[14] Effectively, the Pax Britannica and Pax Americana have jointly been the drivers of globalization.[15] In the process, both Britain and America have spread capitalism, industrialization, intensive agriculture, free trade, liberalism, democracy, Anglo-culture and the English language. But despite these similarities, there are some major differences between the British and American models of development. This is because the two models were driven by different assumptions and different social groups.

'Development' brought about by the British occurred when British merchants encountered weak states or peoples deemed unable to govern themselves well enough to be viable trading partners. Britain annexed such places and then dispatched colonial officials to these territories to 'develop' satisfactory conditions for commerce and trade. Significantly, this British development was driven by an alliance of Britain's upper and middle classes. Middle-class 'gentlemanly capitalists' built businesses and trading networks while the upper classes went to the colonies to build the machinery of bureaucracy and law-and-order. Significantly, these two classes shared no ideological vision of social change. Only Britain's church missionaries were motivated by any ideological zeal to change people in the colonies; but they were never central to the 'development' processes in Britain's empire. As a result, for most of the history of the British empire 'development' did not occur according to any 'ideological plan'; rather, it happened organically as gentlemanly capitalists built their trade networks, British settlers built businesses and farms, and colonial officials established governance and infrastructures (like railways, roads, hospitals and schools) to cope with demands being made on them. Further, Britain's middle class was driven by a desire to make money, not by any utopian social engineering vision; and Britain's governing upper class eschewed Jacobin social engineering projects (generally associated with middle-class utopians). So instead of trying to 'change' or westernize 'natives', British colonial governance generally worked closely with traditional authorities. Consequently, British 'development' was more respectful of indigenous traditions and culture than the Pax Americana approach to development, because Britons were not driven to 'engineer' or change indigenous cultures so as to produce clones of the British middle class. On the other hand, Britons were 'disrespectful' in so far as they made no apologies for intervening in places they deemed 'primitive'. And, unlike contemporary Americans, Britons made no pretence at political correctness when they perceived differences between cultures, races and societies functioning at different levels. Further, British 'development' involved no pretence at 'consultation', and sometimes even by-passed the local 'natives' by importing change/development agents from outside in the form of British managers and indentured or migrant labourers (e.g. Indians).

The post-1945 Pax Americana approach to development has been far more coherently organized, planned and professionalized. This is partly because Pax Americana 'development' has been organized by a group of professional 'developers' who share a relatively coherent 'development ideology'. This coherence is assisted by the fact those driving Pax Americana 'development' tend to be drawn from a relatively narrow social strata – i.e. middle-class professionals educated to share a similar vision of the world (involving 'democracy'; 'universal human rights'; and diffusing modern skills, ideas and technologies).

Although Americans like to believe their way of running the world is less brutal and interventionist than the methods used by the old European empires, Pax Americana 'development' has ironically generally been far more culturally interventionist than British development was. This has occurred precisely because America has run an informal empire. Informal empires imply 'indirect' governance, which means the Pax Americana (ideally) needs middle-class comprador partners in each independent state.[16] This translates into a need to try and systematically build (Westernized) middle-class elites in the Third World through education, and 'nation building' and 'development' exercises. This means changing indigenous people through ethnocentric (i.e. Westernizing) social change projects. Because of the need to build comprador partners, Pax Americana 'development' has often involved Jacobinian social engineering which has been culturally destructive of traditional societies in the Third World.[17] Liberal Jacobins also learned to successfully deploy the rhetoric of 'democracy' as a powerful agent for undermining traditional societies across the globe.[18] Once these traditional elites have been undermined, they are replaced with middle-class elites who then become local agents for secular nation building, and comprador-partners for the Pax Americana. In many cases these new middle-classes compradors have not served the Pax Americana well because they become exploitative and repressive and/or incompetent and corrupt rulers. But because the Pax Americana is an informal empire, it lacks the sort of direct imperial mechanisms Britain possessed to correct such problems. Instead Washington imposes sanctions or launches 'regime change' wars.

Another difference is that, whereas Pax Britannica 'development' deliberately set aside 'native reserves' where traditional cultures could survive alongside the areas of 'British development', Pax Americana development intrudes everywhere. This is hardly surprising given Pax Americana's liberal Jacobins are driven by a compulsion to universalize their vision of a 'better world'. Because America is seen as a 'universal state', Americans believe they are doing the world a service by spreading their 'empire of liberty'. The resultant Pax Americana's 'development' unleashes a complex mix of middle-class cloning (i.e. comprador building); the destruction of traditional elites (though promoting the ideologies of 'democratization' and 'egalitarianism'); an ever-growing network of trade relations; Westernization; Anglicization; the undermining of traditional cultures and indigenous languages; cultural homogenization (in some places) and cultural hybridization (in other places). This 'development' has also unleashed resistance, e.g. Al-Qaeda. If America's 'empire of liberty' is ever 'universalized', there will be two (interconnected) outcomes – American values and practices will be universalized and America itself will be changed ('culturally hybridized') by its global empire.

The mutating 'development industry'

In the two decades after 1945, European empires were dismantled and replaced by the Pax Americana. It was Washington's intention to expand its informal empire over these areas, and from this arose the need to develop a policy framework for how to deal with these decolonized regions. Effectively, America discovered granting self-determination did not necessarily mean the production of functioning states with the capacity for effective self-governance or the capacity to manage their own economies. Instead, decolonization produced 'underdeveloped' states that were not the valuable trading partners America had hoped for. If they were to be turned into valuable trading partners, intervention was required to build a core of (middle-class) people in each new state able to govern effectively and run the businesses, mines and farms America wanted to trade with. The recognition that intervention was required gave rise to the development industry.

But in the 1950s and 1960s America was not going to explicitly frame discussions of 'development' in terms of the obstacles that 'underdevelopment' posed to building their informal empire, because:

• Americans had argued for the self-determination of these states precisely as a means to end empires.

- Americans had only recently been arguing empires represented an unjust system of European domination and exploitation.

- If America was seen to be behaving imperially, Third World states might align themselves with the Soviet bloc. In fact, the Third World became the key sphere for American–Soviet Cold War rivalry.

So instead, the issue of underdevelopment (and its solution) was reframed within a discourse of modernization. This made it sound as if 'development' was driven by Third World needs rather than Pax Americana (trading) needs.

Development as modernization

Modernization is liberalism's theory of change. It is premised upon a binary opposition between 'traditional' and 'modern' societies. To be 'modern' is supposed to be better than 'traditional'. Within modernization discourse, America is the ultimate modern state – it is seen to have advanced furthest in a teleological chain leading from 'backwardness' ('traditional') to 'advanced' ('modern').[19] This picture of the world encodes similar assumptions to those that drove the British empire – i.e. Britain was deemed a civilized and advanced society which, when it encountered backward and primitive societies, annexed them in order to develop and uplift them. This was often called the civilizing mission of empire. American modernization theory sanitized, disguised and replaced this 'civilizing mission' idea by deploying the language of positivist science.[20] But ultimately, 'modernization' is a language of (informal) imperialism serving to justify Americans telling the rest of the world how they ought to be organizing themselves. This new language of imperialism encoded Western superiority,[21] and assumed there was only one pathway to modernity[22] – i.e. following the path America had already taken. The latter implied America was the benchmark to be reached, or 'universal state' to be cloned. And the cloning mechanism was to be found in the scientific method of 'development'. This method offered a blueprint to facilitate liberal-capitalist 'take-off'.[23]

Modernization theory presented itself as benevolent and grounded in universally valid scientific laws (i.e. it claimed all societies passed through the same stages of development).[24] Effectively, this encoded into a 'scientific theory' the idea of America's manifest destiny as a 'universal state' worthy of being copied by all others. Modernization theory was American middle-class utopianism which postulated the 'American way' as the endpoint of a progressive teleology. So just as the British had previously seen their empire as a progressive force in the world, now it was America's turn to be this progressive force – and to take up the role of being a 'civilizer', 'developer' and agent of 'universal' values. But in the American version, social engineers sought to actively plan and implement social change so as to bring about their (utopian) vision for a better (universalized) world.

This notion of being a 'developer' of the world was formulated at a particular moment in time – i.e. a post-World War II world where the only obstacle to implementing Wilson's dream was Soviet power. Modernization theory therefore encoded three American concerns:[25]

- transforming Third World decolonized states into reliable trading partners within America's global trading network;

- preventing the spread of communism to the Third World ('containment') by ensuring the new states were developed according to the principles of democratic capitalism;

- a desire to spread American socio-political organization and values (i.e. the American 'way of life').

So modernization was the American dream writ large. If the 'American way' could be cloned across the world then, the liberal utopians would argue, one could eventually end up with global peace – this would be an American Peace (Pax Americana) where there would no longer be any reason to fight wars because the whole world would agree on the rules governing the global trading network; America's vision of 'human rights' would have been universalized; all self-determining states would be ruling elites governed by people educated to share American values and aspirations; and ethnic, cultural and religious conflicts would be a thing of the past because a process of globalized cultural homogenization/hybridization (i.e. Americanization/ secularization). This liberal-utopian vision assumes some kind of Francis Fukuyama-type 'end of history' or 'end of ideology' can be attained where wars end, because all countries have become the same and have McDonald's hamburgers! For the utopians, promoting modernization was the way to socially engineer this 'better world' into existence. So modernization theory was not about analysing the Third World; it was about what America was already like,[26] and about the modernizers' desire to clone America globally. This did not mean 'foreign-ness' would disappear, but it did mean foreigners would become more like Americans, and that 'deficient' (i.e. traditional) cultures would disappear.[27]

The key drivers of this modernization vision were Walt Rostow, Lucian Pye, Daniel Lerner, Gabriel Almond and Edward Shils.[28] Some were Cold War warriors.[29] The origins of this theory lay in American sociology and so it encoded functionalism, the idea of linear evolutionary change, an optimistic belief in progress, and the assumption that universal models could be built because all humans were essentially the same (irrespective of different historical, environmental or cultural factors).[30] Rostow[31] and Lerner[32] laid the foundation for modernization theory by establishing the 'traditional' versus 'modern' dichotomy. Significantly Rostow's five-stage model of moving from traditional to modern ended with a mass consumer society – clearly an ideal situation for an American global trading empire. Pye was instrumental in shifting the focus towards what developers needed to do to bring about 'political modernization'. American-assisted nation building was deemed to be central to the process of modernizing the Third World.

Modernization theorists saw traditional culture as an obstacle to modernization and modern economic growth. Their fundamental concern was with how to remove the obstacles, so a Rostovian take-off could be initiated. The aim was to develop 'primitive' (traditional) people so they could 'catch up' with and 'imitate' the developed world.[33] Hence a core objective was diffusing 'modern values' to elites in the Third World.[34] The modernizers also put great emphasis on transferring capital and technology to the Third World, and diffusing the cultural capital required to operate this technology and to run Western economies. In many ways modernization was about diffusing not only Western technology and skills, but also diffusing Weber's Protestant work ethic.[35] In this regard education and mass media were important agents for change. Ultimately the development industry sought to diffuse modernity in a variety of ways, including the building of (Western) schools in the Third World; encouraging Third World people to attend Western universities; dispatching agricultural extension officers; funding NGOs as development agents; and sending Western 'role models' into the Third World, such as the American Peace Corps.[36]

An important feature of modernization theory was its utopian belief in teleological progress. These modernizers held true to the spirit of American (Enlightenment) optimism in believing the world was perfectible, and Americans had discovered the way to perfect it. A key feature of this belief was traditional societies were fated to vanish because, advanced/civilized societies (i.e. modern America) were 'destined' (according to modernism's teleological logic) to replace traditional/'backward' societies. This ideological belief that traditional societies were destined to vanish because of the 'intrinsic deficiencies' of 'backward'/primitive cultures served to justify the modernizers' Jacobin interventionism,[37] and served to hide their role as social engineers who were effectively destroying other peoples' cultures. Those inside the development industry with a missionary belief in what they were doing simply did not recognize the cultural arrogance that underpinned their modernist-development schemes. So when, as social engineers, they designed 'development' interventions to detach Third World people from traditional family, religious and cultural bonds,[38] they believed they were doing a good thing by shifting these people towards the modern world. As Jacobins they showed no concern about the destruction of indigenous cultures and languages or the individual social dislocation and pain they caused. And because American modernizers saw no value in traditional society, they left no spaces (such as the British empire's 'native reserves') where people had the choice to opt out of 'development'. In the Pax Americana, traditional culture was fated to disappear because the liberal-Jacobin development industry was going to work hard to make sure it did disappear. The liberal-development industry was extraordinarily disrespectful of others if they happened to be traditional people. These traditional people apparently had no right to survive in the face of the universalizing of American middle classism. The outcome of 'development' was often a legacy of people who were both traumatized and not able to function in either traditional or Western societies. Many of these people now live marginal lives in the shanty towns that surround cities like Nairobi, Johannesburg, Karachi, Manila and Jakarta.

Critics of modernization

Although the modernization paradigm was dominant amongst Western academics from 1950 to the mid-1960s, it was not without its critics. On the right emerged opposition to Third World 'aid' on the grounds that aid undermined local entrepreneurship. On the left, dependency theorists argued Western development served to tie Third World countries into subservient relationships with First World capitalists which facilitated the exploitation of the Third World.[39]

An American Marxist, Paul Baran, initiated dependence theory, which then grew into an influential anti-modernization paradigm.[40] Baran argued Third World underdevelopment and First World development were interrelated processes. He argued the underdeveloped peripheries remained locked into socio-economic relationships with the First World core because Western imperialism effectively continued after the end of the European colonial era. From this grew the idea that underdevelopment was caused by the decisions made by First World capitalists. Hence, Third World backwardness was deemed to be caused by Third World dependency on the First World – i.e. First World development/growth and affluence was seen to be the result of capitalist exploitation in which wealth was being transferred from the Third to First Worlds. The most sophisticated formulation of this argument was developed by a non-Marxist, Immanuel Wallerstein, who recognized the world had been enmeshed into a single (capitalist) economic system[41]– a globalization process that had begun in the fifteenth century when European imperialism got underway. Wallerstein's world systems theory proposed equal development was impossible within this global capitalist system because the system encoded unequal exchange between the core and the periphery. Dependency theory became very influential in Latin America, where it was deployed by intellectuals like Andre Gunder Frank.[42]

The Latin American dependency theorists argued modernization taken to the Third World by the development industry was bad because it caused underdevelopment on the peripheries and generated growing inequalities in Third World countries. These dependency theorists argued if Third World countries wanted real development, they needed to cut themselves off from America's global trading network and achieve self-reliance by developing themselves. This led to the call for a new international economic order (NIEO) which, if implemented, would have seriously disrupted the Pax Americana's global trading network. Dependency theory and NIEO consequently became enmeshed in the Cold War competition for influence and control over the Third World. From the 1970s onwards the expanding influence of dependency theory across the Third World became a growing problem for the Pax Americana.

The Cold War struggle between modernization and dependency theorists hinged on two opposing explanations about the causes of underdevelopment. The modernization theorists saw the problem as being *internal* to these underdeveloped states – i.e. they believed the indigenous people of these states lacked the appropriate cultural capital, skills and know-how to effectively manage their own political and economic systems. Amongst other things these deficiencies meant they were unable to accumulate capital. This lack of capital and skills were deemed the key obstacles to Third World growth and development. The development and aid industries proposed intervening from the outside to rectify these deficiencies. The dependency theorists, on the other hand, believed the problem was not internal to these states; rather, the problem was *external* – it was caused by a global capitalist system that exploited Third World states. The dependency theorists did much to popularize the idea across the Third World that Western imperialism was responsible for pauperizing Third World peoples by destroying their indigenous economies.

The idea that globalized capitalism was responsible for pauperization and underdevelopment served as a very useful ideology for bringing together Marxists and Third World nationalists during the Cold War era.[43] Politicians in Africa, Asia and the Middle East looking for an excuse for the poor performance of their countries found dependency theory invaluable. This theory helped them to deflect attention away from their own poor performance, and fed into a culture of victimhood. The latter was used to argue the West was morally obliged to provide aid to the Third World because the West was responsible for their poverty. Ironically this served to create another form of dependency in which many Third World people learned not to take responsibility for their own lives, but instead waited for outsiders to come and 'fix' things for them and even to feed them.

Dependency theory may have been correct in pointing to the inter-connectedness of the global economy brought about by the building of globalized trade networks by Britain and America. However, when dependency theorists grafted onto this the notion the West could be blamed for pauperizing the Third World, they were simply constructing an ideology useful for political mobilization. This ideology was only tenable if contradictory evidence was ignored:

- Labour rates were not necessarily worse in the Third World,[44] especially when one factored in the often low labour productivity rates in parts of the Third World caused by cultural capital deficits.

- Poverty and underdevelopment existed in parts of the world largely un-touched by the west (e.g. Tibet, Afghanistan and Ethiopia).[45] Pauperization theory did not explain this.

- The behaviour of Third World politicians and leaders was ignored as an important factor responsible for creating negative conditions that undermined development and created poverty.[46]

- Capitalist economies require certain conditions for success, such as the security provided by good governance; a legal system protecting property rights; a labour force with an appropriate work ethic and skills; transport and communication infrastructures; etcetera. Many Third World contexts have not provided these conditions. This was precisely one of the reasons Britain's empire annexed many regions – i.e. to establish the conditions required for economic development and trade.

- Western imperialism did carry out much successful development across the globe – i.e. building infrastructures and creating many viable new economies. Significantly, a number of the economies and infrastructures they built collapsed *after* decolonization (which caused an increase in poverty in places like Africa).

Dependency theory had always serviced the alliance between Third World nationalists and Marxists. So when the Soviet Union collapsed, dependency theory fell on hard times and the NIEO idea became untenable. Third World leaders found themselves confronting the harsh new reality that the 'Cold War leverage' American–Soviet competition had provided them, had now evaporated. Washington was no longer prepared to overlook the corruption, poor governance and even tyranny practised by many of their Third World middle-class compradors. Washington had previously ignored this out of a fear that if they complained, compradors would simply re-align themselves with the Soviet Union. When the Cold War ended, all Third World states found that aid as a mechanism to 'buy allegiance' ended, plus they had no choice but to now negotiate new relationships with the Pax Americana. And what America now demanded was competent compradors who could manage their states so as to provide reliable trading partners. As a result, the 1990s saw many regime changes across the Third World, and saw modernization put firmly back onto Washington's agenda. (This was coupled with the discourse of encouraging 'good governance'). These late twentieth-century Washington policies would have been instantly recognizable to nineteenth-century Britons who argued Britain's empire needed to intervene in African and Asia to improve conditions for trade.

Modernization revived

The collapse of the Soviet Union and rise of postmodern theory made Marxism unfashionable in intellectual circles, and so dependency theory, which had been the only serious anti-modernization theory, found itself out of favour.

It was Francis Fukuyama who heralded the rehabilitation of modernization theory when he proclaimed liberalism triumphant.[47] Fukuyama effectively proclaimed the idea of the USA as the 'universal state' which the rest of the world should emulate. Significantly, he also saw the spread of Western technology as the mechanism that 'guarantees an increasing homogenization of all human societies'.[48] Naturally, the end goal of this homogenization was the cloning of America and the universalizing of liberalism. And so the old idea of development as modernization (and liberalization) – entailing the diffusion of Western technology and skills – was revived.

However, by the 1990s liberal capitalism had itself evolved. And one of the changes this evolution had brought about was that capitalist businesses and the liberal state increasingly outsourced much of their work. This principle of outsourcing also came to underpin the development industry; and the bodies to which 'development work' was increasingly outsourced were non governmental organizations (NGOs). In fact, not only did Washington's traditional development and aid bureaucracies turn to NGOs for the delivery of their projects, but the US State Department and US Military also came to see NGOs as important partners in the execution of American foreign policy.[49] This was expressed in the 2001 *Joint Doctrine for Civil–Military Operations* which laid procedures for joint American military–NGO operations. This shift to working with NGOs was to impact on the modernization paradigm, because many of those working in the NGO sector were on the left of the political spectrum, which meant they were sympathetic to one or more of the following: green politics; a liberalized version of dependency theory (which believed western greed was responsible for Third World poverty); and participatory democracy. From this arose a new conceptualization of Third World interventionism – as articulated by the Swedish Dag Hammarskjöld Foundation and German Green movement – called 'Another Development'.[50] This meant although modernization theory had been revived, it was re-articulated to make it palatable to NGO partners who would be implementing it. The result has been a revitalized modernization paradigm in which some of the errors of the past are acknowledged and efforts are made to correct these, by incorporating the perspectives of 'Another Development'.[51]

The effect has been to turn the NGO sector into something akin to the Pax Americana's Colonial Office. America still needs to build middle-class elites (to function as its comprador partners).[52] Since the 1990s many of the old incompetent and corrupt Third World elites have been removed – some peacefully (e.g. Uganda) and others violently (e.g. Iraq). This meant a major exercise in training up new middle-class elites. Within this process the NGO sector has become central, because many Third World-based NGOs have becoming vehicles for simultaneously grooming and training new elites and for destabilizing regimes Washington deems illiberal. Consequently, since the 1990s, NGOs have been playing an important role in facilitating 'upward mobility' into the ranks of the Pax Americana's new compradorpartners,[53] and for mobilizing mass popular 'democratic' uprisings (i.e. 'liberalization campaigns') against regimes Washington does not like.[54] These NGOs have also helped disseminate the discourse of human rights – which effectively universalizes American middle-class values and American-style democracy.[55]

Interestingly, the old and revived modernization paradigms share much in common since both, after all, service the same American informal empire. But there are also differences caused by Washington having learned (in an era when outsourcing is fashionable) to even outsource elements of its informal empire's governance to the NGO sector. The result is that:

- NGOs foster a new type of cultural and economic colonialism – under the guise of a new internationalism. Hundreds of individuals sit in front of high-powered PCs exchanging manifestos, proposals and invitations to international conferences with each other. They then meet in well-furnished conference halls to discuss the latest struggles and offerings with their 'social base' – the paid staff – who then pass on the proposals to the 'masses' through flyers and 'bulletins'. When overseas funders show up, they are taken on 'exposure tours' to showcase projects where the poor are helping themselves and to talk with successful micro-entrepreneurs (omitting the majority who fail the first year). The way this colonialism works is not difficult to decipher. Projects are designed based on the guidelines and priorities of the imperial centres and their institutions. They are then 'sold' to the communities. Evaluations are done by and for the imperial institutions. Shifts of funding priorities or bad evaluations result in the dumping of groups, communities, farmers and cooperatives. Everybody is increasingly disciplined to comply with the donors' demands and their project evaluators. The NGO directors, as the new viceroys, supervise the proper use of funds and ensure conformity with the goals, values and ideology of the donors.[56]

So now we have an outsourced 'modernization and development' industry which helps to make Washington look even more removed from its informal empire. Much of the NGO-driven development process now appears so removed from Washington that many development-missionaries inside the NGO sector are unaware of their role in promoting the Pax Americana; their role in the diffusing the skills and values required for cloning democratic capitalism; or their role in 'stabilizing' the peripheries for the Pax Americana (through the delivery of health care, Aids prevention, refugee management, etcetera). But perhaps this is not so surprising – after all, many nineteenth-century Christian missionaries would not have thought of themselves as the agents of imperialism either.

But America is interested in global trade, not only Third World trade. Consequently, the Pax Americana needs to build trading partners and middle-class compradors across the entire world. In this regard it is instructive to look at American interventions into post World War II Germany and Japan because these interventions reveal much about how the Pax Americana would (if it could) reconstruct – i.e. 'liberalize' – all societies into clones of the American 'universal state'. At the end of the day America's interventions to build Germany and Japanese middle-class ruling elites, share much in common with the underlying assumptions of the development industry.

Notes

1 Gallagher, J., *The Decline, Revival and Fall of the British Empire* (Cambridge: Cambridge University Press, 1982), 7.
2 Lugard, F.D., *Dual Mandate in British Tropical Africa* (Edinburgh: W. Blackwood & Sons, 1922).
3 Owen, N., 'Critics of Empire in Britain', in Brown, J.M. & Louis W.R., *The Oxford History of the British Empire, Vol. IV* (Oxford: Oxford University Press, 1999), 193.
4 Gallagher, *Decline*, 148.
5 Goldsworthy, D., *Colonial Issues in British Politics 1945–1961* (Oxford: Clarendon Press, 1971), 363.
6 Worsley, P., *The Three Worlds* (London: Weidenfeld & Nicolson, 1984), 307.
7 Onuf, P.S., *Jefferson's Empire* (Charlottesville: University of Virginia Press, 2000), 53.
8 *Ibid.*, 53.
9 Ryn, C.G., *America the Virtuous* (New Brunswick: Transaction Publishers, 2004), 21.
10 Gray, J., *False Dawn* (London: Granta, 2002), 132.

11 *Ibid.*, 2.
12 Latham, M.E., *Modernization as Ideology* (Chapel Hill: University of North Carolina Press, 2000), 14.
13 The 'Western believers' can, of course, be Third World people who have been westernized.
14 Fieldhouse, D.K., *The West and the Third World* (Oxford: Blackwell, 1999), 164.
15 Fieldhouse, *West*, notes there are two conflicting interpretations of globalization based upon free trade. Optimists say such globalization is good for everyone, while pessimists say it is not good for everyone. This book is not concerned with debating which of these positions is correct. However, what this book does note is that both the Pax Britannica and Pax Americana have promoted globalization based upon free trade, and both have grounded their actions in the optimistic assumption that such globalization is good for everyone.
16 Bacevich, A.J., *American Empire. The Realities and Consequences of US Diplomacy* (Cambridge: Harvard University Press, 2002), 41.
17 Middle-class Jacobins have also successfully unleashed the rhetoric of 'democratic capitalism' against traditional elites of Europe.
18 Ryn, *America*, 25.
19 Latham, *Modernization*, 58–59.
20 Engerman, D.C. *et al.*, *Staging Growth* (Amherst: University of Massachusetts Press, 2003), 35.
21 *Ibid.*, 38.
22 *Ibid.*, 39.
23 Latham, *Modernization*, 210.
24 *Ibid.*, 16.
25 *Ibid.*, 19.
26 Engerman, *Staging*, 57.
27 Latham, *Modernization*, 213.
28 Samuel Huntington (*Political Order in Changing Society*) produced a more sophisticated modernization theory in the late–1960s.
29 Leys, C., *The Rise & Fall of Development Theory* (London: James Currey, 1996), 10.
30 Latham, *Modernization*, 30–35.
31 Rostow, W.W., *The Stages of Economic Growth. A Non-communist Manifesto* (Cambridge: Cambridge University Press).
32 Lerner, D., *The Passing of Traditional Society* (New York: Free Press, 1958).
33 Servaes, J., *Approaches to Development* (Paris: Unesco, 2003), chapter 7–2, 3.
34 Leys, *Rise*, 10.
35 Latham, *Modernization*, 62.
36 *Ibid.*, chapter 4.
37 *Ibid.*, 59.
38 *Ibid.*, 210.
39 *Ibid.*, 5.

40 Baran, P., *The Political Economy of Growth* (New York: Monthly Review Press, 1957).

41 Wallerstein, I., *The Modern World System*, 2 *Vols* (New York: Academic Press, 1974, 1980).

42 Frank, A.G., *Capitalism and Underdevelopment in Latin America* (New York: Monthly Review Press, 1969).

43 Smith, T., *The Pattern of Imperialism* (Cambridge: Cambridge University Press, 1981), 82.

44 Leys, *Rise*, 10.

45 Engerman, *Staging*, 67.

46 Smith, *Pattern*, 80.

47 Fukuyama, F., 'The End of History?', *The National Interest* (Summer 1989).

48 Fukuyama, F., 'On the possibility of Writing a Universal History', in Melzer, A.M. *et al.*, *History and the Idea of Progress* (Ithaca: Cornell University Press, 1995), 16.

49 Quarto, F.C., 'US Military/NGO Interface. A Vital Link to Successful Humanitarian Intervention' (Unpublished MA dissertation, US Army War College, Pennsylvania, 2005), 1–2, 6.

50 Servaes, *Approaches*, chapter 7–10, 11.

51 *Ibid.*, chapter 7–31.

52 It is worth noting that Washington needs middle-class compradors not only in Third World states, but also (ideally) in former Second World states.

53 Petras, J. & Veltmeyer, H., *Globalization Unmasked* (Halifax: Fernwood Publishing, 2001), 129.

54 *Ibid.*, 130.

55 *Ibid.*, 131.

56 *Ibid.*, 132–133.

9

Cloning America 2: the Germany/Japan model

There was a time when many said that the cultures of Japan and Germany were incapable of sustaining democratic values. Well, they were wrong. Some say the same of Iraq today. They are mistaken. (George Bush, 26 February 2003)

The contradictions of the democratic revolution from above were clear for all to see: while the victors preached democracy, they ruled by fiat; while they espoused equality, they themselves constituted an inviolate privileged caste … Like their colonial predecessors the victors were imbued with a sense of manifest destiny. (John Downer, *Embracing Defeat*)

The Pax Americana's global trading system works best when its constituent parts govern themselves as liberal-capitalist states. Although the Pax Americana can clearly function when this is not the case, it is a lot easier for America to regulate its informal empire when its constituent components govern themselves according to the logic of liberal capitalism. Woodrow Wilson recognized this when conceptualizing how an American informal empire might work, and thereby effectively set the tone for twentieth-century American interventionism abroad. Wilson, and the Wilsonians who have followed him, have been motivated by 'a compelling ethnocentric humanism – the desire to help other nations achieve the blessings the US enjoyed, whether they wanted them or not'.[1] Hence, Wilson repeatedly used force to implement his foreign policies. He justified this by arguing 'America was unique because it directed its power towards the greater good of mankind, not towards aggrandizement and oppression'.[2] However, it must be noted that, although America sometimes deploys enforced regime change, it has generally preferred to implement its liberalization agenda via persuasion, education, development programmes, and by defusing American values through the global culture industry. None-the-less, within the Wilsonian model, 'renegade nations' (i.e. those refusing to play by the rules deemed acceptable) can legitimately be forcibly dealt with and made to conform.[3] This is how Franklin Roosevelt and Cordell Hull conceptualized the struggle against Germany and Japan in World War II. Another feature of the Wilsonian model is that when the USA has opted to violently impose its preferred 'moral universe' and economic model, such regime change has been brought about by American-led multilateral coalitions. The most significant (and successful) examples of this being post-World War II West Germany and Japan.

In 1945 America was supremely powerful. At last it looked as if the establishment of a Pax Americana was a realistic proposition, after all, Western Europe (from which Europe's empires were controlled) was occupied by American troops, and two of the world's most significant states – Germany and Japan – lay prostrate at America's feet. How America dealt with Germany and Japan within such a context was very revealing of America's vision for a new world order. What America did, was deploy its power to try and clone itself – West Germany and Japan were forcibly reconfigured into liberal-capitalist states so they could be turned into reliable trading partners. Effectively, America launched two massive nation-building programmes which ironically (given American opposition to imperialism) shared many characteristics with the way Britain's empire had, in an earlier era (politically and economically) reconstructed its colonial possessions into valuable trading partners.

What the German and Japanese reconfigurations revealed was that, for the Americans, nation building meant liberalization – i.e. America's liberal political and economic model was to be imposed whenever America found itself in a position to achieve such an outcome. But if liberalization is the ideal, America's actual record of 'exporting democratization' has been poor[4] – with eighteen American-driven regime changes producing only three functioning liberal democracies (in Germany, Japan and Italy).[5] Yet despite this poor record, the German model of enforced liberalization has remained alive and well in Washington, and featured prominently in American thinking about the 2003 Iraq War.[6] Given that Donald Rumsfeld and George Bush both spoke about the relevance of German democratization/deNazification for Iraq, it seems worthwhile examining this model.

Liberalism enforced

The enforced liberalization of West Germany and Japan was central to constructing a Pax Americana because these two states lay at the heart of building American trade networks into Europe and East Asia. The Pax Americana would clearly be greatly empowered if West Germany and Japan could be transformed into liberal democracies (governed by elites allied to America), enmeshed within American trade and military networks, and hegemonically secured by the presence of American military bases. Just as the nineteenth-century Pax Britannica had its key anchor-points, so too did the Pax Americana. West Germany and Japan became core anchors for building America's post-1945 global hegemony.

From a Wilsonian point of view, the problem with pre-World War II Germany and Japan is they were both run by illiberal elites. Even worse, these nationalist and fascist elites had sought to build empires (into Eastern Europe and China). Such empire-building was a profound threat to America's global free-trade model, especially to America's desire to penetrate the Chinese market. If the German and Japanese empire-building had been successful, and the other European empires had remained in place, America was in real danger of being locked out of the bulk of markets across the globe. Hence, smashing these German and Japanese nationalist elites was enormously helpful for building an American informal (trade) empire. Consequently, a core feature of America's 1945 liberalization model was obliterating the old German and Japanese ruling elites and seeking to prevent the re-emergence of nationalism/fascism in these countries. A second feature was Germany and Japan were to be rendered militarily incapable of future empire-building or of challenging American power. Thirdly, liberalization necessarily involved building new German and Japanese elites who would be prepared to function within the framework of America's (Liberal) informal trading empire. Fourthly, liberalization involved building new constitutional, political, legal, social and economic infrastructures which would underpin these new elites, as well as support the integration of Germany and Japan into the Pax Americana's trading network. This involved a process of massive social engineering and creative destruction – i.e. destroying the old (illiberal) networks and infrastructures and replacing these with new (liberal) networks and infrastructures. This was achieved by top-down revolutions, necessarily involving substantial military coercion to enforce German and Japanese compliance. Opposition to the liberalization process was not tolerated – with two hundred thousand civilians in Western Germany alone detained to prevent disturbances.[7] In the case of Japan, America's military supplied the coercive machinery, while in West Germany an American-dominated alliance (of American, British and French forces) supplied the coercive machinery.

Americans conceptualized these German/Japanese interventions as 'democratization', which meant promoting liberal-democracy, individualism, consumerism, and free-enterprise capitalism. These were outside-driven revolutions predominately shaped by New Deal liberals and leftists for whom American-style 'democratic ideals' and the American way of governance were seen as having 'universal' applicability;[8] and for whom the encouragement of 'economic democracy' was deemed important. This meant encouraging American-style political parties and trade unions;[9] and discouraging concentrations of economic power (through the dispersal of wealth to a middle class). When applied, American 'democratization' translated into attacking fascists and communists and promoting the interests of centrists (Christian Democrats and Social Democrats).[10] 'Democratization' took precedence over rebuilding the war-ravaged economies[11] because America's first priority was creating new political elites who could function as American allies[12] in the process of liberalizing Germany/Japan, and ensuring these states were in 'safe' (centrist) hands when economic reconstruction was undertaken. In this way, when Germany and Japan were restored to major economic players in the world, their power would be harnessed for the Pax Americana rather than used to construct alternative centres of power.

Broadly, German and Japanese regime change went through three phases. Firstly, occupation forces established themselves and took control of governance in a manner highly reminiscent of how the British had dispatched colonial administrators to its imperial possessions. 'Little Americas' were established in Germany[13] and Japan,[14] where US military and civilian personnel lived in colonial splendour. Numerous stores, theatres, hotels, golf courses, etcetera were declared off limits to the 'natives' and the American occupiers employed servants paid for by the German and Japanese governments.[15] In Japan a sense of racial superiority made the occupation more obviously 'colonial', with 'General McArthur[16] and his command ruling their new domain as neo-colonial overlords, beyond challenge or criticism'.[17] Hence, while the victors preached democracy, they ruled by fiat; while they espoused equality, they themselves constitute an inviolate privileged caste.[18] Hence, just as nineteenth-century European imperialists were imbued with a 'civilizing mission' when they reconstructed their colonial possessions, so these American-driven regime changes were similarly premised on the assumption that American culture, values and styles of governance were superior to that which was being replaced. The second phase involved smashing the old socio-political networks with a view to removing those who might pose a challenge to the liberalization process. This destructive process was achieved by internment; purges; discrediting or politically banishing the old elite; seizure of assets; decartelization and land reform.[19] Phase two also involved facilitating the emergence of new (liberalized) elites, by creating new career opportunities for those whom it was believed would help build a new liberal order. Phase three was entered when the occupying forces felt secure enough to begin the process of transferring power (decolonization?) to the new (liberalized) elites. For this to occur the new elites had to be deemed trustworthy allies, and also demonstrate they had sufficient legitimacy and governance acumen to run the reconfigured liberal states as reliable components of the Pax Americana global trading system.

In Germany the process of creative destruction was initiated with directive JCS1067 which established the legal basis for American democratization activities. In Japan it was the 11 October directive which initiated democratization, demilitarization and purging the old elite. In both cases these directives empowered American occupying authorities to micromanage liberalization.

Liberalization necessarily began with destroying the old ruling elite. This involved removing (purging) from office anyone who had held positions of responsibility or authority in a range of sectors – politicians, government bureaucrats, judges, policemen, military officials, university academics, school teachers, journalists, film-makers, businessmen and industrial managers. Effectively, the democratization processes 'called for the removal and replacement of practically the entire leadership of both countries'.[20] In both countries 'the purge' of undesirable individuals was geared to creating a space for a new group of leaders to come to the fore.[21] The process began with the banning of undesirable political parties, the seizing of their records and the confiscation of their assets.[22] These parties were also forbidden from reconstituting themselves. In order to remove the old elite and build a new one, it was imperative that America exercise a monopoly of coercive power. For this reason it was vital to break-up and disrupt the coercive capacity of the former regime – i.e. render the old military and police forces incapable of resisting the new order. Under the original plan the German and Japanese military machines were to simply be abolished. (This plan was later modified.) But since law and order needed to be maintained, police forces could not be abolished. Instead the Americans decentralized police structures, purged those police deemed most 'unreliable' and implemented visitor programmes which sent German policemen to America (to learn American practices) and brought American policemen to Germany.[23]

The occupiers turned quickly to identifying and isolating 'undesirable' Germans and Japanese.[24] In Germany, many people were subject to immediate arrest and internment by virtue of the posts they had occupied – by the end of 1946, 95,000 people were interned in concentration camps in the American zone; 64,000 in the British zone; 19,000 in the French zone and 67,000 in the Soviet zone.[25] In addition, a massive machinery of screening, classification and categorizing of the German and Japanese populations was introduced. In Germany, a programme of deNazification was put in place and all thirteen million adults in the American zone were required to fill in an autobiographical questionnaire (*fragebogen*) geared to identify who had supported the Nazis.[26] Ration cards could only be obtained after filling this in. Processing these forms called for a substantive bureaucracy of military and civilian personnel.[27] The immensity of this 'vetting' process became such a burden for America's occupation administration that in mid-1946, they handed their deNazification programme over to Germans, working under American supervision.[28] (In general, those

Germans employed were left-wingers and social democrats who had an axe to grind with the Nazis.) The 22,000 people who staffed this deNazification machinery had the power to imprison, permanently exclude people from holding certain positions, impose fines and confiscate property.[29] Similar screening processes were carried out in the British, French and Russian zones of occupied Germany (but not on the same scale as the American process). In Germany the population was classified into four categories as follows. (1) Leading Nazis were executed or imprisoned, following war crime trials geared to establishing the guilt of the old regime.[30] (2) Some Nazis deemed less dangerous were temporarily removed from society – i.e. they were detained until regarded as rehabilitated. (3) 'Undesirables' were purged from their jobs, and those classified as Nazis were banned by law from exercising political or economic influence in Germany.[31] Until cleared by a tribunal, anyone suspected of being a Nazi supporter could not occupy any position of importance;[32] this included holding any public office, or holding any position of importance in quasi-public and private corporations.[33] (4) Those identified as untainted by Nazism were deemed 'reliable' and so eligible to become part of the new liberalized ruling elite being groomed by the occupiers.

The numbers of people impacted by deNazification was significant. In the American zone 292,089 people were removed from important public or private positions and 81,678 excluded from being employed in such positions. In the Russian zone 307,370 were removed and 83,108 excluded.[34] In the British zone 320,000 were purged; in the French zone 70,000. Overall, the effect was to destroy the former Prussian elite and completely obliterate all vestiges of the former Nazi government.[35] In fact, 'there seems to be no record in modern history of the complete destruction of a government structure from top to bottom in a major country aside from Germany'.[36]

A similar process of screening and categorization was initiated in Japan. Top political and military leaders were hauled before show trials with some being executed and others being imprisoned.[37] Significantly, the head of Japan's political machinery, the Emperor, was not dealt with in this way because the Americans realized (given the Emperor's status) this would have made stabilizing post-war Japan impossible. So instead, the Emperor was rehabilitated and turned into a secularized liberal constitutional monarch.[38] Lower-level Japanese 'undesirables' were, as in Germany, purged. But in Japan much more emphasis was place on smashing the old economic elite – the *zaibatsu* – than had been the case in Germany, because the *zaibatsu* were seen as 'feudal' and constituting the heart of the old (anti-liberal) Japanese elite. The anti-*zaibatsu* programme forced Japan's economic elite to sell their shares; broke up monopolies, trusts, cartels and holding companies; and even dissolved the nine largest Japanese corporations.[39] Effectively, ownership of

Japan's economy was dispersed among a large group of smaller shareholders which had the effect of expanding the middle class[40] – precisely the group America needed to create as a support base for liberalism, and from which could be drawn future political allies of the Pax Americana. The Americans also broke up the old Japanese rural landowning elite through land reform, which created 'little capitalists'[41] – i.e. a rural middle-class support base for liberalism.

It is significant to note which groups were the main focus of the deNazification purges – namely, politicians, teachers, journalists, academics, judges, policemen and managers. The education and media sectors were especially targeted for liberalization, demonstrating a strong determination to eradicate those who might propagate illiberal (nationalist and fascist ideas), while trying to ensure those employed in schools, universities, newspapers, magazines, radio stations and the film industry would be amenable to the propagation of liberal ideology. Schools posed a particular challenge because 80 per cent of German teachers in 1945 were believed to be Nazi sympathisers. Ultimately, 50 per cent of teachers in the American zone were purged, which produced an enormous understaffing problem.[42] The journalist profession was also 'purged on a grand scale with the result that some completely inexperienced men were given editorial jobs'.[43] But at least they were ideologically reliable. All the media that had operated under the Nazi regime were simply closed down, and new media could not start up until granted a printing or broadcast licence by the Allied occupiers. In Western Germany this licensing system meant the growth of a liberal media (dominated by the Springer group),[44] while in East Germany it meant the growth of a communist media. In Japan the media were similarly targeted and 1066 journalists purged.[45] The Japanese purge fist removed nationalist/fascist journalists and later communists (thereby leaving the media staffed by centrists amenable to liberalization).[46]

The American-run purge in Japan looked much like its German equivalent. In all 220,000 Japanese people were purged from the military, politics, schools, universities, newspapers, magazines, radio, the film industry,[47] and from two hundred designated business corporations. Millions of Japanese had to fill out screening questionnaires, although the Japanese vetting process was not as rigorously carried out as in Germany – with only 3.2 per cent of the Japanese population ultimately screened.[48]

The purges created a huge underclass of bitter purgees, with many talented and senior people finding themselves confined to junior jobs.[49] Many became broken men, although others did work their way back up the career ladder – it being estimated that about half of those removed by deNazification were back in senior positions by 1954.[50] However, purgees necessarily had their lives serious disrupted, and the effects of having one's career advancement blocked for six or more years meant most found they got left behind in the race. The purges also destroyed networks underpinning career advancement. Most purgees could never catch up or seriously compete with members of the new liberalized elite who had been nurtured by the Americans.[51] Overall the purges were far more successful in smashing the old German elite than was the case in Japan.[52]

The purges were not just punitive; they were part of a clear ideological struggle geared to proselytizing the American political faith of liberal democracy.[53] The objective was to transform the German and Japanese political cultures. The American High Commissioner in Germany (who functioned as the de facto Governor of an American colony), John McCloy, stated his objective as 'influencing the German mind' – he wanted to change how Germans thought,[54] by shifting mainstream German thinking away from nationalism (and towards liberalism), and making them feel guilty about their past.[55] In Japan, General MacArthur similarly saw his role as inculcating new (liberal) social norms[56] – 'to get at the individual Japanese and remold his ways of thinking and feeling'.[57] The US War Department even made a film for viewing by the occupation forces in Japan called *Our Job in Japan*. This film focused on 'the Japanese brain' as the 'problem', and promoted the idea that America's mission was to 'civilize the Jap' by teaching American values and democracy.[58]

It was recognized winning the ideological battle in both Germany and Japan meant destroying the old media and education systems, thereby ensuring the education and mainstream media systems would in future promote a liberal vision of the world. Consequently, one of the first actions of the occupation forces upon entering Germany was to close all existing media[59] and educational institutions so teachers, academics and journalists could be screened (and 'undesirables' purged). All existing school books were destroyed and replaced with liberalized texts. But closing the existing media left an information gap. This was filled in the first instance by the US military publishing its own newspapers and magazines (in German). Further, American propaganda films encouraging German guilt for the war and Holocaust were screened. (Ration cards needed to be stamped to prove the bearers had seen these atrocity films.)[60]

In Japan, the old media were not closed. Instead, they continued to operate under strict US censorship which made it impossible for undesirable views to be aired and prevented any criticism of the occupation forces and their activities.[61] Under American tutorage, a genre of middle-of-the-road Japanese journalism emerged that complemented the wider liberalization of Japanese society.[62] The same journalistic genre emerged in Germany.

In Germany, the liquidation of the old media system meant a new media needed to be built. This new system grew up under strict ideological guidance in the form of a licensing system. The Americans used their licensing system to discourage the re-emergence of a European-style press in which publications were clearly identified with particular ideologies.[63] Instead, a genre of American-style journalism was encouraged that shunned the explicitly partisan approach in favour of centrist 'general' news. Only journalists with explicitly anti-Nazi credentials were allowed to re-establish themselves.[64] Book publishers, booksellers, film-makers and film-importation were also controlled through the licensing system.[65] This licensing system was also used to shift German radio into an overwhelmingly American-style entertainment medium.[66] In Japan, however, the Americans used radio extensively as their chief propaganda medium in a programme called 're-education for democracy'.[67] However, over time, Japanese radio was encouraged to shift towards the American popular culture format.[68]

A key feature of the top-down liberalization of Germany and Japan was the reconfiguration of their school systems which included a radical revision of the curriculum, the replacement of textbooks and the replacement or re-education of teachers.[69] The aim was to remove illiberal (especially nationalist) values from the curriculum and ensure that future generations of German and Japanese children were taught values promoting liberal democracy, individualism and American egalitarianism.[70] It was understood that liberalizing the economy and liberalizing the education system needed to take place in tandem, so the next generation of children emerged from school with values complementing the needs of the new socio-economic structures America wanted to implant.[71] Educational experts were sent from America to oversee the recasting of Japan and Germany's education system in the image of the American system.[72] In both Germany and Japan, these experts were viewed as 'philistine overlords' who were introducing a lower-quality education system.[73] In Germany old school textbooks were seized and destroyed, and the schools were kept closed until new (American produced) textbooks were available. A feature of the new textbooks and curriculum was the promotion of 'guilt' which was to impact on German political culture for decades.[74] Further, the mass purge of teachers made even those not purged so fearful, that for decades afterwards, a form of self-censorship became a feature of German schooling – the teaching of twentieth century German history, or the discussion of issues that might cause displeasure to the new liberalized political elite were avoided.[75] In Japan, classes were suspended for months in the three subjects (history, geography and ethics) deemed 'nationalistic'.[76] Only when new textbooks were printed were these three subjects reinstated. In other subjects, Japanese students were required to go through their textbooks with the guidance of their teachers and 'blacken over' (*suminuru*) any passages deemed nationalistic or undemocratic.[77] Meanwhile, the new American administration worked overtime to introduce coeducational egalitarianism, a new liberalized school curricula, and new school textbooks. A key problem they faced was that of trying to inculcate American values into a society where individualism and egalitarianism clashed with Japanese culture.[78] The new textbooks were designed to inculcate liberal-democratic values. One such text was called *Democracy Reader for Boys and Girls*.[79] At the same time a programme of re-educating those Japanese teachers (who had not been purged) was launched. A feature of this re-education was a *New Educational Guidance* manual distributed by the Ministry of Education in 1946 which extolled teachers to reflect about the shortcomings of the old Japanese society. The manual said teachers were now expected to promote individualism, democracy and the elimination of nationalism and militarism.[80] Although the transformed education system did inculcate a liberalized worldview, it also bred conformity because teachers (and pupils) felt a need to avoid upsetting the occupying overlords.[81]

Given that America runs an informal empire which depends upon management by indigenous comprador-allies (rather than the colonial managers and officials), the Americans realized the only way to bring about a permanently liberalized Germany and Japan was to create new localized self-sustaining ruling elites committed to liberal-capitalism. So just as Americans recognized they needed to build (Westernized) middle classes in the Third World to act as Pax Americana (compradors) allies, so too did the same hold true in Germany and Japan. Thus McCloy went out of his way to strengthen Germany's 'pro-Western elites, building up their prestige in the eyes of their own people and helping them obtain political legitimacy which the Weimar government had lacked'.[82] In 1945 Germany already possessed (from the Weimar period) a sizeable core of middle-class liberals who could be drawn upon to build a new pro-American ruling elite. But in Japan, no sizeable (Weimar-type) liberalized middle class existed, making the task of encouraging the rapid emergence of a liberalized middle class more urgent.

Overall, one of the most successful aspects of the post-World War II reconstructions of Germany and Japan was the way in which institutional reforms both promoted the rapid growth of liberalized middle classes and the emergence of new leaders. Effectively, the Americans radically rearranged the opportunity structures of these societies to attract, identify and nurture the emergence of new liberalized elites and leaders.[83] They also built new institutions to sustain these new elites.[84] And the purges removed the competition,[85] holding seasoned (conservative) politicians inactive while their (centrist) juniors gained experience.[86]

Amongst the most important infrastructural changes brought about to sustain America's new middle-class allies were the imposition of new liberal constitutions[87] and the active encouragement of centrist political parties. In Germany the Americans promoted the interests of the Christian Democrats, while the British promoted the interests of the Social Democrats.[88] In Japan, liberals grew powerful during America's military occupation, but once Japanese sovereignty was restored, these liberals found themselves needing to make some concessions to conservatives.[89] During the first few years of the occupation of Germany and Japan, there was a clear policy of 'temporarily sterilizing public office against political infection' by conservatives, nationalists or fascists.[90] This was achieved by disrupting conservative forces through the screening/purge process and through detentions. Keeping the right wing out of politics for a number of years gave the centrist newcomers a leg up, so by the time conservatives were allowed back into politics 'the higher positions had already been filled by men and women with good political records, and the offenders, where they could be reabsorbed, were placed under them'.[91]

> During the critical moments when political parties were reorganizing, the most undesirable elements in the national leadership were banished and discredited, and their influence receded as newcomers gained in self-confidence.[92]

Effectively, the Americans promoted those politicians and political parties whom they believed would best serve the interests of the Pax Americana.

> Those individuals who had the support of the occupying power(s) gained the advantage in implementing their programs, if not the exclusive opportunity to do so. Once the democratic process had been restored, this development could theoretically be altered by popular ballot. However, the occupying authorities were able to continue to influence those Germans and their political parties whose postwar vision corresponded most closely to their own. This influence, which was clearly evident in election results, was most direct from 1945 until 1949, but it continued in less overt ways until at least 1955.[93]

There were two ways in which compliant political leaders were identified. The first was to find émigrés – people who had moved to England or America because they opposed Nazism.[94] Such liberalized émigrés were now encouraged to return to Germany and take up politics. The second was to seek out 'reliable' persons who had resisted the former German or Japanese governments, and encourage them to become involved in politics.[95] One of the problems with this approach was it often elevated into positions of authority inexperienced people as well as those who would not normally have been regarded as good leadership material.[96] The man who became America's greatest political asset in Germany,[97] Konrad Adenauer, was such a person – so although American High Commissioner, McCloy regarded him as 'a little weak mentally, morally and physically',[98] Adenauer could become West German Chancellor because he was deemed a 'reliable' ally of the Pax Americana. Many of the political leaders who were 'discovered' by the occupying powers or who came forward during the early years of the occupation, 'continued to forge ahead' once German sovereignty was restored.[99] But significantly, although the Germans and Japanese accepted these new liberalized elites, they did not view them as better than the old elites, and were, if anything, moderately critical of them.[100] So although America's top-down revolutions did ultimately produce viable liberalized elites (allied to the Pax Americana), they never succeeded in discrediting the former Japanese or German elites in the way America had intended.[101]

The manner in which America sought to radically transform Germany and Japan (and more recently transform Iraq and Afghanistan) reveals much about America's political vision. It is a vision that reaches back to Jefferson's 'Empire of Liberty' notion. America's behaviour in Germany and Japan after World War II simply confirmed a belief in America's 'right' (and teleological 'destiny') to engage in a moral crusade to export their model of democracy and social organization to the world. Americans appear not to view their make-over of other people's political cultures as arrogant, but instead see such make-overs as something the recipient people should be grateful for. In this sense the Pax Americana replicates aspects of the Pax Britannica's 'civilizing mission.'[102]

Modifying the model

America's plan to build an informal (trading) empire after World War II immediately ran into the obstacle of an empowered Soviet Union expanding its empire into Eastern and central Europe. Then to make matters worse for America, a communist government took control of China in 1949. Given the prominence of the Chinese market in America's vision of an informal empire, the 'fall' of China to communists was a catastrophe.[103] However, the key event triggering a rethink of US foreign policy was the start of the Korean War in 1950 which suggested a Soviet and communist-Chinese challenge to the building of a Pax Americana. This produced a significant redesign of America's plan for Japan and West Germany. Until 1950 the plan had been to completely demilitarize Germany and Japan and to eliminate from their political cultures all influence from conservative militarists (who had been key members of the old elites). But Korea changed all this, because America now needed a re-militarized Germany and Japan to help defend the Pax Americana against communism.[104] Remilitarizing Germany and Japan also meant abandoning earlier American policy on destroying German and Japanese industrial capacity underpinning armaments production.[105]

Once America decided West Germany and Japan were required as full allies within the Pax Americana system, it required a rethink on (1) destroying the old German and Japanese elites and (2) what sort of economic reconstruction would be allowed. American pragmatism came into play and Washington decided the Germans and Japanese possessed the skills needed to build the sorts of economies required to underpin military forces. Consequently, the reconceptualized American model allowed Japan and Germany to rebuild themselves into leading economic powers (ranked numbers 2 and 3 today). But instead of being autonomous powers (who could challenge American power), Germany and Japan would now be reconstructed within the Pax Americana – their (rebuilt) economies would be so enmeshed within America's global trading network that autonomous action (detrimental to American interests) would be impossible. Similarly, their (rebuilt) political and military structures would be so enmeshed with those of America that autonomous action would be impossible. It was a model that enormously expanded American power, because America's 'Empire of Liberty' would, as a result, de facto 'control' the top three most powerful economies in the world.

As soon as West Germany and Japan became part of America's anti-communist defences, a rethink of the purge was called for. Many of the original ideals of 'democratization' and 'demilitarization' were jettisoned.[106] The effects of this in Japan were especially dramatic because of the pressing need to use Japan as a forward base to fight the Korean War. This saw the Americans align themselves with Japanese conservatives; the Japanese economy was increasingly handed back to big capitalists and state bureaucrats; and many Japanese were even 'depurged'.[107] Japan was encouraged to rebuild its armaments industry to supply the Korean War,[108] and was allowed to rebuild its economy with strong elements of mercantilism.[109] Consequently, the old Japanese elite was never obliterated in accordance with the original model – instead, elements of it were rehabilitated. These rehabilitated conservatives developed a working relationship with the liberalized elite America had been building, and from this emerged a new 'hybridized' Japanese elite willing to function as comprador-partners within the Pax Americana. Significantly, the heart of the new Japanese elite lay in the Ministry of Trade (which administered Japan's enmeshment within America's multilateral global trading network), rather than the Ministry of Home Affairs (which had operated as the core of the old Japanese elite).[110]

A similar pattern was seen in West Germany where Americans were forced to recognize that the old political culture was resilient.[111] This meant a working arrangement needed to be developed between the (liberalized) centrists and the former right-wing elites. Effectively, it was realized Nazism had penetrated deeply into German society, with twelve million Germans (out of a population of 80 million) having been members of the Nazi party or its affiliates.[112] Nazism had effectively been a mass movement in Germany which meant a full-scale purge went beyond the removal of merely an elite and instead hurt a wide array of non-elite Germans.[113] It became clear West

Germans were resentful about the purges, the Nuremberg trials and notions of collective guilt.[114] Hence, McCloy realized if West Germans were to be kept inside the Pax Americana as allies, the original hardline policy on purges and imprisonment of Nazis would need to be moderated. McCloy's release of Nazi war criminals from jail signalled a new pragmatism geared to strengthening the position of America's ally, Konrad Adenauer.[115] Effectively McCloy strengthened the hand of America's centrist allies by softening the deNazification programme. There was also the pragmatic realization that maintaining an effective government bureaucracy, and rebuilding the economy, required the skills of many former Nazis. As a result, deNazification was only ever partially carried out[116] and the old elite were never completely dislodged from the bureaucracy[117] or the military.[118] More successful was the deNazification of the political system where Nazis were effectively purged, and a liberalized ruling elite created.[119] The outcome of McCloy's pragmatism was to consolidate the liberalization of West Germany and to make West Germany a more reliable participant within the Pax Americana.

Although America was compelled to modify its original model in order to contain the Soviets, the rise of communist power actually turned out to be helpful to the development of a Pax Americana, because it helped America co-opt the old German and Japanese right wing into an alliance with liberalized centrists. Without doubt a widespread West German fear of a Russia invasion helped reduce both liberal and right-wing German resentment about America's occupation of their country.[120] Given a choice between American and Russian occupation, American occupation seemed preferable.[121] It was this that led to the phenomenon called an 'Empire by Invitation'[122] – where (liberal and conservative) ruling groups around the world, fearful of Cold War communist invasion, revolution or insurgency, actually welcomed their inclusion into the Pax Americana. (Conversely, there were left-wing ruling groups around the world who during the Cold War opted for inclusion into the Soviet rather than American sphere.)

At any rate, American-led intervention successfully liberalized both the ruling elites and political systems of West Germany and Japan. And even though many conservatives from the pre-war elites were eventually absorbed into these post-war elites, they were absorbed on terms favourable to America's liberalization agenda. Ultimately, both the new elites and general populous of Germany and Japan became accustomed to the discourses and practices of liberal democracy[123] and these liberalized values became self-sustaining. Since Washington recognized the importance of diffusing and reinforcing such values, they ran major visitors and exchange programmes geared to exposing large numbers of Germans and Japanese to 'the American way of doing things'.[124] The impact of these programmes on shifting attitudes should not be underestimated.

Linchpins of the Pax Americana

For the first few years after World War II, America functioned much like an imperial overlord in East Asia and Western Europe – using its economic and military dominance to reconfigure the socio-political and economic relationships of these regions in accordance with the needs of the emerging Pax Americana. A feature of this reconfiguration process was the enormous American occupation armies in Japan and Germany, which turned America into a de facto European and Asian power. For a number of years West Germany and Japan were outright American imperial possessions.[125] Then during the 1950s America began the process of decolonizing these two possessions in a process that paralleled the way America was forcing Britain, France, Belgium and the Netherlands to decolonize its Afro-Asian empires. These decolonization processes (in Africa, Asia, Germany and Japan) were geared to leaving behind compliant ruling elites prepared to function within the framework of a Pax Americana.

The decolonization of West Germany was especially complex, because the reconstruction of Germany was enmeshed within America's wider reconfiguration of all Western Europe into the Pax Americana. Ultimately, the way America redesigned and integrated Western Europe was masterful.[126] (1) West Germany could have its sovereignty restored in 1955 safe in the knowledge it was in the hands of a liberalized ruling elite. (2) From 1949 West Germany was locked into NATO, thereby allowing German rearmament (for the struggle against the Soviets), while making it impossible for West Germany to (unilaterally) use its military forces against other West European nations. (3) From 1951 West Germany was locked into the European Coal and Steel Community (ECSC) which made it impossible for the Germans to (unilaterally) use their coal resources and steel manufacturing capacity for military purposes. (4) From 1957 West Germany was locked into the European Economic Community (EEC) which limited West Germany's capacity for unilateral political and economic action. Effectively, West Germany could now be allowed to grow into a major economic power, because America had developed mechanisms to tame and constrain the giant. (5) The EEC also provided the fulcrum within which France, Italy, the Netherlands and Belgium could redesign their economies – economies traumatized by the decolonization of their empires. (6) West European economies were 'Americanized' by the transfer to Europe of American organizational styles, habits, values, accounting and statistical methods, and banking practices.[127] This greatly facilitated the integration of Europe into America's global trading network. (7) Western Europe became 'institutionalized' within a 'Western Club' that tied North America to Western Europe within a network of trade, military and political connections.[128] (8) Importantly, the West Europeans accepted American 'leadership' which helped immeasurably in consolidating the Pax Americana.[129]

The key that made it possible to allow German rearmament and the rebuilding of Germany's economic might was the establishment of NATO. Until then, other European states (especially France) saw the rebuilding of a powerful Germany as a threat. NATO (plus the ECSC and EEC) were designed as mechanisms to tame[130] Germany within a set of binding multilateral arrangements that diluted German sovereignty and made it impossible for West Germany to use its power in ways America (or France or Britain) disapproved of.[131] The whole edifice of European integration that sprang from this 'taming' process (leading ultimately to the EU) was the outcome of America being prepared to use its power to compel Europeans to cooperate.[132] For America, the key benefit was the creation of an economically valuable trading partner in the form of the EEC/EU, which also collaborated in stabilizing the Pax Americana's wider global multilateral trading network.

The establishment of NATO also saw the Americans successfully create a multilateral military force (under American command) which led to America permanently basing a substantive part of its military forces outside America. Effectively, America's military never went home after World War II – they stayed in Europe as one of the anchors to which the Pax Americana could be tethered. So NATO became an extraordinarily important mechanism for building the Pax Americana, because it served as the means by which America could (1) become Europe's 'pacfier'; (2) simultaneously manage the power of West Germany and the Soviet Union; (3) protect its multilateral trade networks in Europe; bring anti-communist Germans into the American alliance;[133] and (4) ensure a powerful EU could never become a third force able to challenge American power.[134]

The decolonization of Japan was less complex than was German decolonization because the main opponent to Japanese rearmament – China – was not inside the Pax Americana. But before restoring Japanese sovereignty in 1951, America made sure Japan was so tightly locked into an American military embrace that it would be impossible for Japan to use its power (economic or military) in ways America disapproved of.[135] The key feature of America's containment of both Japan and China was permanently maintaining a large American military presence in Okinawa,[136] Guam and South Korea. These forces gave America a huge forward strike capacity in East Asia, effectively making America an 'Asian' power.

Ultimately, both Germany and Japan become linchpins within America's informal empire – indeed both were crucial to American global power, given their economic strength[137] and the important role that American military bases in Germany and Japan played in anchoring the Pax Americana in Europe and Asia.

Americanization

The core feature of the Pax Americana project is building (and maintaining) a global multilateral trading system which, although it has a dispersed system of control,[138] is substantively governed from New York. American military power is geared to coercively underpinning this American-led trading system that sustains American economic, political and military power. Indisputably American power is built upon the global reach of American economic and military networks and the expanding hegemony of American practices and procedures. The remodelling of Germany and Japan were, in fact, pioneering instances of America's learning to use its post-1945 capacity to project American military power across the globe; and then using this power to deliberately enforce the liberalization of another nation's governance (political and economic) structures. What America's successful liberalization of Germany and Japan showed was the value of changing governance structures in order to build thriving liberal-capitalist societies with which America could trade. The British had already made this discovery in an earlier era, which is why much of the history of Britain's empire was focused on reconfiguring the structures of Britain's imperial possessions (in order to facilitate British trade).

The German and Japanese transformations also showed the importance of modifying the social, political and economic value systems that underpin these governance structures (in order to maximize synergies between governance structures and values). And it is in this area where the Pax Americana has been immensely successful – in the spreading of American values. Since 1945, America has not merely been a military and economic giant; it has been an extraordinarily successful proselytizer of the 'American way' of doing things (politically, culturally and economically). Essentially, as the Pax Americana has opened its global trading routes, it has simultaneously opened up global communication routes through which American culture and the 'American way' of doing things (i.e. 'Americanization') has spilled out across the globe. The importance of this proselytizing work should not be underestimated, because once a community is able to deploy the 'American way' of doing things, that community will become more effective at interfacing with Americans (economically and politically). Furthermore, Americans will necessarily 'trust' a community with high levels of 'Americanization' more than a community with low levels of Americanization.[139] So within the context of the Pax Americana, americanization makes good economic sense – since it oils the machinery of America's informal trading empire.

America did not merely liberalize Germany and Japan, they americanized these societies. American intervention in West Germany is especially noteworthy because it included a significant attempt to deliberately Americanize German culture. This stands in contrast to the usual processes of Americanization, in which cultural change and hybridization does not derive from planned top-down imposition, but rather from the easy availability of Anglo-American media and American popular culture (such as Hollywood movies and television) across the globe.

The Americanization of Germany can be traced to three sources – a deliberate post-war programme of cultural intervention; the impact of America's large occupation army; and the widespread availability of American media and popular culture.

Those driving American policy in West Germany were clearly very serious about using their occupation to have as much of a cultural impact as possible. The aim was to turn Germans into reliable members of America's new world order by promoting values helpful to the Pax Americana such as liberal democracy, individualism and consumerism, and by replacing German nationalism with support for global trade, international peace and European cooperation.

America's cultural transformation programme was launched even before the occupation began, with German prisoners of war being put through re-education programmes in which they were shown American films and taught about American society, history and liberal democracy.[140] Then, from 1945, America launched a number of major cultural interventions within Germany itself. The most important interventions were (1) the American Educational Mission to Germany, geared to deNazifying and americanizing German schools and universities, and (2) the deNazification and liberalization of West Germany's media. A key outcome of these education and media reconfigurations, was a substantive inflow of American values and ideas through the newly licensed media and the new school (and university) curricula. The extraordinarily successful transformation of West Germany's media was especially noteworthy, such that the 'new generation of post-war journalists, editors, and publishers orientated for the most part towards the West and the USA'.[141] Adult Germans would have been less susceptible to (and more cynical of) this enforced cultural realignment because they had experienced a 'pre-American' media/cultural environment;[142] plus they would have understood the propagandistic nature of this top-down cultural revolution. However, children being born into this new media and school environment would have been more likely to accept (and internalize) the values being propagated. It has been suggested that even though adult Germans turned a deaf ear to American attempts to change them, young urban Germans were very receptive.[143] And clearly, it was by successfully

Americanizing (and liberalizing) the worldviews of the new generations, that the Pax Americana could best stabilize its hegemony over Western Europe. Hence, as one 1960s commentator said:

> If West Germany is beyond question the most American country outside America, it is the young Germans who are most completely Americanized. Meeting them in the evening, in the American made pin-table saloons, or skylarking on their noisy motor-bikes, you come across so many James Deans, Marlon Brandos and Marilyn Monroes that you scarcely know which country you are in.[144]

In addition to its educational and media reconfigurations, America also made other cultural interventions. One was the America House (*Amerika Haus*) programme. This programme originated with the US Army's Psychological Warfare branch that set up a reading room for German civilians in Frankfurt.[145] The idea was to make American cultural material (newspapers, magazines, books, pamphlets, films, documentaries, phonograph records and children's books) easily available in English, German and French. This first reading room grew into a large US Information Centre program with America Houses being opened all over the American occupation zone. The America Houses were comfortable places to read and view material, but material could also be borrowed and taken home. Bookmobiles distributed materials to outlying areas. The America Houses also ran English classes and screened films (which became popular in war ravaged cities with little entertainment). They also ran exhibitions of American art; brought visiting American singers and musicians on tours to Germany; ran lecture tours by American speakers; and organized programs for children and mothers. Thousands of performances of American plays were also staged across Germany.[146]

Germany was also flooded with American books, periodicals and literature via Education Service Centres which made these materials easily available to teachers across Germany.[147] Over 1400 works of American literature were translated into German.[148] The American High Commission in Germany also provided resources to promote the establishment of new (Americanized) universities, youth groups, and liberal media.[149] The liberalized media were encouraged to promote American notions of freedom and liberty.[150] American-style magazines were launched such as *Heute* (based on *Life* in the USA) and *Der Spiegel* (based on *Time*).[151] These new magazines disseminated American values. *Der Spiegel*, in particular, became a major source of Americanisms.[152] American Studies was introduced at German universities with funds being made available to encourage visiting academics to help establish such programmes.[153] Exchange programmes also featured very prominently in American attempts to promote the American 'way of doing things' – Germans were sent to America (including teachers, police officers, journalists, political and community leaders). American teachers and other specialists were sent to Germany to confer, and German teenagers sent to live with American families for a year.[154] A wide range of decision-makers from business, trade unions, social organizations, and the legal profession were sent to America on study tours which played a crucial role in transferring American organizational styles and procedures to Germany.[155]

But 'the period of Occupation, marked by economic colonization, cultural imperialism, and the re-education programme, was the prologue to a more developed Americanization'.[156] Ultimately West German culture was transformed at a much deeper level by American economic penetration through investment and advertising.[157] This produced an 'irresistible flow of images supplied by American mass culture [which] included Coca-Cola, Hollywood stars, *Time* magazine, streamlined cars, and Lucky Strike cigarettes'.[158] What was implanted into the German psyche was the self-referential world of American 'consumer democracy'.[159] As one newspaper described 1957 West Germany:

> The streets are wide, lined with glass buildings, gleaming with metal, everywhere department stores … All this is no longer German, it is American. The shop windows, glowing and shining, give an impression of excess … the new streets appear crude and bombastic.[160]

This was more than a superficial change in the appearance of the streets. 'The replacement of "Aunt-Emma" shops and their products by the "Supermarkt", full of consumer goods, would gauge the modernization and Americanization of economic and social reality in Germany.'[161] Effectively, German culture was reconfigured by American competitive materialism, secular liberalism and individualist consumerism. It was American goods, and the cultural behaviours associated with these goods, that were the 'revolutionary missionaries for the American way of life'.[162] And in West Germany, the presence of a large occupation army (that was still in position half a century after arriving) provided role models for how Americans lived their consumer democracy. And so, not surprisingly, West Germany became the most Americanized country in Western Europe,[163] which is not to say American culture completely supplanted German culture. Rather, what emerged was a hybridized culture and mixed socio-economic system that was discernibly different from the pre-Pax Americana era.

The same pattern emerged in Japan, where a hybridized culture and mixed socio-economic system emerged. This hybridized culture emerged from two different waves of Americanization. The first was 'forced' Americanization during the occupation associated with the redesign of educational curricula, and the liberalization of the media and political systems.[164] The learning of

English was also a vehicle through which Americanization was imbibed,[165] but even the Japanese language was reconstructed by the need to deal with a host of new liberalized infrastructures. The second (and perhaps more powerful) wave of cultural transformation occurred through the imbibing of American mass culture. The long-term presence of Americans associated with the occupation of Japan, the Korean War and the Vietnamese War, provided ordinary Japanese people with many role models of how Americans lived their consumer democracy. Their impact on Japanese culture was profound, with Japanese popular culture being radically transformed by this on-going encounter with Americans.[166]

As was the case in Germany, the Americanization of Japan produced a society that understood the 'American way' of doing things, and so the Japanese became highly adept at effectively interfacing with Americans. Japan, with it hybridized culture, was able to function as the nodal hub for America's penetration of East Asia.

The integration of Germany and Japan into the Pax Americana tell us much about America's 'Empire of Liberty', the governance of this empire, and the way America uses its economic, military and 'soft' (cultural) power to ensnare the components of the Pax Americana into a web of economic, political, military and cultural relationships that hold the informal empire together. In the case of Germany and Japan, their conquest and integration into the Pax Americans went well for America. Time will tell if America will be as successful with its attempts (sixty years later) to reconfigure Afghanistan and Iraq.

Notes

1 Calhoun, F.S., *Uses of Force and Wilsonian Foreign Policy* (Kent: Kent State University Press, 1993), 20.
2 *Ibid.*, 2.
3 *Ibid.*, 4.
4 Etzioni, A., 'A Self-restrained Approach to Nation-building by Foreign powers', *International Affairs*, 80, 1 (2004), 6.
5 *Ibid.*, 6.
6 Phillips, D.L., *Losing Iraq* (New York: Basic Books, 2005), 145.
7 Montgomery, J.D., *Forced to be Free. The Artificial Revolution in Germany and Japan* (Chicago: University of Chicago Press, 1957), 39.
8 Dower, J.W., *Embracing Defeat. Japan in the Wake of World War II* (New York: W.W. Norton, 1999), 220.
9 Trade Unions were also encouraged as a mechanism to undermine the power of the old economic elites which had underpinned the former German and Japanese regimes – see Montgomery, *Forced*, 173.
10 'A democratic German was seen to be non-Nazi, pro-American and non-

Communist' according to Boehling, R., 'US military occupation, grassroots democracy and local German government', in Diefendorf, J.M. *et al.*, *American Policy and the Reconstruction of West Germany, 1945–1955* (Cambridge: Cambridge University Press, 1993), 305.

11 Diefendorf, J.M., 'America and the Rebuilding of Urban Germany', in Diefendorf, *American*, 351.

12 The process of building political allies during the occupation of Germany and Japan reveals much about the way the Pax Americana puts great store in finding and encouraging the emergence of comprador allies.

13 Zink, H., *The United States in Germany 1944–1955* (Princeton: D. Van Nostrand Co, 1957), 141.

14 Dower, *Embracing*, 206–207.

15 *Ibid.*, 207.

16 McArthur actually described himself as 'blank on Japan' and he surrounded himself with a staff who similarly had no knowledge of Japan. See Dower, *Embracing*, 223–224. Since the objective was to 'Americanize' Japan, a knowledge of Japanese society was not required. A similar pattern was observed in Europe where the occupying administrators were generally ignorant about European political culture. See Ebsworth, *Restoring*, 9.

17 *Ibid.*, 27.

18 *Ibid.*, 211.

19 Montgomery, *Forced*, 190.

20 *Ibid.*, 15.

21 Kawai, K., *Japan's American Interlude* (Chicago: University of Chicago Press, 1960), 91.

22 Zink, *United*, 152.

23 *Ibid.*, 304–306.

24 Montgomery, *Forced*, 17.

25 Grosser, A., *Germany in Our Time* (Harmondsworth: Pelican Books, 1974), 70.

26 *Ibid.*, 21.

27 Zink, *United*, 159.

28 *Ibid.*, 161.

29 *Ibid.*, 162.

30 In Germany and Japan these were perceived as show trials driven by victor's justice. And have been criticized as somewhat 'Hollywoodesque'. See Dower, *Embracing*, 461.

31 Montgomery, *Forced*, 22.

32 *Ibid.*, 23.

33 Zink, *United*, 156.

34 *Ibid.*, 165.

35 Grosser, *Germany*, 286.

36 Zink, *United*, 169.

37 Kawai, *Japan's*, 22.

38 Dower, *Embracing*, 330–331.

39 Kawai, *Japan's*, 142–147.

40 *Ibid.*, 158.
41 *Ibid.*, 174.
42 Zink, *United*, 197–198.
43 Grosser, *Germany*, 380.
44 *Ibid.*, 381–383.
45 Dower, *Embracing*, 433.
46 *Ibid.*, 434–438.
47 Kawai, *Japan's*, 92.
48 Montgomery, *Forced*, 26.
49 Ebsworth, R., *Restoring Democracy in Germany* (London: Steven & Sons Ltd, 1960), 17.
50 Montgomery, *Forced*, 113.
51 Kawai, *Japan's*, 95–97.
52 Schwartz, T.A., *America's Germany* (Cambridge, MA: Harvard University Press, 1991), 175.
53 Montgomery, *Forced*, 9.
54 Schwartz, *America's*, 85.
55 *Ibid.*, 156.
56 Dower, *Embracing*, 80–81.
57 *Ibid.*, 206.
58 *Ibid.*, 215–217.
59 Zink, *United*, 235.
60 Willett, R., *The Americanization of Germany, 1945–1949* (London: Routledge, 1992), 25.
61 Kawai, *Japan's*, 52, 213–214; Dower, *Embracing*, 180, 211.
62 Kawai, *Japan's*, 218.
63 Zink, *United*, 236
64 *Ibid.*, 236.
65 *Ibid.*, 239.
66 *Ibid.*, 242.
67 Kawai, *Japan's*, 221.
68 *Ibid.*, 222.
69 Zink, *United*, 202–205; Kawai, *Japan's*, 25.
70 Kawai, *Japan's*, 191, 202–203.
71 *Ibid.*, 183, 225.
72 *Ibid.*, 187.
73 *Ibid.*, 206.
74 Grosser, *Germany*, 330.
75 *Ibid.*, 329.
76 Dower, *Embracing*, 247.
77 *Ibid.*, 247.
78 Kawai, *Japan's*, 226, 232, 233.
79 Dower, *Embracing*, 249.
80 *Ibid.*, 248.
81 Kawai, *Japan's*, 197–198.
82 Schwartz, *America's*, 296.

83 Montgomery, *Forced*, 107.

84 *Ibid.*, 2.

85 *Ibid.*, 107, 149.

86 *Ibid.*, 44.

87 Zink, *United*, 179–180; and Dower, *Embracing*, 346–347, 376.

88 Zink, *United*, 338.

89 Kawai, *Japan's*, 242.

90 Montgomery, *Forced*, 25.

91 Ebsworth, *Restoring*, 13.

92 Montgomery, *Forced*, 90.

93 Boehling, 'US military', 287–288.

94 Ebsworth, *Restoring*, 6.

95 Zink, *United*, 171.

96 Montgomery, *Forced*, 43, 68.

97 Rupieper, H., 'American Policy towards German Unification, 1949–1945', in Diefendorf, *American*, 50.

98 Schwartz, *America's*, 127.

99 Grosser, *Germany*, 87.

100 Montgomery, *Forced*, 30–33, 92.

101 *Ibid.*, 32–35.

102 Dower, *Embracing*, 33; and Kawai, *Japan's*, 13–14.

103 After losing China, the Americans became deeply fearful about also losing Germany with its substantive resources and manpower. Schwartz, *America's*, 129.

104 Schwartz, *America's*, 126.

105 For example, Morgenthau's plan to dismantle German industry. See Zink, *United*, 154.

106 Dower, *Embracing*, 525.

107 *Ibid.*, 525.

108 *Ibid.*, 542.

109 *Ibid.*, 546.

110 *Ibid.*, 560.

111 Prowe, D., 'German Democratization as Conservative Restabilization', in Diefendorf, *American*, 308.

112 Schwartz, *America's*, 46.

113 Montgomery, *Forced*, 67.

114 Schwartz, 'John McCloy and the Landsberg Cases', in Diefendorf, *American*, 437.

115 *Ibid.*, 436; and Prowe, 'German', 452.

116 Montgomery, *Forced*, 181.

117 *Ibid.*, 73.

118 *Ibid.*, 185.

119 *Ibid.*, 185.

120 Zink, *United*, 355.

121 It must be remembered that a virulent anti-communism was promoted during the Nazi era.

122 Schwartz, *America's*, 299.

123 Prowe, 'German', 309.

124 Zink, *United*, 207, 212–213, 223–224, 306; and Schroter, H.G., *Americanization of the European Economy* (Dordrecht: Springer, 2005), 50–51.

125 See Schwartz, *America's*, 304–305; Grosser, *Germany*, 75; and Dower, *Embracing*, chapter 6.

126 Mai, G., 'American Policy towards Germany and the Integration of Europe, 1945–1955', in Diefendorf, *American*; and Gillingham, J., 'From Morgenthau Plan to Schuman Plan: America and the Organization of Europe', in Diefendorf, *American*.

127 Schroter, *Americanization*, chapter 2.

128 Schwartz, *America's*, 303.

129 Mai, 'American', 102.

130 Rupieper, 'American', 47.

131 Schwartz, *America's*, 150–151.

132 *Ibid.*, 203.

133 *Ibid.*, 298–300.

134 Mai, 'American', 101.

135 Dower, *Embracing*, 552.

136 Japan did not regain sovereignty over Okinawa.

137 The top three ranked economies in the world are – America, Japan and Germany.

138 The key locations of power within the Pax Americana's 'governing' financial network are New York, London, Tokyo and Frankfurt.

139 Americanization does not mean replacing indigenous cultures with American culture. Rather, Americanization is a hybridization process in which the 'American way' of doing things mixes with local cultural practices. Hence different societies are Americanized in different ways.

140 Willett, *Americanization*, 17.

141 *Ibid.*, 85.

142 Interestingly, pre-1945, Germans had been socialized to look down upon American culture. In 1945, the idea that Americans had a low-taste 'mongrel culture' that was inferior to European culture was widely held in West European societies like Germany, France and Britain.

143 Schroter, *Americanization*, 55.

144 Heinz Abosch quoted in Willett, *Americanization*, 122.

145 Zink, *United*, 245–247.

146 Willett, *Americanization*, 61–62.

147 *Ibid.*, 214.

148 Willett, *Americanization*, 55.

149 Schwartz, *America's*, 301.

150 Willett, *Americanization*, 77.

151 *Ibid.*, 81.

152 *Ibid.*, 85.

153 *Ibid.*, 19.

154 Zink, *United*, 207, 223–224, 306.

155 Schroter, *Americanization*, 50–51.
156 Willett, *Americanization*, 14.
157 *Ibid.*, 17.
158 *Ibid.*, 11.
159 *Ibid.*, 127.
160 *Ibid.*, 126–127.
161 *Ibid.*, 85.
162 *Ibid.*, 27.
163 Schwartz, *America's*, 301.
164 Dower, *Embracing*, 24, 207, 211.
165 *Ibid.*, 173.
166 *Ibid.*, 148.

10

Cloning America 3: Hollywood and soft power

There exists in the world today a gigantic reservoir of good will towards us, the American people. Our motion pictures have played an important role in building up this reservoir of friendliness. (Wendell Willkie, *One World*, 1943)

Soft power includes shaping others perceptions ... generally soft power resources are slower, more diffuse, and more cumbersome to wield than hard power resources. (Joseph Nye, *Soft Power*)

Because the Pax Americana is an informal empire, exercising global hegemony is a complex business. Hence, Washington deploys all manner of 'global governance' tools, including financial and trade regulations, negotiations and diplomacy, military coercion, financial coercion (sanctions), dollar diplomacy and cultural influence. But within this spectrum of tools, one of the defining characteristics of the Pax Americana is that 'soft' (cultural) power plays a really major part in building and maintaining America's global hegemony. This is partly because exercising global hegemony through 'ideas' and 'influence' is far more cost-effective than deploying the military. However, the Pax Americana has also made 'culture' an important hegemonic tool, because Americans are so extraordinarily adept at using 'soft' power (having created a culture industry that delivers global 'influence' and makes a profit from doing so). Americans have accumulated impressively high levels of expertise in this area.

During the twentieth century, Americans constructed a huge media and culture industry with the two main production hubs in Los Angeles and New York. This multifaceted culture industry is often collapsed into the rubric 'Hollywood'. This industry's influence is now global, because 'American media are everywhere'.[1] American-made images and their accompanying sound-tracks (carried by film, television, videos, DVDs and the internet) now reach every corner of the globe.[2] Clearly these images and sounds are not value neutral. They expose the world to American products, how to use these products, and the lifestyles accompanying the use of such products. Hence, they overtly and subliminally diffuse models of behaviour, dress codes, eating habits and values. And they do so within a format that is highly entertaining and pleasurable. In this way, an American zeitgeist is diffused – a way of seeing the world that naturalizes consumerism, materialism, secularism, individualism and middle classness; which are all values, conveniently helpful for promoting global trade; and hence for underpinning the Pax Americana.

All empires have cultural impacts. All imperial nations have spread their language; values, religions and discourses; 'ways of doing things' (practices); technic (economic skills); food; leisure activities; fashion; architecture; legal codes; governance styles; etcetera. And these cultural impacts modify the way subject peoples experience the world which, over time, produces cultural-behavioural shifts. Interestingly, when empires die, the cultural changes they have introduced tend to remain. Outstanding examples are the cultural residues left by the Roman, Ottoman, Spanish and British empires.

In the case of formal empires, such cultural impacts are generally diffused by direct contact with imperial officials dispatched to govern the empire, or by direct contact with colonial settlers. By dispatching officials and colonists to the farthest reaches of their empires, formal empires effectively created cultural role models who were mimicked by subject peoples. (They were mimicked because as conquerors they had power, and hence status). Formal empires also systematically exported their language, legal codes, fashion, food, architecture, etcetera, and often created education systems to teach their subject peoples those skills and values deemed appropriate by the imperial officials. So acculturation in formal empire was often driven by imperial policies explicitly geared to diffusing new cultural practices.

In the case of informal empires there is no systematic export of officials, colonial settlers, or imperial institutions able to force cultural change. However, the global media industry associated with the Pax Americana has provided a new mechanism for achieving the same results. Hollywood and the American culture industry effectively provide new types of role models in the form of film/television characters and celebrities. And because these characters/celebrities are now globally diffused right into people's homes (by television and internet), the acculturation effect (of media images) may ironically turn out to be more powerful than the acculturation effect of directly encountering/observing a British or Ottoman imperial official/settler. Because exposure to American media is more pleasant, and appears more 'innocent' than exposure to an imperial official, there may be greater openness/willingness to absorb such media-delivered culture. This would explain the 'Americanization' of so many people across the globe since 1945. The importance of successfully diffusing American culture and values should not be underestimated, because this greatly enhances America's abilities to win friends, allies and comprador-partners – which effectively translates into 'soft power'.

Soft power

America possesses both hard and soft power. Hard power is built upon military and economic might. Nations possessing such hard power can usually get others to change their position through either threats ('sticks) or inducements ('carrots').[3] America has more hard power at its disposal than any other nation in history. Militarily, America's capacity to mobilize violence and project this violence to any part of the globe is unrivalled. In 2007 it spent $439 billion on military expenditure, which is almost the equivalent of what the entire rest of the world spends on military forces combined.[4]

America also possesses soft power in more abundance than any other nation. 'Soft power rests on the ability to shape the preferences of others.'[5] It means having the ability to get others to want the same outcome that you want – soft power provides the ability to co-opt people. This means not needing to coerce people. At the heart of America's soft power lies its culture industry – an industry that projects images of America into the world; images that others find 'attractive'. America has developed a phenomenal capability to project 'attractiveness'. This translates into the ability to get others to 'buy into' its values, which makes it easier for America to sell its policies as legitimate.[6] Hence, America can lead by example, and so can often get its way without having to use threats and violence. Effectively, soft power grows out of an ability to attract, co-opt and set agendas,[7] all three of which are tied to two of America's key strengths: namely, its ability to project positive images into the world (through the culture industry) and having a strong economy, which provides the resources for largess, leverage, influence (or sanctions).

Because the Pax Americana is an informal empire, Washington needs comprador-partners in every independent state across the globe. The best compradors are those who aspire to consume the sorts of goods middle-class Americans consume; who live urban middle-class lifestyles; and who share similar values to middle-class Americans. Consequently, the Pax Americana relies upon building middle-class values across the globe. If this can be achieved, the Pax Americana's imperial nature can be obfuscated behind the networking of like-minded (middle-class) people from around the globe who aspire to joining the American-run global trading network. Effectively a global (networked) elite is constructed out of successful comprador-building which, in turn, becomes intertwined with the mobilization of soft power.

America's soft power has emerged from building a pool of overseas goodwill. Essentially America has proved to be adept at constructing a sense of 'affinity' and 'comfort' with American culture and ideas. There are a number of ways this happens:

- Constant exposure to images of America and Americans creates a sense of 'familiarity', and identification with American celebrities can generate a sense of 'bonding' with America. Since America is by far the world's number one exporter of films and television programmes its capacity to globally project positive images is phenomenal.[8] And since 'pictures often convey values more powerfully than words' Hollywood has a huge capacity to 'americanize', modernize and 'de-traditionalize' people across the world.[9] Further, American popular culture portrays Americans as open, mobile, individualistic, anti-establishment, pluralistic, voluntaristic, populist and free.[10] These are all values with great appeal to middle-class people across the world – the very people America seeks as comprador-partners.

- America has for decades run a foreign visitors' programme on an industrial scale. Foreigners identified as movers-and-shakers and potential future leaders are brought to America on 'familiarization tours' geared to building positive feelings and networking comprador-linkages. However, America dramatically cut its spending in this area after the Soviet Union's collapse – abolishing the US Information Agency, and cutting cultural and academic exchanges down to only twenty-nine-thousand in 2001.[11] Nye has argued this is an enormous error at a time of growing anti-Americanism.[12]

- Millions of foreign students study at American universities. This is encouraged because it is understood university graduates are more likely to end up in leadership positions back home, and US education promotes American middle-class values. The millions who have studied in America over the years undoubtedly constitute an enormous reservoir of goodwill.[13]

- Foreign scholars are encouraged (and financially assisted) to spend time in America. Over eighty-thousand such scholars go to America each year, which helps diffuse American values throughout the world's middle-class communities.

- Not only is America the world's leading importer of migrants, but it deliberately encourages immigration from every country in the world. This means people from all over the world 'recognize' Americans who 'look' like them. It also generates familial networks with all countries, which creates significant comprador-building opportunities.

- As an immigrant nation, America has borrowed freely from the traditions of waves of migrants; with such borrowings having almost come to define 'American-ness'. Thus pizza, burritos, frankfurters and bagels now seem American. This is significant because once 'American culture' is viewed as being mongrel, hybridized and globalized, the idea of becoming 'americanized' starts to shift. Hence, instead of 'americanization' being negatively viewed as an 'imperialist' imposition, it can now be positively interpreted as joining 'globalized culture', and even become fashionable for some.

- American (military and economic) power confers status. Throughout history, power confers prestige and status upon the culture of leading nations. This makes the citizens of other states desire to consume and even mimic the culture of the more powerful.[14] So soft power is partly derivative of hard power.

- America is the largest seller of music to the world.[15]

- America publishes more books than any other country.[16]

- America hosts more websites than any other country.

- Americans are the most prolific publishers of academic journal articles in the world.[17]

Although much American soft power derives from non-government sources – e.g. Hollywood film studios or the music industry – some soft power is consciously organized by the government in the shape of government information, public relations, public diplomacy[18] and military psychological operations.[19] In this regard, it is interesting to note, American foreign policy officialdom has traditionally been divided into four camps: Hamiltonian realists, Jacksonian populists, Jeffersonians and Wilsonians. The realists (who focus on power and security) advocate doing whatever is necessary to achieve American interests. Populists set policy according to the whims of public opinion. Jeffersonians wish to make America a shinning beacon of democracy for others to follow. Wilsonians want to actively globalize liberal democracy. Both Jeffersonians and Wilsonians emphasize the deliberate creation and use of soft power.[20] But because soft power is tied to how foreigners interpret American messages – and messages can be interpreted in multiple ways – soft power is a fluid and unpredictable resource for American policy-makers. In general, however, America's culture industry has proved to be extraordinarily successful at generating products and ideas that consistently appeal to middle-class audiences around the world. And since it is this middle-class sub-culture that American policy-makers are the most interested in, American media messages have, on the whole, proved to be key soft power assets.

Global media

Although American soft power has a variety of different sources, America's key soft power asset is American dominance over a significant part of the global media industry including film and television production; news agencies; book publishing; and internet websites. This is important because media plays a major role in organizing culture. Tunstall suggests the world's media operate at three levels:[21] (1) at the international level an American-led cartel dominates; (2) at the national level one finds media that are hybridized (i.e. hybrids of local national cultures and American culture); and (3) at the local level one finds ethnic media. From the perspective of operating an informal empire, it is levels one and two that are significant, because they guarantee 'American media are everywhere'.[22] Effectively, 'Hollywood has conquered the world',[23] with American products especially dominant in the world's film and television sectors.[24] In Europe for example, 75 per cent of movie tickets sold in 1995 were for American made films, and 70 per cent of the movies screened on European television were American made.[25] American images are quite literally a globalized phenomenon. Global news flows are also dominated by Anglo-American media with three of the four big print-based news agencies (AP, UPI, Reuters and AFP) being Anglo-American; and both the major television news agencies (Reuters and WTN) being Anglo-American.[26] These shape the presentation of news around the globe.[27] And the recent reconfiguration of the media system, namely the internet, is also largely American driven with American companies like Microsoft and Google at the heart of this system.

Not only is Tunstall's observation that the 'media are American'[28] still true; but because the global media system is 'an American, or Anglo-American, built box'[29] there seems to be little prospect of escaping Anglo-American media dominance, given there seems no prospect of anyone else building another 'box'. What is more, the growth of the internet as the recent media platform has only served to enhance this dominance of Anglo-American media messages and Anglo-American cultural content. This dominance is illustrated by the fact global media networks are dominated by ten or so vertically integrated media conglomerates, most of which are based in America.[30] Similarly, the top seven world wide web (WWW) providers are American based. Equally important, since the end of the Cold War, America's commercialized and liberalized model of media (and internet) organization has increasingly been cloned across the globe.[31] This cloning process, coupled with the growing global impact of American advertising,[32] has generated a growing homogenization of the world's culture industries. Consequently, even though Hollywood for example, has become less American owned,[33] this does not alter the fact that the 'box' remains essentially American in terms of its key practices and discourses. In fact, as America succeeds in building middle class comprador clones across the globe, it matters less and less who owns Hollywood, because a 'foreign' owner who is, for example, a member of the ('Americanized') Japanese, German, British or Australian middle classes is unlikely to have attitudes and values markedly different to an American owner anyway. What is clear is that the global media now have a distinctively 'American' feel, and the Anglo-American global media 'box' helps create the frame within which the world is seen. Although this does not mean the Anglo-American global media is able to force the rest of the world to accept its worldview, it grants America many possibilities for agenda setting, and for presenting America and American values in a positive light.

How did this Americanized global media come about? The initial growth of Hollywood into a global phenomenon was made possible by the fact Britain's empire spread the English language across the world.[34] During the 1920s Hollywood used this shared language to spread its influence to Britain's possessions in Australasia, Asia and Africa. Then, during World War II, Rockefeller made a concerted effort to establish his presence in the Latin American media market. He was successful, and by the end of the War America dominated Latin America's radio and news networks.[35] But although America's media leadership had been growing for a hundred years, the real take-off of American media dominance began after World War II.[36] During and after this war, American troops were stationed in Britain, Western Europe, Japan, Australia, India and Korea. They carried American media and popular culture with them and thereby helped trigger the first phase of what grew into the post-war phenomenon of Americanization. In this regard, the impact of America's occupation of Germany and Japan has already been noted in chapter 9.

The impact of American troops, Hollywood movies and American popular music on wartime Britain turned Britain into a heavy post-1945 importer of American media products.[37] This British cultural shift was significant because, at that stage, Britain still ran a global media system across its empire. Consequently, any Americanization of Britain's media content automatically translated into the onward flow of American products into Britain's empire. So as the American and British media gradually merged into an increasingly integrated industry following the war,[38] London became an important linchpin for spreading American media products into both the former British empire and into the rest of Europe.[39] In fact, it could be argued that today's global media operate within an Anglo-American 'box' precisely because of the pioneering work done by Britain's empire in building media infrastructures across its empire, which later carried American content. Effectively, the Pax Americana inherited this British legacy, with Americans simply 'Americanizing' and expanding the communications network originally built by Britain's empire.[40] However, English is now spreading beyond the old British empire zone because it is increasingly being adopted by middle-class people across the world (due to the status conferred upon English by the Pax Americana). This means an ever-expanding global audience for American media products.[41] Consequently, the Anglo-American media box looks set to have an increasingly profitable future, as even medium-sized nations who produce their own media, now also buy American media products.[42]

Why Hollywood works

Given the importance of American films and television within the process of spreading American culture and promoting American 'attractiveness', it seems useful to explore the reasons why Hollywood has been so successful. Why are the products of America's film and television industry so appealing to audiences across the globe?

Tunstall suggests the origin of Hollywood's success was that its films were developed to provide cheap entertainment for immigrants to America.[43] Having built a large American audience as its core market, Hollywood could then sell these films to the rest of the world cheaply. Because it was already making a profit at home, Hollywood could then undercut the prices of its overseas competitors.[44] Unable to compete, many non-Hollywood film-makers went bankrupt and Hollywood cornered the global market.

Hollywood's success derived from an important feature of American society: namely, America was a nation of migrants. Many of these migrants were non-English speakers and were poorly educated. Consequently they were unable to understand complex texts (filmic or print). Many migrants also experienced poverty and homesickness, so they wanted entertainment that made them feel better. Essentially this immigrant audience wanted easy-to-understand media texts that made them feel good. These texts needed to be 'transparent',[45] i.e. easily interpretable regardless of the migrant's culture; and comprehensible to people for whom English was a second language. Hollywood films learned to deliver a limited number of clear simple feelings through story-lines that were simple to understand and ended happily.[46] They were scripted to be instantly 'emotionally' transparent by appealing directly to feelings and emotions and by deliberately avoiding being intellectually taxing. One needed no particular prior knowledge to understand these texts. In other words, Hollywood became expert in producing low-culture, low-taste media texts, not requiring good language skills or good education to be understood. Visualized action and clear (even hyped) emotions became a hallmark of these products. This Hollywood genre later came to also inform American television. Consequently, a nation of migrants gave rise to a media genre that – because it is simplistic, emotive and 'transparent' – is now easily understood by people across the globe for whom English is not their first language. And because these media texts avoid complex cultural messages (i.e. little cultural capital is required to understand them), they can appeal to huge audiences and support a profitable culture industry. Not surprisingly these films have been described as 'entertainment for the moron majority'.[47]

America's culture industry has been successful because it learned to mass produce popular culture within an industrialized process.[48] As a profit-driven industry, it has learned to design products appealing to mass audiences. This means constructing uncomplex communication, designed for the lowest common denominator. Effectively, American culture industry products are formulaic, mass-produced, commercialized and success is measured by profitability.[49] The purpose is to entertain, not enlighten. So whereas high culture is built on attributions of truth, beauty and seriousness (and targets audiences with enough cultural capital to decode them),[50] popular culture is built on instant gratification,[51] a rejection of 'hierarchies of taste',[52] (and is designed for audiences with minimal cultural capital). Consequently, American popular culture, as encoded into Hollywood film and television, has a number of characteristics:[53]

- a preference for things tangible and real as opposed to traditional and formal;

- a focus on gratifying the body rather than the mind;

- the delivery of moral certitude – i.e. 'good guys' and 'bad guys';

- plots mobilize clear and predictable feelings;

- messages are simultaneously 'patriotic', yet critical of authority;

- an obsession with 'speed' and 'instantaneousness' (instant gratification) leads to forgetfulness and a-historical thinking;

- a tendency towards utopian thinking and the desire for happy endings (and wish fulfilment);

- an ideology of 'democratic egalitarianism' which promotes banality, superficiality and (sometimes) vulgarity (in the name of 'giving people what they want').[54]

Hollywood films and American television represents the quintessential 'culture of the free market' within which middle-class people glorify their 'ordinariness' through an 'ideology of democratic egalitarianism'[55]– an ideology that assumes the best thing that could happen to the world is to universalize American middle-class values and lifestyles. It is a cultural form solidly rooted in mainstream America – where 'there is neither a wealth of highly educated people nor a plague of uneducated ones, but a great mass in the middle'.[56] American popular culture both affirms these Philistine middle-class' values and prejudices, and promotes middle-class ideology[57] which is why Hollywood products are so appealing to middle-class people around the globe.[58]

The success of Hollywood products around the globe is indisputable, with American popular culture being America's second most important export,[59] and with Hollywood's global influence continuing to expand.[60] The fact that this Hollywood genre was designed (mostly by Jewish immigrants) to appeal to (other) immigrants, by being easy-to-understand, banal, etcetera, now turns out to be its greatest strength in the global market, since it turns out this makes Hollywood-type products translate easily into other cultures.[61] So just as Hollywood films earlier helped socialize many immigrants into the American middle-class dream, Hollywood now performs a similar 'cloning' function overseas by helping to disseminate American middle-class values globally. Effectively, Hollywood is selling a brand to the world which mixes liberalism, democracy, pleasure and utopia.[62] Hollywood movies are not just well packaged innocent stories – they encode the values of consumer capitalism and liberalism. These movies have been playing an important role in diffusing America's assumptions about the world, and in liberalism's conquest of the world.[63]

But significantly, this Hollywood system has now expanded beyond Hollywood itself. It is no longer only America's home-grown film and television products that now promote the values associated with this Hollywood genre. Effectively, Hollywood now outsources some of its production to other parts of the Anglo-American media 'box'. This means Hollywood-genre products are now often made in Australia, New Zealand, Canada or Britain. Further, other countries are now copying the Hollywood genre. Hence, much media content around the globe increasingly has a Hollywood flavour,[64] i.e. America's film/television genre is now so hegemonic it has become an 'international style'.[65]

Hollywood's impact 1: zeitgeist

Every culture has a specific 'feel' or 'flavour' which derives from the cultural 'ethos' of a particular society. This ethos flows from the dominant worldviews held by people in that culture; their styles; what inspires them; and their interpretive frameworks. This can best be summed up by the German words *Zeitgeist* (spirit of the times) and *Weltanschauung* (way of looking at the world).[66] America's zeitgeist can be found in its media products.

However, America's culture industry has global reach, which means America's zeitgeist is being exported to the world. Unsurprisingly, America's zeitgeist has become the zeitgeist of the Pax Americana and the American culture industry is a key purveyor of this 'spirit of the times'.

Because America's culture industry has global reach, America has become a net exporter of 'effects'.[67] Four main effects can be identified.[68] Firstly, Hollywood exports American values that promote materialist consumerism, secularism, individualism and the ideology of democratic egalitarianism. Secondly, because this culture industry seeks to attract the largest possible audience through mass entertainment, American media increasingly produce infotainment, 'happy news', and media content that mixes coverage of celebrities, sex, violence, low-taste vulgarity, crime, travel, wealth and consumption. These all feed into a *Weltanschauung* favouring competitive individuals who struggle for success and happiness (where success is defined in terms of material rewards, and happiness defined by the individual's 'right' to fulfil his/her fantasies and wishes). Thirdly, America's culture industry carries messages naturalizing 'globalization' (i.e. America's liberal-capitalist global trading system). Fourth, the growing diffusion of America's zeitgeist, coupled with the socio-economic processes of globalization, is undermining and eroding local cultures (through homogenizing and hybridizing influences). Hollywood tends to act as a missionary for modernity by proselytizing an American 'lifestyle' and promoting American-style consumption. This often undermines traditional ways of doing things.

Obviously, America's culture industry does not have the power to make everyone in the world agree with the American 'way of looking at the world', and clearly not everyone has internalized this weltanschauung. However, America's zeitgeist has been globalized by this culture industry, and it would be difficult for anyone living in today's world to be completely unaware or untouched by this zeitgeist. But even if not everyone buys into American values, what does appear to be a growing phenomenon is America's zeitgeist is becoming a kind of globalized 'ethos' that middle-class people around the world feel comfortable with. Since the Pax Americana is an informal empire it needs to try and bind its middle-class comprador-partners into a global network of shared values. Creating such a shared pool of meanings necessarily serves as a mechanism to help hold together America's multicultural empire. In this regard, one of the key roles being played by Hollywood has been to build such a global pool of meanings – meanings that are constantly being drawn upon by middle classes (both emerging and established) around the world when they construct their identities as comprador-partners of the Pax Americana. From this a kind of Pax Americana zeitgeist is emerging, which helps build and hold together a global network of American comprador-partners.

Hollywood's impact 2: cultural imperialism

Because Americans run an informal empire they do not directly impose their culture on the world.[69] Rather, the Pax Americana exercises its global hegemony in indirect ways. The same holds true for the way American cultural influence is diffused.

In order to understand the way the Pax Americana's cultural machinery works to produce a form of cultural imperialism, it is necessary to begin with the global economic system America created after 1945. This trading and financial system was designed to service the needs of American liberal capitalism. Technically no independent country can be forced to join this system. But there are benefits to joining and penalties for refusing to cooperate with this American-designed trading system. Coercion comes in many forms and the Pax Americana has shown a willingness (and skill) to deploy the mechanisms of the global financial and trading system as a weapon. Alternatively, America dispenses financial inducements to those who collaborate. This may not be the sort of power associated with a formal empire, but it is power and it is imperial. Clearly, not every independent state has generated the same sort of ruling elite; however, the Pax Americana (through its global regulatory system and system of inducements) has been remarkably successful in producing middle-class comprador-partners in a wide variety of independent states across the world. These ruling elites have opted to collaborate with America (as compradors). This does not make them dupes,[70] because compradors are motivated by rational career choices when they chose to be partners (just as African slave traders made rational career decisions when collaborating with Europeans and Arabs in running Africa's slave trade). It is these comprador-partners who are central to the processes of cultural imperialism.

As noted, the Pax Americana resembles, in many ways, a huge global alliance of middle-class people who share similar lifestyles. Many comprador-partners were drawn from the middle classes, while others learned to become middle class.[71] Whatever path they took to get there, middle class-ness is a common characteristic of those occupying the governance structures of the Pax Americana across all continents.

These comprador-partners tend to regularly expose themselves to products of the American culture industry. Many of these compradors aspire to adopting American life-styles (given the status that power confers upon imperial cultures). But whether they 'aspire' to it or not, members of the Pax Americana comprador alliance imbibe heavily of American culture – consuming American television, films and internet products and enjoying the benefits of America's consumption-based culture. Effectively, a 'cloning process' can be observed in which the comprador classes absorb America's middle-class materialist values. American media (film, television and the internet) are the 'cultural reservoirs' from which they consume these values. What often emerges from this is hybridized culture – i.e. many comprador classes effectively build new cultures by combining American cultural material with their indigenous cultural materials. Consequently, 'Americanization' does not look the same everywhere. However, some American cultural influence is discernible in all states, from which is emerging a globalized cultural 'convergence' or 'synchronization'.[72]

Comprador-partners reconfigure their economies to suit the Pax Americana's needs because it is in their interests to do so. These configurations impact on how people function and live within these states. The cultural shifts produced by the Pax Americana are most visible where modernization is occurring in Third World contexts. These cultural shifts are not imposed by America. Instead, they are the result of comprador allies implementing socio-economic policies that more effectively mesh their states into the Pax Americana. So cultural change is brought about in a two-step process – Washington influences its compradors, who then create altered socio-economic and cultural conditions that stimulate cultural shifts (associated with economic modernization). Media and education are often important mechanisms for inducing such changes. The result is a form of two-step cultural imperialism.

So 'supportive forms of culture' associated with new values and habits are being imported to assist with Pax Americana imperial control.[73] However, the cultural changes associated with the Pax Americana should not be seen as planned 'invasions' of foreign culture[74] that undermine the 'cultural sovereignty' of these states.[75] Rather, these changes are brought about by one section of the indigenous population (the comprador-partners) who, as agents of the Pax Americana, actually 'invite' the empire in. Their own consumption and adoption of American values is voluntary. Consequently, 'Americanization' and cultural hybridization is not something one can simplistically 'blame' on Americans. On the other hand, the cultural devastation being wrought on traditional cultures across the world is not happening by invitation. Rather, this devastation is been driven by an alliance of local compradors and Western 'development' agents from the metropolitan core.[76] In this regard, 'nation building' (discussed in chapter 8) is a significant driver of cultural imperialism. These nation building projects involve local compradors trying to invent new 'national cultures'. By importing American culture they unleash cultural hybridization; while their countries' traditional cultures are modernized out of existence. Consequently, the cultural imperialism of the Pax Americana is a mixture of invitation and imposition, depending on which sub-culture one belongs to.

The outcome of this cultural imperialism is Americanization. This Americanization represents the cultural fallout from the second wave of globalization; just as Britishization was the fallout from the first wave. Both Americanization and Britishization have been associated with the spread of modernization and globalized trading. Together, the Pax Britannica and Pax Americana have spread Anglo culture globally. It is a project of creative destruction that is still in progress.

Hollywood's impact 3: Americanization

Americanization is the outcome of propagating American ideas, customs, social patterns, language, industry and capital around the world.[77] Defining exactly the 'content' of americanization is difficult for two reasons. Firstly, America does not itself have a single, uniform or static monoculture. Secondly, there are multiple responses to American culture around the world, so different cultural contexts are impacted differently. Hence, Americanization is a complex process rather than a clear-cut phenomenon. None-the-less, it is possible to describe the broad outlines of the cultural residues left by the americanization process.

Perhaps the place to start is inside America because the process of americanization also occurs inside America itself. A key feature of America is that it is a nation of immigrants. This means 'being American' is, in many ways, the outcome of being inducted into a new culture – of being born 'anew'; in ways that Americans see as being better than the 'old cultures' being 'replaced'. Each new wave of inductees changes the 'American-ness' the next wave gets inducted into. However, that does not mean that 'American-ness' does not have a core. Essentially, American culture has a Northwest European, specifically Anglo, core.[78] At heart it is an Anglo-Saxon culture modified by its relocation to a new continent, and by the infusion of non-Anglo influences.[79] America's Hispanic, African-American and Native American subcultures are dominated by a mainstream white (Anglo) culture.[80] However, since the 1960s there has been a growing tendency to de-emphasize (and even try and 'hide') America's Anglo roots by trying to promote instead, the idea of cultural hybridity.[81] This is tied to the notion America is building an 'international culture' by specifically drawing migrants from every country in the world.[82] This idea has been codified into the ideology of multiculturalism, which promotes the idea of America as a culturally hybridized 'post-ethnic nation'.[83] America's post-ethnic nation ideology reached new heights with the election of President Obama. This ideology services the needs of the Pax Americana by creating a new set of myths about American society and its relationship to the world. Obama exemplifies how this ideology works because despite having an African father, Obama is culturally indistinguishable from a white middle-class American. But because he looks different, Obama can be used to sell the post-ethnic nation 'brand' and so make the Pax Americana look less 'imperialist' to non-Americans. Naomi Klein, in her analysis of American advertising, notes how his 'brand America' promotes a set of new myths through a

> tangle of Cape Cod multiculturalism: scrubbed black faces lounging with their wind-swept white brothers and sisters in that great country club in the sky,

and always against the backdrop of a billowing American flag. 'By respecting one another we can reach all cultures and communities', the company says, 'we promote the concept of living the American dream'.[84]

The post-ethnic nation myth serves two purposes. Firstly, it offers an apparent 'cure' to America's guilt over slavery.[85] Secondly, it makes American imperialism look more benign and disguises the 'ethnic continuity' between the Pax Britannica and Pax Americana's globalization projects. If the ideology is to be believed, both the American nation and American imperialism are being de-racialized, 'multiculturalized' and 'post-nationalized' such that a new (utopian) post-conflict world is being built. This provides the Pax Americana with a new missionary impulse – a new 'civilizing mission' geared to universalizing the American dream. In this dream the world is run by a multiracial network of middle-class comprador-partners scattered around the globe who all share America's 'post-national' and 'democratic-capitalist' vision of how societies ought to be run.[86] It is the perfect ideology for running an informal empire and promoting Wilsonian liberalism.

However, the notions of post-ethnic nation, multiculturalism and cultural hybridization make the Pax Americana's version of globalization far more culturally destructive than the Pax Britannica's because these notions trivialize (and relativize) the differences between cultures. America's post-ethnic nation vision encodes the idea history and culture 'do not matter', or even worse are 'bad' (because cultural differences and cultural boundaries 'cause' conflict).[87] Effectively, this post-ethnic nation idea decontextu-alizes people by devaluing the complex relationships between history, cultural difference and place. In its stead Americans are building a culture of 'uniformity and placelessness' of shopping malls (that look much the same), and synthetic landscapes and pseudo-places (e.g. 'disneyfication' and 'museumization').[88] Filling the world with shopping malls may be an efficient way to promote consumption, global trading and a mobile workforce, but it erodes both the sense of living in a distinctive-place and of 'belonging' to a culture rooted temporally and geographically. In place of 'rootedness' comes a homogenizing culture built on second-hand media-images geared to generating conspicuous consumption in the 'here and now'– a culture that de-historicizes by inducing a 'forgetfulness', or even 'contempt' for cultural heritage and 'difference'. Americans appear to have decided to forget the past histories, traditions and cultures of their (migrant) ancestors, in favour of a new polyglot 'American' culture of the 'here-and-now'. And because America's here-and-now secular materialism is, at heart, anti-tradition, this has resulted in Americans showing less respect for other people's cultures and traditions than the British did. Consequently, across the world, Pax Americana-type development and modernization has proved immensely destructive to other people's traditions and ways of life[89] (whereas the Pax Britannica allowed greater opportunities for other cultures and traditions to exist alongside the empire's mainstream Anglo-culture).

Americanization also alters people's lifestyles and perceptions (weltanschauung) by promoting consumerism. Across the world American visual media (films, television and advertising) actively promote (American-style) consumer-driven lifestyles, and the products supporting such a lifestyle (from fashion and mobile phones to processed foods and modes of recreation). But this Americanization not only diffuses consumerist values, it also alters the actual ways in which people consume. Hence, in the latest waves of Americanization, consumption is associated with glitzy shopping malls, franchises, fast food, superstores, theme parks and casino hotels.[90] The effects of this are the homogenization of the consumption experience such that the products being consumed, and the experience of purchasing them, are now remarkably similar in Atlanta, Johannesburg, Singapore or Munich. The result has been to reconfigure our cities, architecture and socio-cultural landscapes, and alter the way people now interact with each other and with their material world. These changes, broadly labelled McDonaldization,[91] change business practices and how ordinary people consume and behave in everyday life.[92] McDonaldization, (which is part of the growing phenomenon of American franchising), is globally diffusing and naturalising American cultural forms. This is leading to a kind of homogenized global monoculture.[93] McDonald's is not just about the fast/efficient preparation and serving of hamburgers; it is also alters how customers relate to food, time and consumption generally. It embeds (American-style) cultural modernization; and encodes an American weltanschauung every bit as powerful as a Hollywood movie. It makes doing things 'the American way' both familiar and natural for people (especially middle-class people) across the world. In this way the Pax Americana becomes more than an informal (trading) empire, it becomes a major force for cultural change.

So what are the sources of the cultural changes associated with the Pax Americana?

Firstly, soft power must be recognized as an important feature of the Pax Americana. Not only have the Americans built highly effective machinery for diffusing their ideas, customs and socio-economic practices around the world, but they have become extremely skilled at producing media images and messages that resonate with global audiences. Americans are an upbeat people with a flair for selling positive images of themselves and their way of life. They have learned to use 'culture' and the culture industry as a tool to promote themselves, their products, and their trading empire. The importance of this 'marketing' dimension of American hegemony should not be underestimated.

Americans recognize the importance of the media and media products as hegemonic tools. Their awareness of the value of Hollywood to American interests can be seen in the enormous energy Washington invests into promoting the interests of this industry in international negotiations. Further, the way America acts towards media and culture industries during warfare reveals an assumption that 'media/cultural influence' is important – e.g. huge energy was put into reconfiguring media and education production in post-war Germany and Japan; plus media and education were similarly targeted for reconstruction in Iraq; and enemy media installations were specifically targeted for destruction during the Iraq and Kosovo wars. These are the actions of a nation that thinks 'media matters' and that the media has the 'power' to influence. So it should come as no surprise to discover that almost as soon as American film-making emerged, Washington recognized the potential these films offered for American propaganda. It was none other than Woodrow Wilson who decided an official partnership was needed between Washington and Hollywood to spread American values to the world. To achieve this Wilson created a Congressional Committee on Public Information with the mandate of spreading the 'Gospel of Amercianism' abroad.[94]

The importance Americans attach to the media and culture industry is not surprising given how successful this industry has proved to be in helping to build an American zeitgeist across the world. Perhaps the most noteworthy thing about the growth of this global zeitgeist is that, for the most part, Americanization is not imposed. Rather, Americanization is the outcome of millions of people across the world willingly adopting American consumer culture; choosing to consume American media products; copying the fashions and behaviours they see reflected on Hollywood screens; and aspiring to adopt American middle-class lifestyles. This seems to happen because Americans successfully present their way of life as inherently 'exciting' and 'new'.[95]

Hollywood serves as an extraordinarily effective marketing tool for showcasing consumer goods and middle-class lifestyles. Effectively Hollywood creates aspirational people across the globe who desire the products and lifestyles they see in American media images. From this comes a willingness (and even desire) to be Americanized. Not everyone in the world responds like this. But millions do. And from these millions America recruits its comprador-partners.

Those who adopt America's consumerist lifestyle not only change their consumption patterns; they also enter into a process of cultural change. The outcome of this is Americanization – a process that is undermining traditional cultures across the globes, while simultaneously creating a range of hybrid cultures. Common to all these hybrid cultures are powerful American influences, which graft themselves onto local cultures. Although indigenous cultures may not be completely destroyed by the hybridizing process, they are modified. This means each local culture becomes less unique,[96] and a creeping global Americanization becomes apparent. Effectively, in cultural terms, the Pax Americana seems to be associated with a process of creative destruction – as old traditional cultures are damaged and destroyed; while at the same time as a (creative) process of Americanization and cultural hybridization asserts itself across all the continents of the world.

The result is the globalization of Americanized culture grounded in a Philistine middle class-ness; driven by a shallow and glitzy consumerism; and made manifest in the lowbrow popular culture of Hollywood movies, American television series and populist infotainment. It is indisputable that America's cultural accent is now ubiquitous across the globe, and 'America is now everyone's second culture'.[97] That this has come to pass is testament to the fact America's (globalized) culture industry is undoubtedly one of the most effective vehicles ever devised by any empire to diffuse its values and weltanschauung. America's soft power capacities to market its consumerist lifestyle and recruit comprador-partners is impressive.

Notes

1 Olson, S.R., *Hollywood Planet. Global Media and the Competitive Advantage of Narrative Transparency* (Mahwah: Lawrence Erlbaum Associates, 1999), vii.

2 Although no one denies American culture industry images reach everywhere, there is debate about the level and nature of their influence. 'Cultural imperialist' theorists say the global spread of American culture is obliterating other cultures, while 'active audience' theorists argue the media does not possess the 'power' to change attitudes and cultures because audiences 'interpret' the media for themselves thereby thwarting its 'influence'. Both are extreme positions. The reality is, the media has an enormous capacity to influence audiences, but this influence is not 'total' or 'absolute'.

3 Nye, J.S., *Soft Power* (New York: Public Affairs, 2004), 5.

4 The Stockholm International Peace Research Institute calculated America spent 47 per cent of the world's total military spending in 2003.

5 Nye, *Soft*, 5.

6 *Ibid.*, x.

7 *Ibid.*, 8.

8 *Ibid.*, 33.

9 *Ibid.*, 47.

10 *Ibid.*, 47.

11 Nye, J., 'The Decline of America's Soft Power', in Skidmore, D., *Paradoxes of Power* (Boulder: Paradigm Publishers, 2007), 28–29.

12 *Ibid.*, 27–29.

13 Nye, *Soft*, 45.

14 Tunstall, J., *The Media are American* (London: Constable, 1994), 14.

15 Nye, *Soft*, 34.
16 *Ibid.*, 34.
17 *Ibid.*, 34.
18 *Ibid.*, 107–113.
19 *Ibid.*, 116.
20 *Ibid.*, 140.
21 Tunstall, *Media*, 18.
22 Olson, *Hollywood*, vii.
23 *Ibid.*, 1.
24 Herman, E.S. & McChesney, R.W., *The Global Media* (London: Cassell, 1997), 41.
25 Olson, *Hollywood*, 1.
26 Herman, *Global*, 49.
27 Tunstall, *Media*, 45.
28 *Ibid.*, 13.
29 *Ibid.*, 63.
30 Herman, *Global*, 104.
31 *Ibid.*, 137.
32 *Ibid.*, 58.
33 *Ibid.*, 40.
34 Tunstall, *Media*, 125.
35 *Ibid.*, 140.
36 *Ibid.*, 137.
37 *Ibid.*, 129.
38 *Ibid.*, 131.
39 *Ibid.*, 133.
40 As Tunstall (*Media*, 131) notes, the Anglo-American global media 'box' looks like an English-language cartel consisting of America, Britain, Australia, Canada and New Zealand.
41 Herman, *Global*, 52.
42 Tunstall, *Media*, 62.
43 *Ibid.*, 66.
44 *Ibid.*, 42.
45 Olson, *Hollywood*, 18.
46 *Ibid.*, 70.
47 Twitchell, J.B., *Carnival Culture* (New York: Columbia University Press, 1992), 130.
48 The Frankfurt School developed an important critical analysis of this culture industry. See Adorno, T. & Horkheimer, M., 'The Culture Industry: Enlightenment as Mass Deception', in Adorno & Horkheimer, *Dialectic of Enlightenment* (London: Verso, 1979).
49 *Ibid.*, 43.
50 *Ibid.*, 43.
51 *Ibid.*, 38.
52 *Ibid.*, 40.
53 Olson, *Hollywood*, 72–75.

54 Twitchell (*Carnival*) suggests American popular culture is equivalent to 'carnival culture' which has effectively made the common, the vulgar and the banal ('low taste') into the mainstream cultural norm of American television. This has driven out 'high taste' culture.

55 Twitchell, *Carnival*, 7.

56 Olson, *Hollywood*, 76.

57 *Ibid.*, 74.

58 *Ibid.*, 85.

59 *Ibid.*, 83.

60 Herman, *Global*, 43–45, 183.

61 Olson, *Hollywood*, 21–22.

62 Campbell, N., Davies, J. & McKay, G., *Issues in Americanisation of Culture* (Edinburgh: Edinburgh University Press, 2004), 30.

63 Mandelbaum, M., *The Ideas that Conquered the World* (Oxford: Public Affairs, 2002).

64 Herman, *Global*, 43.

65 Olson, *Hollywood*, 7.

66 Cowen, T., *Creative Destruction* (Princeton: Princeton University Press, 2002), 48.

67 Herman, *Global*, 153.

68 *Ibid.*, 153–155.

69 There are a number of different ways 'cultural imperialism' has been conceptualized. Tomlinson, J., *Cultural Imperialism* (London: Continuum, 1991) provides a good overview of these, and discusses why the imposition/domination model is unsatisfactory.

70 Tomlinson, *Cultural*, 141.

71 The rich will often even 'talk down' their affluence to 'appear' middle class.

72 Hamelink, C., *Cultural Autonomy in Global Communication* (New York: Longman, 1983).

73 Tomlinson, *Cultural*, 3.

74 *Ibid.*, 23.

75 *Ibid.*, 6.

76 In this regard those criticizing global capitalism and modernization for bringing about cultural imperialism have valid points. Tomlinson, *Cultural*, 24–27.

77 Ritzer, G. & Ryan, M., 'Americanisation, McDonaldisation and Globalisation', in Campbell, *Americanisation*, 47.

78 This Anglo-core derives from migration from the British Isles (including Ireland).

79 The most significant non-Anglo influences came from nineteenth-century northern European migrants (especially Germans and Scandinavians), with the largest infusion of migrants into America being Germans. Then the first half of the twentieth century saw the arrival of southern and eastern Europeans (especially Italians and Russian Jews). After the mid-1960s came Latin Americans and Asians.

80 Campbell, *Americanisation*, 16.

81 Olson, *Hollywood*, 166.

82 Campbell, *Americanisation*, 19.

83 *Ibid.*, 19.

84 *Ibid.*, 28.

85 Where Britons have obsessed over class, Americans obsess over race. America's obsession to 'overcome' race and cultural conflict derive from America's slave history.

86 The Hollywood product best encapsulating this Pax Americana post-ethnic/multicultural ideology is *Star Trek*. As America's multicultural and imperialist ideologies mutated over time, *Star Trek* encoded these ideological shifts. Hence, the different *Star Trek* television series encoded updated versions of America's vision for running an informal empire (called 'The Federation' in *Star Trek*).

87 Twitchell (*Carnival*, 55) has noted the central role played by Hollywood in breaking down cultural 'boundaries' and devaluing the traditional canons of Anglo 'high culture'. He attributes this to the disproportionate role played by Jewish migrants and homosexuals in the Hollywood industry; arguing because both Jews and homosexuals were especially sensitive to being marginalized by mainstream Anglo society, they were natural 'boundary' crossers. This has led to Hollywood actively destroying the traditional cultural boundaries of Anglo culture and replacing high-culture canons with Hollywood popular culture that revels in producing banal, low-taste and vulgar culture – or what Twitchell calls 'carnival culture'. Since Hollywood's carnival culture naturally undermines 'boundaries' and 'cultural canons', it has served to promote the intermeshed processes of cultural breakdown (of established, traditional cultures) and cultural hybridization. This is functional for the Pax Americana.

88 Campbell, *Americanisation*, 17.

89 The implicit assumption seems to be – if Americans think cultural differences and history are unimportant, then everyone else in the world should also think they are unimportant.

90 Campbell, *Americanisation*, 47–48.

91 Ritzer, G., *The McDonaldization Thesis* (London: Sage, 1998).

92 Campbell, *Americanisation*, 18.

93 Olson, *Hollywood*, ix, 9.

94 Fraser, M., *Weapons of Mass Distraction* (New York: Thomas Dunne Books, 2003), 40–41.

95 Campbell, *Americanisation*, 13.

96 Cowen, *Creative*, 72.

97 Ritzer, 'Americanisation', 53.

11

The Empire strikes back: 9/11 and beyond

What the British Empire proved is that empire is a form of international government that can work – and not just for the benefit of the ruling power ... it must be said that the experiment of running the world without the [British] Empire cannot be judged an unqualified success. (Niall Ferguson, *Empire*)

Roosevelt's model for a post-war world was predicated upon 'a grand illusion' and 'charming belief that the United States could reap the rewards of empire without paying the costs of empire and without admitting it was an empire'. (William Williams, *Empire as a Way of Life*)

The Soviet Union's collapse transformed America into the world's only superpower because after 1991 no other country, or even alliance of countries, was able to challenge American global military superiority or American economic might. Conditions may not have been right for implementing the Rooseveltian new world order after World War II, but in the 1990s they were. At last conditions existed where a Pax Americana could potentially be built on a global scale. For Wilsonian liberals their time had come. So when a Wilsonian, Bill Clinton, became president in 1993, he immediately turned his hand to rolling out the Pax Americana on a global scale. The term used by Clinton and his speechwriters for this roll-out was 'globalization'.[1] Under Clinton, liberal-American hubris was given an enormous boost. Wherever one lived in the world in the 1990s, this American hubris could be felt. It was a hubris that was bound to generate some form of backlash.

Both Democrats and Republicans share a belief in American exceptionalism, and hence believe Americans have a calling (or even a 'right') to spread American values, democracy and open markets to all corners of the world. They also believe it is feasible to promote these worldwide.[2] Although Democrat and Republican versions are not quite the same (as reflected in table 11.1), the differences are more significant to Americans than outsiders. In essence, whichever party governs, American foreign policy is underpinned by a shared assumption that Lockean liberalism is good for all humankind.[3] American foreign policy simply reflects the fact American liberalism, as an

Democratic Party	*Republican Party*
Doing 'good' in the world = • Promoting American values in the world (e.g. democracy and liberalism) • Building global open trade • Liberalizing the world by building a global alliance of like-minded middle-class liberals	Doing 'good' in the world = • Promoting free-market capitalism across the world • Helping American businesses operate globally • American values seen to follow trade
As social democrats, Democrats make spaces for bureaucrats and functionaries (e.g. 'development' workers and UN staffers) to 'colonize' opportunities in an informal empire	As free marketers, Republicans are less inclined to trust bureaucrats and functionaries. Instead they promote informal empire spaces for multinational corporations and business to engage in global trade
Multilateralism preferred	Unilateralism if possible; multilateralism when necessary
Favour using bodies like UN and World Court to universalize American values	Only accept UN and World Court authority when it suits American interests
Vision of globalization skewed by interests of urban intellectual elite and American working class	Vision of globalization skewed by interests of American business and middle America

Table 11.1 Two versions of American hubris

enlightenment ideology, looks forward to building a universal civilization,[4] and indeed is driven by a missionary zeal to universalize itself.[5]

Clinton and his Secretary of State, Madeleine Albright, were classical liberal internationalists. Their foreign policy upheld the familiar Wilsonian mix of open markets, liberal democracy and multilateral internationalism.[6] But Clinton also became a hyperinterventionist driven by both a humanitarian zeal and a willingness to use violence to promote his idealism.[7] The Clinton Doctrine was thus characterized by humanitarian multilateralism and aggressive interventionism.[8] Like Woodrow Wilson, Clinton was quite prepared to use violence to force people to adopt America's vision of freedom and justice. Consequently, under Clinton, the Pax Americana assumed the mantel of a moral imperialism, with Washington aggressively promoting the idea that America's vision of human rights and democracy should be adopted universally.[9] Effectively, America came to see itself as a 'vanguard of history'.[10]

Liberal hubris

Although American self-confidence soared after 1991, it was not until Clinton's presidency that an assertive Wilsonian hubris manifested itself. Under both Clinton and his successor, Bush, an expansionist Pax Americana, underpinned by an arrogant liberal hubris, manifested itself. At heart, this liberal hubris derived from America's overwhelming military power. So although America may not have possessed a formal empire at the start of the twenty-first century, the global reach of its military power meant no country could afford to ignore Washington. This gave Washington the capacity to make America's informal empire truly global, and thereby unleash a second wave of globalization.

As moral imperialists Clinton's team were missionaries for American values; seeing America as an 'indispensable nation' and a 'force for good' in the world.[11] Clinton was clearly prepared to spread the Pax Americana, liberalism and market democracy by force.[12] However, significantly, when Clinton used violence to promote the Pax Americana, he did so in ways that kept the costs for Americans as light as possible. Thus, where possible, Clinton used air power not ground forces.[13] Clinton also developed a new form of privatized warfare,[14] which saw the Pax Americana turn to contractor-supported foreign armies,[15] plus a growing reliance on the use of surrogates[16] and proxies, supported by American advisors.[17] The Clinton team cleverly learned to deploy a form of violence that dramatically minimized American casualties. Further, the Pax Americana, under both Clinton and Bush, invented a new kind of governance for troubled regions of the empire – this saw the birth of a new class of uniformed proconsuls[18] presiding over vast quasi–imperial domains[19] e.g. Bosnia, Kosovo, Afghanistan and Iraq.

Central to American global power is its awesome military capacity. With 702 overseas military bases in 130 countries,[20] American violence can reach globally. Especially important in securing its global hegemony has been the fact American occupation armies in Europe and Asia never went home after World War II. Even after the Cold War ended, America retained a two hundred thousand-strong military force in Western Europe and Northeast Asia. This secured America's global trading network and the (American-built) liberal hegemonies of Japan and Germany.

Americans had every reason to feel self-confident at the dawn of the twenty-first century. They had established a global liberal hegemony that was American led. It was an entrenched hegemony with North America,

EU and Japan as the linchpins of what was a truly global trading network. This trading network both fed and relied upon American military power. The way Europe was tied into this network served to illustrate how the Pax Americana functioned as an extraordinarily successful (and complex) informal empire that operated as a rule-based international order.[21] The EU (along with NATO) secured the Rooseveltian dream of:

- locking Europeans into a multilateral network that

- simultaneously tamed Germany politically, yet released its economic potential

- promoted liberal-hegemony across the continent, and

- meshed Europe into a set of (American-led) military and economic arrangements that

- harnessed European productive capacities for America's global hegemony, and

- effectively preventing Europeans from producing an alternative power centre capable of challenging American power.[22]

What the Pax Americana provides is a global coordinating framework within which liberals have learned to work together to promote (a shared) globalized liberal capitalism. In this way America attracts to itself the support of liberals across the globe. Effectively, because the Pax Americana services the interests of liberals everywhere, it becomes an empire welcomed by liberals everywhere. This is the basis of America's 'consensual empire' or an 'empire by invitation'[23] which has led to two interrelated phenomena. Firstly, the Pax Americana is a coordinating network for globalized liberalism, i.e. Washington, has effectively 'assembled a class coalition around the world'.[24] Secondly, across the world we find ruling elites who are increasingly Americanized. These elites not only look increasingly alike, but they are building look-alike societies grounded in plebiscitary democracy, proceduralized liberalism, consumerism and low-taste culture fed by Hollywood.[25]

Under Clinton, America moved aggressively to expand the Pax Americana, promote globalization and roll out what Clinton called the 'information super highway' – an American-built system of instantaneous global communication facilitating American coordination of their empire (in much the way Britain's empire used a global telegraph system). Clinton also articulated the goal of building a 'global middle class' and of trying to make billions of people around the world more and more like 'us' (i.e. American middle class).[26] Under Clinton the Pax Americana economically colonized as much of the old communist bloc as possible. Liberal allies were actively sought out, and the growth of middle-class comprador-partners encouraged across

Eastern Europe. Wherever possible the hand of East European liberals was strengthened, and they were encouraged to enmesh their nations into the existing multilateral networks of liberal hegemony (e.g. NATO and EU). At the same time Clinton's administration also intervened across the Third World to promote liberalization and democratization – which meant encouraging the growth of (middle-class) comprador-partners prepared to acquiesce to America's 'vision' and the Pax Americana's economic needs. Clinton surrounded himself with people who had designed the Washington Consensus and structural adjustment.[27] The interventions of this Clinton-team in the Third World generated a rash of regime changes and a new variety of compliant (middle-class) Third World ruling elites (some of whom later moved on to apparatchik jobs in the Pax Americana's multilateral structures like the World Bank, WTO, UN, Food and Agriculture Organisation (FAO), etcetera). Countries failing to deliver compliant comprador-partners for the Pax Americana found themselves at the receiving end of American force, e.g. Haiti and Serbia. More commonly, ruling elites simply adjusted themselves to the new realities of American power and acquiesced, e.g. Libya and Vietnam.

The response of communist China to this expansionist Pax Americana was interesting. The Chinese Communist Party recognized the folly of resisting American expansionism, so they agreed to China being incorporated into the Pax Americana's trading network. After World War II America had wanted Britain to return Hong Kong to China, but had moved away from this position when China became communist. Now with China's acquiescence to the Pax Americana, things changed again; and so in 1997 Hong Kong was returned to China – a move that greatly accelerated the penetration of capitalism into China. The outcome was the transformation of southern China into one of the Pax Americana's major industrial production areas. Washington (and its partners in London and Canberra) clearly wished to see the emergence of a huge Chinese middle class to serve as the Pax Americana's acquiescent comprador-partners. Although such a middle class is being built, there are no signs China's communist elite can be transformed into a compliant (liberalized) comprador group. Instead America may, in the long-term, be creating a (non-liberal) alternative power centre. And should China's 'resource diplomacy' mutate into Chinese imperialism (or even colonialism [28]), the implications for the world's balance of power and the Pax Americana will be significant.[29]

American 1990s expansionism dramatically boosted the processes of globalization. Effectively, the Pax Americana as globalization II expanded the reach of liberal-capitalist trade; and widened the reach of the rules, regulations and procedures underpinning liberal capitalism. Although the effects of this were most keenly felt in the former Soviet empire, the Third

World and China, its impacts were also felt within the Pax Americana's liberal heartlands in the following ways:

- by rearranging the global division of labour, parts of North America, EU and Australia were deindustrialized (as factories were shifted to China);

- huge labour flows rearranged the demographics of North America, EU and Australia. An emerging backlash against the resultant cultural changes has some potential to destabilize liberalization and globalization;

- building the 'information super highway' generated cultural changes (beneficial to liberal capitalism);

- there has been a growing cynicism and unease about Western political and economic elites promoting globalization.

Effectively, after 1991 the Pax Americana acted like a proselytizing agent for liberalism, capitalism, democracy and materialist consumerism. Under both Clinton and Bush a rather militant Conquistador-type proselytization emerged in which (since Western liberal values were assumed 'universally' valid), liberalization and democratization were often violently enforced. Interestingly, the resultant 'pan human universalism'[30] (encoded into the notion of 'universal human rights') came to be promoted not only by Americans, but also by their liberal partners in the EU, Australia and Canada.

The result was a proselytizing and moralizing imperialism under both the Clinton and Bush versions of the Pax Americana, which had more in common with Jacobin libertarianism than with classical liberalism.[31] In Europe this libertarianism is called 'social liberalism' and in America called 'liberalism'.[32] It is a form of liberalism stressing democracy and equality, desirous of big activist governments, and wanting 'outdated' regimes in the world to give way to progressive ones.[33] This libertarianism has becoming a new Jacobinism in America (and other Western democracies) – an ideology transforming democracy into a worldwide moral crusade.[34] The Pax Americana has served as a key facilitator of this crusade. Interestingly, although Jacobinism is traditionally associated with socialists or liberals, in America this new Jacobinism also found expression amongst people calling themselves conservatives or neoconservatives.[35] This facilitated alliances between people who seemed to adhere to different ideological positions, such as George Bush and Tony Blair.

For the new Jacobins (like Clinton, Bush and Blair), Western democracy came to be seen as inherently 'progressive' and a system deserving to be 'universalized'.[36] This produced a new kind of zealous liberalism whose adherents were absolutely convinced they knew what was best for all humankind; expected everyone else to recognize the inherent superiority of Western democracy; and believed it was justified to rid the world of unenlightened and undemocratic societies.[37] From within the *Weltan-schauung* of this 'democratism',[38] universalizing egalitarianism, plebiscitary democracy, human rights and majority rule was necessarily 'progressive'.[39] Hence, Jacobin idealists believed (like Wilson) it is acceptable to force people to be free.

As a Jacobin project, globalization II, has involved rolling out market democracy, capitalism and liberalism across the world. The new Jacobins even produced an imperialist ideology which advocated 'democratic capitalism' should replace traditional institutions and habits, old elites and old forms of social organization.[40] This Jacobinist ideology of 'democratism' helped roll out the Pax Americana in three ways. Firstly, it reconfigured the governance of Pax Americana heartlands by producing a new kind of ruling elite in places like America and Britain.[41] Secondly, democratism promoted liberalized comprador ruling elites across all regions of America's informal empire. Thirdly, by attacking traditionalism across the globe 'democratism' undermined alternative elites unsupportive of rolling out modern capitalist trading systems and secular materialism. The new Jacobins saw capitalism as an especially useful change agent because it served as such a powerful force for making-over (i.e. modernizing) traditional societies.[42]

Effectively, these new Jacobins (as modernists) have been intent on destroying traditional values, institutions and elites whether these are Western, Asian, Middle Eastern or African. And because the new Jacobins believe they have discovered a pan-human universalism, theirs has been a form of imperialism potentially far more culturally destructive than the British empire's globalization I. This is because 'democratism', as a 'univer-salizing' project, has not been intent on leaving 'spaces' for the survival of any remnants of traditional culture, traditional elites or traditional society in the way the British empire did. This is one of the reasons the Pax Americana has been such a powerful agent for cultural imperialism.

The 'American Peace' and its discontents

All empires generate resistance. However, formal empires are easier to attack because their power structures, personnel and symbols are easily identifiable. The Pax Americana exercises control more indirectly – through comprador-partners and proceduralized rules and regulations administered by global multilateral organizations like IMF, World Bank, WTO and UN. This renders much American power opaque, thereby making their informal empire more difficult to attack.

An interesting feature of Pax Americana governance is how multilateralism has been used to entrench an 'American peace'. Since 1945 governments have been locked into a global regulatory system designed by Wilsonian liberals and ratified by the Allies. This (American-designed) system effectively freezes the arrangements agreed to by the winners of World War II. This clearly benefits the Pax Americana by freezing existing boundaries and making it difficult for those opposed to the status quo to start a (legal) war. The current arrangements encoded into the UN and World Court, lock governments into multilateral arrangements, making their behaviours highly circumscribed and predictable. Consequently, the Wilsonian system is a deeply conservative international order reminiscent of the nineteenth-century Congress system. All political systems produce winners and losers, and the international system designed by Roosevelt's team makes it difficult for 'losers' within the Pax Americana to challenge the system. However, this does not mean they will all give up. The Pax Americana necessarily generates opponents, and despite difficulties, some find ways to hit back.

Liberalism may have defeated fascism (in 1945) and communism (in 1991), and liberals may have been immensely successful in undermining traditionalists everywhere, but these alternative worldviews have not (yet) gone away. Liberalism is hegemonic, but has not obliterated all alternative thinking. Liberals, as the current winners, may wish to proclaim 'peace' and deploy peacekeepers to freeze their victories, but Fukuyama's prediction of the 'end of history' was premature. A finalized 'liberal peace' is not yet available because 'America's peace' does not suit everybody; liberalism still has opponents; and the Pax Americana has its discontents.

So does the Pax Americana have any serious challengers?

Currently the Pax Americana is unrivalled because no other state (or even coalition of states) can match American power. America is a hyperpower, and for the moment, is unchallengeable. Consequently, the Pax Americana as a global liberal hegemony seems set to define the nature of global power relations for the foreseeable future. States not complying with America's liberal 'vision' for the world can expect to feel the discomfort of American pressure, e.g. North Korea and Iran.

The only state currently able to offer any meaningful resistance to Washington's will is Russia (because Russia still possesses the Soviet-built nuclear arsenal). Russia is clearly discontented with the Pax Americana's intrusion into Eastern Europe, the Caucuses and central Asia. But Russia is no longer a global power able to drive America out of the region. Instead Russia is, at best, a regional power currently engaged in trying to reincorporate into its sphere of influence some of the areas lost when the Soviet empire collapsed.

During the 1990s the Pax Americana made huge gains in Eastern Europe, absorbing large swathes of the former Soviet empire and incorporating these into NATO and the EU. Also, during the Yeltsin era, the emergence of Russian oligarchs created potential comprador-partners for the Pax Americana. However, Putin successfully pushed back the forces of liberalization in Russia by destroying these oligarchs and reasserting some measure of Russian autonomy from the Pax Americana. Further, Moscow's creation of a Collective Security Treaty Organization (incorporating Russia, Belarus, Kazakstan, Kyrgyzstan, Tajikistan and Armenia), created some basis for a bloc of states that may in the future be able to resist American hegemony in Eurasia. That Russia is trying to position itself outside the Pax Americana suggests American-Russian conflict will re-emerge in an arch stretching through Ukraine, Georgia, Azerbijan, Iran, Turkmenistan and Tajikistan.

Apart from Russia, the only other serious powers are the EU and China. China's rapid economic development (ironically being driven by Pax Americana globalization), is likely to eventually make China into a significant centre of power. Of course, Washington hopes China's economic growth will build a Chinese middle class who can be turned into comprador-partners within America's informal empire. But whether China's Communist Party allows this to happen is a moot point. A more likely scenario is that China will follow Putin's example, and disallow the liberalization of China on American terms. Whether this will turn China into an opponent of the Pax Americana only time will tell. As for the EU and Germany (the EU's core nation), Washington appears to have built a secure liberal hegemony – i.e. liberal comprador-partners are deeply entrenched in a range of European states, and for the foreseeable future European liberals seem perfectly capable of maintaining their hegemony over anti-liberal Europeans. Further, (liberal-run) multilateral organizations like NATO and the EU provide Europe's liberals with important organizational bases from which to bolster their hegemony across the whole region. Consequently, Europe looks set to remain solidly part of the Pax Americana, even though Europe contains a number of groups likely to offer some future resistance to the Pax Americana (e.g. Islamicists, fascists, communists and traditionalists).

A key feature of the contemporary Pax Americana is that no state actor is able to challenge America's hyperpower. Compared to America all other political players are 'weak'. It is this which creates the Pax Americana's fear of terrorism: after all, terrorism has always been the weapon of the weak; and the Pax Americana's key discontents are weak to the point of near defenceless in the face of the sort of power America can bring to bear upon them. Political actors who turn to terrorism are precisely those who are discontented *and frustrated* because they feel their worldview is crushed by another overwhelmingly powerful political force. Any number of discontented (non-state) political actors may have been expected to deploy terror against the Pax Americana (as an *overwhelmingly* powerful and hubristic liberal hegemon); it just happened to be the Islamisists who acted first, on 9/11.

The 2001 Al-Qaeda terror attacks on America reveal much about the sort of opposition America's informal empire seems likely to generate over the foreseeable future. Al-Qaeda was driven by hostility to the political and economic hegemony America exercises globally. (A hostility they share with many Third World political movements.) New York and Washington were seen as the centre of an empire – and hence are deemed to be legitimate targets. Al-Qaeda opposed the Pax Americana's modernization and liberalization of the world as a form of 'cultural imperialism'. Specifically, Al-Qaeda rejected liberal secular materialism (which they deemed 'ungodly') which was seen to be encoded into Pax Americana cultural imperialism. They also opposed the Pax Americana's Middle Eastern comprador-partners. These comprador-partners were seen to be in power (despite often being corrupt, incompetent and brutal) because the Pax Americana kept them in power. Hence, the West is blamed for the poor quality of both Third World governance and poverty. Whether or not the Pax Americana is actually to blame for Third World poor governance and poverty is a moot point. However, the reality is, conditions on the Pax Americana's peripheries have become breeding grounds for the sort of beliefs and discontent that feeds terrorism. Third World (and ex-Second World) economic and social instability, plus warlordism and crime, when coupled to population explosions have generated waves of migrants and refugees. Many of these migrants, who now reside in North America, the EU and Australia, carry with them resentments about conditions in their former homelands which they blame on the Pax Americana. It was precisely this mix of circumstances that gave birth to Al-Qaeda and 9/11.

For those who believe America's system of market democracy as inherently superior, and therefore worthy of being replicated across the world, it is difficult to comprehend why America's 'self-evident truths' are not welcomed everywhere. Similarly, for those who believe the ideology of 'One Worldism' it is difficult to understand why anyone would oppose the 'progress' and modernization promised by globalization II. This is why so many Americans were clearly baffled by the 9/11 attacks ('why do they hate us so much?') and by the response of Iraqis to the 2003 War ('why don't they want our democracy?'). Perhaps 9/11 and the Iraq War will force Americans to deal with such baffling issues and also confront the realities of how the Pax Americana has impacted on the lives of people living across their informal empire. Time will tell if Americans learn from these events and develop ways to improve their empire.

9/11 and the Bush Doctrine

The 9/11 terror attacks transformed the presidency of George W. Bush and led directly to two wars and to the Bush Doctrine. And because these two wars – in Afghanistan and Iraq – were unsuccessful for Washington, they generated an American debate about the nature of American power; America's role in the world; and the realization that many non-Americans saw America as imperialist. As a consequence, the Bush presidency will likely be seen as an important moment in the Pax Americana's evolution.

America's foreign policy was reconfigured by 9/11, with Bush's team jumping between different policies as they tried to develop a response:

- At the start of Bush's presidency, the Bush team leaned towards the realistic paradigm of foreign policy and were determined to move Washington away from liberal internationalism[43] – i.e. they rejected Clinton's Wilsonian idealism and Jacobinist 'democratism' and believed America should avoid meddling in the domestic affairs of other nations.[44] Bush had specifically opposed Clinton's interventionism in Haiti, Somalia, Bosnia and Kosovo.[45]

- 9/11 shifted the Bush-team's policy by simultaneously generating a sense of American vulnerability, coupled with a recognition America possessed tremendous power and so could 'hit back'. These two factors tipped the balance away from the realist paradigm and back towards the 'idealists'.[46] So ironically, 9/11 resulted in the Bush administration adopting Clinton's Wilsonian idealism and Jacobinist 'democratism' – i.e. Bush decided to use the enormous power America possessed to 'transform the world'[47] by liberalizing and Americanizing the international system.[48] In the process Bush became intensely Wilsonian.[49] But whereas Clinton-the-crusader operated within Wilsonian multilateralism (i.e. mobilizing Pax Americana comprador support), Bush-the-crusader shifted to greater unilateralism (which naturally upset America's comprador-partners). This effectively modified the internal dynamics of Pax Americana governance.

- When the Iraq war soured, the Bush administration edged back towards multilateralism/comprador consultation. They also shifted away from over-reliance on military power (e.g. Afghanistan/Iraq), and back towards diplomacy underpinned by military power (e.g. Iran/North Korea/Georgia).

But the key shift triggered by 9/11 was America's move towards pre-emption. This was encoded into the Bush Doctrine enunciated in 2002:

> It is an enduring American principle that this duty obligates the government to anticipate and counter threats, using all elements of national power, before the threats can do grave damage ... To forestall or prevent such hostile acts

by our adversaries, the United States will, if necessary, act pre-emptively in exercising our inherent right of self-defence.[50]

At heart the Bush Doctrine contained four features.

Firstly, America would in future use pre-emptive strikes against potential enemies. This altered the nature of the Pax Americana (previously based on the Wilsonian notion of guaranteed national sovereignty) because the Bush doctrine makes sovereignty conditional.[51] The Bush Doctrine effectively proposed that in future governments would have to comply with Pax Americana-made rules of 'acceptable behaviour'. Failure to comply with these rules meant America might launch a war to end their sovereignty (as seen in Iraq 2003).

Secondly, the rules of 'acceptable behaviour' would emerge from a revised form of multilateralism – i.e. a coalition of liberal states would now set the rules. (Bush's team called this the 'coalition of the willing'). Effectively, a globalized 'class coalition' of liberals (constructed by America) would govern the globe within the framework of the 'American peace'. Clearly, international law would be 'liberalized' within such new (global) liberal hegemony. This revised multilateralism derived from the fact that, post-1991, America has the power to act unilaterally. America's comprador-partners had become so weak compared to America that Washington could now choose which compradors it wanted to consult with, and on what terms. This necessarily altered the internal dynamics of the Pax Americana.

Thirdly, the Pax Americana was going to actively promote the spread of democracy, which would include forcing 'regime change' if necessary. The aim was to try and ensure all administrative units of the Pax Americana were governed as 'market democracies' in future. Hence, the idea that America should avoid meddling in the domestic affairs of other nations was now abandoned in favour of liberal proselytization; and Bush became the most Wilsonian president since Wilson himself.[52] References made by the Bush administration to deploying the German-democratization model in Iraq indicated how far the Bush team had moved towards the Rooseveltian (i.e. Wilsonian) model of hyper interventionism.

Fourth, the above three features were all premised upon the fact that America was overwhelmingly powerful, with no other political actor on the planet seriously able to challenge America's military superiority. The Bush Doctrine made it clear, from now on, America intended to use this power to impose its will and to tighten up on the (global) governance of the Pax Americana.

Ultimately, the Bush Doctrine simply reflected the reality that America's military power was so great that it necessarily altered the dynamics of all global politics as well as the operation of the Pax Americana. Amongst those who grappled with the implications of this new global reality were the Project for the New American Century (a conservative think-tank founded in 1997) and Bush's foreign policy advisors, who called themselves 'the Vulcans'.[53] Although there was some overlap between memberships of these two groups, they were not identical. Both these groups were interested in working out what America's new global role should be in the light of America's vast military superiority over everyone else. In this regard, the ideas of Paul Wolfowitz (a member of both groups) were especially important.

In the early 1990s Wolfowitz, as undersecretary of defence in the Bush Snr administration, grasped the enormous implications of the Soviet Union's collapse. Wolfowitz drew up a 1992 defence planning document suggesting a radical departure from America's traditional foreign policy built on the Wilson–Roosevelt model.[54] Effectively Wolfowitz proposed re-writing the rules of the Pax Americana on the basis Washington now had the power to govern global relations exclusively on American terms. Further, Wolfowitz suggested America should ensure it permanently retained global pre-eminence by working to ensure no other power could ever arise to challenge American dominance. Effectively, Wolfowitz proposed America assume the role of 'world policeman', which is exactly what the British empire had previously been. This sounded like a new kind of Pax Americana – one deploying an 'imperialism' somewhat more akin to the Pax Britannica than to a Wilsonian informal empire. By focusing on the new realities of global power Wolfowitz threatened to undermine a long-standing element of American foreign policy, namely the notion of American exceptionalism which held that truth, justice and history were on America's side, and that because America was so inherently 'good', America's will would naturally prevail. Wolfowitz seemed to be suggesting instead of relying on some kind of natural teleology, America should work at building and maintaining its power to ensure it permanently retained a pre-eminent position. From this grew the school of 'American primacy' (associated with the Project for the New American Century) which proposed building an unambiguously 'Americanized' international order that was to be maintained in perpetuity by force.[55] Wolfowitz's realism and honesty were deeply offensive to American idealists and the backlash was so intense that the Bush Snr administration distanced itself from him.[56] However, Wolfowitz had correctly pointed to the new reality of American power and the way this necessarily produced a new kind of Pax Americana. Consequently, although Clinton and his secretary of state, Albright, avoided Wolfowitz-speak, in reality they adopted his 'calculus of power'.[57] So although in reality American foreign policy became increasingly militarized under Albright,[58] she deployed the language of Wilsonian idealism and American exceptionalism (and kept the Wolfowitz discourse of power hidden from public view).[59]

The idea that the Bush Doctrine represented a radical departure from

earlier American foreign policy is an exaggeration. At heart Bush's administration simply pursued a widening of the Pax Americana, much as the
Clinton administration had done. Bush policies were grounded in:

- A desire to expand and secure America's informal trading empire, or as
  he said: 'to build a world that trades in freedom and therefore grows in
  prosperity'.[60] At its core the war on terror was simply an extension of the
  long-standing Pax Americana informal empire project of integrating the
  world and building open trade, with Bush noting the 'terrorists want to turn
  the openness of the global economy against itself'.[61]

- A conviction America was not an empire, but merely interested in spreading
  liberty and free markets.[62]

- A deeply American assumption that given a chance, people everywhere would
  embrace America's values of freedom, democracy and free enterprise.[63]

- The Wilsonian view that America stood for everything 'good' in the world.
  Hence working to promote American values and interests was good for the
  whole world.[64]

- The idea that Washington no longer had to tolerate compradors who were
  'tyrants' (which had been necessary during the Cold War).[65] Hence, like
  Clinton, Bush pursued 'democratization' (now that America had the power
  to do so).

Ultimately, the Bush Doctrine simply confirmed (and strengthened) the
Clinton Doctrine's aggressive interventionism. Essentially both doctrines
enunciate the same departure from Truman's policy of containment based on
the fact that, with the Soviet Union gone, the Roosevelt team's plans could
now be fully operationalized. However, whereas the Clinton team believed
multilateral diplomacy was a useful tool for bolstering the Pax Americana,
Bush's team was less convinced. The Bush team's mistake was to highlight
the fact that America's comprador-partners in Europe were so weak relative
to America that Washington could now afford to ignore them. Going to war
in Iraq without the support of all NATO partners made many American
comprador-partners uneasy because it revealed their actual status within the
Pax Americana. However, the Bush team soon realized that casting aside
multilateralism (as institutionalized by the Rooseveltians) made the Pax
Americana function less effectively. Consequently, Bush's team shifted back
to a 'new variety' of multilateralism that encoded three features: firstly, it
drew upon an 'idealistic' belief that globalizing American values, democracy
and trade was good for everyone; secondly, it was grounded in a 'realist'
recognition of America's awesome power; but, thirdly, it took the feelings of
Washington's comprador-partners into account in order to promote the idea
of the Pax Americana as an 'empire by invitation' (instead of an empire by
conquest).

Problems with the Pax Americana

The Bush administration's wars in Iraq and Afghanistan demonstrated the limits of American hubris, and exposed the shortcomings of the Pax Americana as an informal empire. The Iraq intervention in particular exposed the limitations of an informal empire that depends upon liberalized comprador-partners. The Iraq intervention was a liberalization exercise which, Washington hoped, would lead to the liberalization of the whole Middle East.[66] There were four elements to this Iraqi project:

- creating a middle-class comprador ruling elite. This involved identifying pro-Western modern secularized people prepared to function as comprador-partners. Ahmed Chalabi (and his Iraqi National Congress) initially served this purpose in Iraq. (In Afghanistan Hamid Karzai filled this role). People like Chalabi were expected to help America build an Iraqi bourgeoisie who could serve as America's comprador-partners;[67]

- 'democratization' through building liberal-democratic political infrastructures that replicated America's vision of 'good governance';[68]

- reconfiguring the economy into a free-market capitalism;[69]

- tying the reconfigured (liberalized) state to America's informal trading empire.[70]

The Iraqi project drew upon both America's conceptualization of 'development' (discussed in chapter 8) and a belief that the forced liberalization of Germany and Japan (discussed in chapter 9) could now be replicated in Iraq. George Bush, Condoleezza Rice and Chalabi all spoke about using Germany's deNazification as a model for Iraqi regime change. And so it was that the American-run Coalition Provisional Authority deployed the same techniques used in post-1945 Germany, namely: the Ba'ath Party was banned;[71] its leadership arrested; put on trial; and some executed. The de-Ba'athification programme saw a hundred and twenty thousand Iraqis fired from their jobs.[72] Then Iraq's four hundred thousand military personnel were fired to make way for a new military and police force America was to construct.[73] The old media and education systems were purged; and old school books destroyed and replaced with American-approved books. The Office for Reconstruction and Humanitarian Assistance (ORHA) had the task of developing Iraq in accordance with America's vision of modernist nation building and liberalization. Significantly, ORHA developed a strategy for mobilizing the expertise of NGOs with knowledge of Third World development and nation-building.[74] Development was to be outsourced and NGOs deployed as tools of the Pax Americana.

However, Iraq's liberalization did not go according to plan. Building an

Iraqi liberal bourgeoisie turned out to be more difficult than Washington anticipated, and it turned out to be naive to believe liberal democracy could flourish in any political culture. Washington was unable to build a liberalized group of Iraqi comprador-partners and Chalabi proved incapable of functioning as Adenauer.[75] Instead, 'democracy' simply empowered Iraq's Shiite majority (thereby strengthening Iran); Iraq fragmented into sectarian blocs and became a failed state; and America's military found themselves in the role of an occupation army facing a protracted guerrilla war.

The Pax Americana faced a similar situation in Afghanistan where NATO forces became an occupation army confronting Islamicist guerrillas. Karzai's compradors had no influence beyond Kabul and de facto control of this failed state was exercised by tribal warlords or Islamicists.

In the case of both Iraq and Afghanistan, Washington found itself trapped by the nature of its informal empire. The Pax Americana is an empire premised upon having compradors willing and able to act as America's partners. If these compradors are incompetent, America is unable to replace them in the way a formal empire can replace governors and officials. Similarly, American military actions are constrained by the need to go through the pretence of consulting compradors like Talabani and Karzai. The Iraq and Afghanistan wars highlighted the fact formal and informal empires deploy fundamentally different genres of control and governance; and that Washington needs to be more aware of the advantages, disadvantages and logics of both the 'formal' and 'informal' genres, and realize that drifting back and forth between the two genres is unlikely to produce success. Engaging in 'regime change' is the sort of extreme interventionism one would usually expect from a formal empire. To be carried out successfully, it requires the consistent deployment of formal empire logic. The result of mixing 'formal' and 'informal' genres in Iraq and Afghanistan simply produced failed states.

There are also signs Washington is experiencing growing difficulties maintaining a global 'liberal consensus', and managing its informal empire through compradors. Examples are the collapse of the Doha round of world trade negotiations; a growing 'restiveness' in the Third World as seen in the election of Latin American populists (e.g. Hugo Chavez and Evo Morales); a re-emerging European right wing; growing pressures on EU unity; and the failure of key comprador-partners to maintain viable states (e.g. Pakistan).

These difficulties, especially those encountered in Iraq and Afghanistan, raise some interesting questions Americans presumably need to consider, debate and answer:

- Would there be any benefits to reconfiguring some parts of the Pax Americana into a formal empire? (After all Britain's Indian Ocean empire was transformed from an informal to a formal empire when this became beneficial).

- If America continues to operate an informal empire what are the likely consequences for America? And for the rest of the world?

- Did Britain's empire do a better job of governing the 'processes of globalization' than the Pax Americana is doing?

- Does America have the cultural capital required to run a successful formal empire?

Pax Britannica and Pax Americana: some comparisons

Although the first and second waves of globalization are rooted in the same Anglo global-trading project,[76] the second wave (driven by the Pax Americana) differs from the first wave (driven by the Pax Britannica). These differences – summarized in table 11.2 – can be explained by the fact that, (due to its political culture), America opted to run an informal empire, as opposed to Britain's formal empire. That America adopted the informal empire approach was to have major implications for the world.

So what does a comparison of the Pax Britannica and Pax Americana reveal?

Firstly, the Pax Americana, despite its enormous military power, appears to be a poor global policeman. One of the key roles of empires is to provide the security required for both investing in distant lands and for global trade, e.g. Niall Ferguson argues the security, law and administration provided by Britain's empire created conditions for development, economic growth and trade.[77] Michael Mandelbaum concurs Britain's empire fulfilled this role, and argues that today America fulfils this role.[78] However, unlike Mandelbaum, Ferguson regards Britons as having done a far better job than Americans.[79] Certainly, America's informal empire has been an unsuccessful provider of security when measured by the number of corrupt, tyrannical or incompetent comprador-partners; and the number of failing states. Further, the British (as 'world policeman') clearly did a better job at suppressing seaborne piracy than the Pax Americana has done.

A second difference can be found by comparing the British and American ruling elites. Bernard Porter suggests Britain produced a ruling elite perfectly suited to ruling empires.[80] This elite were prepared to actually move to the ends of the earth as colonial officials to serve their empire and build the infrastructures required for development and trade. They learned the local languages and customs and became advocates for the areas they lived in. They also guarded local cultures, becoming advocates for cultural pluralism in Britain's empire. The Americans have produced no such class of rulers with a natural flair for empire. Instead, the Pax Americana's (political and business) elite prefers to stay in their comfortable American suburbs and rule from a distance – communicating by email, or

Pax Britannica (formal empire)	Pax Americana (informal empire)
British annexed foreign territory and ran up the British flag	Foreign territory not annexed
Dispatched British occupation army	Independent states have their own armies which America often helps train. America uses an alliance system which it dominates (e.g. NATO). American-led (multilateral) occupation armies only rarely dispatched (e.g. Germany, Japan, Afghanistan, Iraq)
British-ran police systems in each occupied territory	Independent states have their own police force which America often helps train
British-ran judicial systems in each occupied territory (with Privy Council in London as final court of appeal)	Independent states run their own judiciaries. But power of International Court to impose 'international will' is growing
British Governor oversaw political process in each occupied territory (Political processes had various levels of 'local participation' and various levels 'autonomy' from Britain)	No American governors in the informal empire. Instead, America encourages 'comprador elites' within independent states
Local economies were restructured to suit British economic interests	Local economies restructured to suit American economic interests, but this is achieved through intervention of American corporations, American Aid, World Bank (rather than direct American government policy-making)
British merchants emigrated to colonies (to network these colonies with London)	American corporations dispatch some staff to foreign states, but control mostly exercised via telecommunications, short-term visits, or comprador managers
British built infrastructures such as railways, ports, roads, hospitals, schools, universities, irrigation, electricity/water/sewerage and telecommunications. This involved building British-run bureaucracies in each colony to administer and develop these territories	America builds no foreign infrastructure and runs no overseas bureaucracy. However, a system of multilateral organizations (UN, World Bank, etcetera) operates as a 'neo-imperial bureaucracy'

Pax Britannica (formal empire)	Pax Americana (informal empire)
Colonial economies tied to London (often via system of imperial preferences)	Foreign economies tied to New York through American-corporations and American dominance of global financial system
Britain ran a global system of maritime trade routes (protected by globally dispersed naval bases), and a global telegraph system	America runs a global system of maritime and aviation trade routes (protected by globally dispersed naval and airforce bases) and a global telecommunications system

Table 11.2 Differences between the British and American empires

paying the occasional quick visit or familiarization tours to the margins of the empire. And because Americans do not move to the margins of their empire, they do not have to live with the consequences of bad decisions and bad rule in these places. British colonial officials lived with the consequences of their decisions. Instead, the Pax Americana has come to be associated with American-supported compradors, some of whom are tyrants and dictators.[81] America has now even begun delivering its violence from a distance – with military personnel sitting comfortably in America and using satellite communication and computers to direct missiles and armed drones to attack targets on the other side of the world. This 'ruling-from-a-distance' phenomenon is the root of America's poor intelligence. (The consequences of which were witnessed in 9/11.) It is a particularly poor form of governance.

The question is, why haven't Americans developed good imperial governance like the British? Interestingly, Washington tried imperial governance in the Philippines and when they discovered how hard it was[82] they gave up.[83]

A third difference between American and British imperialism is America's dependence on comprador-partners. When Britain's empire encountered societies incapable of governing themselves they directly intervened and dispatched their own colonial officials to establish the governance required for development and trade. In the process Britain created a form of international government that worked.[84] The Pax Americana, on the other hand, is a poor form of global governance because it allows poor governance and even failed states to exist. Dismantling the European empires and insisting on a world of self-determining states tied into America's trading network has created great human suffering in vast swathes of the world where poor governance and comprador corruption now exists. 'It must be said that the experiment of running the world without Empire cannot be adjudged an unqualified success',[85] and post-1945 American idealism has much to answer for. Certainly, Pax Britannica colonial officials may have delivered 'paternalistic' and even 'dictatorial' governance, but it was effective governance and was not corrupt. The Pax Americana replaced this with a system of compradors, where some compradors became dictators; many were incompetent and corrupt; and some were so inept they produced failed states. For the inhabitants of poorly governed regions, the failings of Pax Americana's global governance are already clear enough. But the potential future consequences of these failings may be greater – for example, Pakistan has nuclear weapons and teeters on the brink of being a failed state; while badly governed states elsewhere are generating waves of migrants that threaten to destabilize North America and Western Europe. Of real concern is the fact that the Pax Americana, as a form of global governance, currently appears to have no mechanisms to fix the problem of under-performing compradors.

A fourth difference between British and American imperialism is America's almost religious belief that liberal democracy is good for everybody. America's proselytizing zeal for 'democratization' and egalitarianism translated into an attempt to impose a single vision of governance upon the world. Such a formulaic and homogenizing worldview is both naive and likely to generate resistance from non-liberals. Britain's empire, in contrast, ran multiple different kinds of governance structures – with governance being pragmatically designed to suit local circumstances. Hence, Canada was a liberal democracy; Uganda a benevolent autocracy; and South Africa an oligarchy. Ironically, American attempts at global political homogenization are just as much top-down imperialist impositions as anything the European empires ever tried. But they simply do not function as well.

A fifth difference concerns the cultural impacts of British and American imperialism. The Pax Britannica was a curious phenomenon because, on the one hand, Britons seized territorial control, governed directly and actively managed development themselves. Yet British colonial officials tended, as conservatives, to be opposed to liberal or socialist utopian planning and social engineering; and instead deliberately worked with and through local cultures, deploying a form of governance characterized by 'collaboration' with local elites.[86] Consequently, although the British created Westernized 'development zones' in their colonies, they also left 'spaces' where local cultures could thrive. Pax Americana comprador governance is curiously far more interventionist and damaging to local cultures despite its 'rule-from-a-distance' approach. So whereas the Pax Britannica resulted in a form of cultural pluralism (where local cultures continued alongside Anglo culture), the Pax Americana's impact on local cultures has been truly destructive for three reasons. Firstly, the Pax Americana has frequently promoted comprador regimes motivated by nation building. These nation builders are often zealous social engineers who wilfully destroy traditional cultures and ethnic minorities in the states they run. As John Gray notes of liberal-Jacobin nation building: 'National self-determination marches hand in hand with ethnic cleansing and the uprooting of eclectic societies in which different ways of life have long coexisted in peace.'[87] Secondly, liberal Jacobins (driving 'development' from the West) have in general, (unlike the British colonial officers) shown little regard for local traditional cultures which get in the way of their social engineering projects. Thirdly, the global media/Hollywood has produced cultural homogenization and hybridization functional to Third World development. However, it is a moot point whether the vulgar narcissistic consumer culture and 'sceptical relativism' being disseminated by this media is actually functional for the long-term governance of the Pax Americana. In this regard, Bacevich suggests the 'multicultural and value-free nonjudgmental tolerance combined with an ever-widening definition of personal autonomy' being disseminated by American media may be undermining any sense of a 'common higher purpose'.[88] Ultimately, the shallow consumerist culture, now being disseminated globally, may possibly undermine the Pax Americana's capacity to produce a ruling elite capable of coherently governing an empire.

The Pax Americana clearly leaves less room for cultural 'difference' than did the Pax Britannica, and looks set to be an agent of widespread cultural destruction because of America's vision of itself as a 'universal civilization'.[89] Effectively the Pax Americana simply disallows other ways of life; and other ways of political and socio-economic organization[90] as it globally spreads its culture of meaningless shallow consumerism.

A sixth difference springs from American attitudes towards imperialism and towards governance. Britons embraced imperialism and were flexible and pragmatic in their approach to governance. Britain's empire produced a form of global governance that worked well. The Pax Americana, on the other hand, is imperialism done badly because it is an empire 'run by a democracy that embraces the principle of equality and values formal limits on state power. These principles contradict the imperial tendency to hierarchy and the use of unrestrained, extra-legal violence'.[91] Essentially Americans believe in plebiscitary democracy; the ideology of egalitarianism and believe 'imperialism' and 'colonialism' is bad. Many Americans would even deny they run an empire. Consequently, Americans will not do what is necessary to run an empire well. The problem is, the Pax Americana effectively replaced the Pax Britannica, and America now de facto acts as a kind of world government.[92] But because it is in denial about its imperial role in the world, America is doing a very poor job.

The empire that runs the world today is both more and less than its begetter. It has a much bigger economy, many more people, a much larger arsenal. But it is an empire that lacks the drive to export its capital, its people and its culture to those backward regions which need them most urgently and which, if they are neglected, will breed the greatest threats to its security. It is an empire, in short, that dare not speak its name. It is an empire in denial.[93]

Quo vadis?

So what is the solution?

Americans – as the people running the current system of global governance – need to debate a way forward. (The rest of us are simply disenfranchised spectators.) Bacevich suggests there are four American views of their empire – those who:[94]

- deny an American empire even exists;

- acknowledge it exists and say it is evil;

- are enthusiastic it exists and say this empire is good for America and for everyone else;

- say it exists and it is an American burden.

A fifth category could be added: namely, the American empire exists and it needs to be run better. Effectively, Americans need to considerably lift their game and deliver a better form of global governance than we have at present.

It is simply unhelpful to suggest the Pax Americana is evil and needs to be abolished. This would merely generate even more global anarchy than we have at present. Ferguson is correct that a fully self-conscious and effective empire (such as the Pax Britannica) appears to be a better form of global governance than an unself-reflexive informal empire in denial (such as the Pax Americana). Good empires create order and civilization. Human greatness has come from well-run empires. Even if empires have their downsides, the alternative to empire can be worse, because order is better than anarchy. (Simply ask anyone who has lived in a state where law-and-order breaks down because of poor governance.)

It is also time to overcome the notion that 'empire is obsolete'. The ideologies of anti-imperialism and anticolonialism need to be challenged as old fashioned. Post-World War II decolonization did not produce a better world. Instead, it spread poor governance, failed states and nation-building Jacobins who rode roughshod over their own subjects.

It is also time to re-examine Wilsonian idealism and liberal interna-tionalism which produced an informal empire that has not been as effective as the world order it replaced. The Wilsonian notion of sovereign nation states tied into a multilateral global system (i.e. America's informal empire) has not been an unqualified success. Vast swathes of America's contemporary informal empire are characterized by poor governance and poor socio-economic organization. Many of the sovereign states created by post-World War II decolonization have experienced economic decline and some are sliding into becoming feeble and failed states. Around the globe piracy and slavery is growing. Consequently, it would seem the system of global governance built by Wilsonian liberal internationalism needs to be re-evaluated. The Project for the New American Century and Bush's Vulcans began such a re-evaluation during Bush's presidency.[95] Washington seemed to be tentatively trying to conceptualize a post-Wilsonian international order in which America's informal empire might be replaced with a different kind of Pax Americana. However, the Bush team did not do a good job of redesigning the Pax Americana. And when the Iraq and Afghanistan wars did not proceed according to plan, Americans drew back and elected Obama, who effectively promised a return to the old safe ways of multilateralism, informal empire and soft power. The Obama model involves governing the empire through comprador-partners, diplomacy and the imposition of multilateral regulation and 'universal rights' by a global system that all players understand to be undergirdered by American military might. Within this model, those areas of the empire proving difficult to govern are 'fixed' by diplomatic pressure and sanctions, or by deploying 'development' to build new comprador-partners.

Could it be that the Bush team's failures, events in Iraq and Afghanistan, plus America's rejection of the Vulcans, simply confirms the incapacity of America's political system and political culture to deliver a governing elite as competent as Britain's imperial administrators? If so, this does not bode well for the future because, as Mandelbaum notes, America effectively acts as a world government.[96] So if American political culture is unable to produce a ruling class capable of adequately governing their global empire the whole world is in trouble.

Notes

1 Bacevich, A., *American Empire. The Realities and Consequences of US Diplomacy* (Cambridge, MA: Harvard University Press, 2002), 38–39.
2 Dueck, C., *Reluctant Crusaders* (Princeton: Princeton University Press, 2006), 121.
3 *Ibid.*, 21–22.
4 Gray, J., *Black Mass. Apocalyptic Religion and the Death of Utopia* (New York: Farrar, Straus & Giroux, 2007), 30.
5 *Ibid.*, 191.

6 Dueck, *Reluctant*, 114–115.
7 Krauthammer, C., 'Democratic Realism', in Skidmore, D., *Paradoxes of Power* (Boulder: Paradigm Publishers, 2007), 108.
8 Dueck, *Reluctant*, 130.
9 *Ibid.*, 123.
10 Bacevich, *American*, 215.
11 *Ibid.*, 131.
12 Dueck, *Reluctant*, 114.
13 Bacevich, *American*, 155.
14 *Ibid.*, 162.
15 *Ibid.*, 163.
16 *Ibid.*, 157–158, 161.
17 *Ibid.*, 165.
18 These uniformed proconsuls were American and American allies (e.g. NATO and Australian).
19 Bacevich, *American*, 167.
20 Porter, B., *Empire and Superempire* (New Haven: Yale University Press, 2006), 90.
21 Ikenberry, J., 'Imperial Ambitions', in Bacevich, A., *The Imperial Tense* (Chicago: Ivan Dee, 2003), 186.
22 As Ignatieff, M., *Empire Lite* (London: Vintage, 2003), 14–16 notes, Europeans demilitarized themselves so much that America no longer has to heed what Europeans say.
23 Maier, C., 'Imperial Limits', in Bacevich, *Imperial*, 204.
24 Smith, N., *The Endgame of Globalization* (New York: Routledge, 2005), 147.
25 Ryn, C., *America the Virtuous* (New Brunswick: Transaction Publishers, 2004), 158.
26 Bacevich, *American*, 40–41.
27 Guyatt, N., *Another American Century* (London: Zed Books, 2003), 14.
28 China's resource-extraction projects in Africa have encountered the same labour difficulties previously experienced by Europe's empires. China's response has been to send large numbers of Chinese workers into Africa to build the projects themselves. The parallel with Britain's empire is clear.
29 Lee, M.C. *et al.*, *China in Africa* (Uppsala: Nordiska Afrikainstitutet, 2007).
30 Greenfeld, L., *Nationalism* (Cambridge, MA: Harvard University Press, 1993), 446.
31 Ryn, *America*, 26–27.
32 *Ibid.*, 27.
33 *Ibid.*, 27.
34 *Ibid.*, 20–21.
35 *Ibid.*, 21.
36 *Ibid.*, 21.
37 *Ibid.*, 26.
38 *Ibid.*, 71.
39 *Ibid.*, 49.
40 *Ibid.*, 25–26.

41 *Ibid.*, 158.
42 *Ibid.*, 25.
43 Dueck, *Reluctant*, 162.
44 Gordon, P., 'The End of the Bush Revolution', in Skidmore, *Paradoxes*, 267.
45 Phillips, D., *Losing Iraq* (New York: Basic Books, 2005), 14.
46 Gordon, 'End', 208.
47 *Ibid.*, 208.
48 Dueck, *Reluctant*, 160.
49 *Ibid.*, 158–159, 163.
50 Bush, G.W., *The National Security of the United States of America* (Washington: National Security Council, 20 September 2002).
51 Ikenberry, 'Imperial', 192–193.
52 Desch, M., America's Liberal Illiberalism, *International Security*, 32, 3 (2007), 20.
53 Mann, J., *Rise of the Vulcans* (New York: Viking Penguin, 2004).
54 Bacevich, *American*, 44–45.
55 Dueck, *Reluctant*, 119–121.
56 *Ibid.*, 44.
57 *Ibid.*, 45–46.
58 *Ibid.*, 49.
59 *Ibid.*, 46, 49, 51–52.
60 Bush, G.W., 'America's Responsibility, America's Mission', in Bacevich, *Imperial*, 8.
61 Bacevich, *American*, 232.
62 Daalder, I. & Lindsay, J., *America Unbound* (Washington: Brookings Institute, 2003), 45.
63 *Ibid.*, 125.
64 *Ibid.*, 36.
65 *Ibid.*, 121.
66 Lafer, G., 'Neoliberalism by Other Means. The "War on Terror" at Home and Abroad', in Peschek, J., *The Politics of Empire* (London: Routledge, 2006), 57.
67 Phillips, *Losing*, 147.
68 Phillips, *Losing*, 63, suggests State Department Arabists did not believe democratization was possible, but the Pentagon and White House pushed this agenda.
69 Lafer, 'Neoliberalism', 58–60.
70 *Ibid.*, 60.
71 Phillips, *Losing*, 145.
72 *Ibid.*, 145.
73 *Ibid.*, 149.
74 *Ibid.*, 129.
75 Even in Third World societies where the Pax America successfully built middle-class compradors (e.g. the 'patriotic black bourgeoisie' in South Africa), it has proved difficult to build functioning liberal democracies.
76 Gray, J., *False Dawn. The Delusions of Global Capitalism* (London: Granta, 2002), 13–14.

77 Ferguson, N., *Empire* (New York: Basic Books, 2004), 305–307.
78 Mandelbaum, M., *The Case for Goliath* (New York: Public Affairs, 2005), 88–94.
79 Ferguson, *Empire*, 308.
80 Porter, *Empire*, 49–52.
81 *Ibid.*, 90–92.
82 Judis, J., 'History Lesson', in Skidmore, *Paradoxes*, 65.
83 Smith, *The Endgame*, 49.
84 Ferguson, *Empire*, 308.
85 Ferguson, *Empire*, 308.
86 Porter, *Empire*, 55–59.
87 Gray, *Black*, 169.
88 Bacevich, *American*, 84.
89 Gray, *False*, 2–3.
90 *Ibid.*, 202–205.
91 Rosen, S., 'Imperial Choices', in Bacevich, *Imperial*, 224.
92 Mandelbaum, *Case*, 126.
93 Ferguson, *Empire*, 317.
94 Bacevich, *Imperial*, xii.
95 Mann, *Rise*.
96 Mandelbaum, *Case*.

Select bibliography

Allawi, A.A. (2007) *The Occupation of Iraq*. New Haven: Yale University Press.

Anon (1941) *The Atlantic Charter. A full Text of the Joint Declaration of the President of the United States of America and the Prime Minister of Great Britain* (12 August). London: Whitcombe & Tombs Ltd.

Bacevich, A.J. (2002) *American Empire. The Realities and Consequences of US Diplomacy*. Cambridge, MA: Harvard University Press.

Bachevich, A.J. (2003) *The Imperial Tense. Prospects and Problems with the American Empire*. Chicago: Ivan Dee.

Bell, S. (1972) *Righteous Conquest. Woodrow Wilson and the Evolution of the New Diplomacy*. Port Washington: Kennikat Press.

Black, J. (2004) *The British Seaborne Empire*. New Haven: Yale University Press.

Boyce, D.G. (1999) *Decolonisation and the British Empire, 1775–1997*. London: Macmillan.

Brown, J.M. & Louis W.R. (1999) *The Oxford History of the British Empire, Vol. IV*. Oxford: Oxford University Press.

Burns, J.M. (1970) *Roosevelt. The Soldier of Freedom*. New York: Harcourt Brace Jovanovich.

Bush, G.W. (2002) *The National Security of the United States of America*. Washington DC, 20 September (www.whitehouse.gov/nsc/nss.pdf).

Cain, P.J. (1978) 'J.A. Hobson, Cobdenism and the Radical Theory of Economic Imperialism 1898–1914', *Economic History Review*, 31, 565–584.

Cain, P.J. & Hopkins, A.G. (1987) 'Gentlemanly Capitalism and British Overseas Expansion', *The Economic History Review*, 40 (1), 1–26.

Cain, P.J. & Hopkins, A.G. (2002) *British Imperialism 1688–2000*. Harlow: Longman.

Calhoun, F.S. (1993) *Uses of Force and Wilsonian Foreign Policy*. Kent: Kent State University Press.

Callahan, R.A. (1984) *Churchill. Retreat from Empire*. Wilmington: Scholarly Resources.

Campbell, N., Davies, J. & McKay, G. (2004) *Issues in Americanisation of Culture*. Edinburgh: Edinburgh University Press.

Clarke, P. (2007) *The Last Thousand Days of the British Empire*. London: Allen Lane.

Clymer, K.J. (1988) 'Franklin Roosevelt, Louis Johnson, India and Anticolonialism. Another Look', *Pacific Historical Review*, 57, 261–284.

Cohen, A. (1959) *British Policy in Changing Africa*. Evanston: Northwestern University Press.

Cowen, T. (2002) *Creative Destruction. How Globalization is Changing the World's Cultures*. Princeton: Princeton University Press).

Cox, R. (1987) *Production, Power and World Order*. New York: Columbia University Press.

Daalder, I. & Lindsay, J. (2003) *America Unbound*. Washington: Brookings Institute.

Danchev, A. & McMillan, J. (2005) *The Iraq War and Democratic Politics*. London: Routledge.

Davis, L.E. & Huttenback, R.A. (1986) *Mammon and the Pursuit of Empire. The Political Economy of British Imperialism, 1860–1912*. Cambridge: Cambridge University Press.

Den Hollander, A.N.J. (1973) 'On "Dissent" and "Influence" as Agents of Change', in Den Hollander, A.N.J. *Contagious Conflict*. Leiden: E.J. Brill.

Diefendorf, J.M., Frohn, A. & Rupieper, H. (1993) *American Policy and the Reconstruction of West Germany, 1945–1955*. Cambridge: Cambridge University Press.

Dower, J.W. (1999) *Embracing Defeat. Japan in the Wake of World War II*. New York: W.W. Norton.

Dueck, C. (2006) *Reluctant Crusaders*. Princeton: Princeton University Press.

Dunn, F.S. (1963) *Peace-making and the Settlement with Japan*. Princeton: Princeton University Press.

Dutt, R.P. (1953) *The Crisis of Britain and the British Empire*. London: Lawrence & Wishart.

Dutton, D. (1997) *Anthony Eden*. London: Arnold.

Ebsworth, R. (1960) *Restoring Democracy in Germany*. London: Steven & Sons Ltd.

Engerman, D.C., Gilman, N., Haefele, M. & Latham, M. (2003) *Staging Growth*. Amherst: University of Massachusetts Press.

Etherington, N. (1982) 'Reconsidering Theories of Imperialism', *History and Theory*, 21 (1), 1–36.

Etzioni, A. (2004) 'A Self-restrained Approach to Nation-building by Foreign Powers', *International Affairs*, 80 (1), 1–7.

Fanon, F. (1968) *The Wretched of the Earth*. New York: Grove Press.

Ferguson, N. (2004) *Empire*. New York: Basic Books.

Ferguson, N. (2005) *Colossus*. London: Penguin Books.

Fieldhouse, D.K. (1999) *The West and the Third World*. Oxford: Blackwell.

Frank, A.G. (1969) *Capitalism and Underdevelopment in Latin America*. New York: Monthly Review Press.

Frank, A.G. (1972) 'Who Is the Immediate Enemy?', in Cockcroft, J.D., Frank, A.G. & Johnson, D. (eds), *Dependence and Development*. New York: Anchor Books.

Fraser. M. (2003) *Weapons of Mass Distraction*. New York: Thomas Dunne Books.

Fukuyama, F. (1989) 'The End of History?', *The National Interest*, Summer, 3–18.

Gallagher, J. (1982) *The Decline, Revival and Fall of the British Empire*. Cambridge: Cambridge University Press.

Gardiner, D. (1982) 'Decolonization in French, Belgian and Portuguese Africa', in Gifford, P. & Louis, Wm.R. (eds), *The Transfer of Power in Africa*. New Haven: Yale University Press.

Gardner, L.C., LaFeber, W. & McCormick, T. (1973) *Creation of the American Empire. US Diplomatic History*. Chicago: Rand McNally.

Gifford, P. & Louis, Wm.R. (eds) (1982) *The Transfer of Power in Africa. Decolonization 1940–1960*. New Haven: Yale University Press.

Gifford, P. & Louis, Wm.R. (1988) *Decolonization and African Independence. The Transfer of Power 1960–1980*. New Haven: Yale University Press.

Gilpin, R. (2000) 'The Retreat of the State', in Lawton, T.C., Rosenau, J.N. & Verdun, A.C. (eds), *Strange Power*. Aldershot: Ashgate.

Goldstein, J. (2000) 'The United States and World Trade. Hegemony by Proxy?', in Lawton, T.C., Rosenau, J.N. & Verdun, A.C. (eds), *Strange Power*. Aldershot: Ashgate.

Goldsworthy, D. (1971) *Colonial Issues in British politics 1945–1961*. Oxford: Clarendon Press.

Gray, J. (2002) *False Dawn. The Delusions of Global Capitalism*. London: Granta.

Gray, J. (2007) *Black Mass. Apocalyptic Religion and the Death of Utopia*. New York: Farrar, Straus & Giroux.

Greer, T.H. (1958) *What Roosevelt Thought*. East Lansing: Michigan State University Press.

Grosser, A. (1974) *Germany in Our Time*. Harmondsworth: Pelican Books.

Guyatt, N. (2003) *Another American Century*. London: Zed Books.

Harris, K. (1982) *Attlee*. London: Weidenfeld & Nicolson.

Hartz, L. (1955) *The Liberal Tradition in America*. New York: Harcourt Brace.

Hathaway, R.M. (1981) *Ambiguous Partnership. Britain and America 1944–1947*. New York: Columbia University Press.

Helleiner, E. (2000) 'Still an Extraordinary Power, But for How Much Longer? The United States in World Finance', in Lawton, T.C., Rosenau, J.N. & Verdun, A.C. (eds), *Strange Power*. Aldershot: Ashgate.

Herman, E.S. & McChesney, R.W. (1997) *The Global Media*. London: Cassell.

Hess, G.R. (1971) *America Encounters India*. Baltimore: Johns Hopkins University Press.

Hess, G.R. (1972) 'Franklin Roosevelt and Indochina', *The Journal of American History*, 59 (2), 353–368.

Hess, G.R. (1987) *The United States' Emergence as a Southeast Asian Power, 1940–1950*. New York: Columbia University Press.

Hitchens, C. (1990) *Blood, Class and Nostalgia*. New York: Farrar, Straus & Giroux.

Hobson, J.A. (1968) *Imperialism. A Study*. London: George Allen & Unwin.

Hogan, M.J. (1999) *The Ambiguous Legacy. US Foreign Relations in the American Century*. Cambridge: Cambridge University Press.

Horowitz, D. (1970) Attitudes of British Conservatives towards Decolonization in Africa, *African Affairs*, 1 (274), 9–26.

Howe, S. (1993) *Anticolonialism in British Politics*. Oxford: Clarendon Press.

Hugh-Jones, E.M. (1947) *Woodrow Wilson and American Liberalism*. London: English Universities Press.

Hughes, R.T. (2004) *Myths America Lives By*. Urbana: University of Illinois Press.

Hull, C. (1948) *The Memoirs of Cordell Hull* (2 vols). London: Hodder & Stoughton.

Ignatieff, M. (2003) *Empire Lite*. London: Vintage.

Johnson, D.B. (1960) *The Republican Party and Wendell Willkie*. Urbana: University of Illinois Press.

Kawai, K. (1960) *Japan's American Interlude*. Chicago: University of Chicago Press.

Keohane, R.O. (2005) *After Hegemony. Cooperation and Discord in the World of Political Economy*. Princeton: Princeton University Press.

Kimball, W.F. (1984) *Churchill & Roosevelt. The Complete Correspondence I*. Princeton: Princeton University Press.

Kimball, W.F. (1991) *The Juggler*. Princeton: Princeton University Press.

Kirk-Greene A.H.M. (1982) 'A Historiographical Perspective on the Transfer of Power in British Colonial Africa', in Gifford, P. & Louis, Wm.R. (eds), *The Transfer of Power in Africa. Decolonization 1940–1960*. New Haven: Yale University Press.

Kolko, G. (1968) *The Politics of War*. London: Weidenfeld & Nicolson.

Latham, M.E. (2000) *Modernization as Ideology. American Social Science & Nation Building in the Kennedy Era*. Chapel Hill: University of North Carolina Press.

Lawton, T.C. & Michaels, K.P. (2000) 'The Evolving Global Production Structure: Implications for International Political Economy', in Lawton, T.C., Rosenau, J.N. & Verdun, A.C. (eds), *Strange Power*. Aldershot: Ashgate.

Lawton, T.C., Rosenan, J.N. and Verdun, A.C. (2000) *Strange Power*. Aldershot: Ashgate.

Lee, J.M. & Petter, M. (1982) *The Colonial Office, War, and Development Policy*. London: Institute for Commonwealth Studies.

Lefeber, W. (1975) 'Roosevelt, Churchill and Indochina, 1942–45', *American Historical Review*, 80, 1277–1295.

Lenin, V.I. (1975) *Imperialism. The Highest Stage of Capitalism*. Moscow: Progress Publishers.

Leys, C. (1996) *The Rise & Fall of Development Theory*. London: James Currey.

Lipscomb, A.A. & Bergh, A.E. (1903) *The Writings of Thomas Jefferson, Vol. 12*. Washington, DC: Thomas Jefferson Memorial Association of the United States.

Louis, W.R. (1977) *Imperialism at Bay, 1941–1945*. Oxford: Clarendon Press.

Louis, W. & Robinson, Wm.R. (1982) 'The United States and the Liquidation of the British Empire in Tropical Africa 1941–1951', in Gifford, P. & Louis, Wm.R. (eds), *The Transfer of Power in Africa. Decolonization 1940–1960*. New Haven: Yale University Press.

Louw, P.E. (2004) *The Rise, Fall and Legacy of Apartheid*. Westport: Praeger.

Madison, J.H. (1992) *Wendell, Willkie*. Bloomington: Indiana University Press.

Mandelbaum, M. (2002) *The Ideas that Conquered the World*. Oxford: Public Affairs.

Mandelbaum, M. (2005) *The Case for Goliath*. New York: Public Affairs.

McMahon, R.J. (1981) *Colonialism and Cold War*. Ithaca: Cornell University Press.

McIntyre, W.D. (1998) *British Decolonization, 1946–1997*. London: Macmillan.

McKercher, B.J.C. (1999) *Transition of Power. Britain's Loss of Global Pre-eminence to the United States, 1930–1945*. Cambridge: Cambridge University Press.

Montgomery, J.D. (1957) *Forced to be Free. The Artifical Revolution in Germany and Japan*. Chicago: University of Chicago Press.

Moon, P.T. (1927) *Imperialism and World Politics*. New York: Macmillan.

Morel, T.P. (2005) *Red Rubber*. Honolulu: University of the Pacific Press.

Morris, J. (1968) *Pax Britannica*. London: Faber & Faber.

Morris, J. (1978) *Farewell the Trumpets*. London: Faber & Faber.

Newsom, D.D. (2001) *The Imperial Mantle. The US, Decolonization and the Third World*. Bloomington: Indiana University Press.

Nkrumah, K. (1968) *Neo-colonialism*. London: Heineman.

Nye, J.S. (2004) *Soft Power*. New York: Public Affairs.

Olson, S.R. (1999) *Hollywood Planet. Global Media and the Competitive Advantage of Narrative Transparency*. Mahwah: Lawrence Erlbaum Associates.

Onuf, P.S. (2000) *Jefferson's Empire. The Language of American Nationhood*. Charlottesville: University of Virginia Press.

O'Sullivan, C.D. (2008) *Sumner Welles, Postwar Plannning, and the Quest for New World Order*. New York: Columbia University Press.

Paolino, E.N. (1973) *The Foundations of the American Empire. William Henry Seward and US Foreign Policy*. Ithaca: Cornell University Press.

Pakenham, T. (1979) *The Boer War*. Johannesburg: Jonathan Ball.

Peschek, J. (2006) *The Politics of Empire*. London: Routledge.

Petras, J. & Veltmeyer, H. (2001) *Globalization Unmasked*. Halifax: Fernwood Publishing.

Phillips, D.L. (2005) *Losing Iraq*. New York: Basic Books.

Porter, B. (1968) Critics *of Empire. British Radical Attitudes to Colonialism in Africa*. London: Macmillan.

Porter, B. (1975) *The Lion's Share. A Short History of British Imperialism 1850–1970*. London: Longman.

Porter, B. (2006) *Empire and Superempire. Britain, America and the World*. New Haven: Yale University Press.

Roosevelt, E. (1946) *As He Saw It*. New York: Duell, Sloan & Pearce.

Ryn, C.G. (2004) *America the Virtuous*. New Brunswick: Transaction Publishers.

Schroter, H.G. (2005) *Americanization of the European Economy*. Dordrecht: Springer.

Schwartz, T.A. (1991) *America's Germany*. Cambridge: Harvard University Press.

Servaes, J. (2003) *Approaches to Development*. Paris: Unesco.

Skidmore, D. (2007) *Paradoxes of Power. US Foreign Policy in a Changing World*. Boulder: Paradigm Publishers.

Smith, D.M. (1965) *The Great Departure. The US and World War I*. New York: John Wiley.

Smith, N. (2005) *The Endgame of Globalization*. New York: Routledge.

Smith, T. (1981) *The Pattern of Imperialism*. Cambridge: Cambridge University Press.

Spillman, K.L. (1973) 'Wilsonian Ideas and European Politics', in Den Hollander, A.N.J. *Contagious Conflict*. Leiden: E.J. Brill.

Story, J. (2000) 'Setting the Parameter. A Strange World System', in Lawton, T.C., Rosenau, J.N. & Verdun, A.C. (eds), *Strange Power*. Aldershot: Ashgate.

Strange, S. (1982) 'Cave! Hic Dragones. A Critique of Regime Analysis', *International Organization*, 36 (2), 479–496.

Strange, S. (1987) 'The Persistent Myth of Lost Hegemony', *International Organization*, 41 (4), 551–574.

Strange, S. (1988) 'The Future of the American Empire', *Journal of International Affairs*, 42 (1), 1–17.

Strange, S. (1990) 'Finance, Information and Power', *Review of International Studies*, 16, 259–274.

Strengers, J. (1982) 'Precipitous Decolonization. The Case of the Belgian Congo', in Gifford, P. & Louis, Wm.R. (eds), *The Transfer of Power in Africa. Decolonization 1940–1960*. New Haven: Yale University Press.

Takeyh, R. (2000) *The Origins of the Eisenhower Doctrine*. London: Macmillan.

Thorne, C. (1976) 'Indochina and Anglo-American Relations, 1942–1945', *Pacific Historical Review*, 45 (1), 73–96.

Thorne, C. (1978) *Allies of a Kind*. Oxford: Oxford University Press.

Tomlinson, J. (1991) *Cultural Imperialism*. London: Continuum.

Tunstall, J. (1994) *The Media are American. Anglo-American Media in the World*. London: Constable.

Underhill, G.R.D. (2000) 'Global Money and the Decline of State Power', in Lawton, T.C., Rosenau, J.N. & Verdun, A.C. (eds), *Strange Power*. Aldershot: Ashgate.

Walker, E.A. (1953) *The British Empire. Its Structure and Spirit*. London: Bowes & Bowes.

Wallerstein, I., (1974, 1980) *The Modern World System, 2 Vols*. New York: Academic Press.

Walworth, A. (1977) *America's Moment. America's Diplomacy at the End of World War I*. New York: W.W. Norton.

Watt, D.C. (1973) 'American Anti-colonialist Policies and the End of the European Colonial Empires 1941–1962', in Den Hollander, A.N.J. (ed.) *Contagious Conflict*. Leiden: E.J. Brill.

Watt, D.D. (1984) *Succeeding John Bull. America in Britain's Place 1900–1975*. Cambridge: Cambridge University Press.

Weinberg, A.K. (1963) *Manifest Destiny. A Study of Nationalist Expansionism in American History*. Chicago: Quadrangle Books.

Welensky, R. (1964) *4000 Days. The Life and Death of the Federation of Rhodesia & Nyasaland*. London: Collins.

Willett, R. (1992) *The Americanization of Germany, 1945–1949*. London: Routledge.

Williams, W.A. (1980) *Empire as a Way of Life*. New York: Oxford University Press.

Williamson, J. (2004) 'A Short History of the Washington Consensus'. Paper delivered at From the Washington Consensus Towards a New Global Governance Conference, Barcelona, 24–5 September.

Willkie, W.L. (1943) *One World*. New York: Simon & Schuster.

Wilson, W. (1902) *History of the American People*. New York: Harper & Bros.

Winfield, B.H. (1990) *FDR and the News Media*. Urbana: University of Illinois Press.

Winks, R.W. (1976) 'On Decolonization and Informal Empire', *The American Historical Review*, 81 (3), 540–556.

Winslow, E.M. (1931) 'Marxian, Liberal, and Sociological Theories of Imperialism', *The Journal of Political Economy*, 39 (6), 713–758.

Wood, J.R.T. (1983) *The Welensky Papers. A History of the Federation of Rhodesia & Nyasaland*. Durban: Graham Publishing.

Worsley, P. (1984) *The Three Worlds*. London: Weidenfeld & Nicolson.

Young, C. (1988) 'The Colonial State and Post-colonial Crisis', in Gifford, P. & Louis, Wm.R. (eds), *Decolonization and African Independence*. New Haven: Yale University Press.

Zakaria, F. (1998) *From Wealth to Power*. Princeton: Princeton University Press.

Zink, H. (1957) *The United States in Germany 1944–1955*. Princeton: D. Van Nostrand Co.

Index

EU authorised representative for GPSR:
Easy Access System Europe, Mustamäe tee 50,
10621 Tallinn, Estonia
gpsr.requests@easproject.com